Reclaiming the Nation

RECLAIMING THE NATION

The Return of the National Question
in Africa, Asia and Latin America

Edited by
Sam Moyo and Paris Yeros

PlutoPress
www.plutobooks.com

First published 2011 by Pluto Press
345 Archway Road, London N6 5AA and
175 Fifth Avenue, New York, NY 10010

www.plutobooks.com

Distributed in the United States of America exclusively by
Palgrave Macmillan, a division of St. Martin's Press LLC,
175 Fifth Avenue, New York, NY 10010

British Library Cataloguing in Publication Data
A catalogue record for this book is available from the British Library

ISBN   978 0 7453 3083 9   Hardback
ISBN   978 0 7453 3082 2   Paperback

Library of Congress Cataloging in Publication Data applied for

10   9   8   7   6   5   4   3   2   1

Designed and produced for Pluto Press by
Chase Publishing Services Ltd, 33 Livonia Road, Sidmouth, EX10 9JB, England
Typeset from disk by Stanford DTP Services, Northampton, England
Simultaneously printed digitally by CPI Antony Rowe, Chippenham, UK
and Edwards Bros in the USA

Contents

Preface

This book is the second in a series of tri-continental research initiatives undertaken by the African Institute of Agrarian Studies (AIAS) in Harare, Zimbabwe. It is the result of a partnership with the Department of International Relations at the Catholic University of Minas Gerais (PUC Minas) in Belo Horizonte, Brazil, and the Centre for Policy Studies in Johannesburg, South Africa. The three institutions have supported this project in its different stages, including its initial conceptualisation and network-building, the organisation of a conference, hosted by PUC Minas in May 2007, the subsequent translation of chapters, and the publication of the book. Generous support has also been extended by official sources in Brazil, namely CNPq (National Council of Technological and Scientific Development) and FAPEMIG (Foundation for Research Support of the State of Minas Gerais).

This second tri-continental project has aimed to address issues that arose from the first, which focused on the agrarian question and the rise of rural movements under neoliberalism – see our *Reclaiming the Land: The Resurgence of Rural Movements in Africa, Asia and Latin America* (London and Cape Town: Zed Books and David Philip, 2005). Specifically, the character of the state under neoliberalism, and the rise of new (or revived) nationalisms against neoliberalism, were discussed in relation to agrarian change, but were not investigated in a holistic and systematic manner. Thus, another comparative study dedicated to these issues became necessary and urgent. We hope that this second volume will begin to fill the gap.

It is important to say a few words, as editors, on the nature of the book. Our insistence on addressing properly the national question has been driven by our profound disquiet with its fate over the last 30 years. Clearly, this fundamental political and economic question of the modern world suffered severe setbacks, just two decades after decolonisation and the end of empire. The neoliberal assault, together with its newly-found allies – on the one hand, the post-modernist trend; on the other, a much older false cosmopolitanism practiced by dominant sections of the Marxist left – succeeded in submerging the national question under a flood of illusions regarding the 'globalised' nature of the world economy 'beyond' states and nations, centres and peripheries.

It is clear to us that the enhanced integration of the South into the commercial and financial centres of the world economy, rather than superseding states and nations, could only be effected by mobilising state apparatuses *against* nations, and by reinforcing tendencies towards national disintegration and international differentiation. Social, racial, ethnic and regional cleavages; state violence, rural conflict, urban crime and communal strife; serial economic crises and institutional ruptures – these have all been intrinsic to globalisation, as have the rise of the semi-peripheries, new monopolies, new middle classes and, of late, new South-South relations. The re-militarisation of US/Western foreign policies against the South, the proliferation of sanctions regimes and the scramble all around for energy resources, minerals and irrigated land – these, too, have been intrinsic to globalisation.

Until recently, the task of bringing the national question back to life, as a specifically *economic* question, was left almost entirely to the radicalising social forces in the peripheries of the system; perhaps unsurprisingly, they were based mainly, though not exclusively, in the countryside (see our *Reclaiming the Land*). Even the World Social Forum (WSF), the main global network of social movements of recent years, did not manage to grasp the national question fully: the radicalisation of social forces ran ahead, even away, from the WSF. Such social forces are now recuperating lost ground and going far beyond abstract 'identity' politics and 'plural' democracy to reclaim natural resources, namely land, energy and mineral deposits, and even to restructure the apparatus of the state in the name of the oppressed – most often the racially oppressed – with all the contradictions that such a process entails. The recent phenomenon of 'radicalised states' – a term that remains contested – is most evident in South America (see Venezuela and Bolivia in this volume), but it has its parallels in Africa (Zimbabwe) and Asia (Nepal).

The emerging semi-peripheries have also been broaching the economic dimension of the national question, but in an entirely different manner: by re-connecting the South through trade, finance and investment. This is an aspect which we do not fully explore in this book – it awaits another tri-continental research project – although it is increasingly evident that, as a process led by newly-aspiring business interests, its political orientation remains ambiguous: there is new space for manoeuvre, but also limits to solidarity. The questions which we explore have more to do with the internal dynamics of these states and less with their external relations. By contrast to the radicalised states, these emerging semi-peripheries (Brazil, Argentina, India, Turkey) seem to be 'stabilising', by co-opting or disorganising radicalisation, even after serial bouts with crisis, and seeking control over their regional neighbourhoods as well.

But beyond the economic dimension of the national question, there are states and peoples still struggling to maintain their territorial integrity or obtain political independence, long after the formal end of empire. These struggles are not only inseparable from the others, they are of a higher global priority, requiring unalloyed, principled solidarity. They are the 'fractured' states – not exactly 'failed', as the pundits would have it – those that succumb to the disintegrating forces of peripheral capitalism and external interference (Sudan), as well as the unresolved cases of colonised/occupied peoples (Palestine), who have now been joined by the newly invaded and re-colonised, for whom imperialist strategy has found no other way, once again, but to extinguish their sovereignty altogether.

We ought to be asking: why do some states radicalise, while others stabilise, fracture or come under occupation? Of course, fracture may lead to occupation, and vice versa, just as radicalisation may give way to all of the above, or stabilisation to radicalisation. But these are not a matter of chance, or historical stages, or detours, or discursive flurries. Are there deeper structural tendencies, deriving from the economic and social disarticulation that holds within the periphery, or perhaps the constitution of the business classes, or the organisation of the popular classes, which make certain countries more propitious to inclining one way or another? Are certain semi-peripheral countries, with their more established business classes, which have even entered the monopoly phase, and now boasting a 'shining' populism, more capable of evading radicalisation? Are there specific ideological conditions, such as those deriving from racial or caste consciousness, which play a special role in unifying social forces across the rural-urban divide, and tilting the balance? What are the potentialities and limits of the new international relation of forces – regional and North-South – in determining the direction of change? And if change is to be progressive, what is to be made of the state as a conservative bureaucratic apparatus? For whom and for what purpose should its relative autonomy be exercised? These are just some of the questions that need now to be taken seriously, as the 'globalisation' floodwaters retreat.

Our choice of country case studies has not aimed to be exhaustive; indeed, every country would have been interesting and deserving in its own right. We have intended, within the means of our networks, to be representative of the main tendencies observed and suggestive of the conceptual and political issues at stake. Our own editorial introduction on the 'fall and rise of the national question' sets out these issues succinctly, as does the concluding chapter by Samir Amin on the 'way forward'. The heart of the book, the eleven country case studies, is organised into three sections, one each for Africa, Asia and Latin America, which, in turn, are introduced by regional overviews by Thandika Mkandawire, Korkut Boratav and Atilio Boron, respectively. Readers will note that we place great value on the relationship of the contributors to their subject matter: they are researchers and political activists based in the countries and regions concerned, or otherwise have a life-long organic relationship with them.

Sam Moyo and Paris Yeros
June 2010

Introduction

1
The Fall and Rise of the National Question

Sam Moyo and Paris Yeros

ON THE CUSP OF HISTORICAL CHANGE

The current economic crisis has raised the possibility of pursuing autonomous development paths in the peripheries of the world economy. But it has also shown the difficulties of such development. For the states and societies of Africa, Asia and Latin America have undergone deep transformations over the last three decades, which reversed many of the social and economic gains of the postwar period and weakened their bureaucratic capacities in confronting the global crisis. What is more, contemporary attempts at forging a new path, especially among 'radicalised' states, have been met with concerted, externally-led destabilisation campaigns, which have aggravated internal contradictions and accentuated their socio-political polarisation.

It is clear, however, that the national question is becoming once again a crucial determinant of the current systemic crisis. Thus, to understand the character of the crisis, we must look far beyond metropolitan states. It is well acknowledged that the financialisation of capital since the 1970s reorganised class balances within metropolitan states and projected outwards a new mode of accumulation and regulation, parasitic in nature, whose effect was to postpone and displace the resolution of the postwar crisis (Brenner 2006, Gowan 1999, Harvey 2005). What is less acknowledged is the response from the states and societies in the periphery of the system: these have been crucial not only in perpetuating the new order but also in undermining it. We must look at these more closely to gain a fuller grasp of the nature of the crisis.

The demise of the long postwar economic cycle was foretold, but its timing and character could not be foreseen with any precision. A key political dimension throughout has been the rise of the third world. Nation-building, non-alignment in the Cold War and the numerous liberation struggles had determinant, if contradictory, effects on the course of global expansion and crisis. They were contradictory, because they threatened to break free from monopoly capital, at the same time as they compelled its expansion to regions which initially were 'off the map'. And they were determinant, because whether by threat or compulsion, they elicited a robust strategic response from the North Atlantic alliance, including covert operations, military intervention and ultimately over-extension, which sapped its own ideological and economic vitality (Amin 2003, Arrighi 2003).

The subsequent down-cycle of financialisation was similarly a third-world affair. The new Washington Consensus set as its main objective to create the conditions for parasitic capitalism to penetrate the peripheries of the system. And even though new industrial centres sprouted in Asia, stagnation and regression took over much of the global South, while financial crises swept across both to throw 'developing' and 'emerging' economies into disarray. It was a matter of time before the social effects would gain a political expression, with consequences for the system as a whole. Some of these expressions were chauvinistic, fundamentalist and even genocidal; but others had a progressive global agenda, led by diverse social movements, including the most militant among them, rural movements (Moyo and Yeros 2005). At the turn of the century, these contradictions would mature: fundamentalism would strike indiscriminately at the symbols of financial and military power within the United States, and social movements would launch an 'International' of their own, the World Social Forum, and in some cases go further to radicalise states.

It was also a matter of time before the decaying order would assume a new 'geopolitical' dimension, with the periphery as its object. The United States would embark on the invasion of Afghanistan and Iraq with 'shock and awe' tactics whose intended targets was not just 'terror' in the Western Asian region, but a restless world system (Wood 2002). This military adventure would have the contrary effect of eroding the international political alliances that had hitherto sustained the Washington Consensus, especially in the periphery. Three large states in the East, China, Russia and India, would reposition themselves as economic and strategic competitors, while a series of small states, mainly in South America, but also in Africa and Asia, would deepen their process of radicalisation – largely, but not exclusively, born of rural movements. Despite their small size, these radicalised states have threatened Western strategic control over large swathes of the periphery and, hence, the ability of the centre to continue to displace the social effects of the crisis.

We are now on the cusp of historical change. The Washington Consensus has suffered setbacks within the West, evident in the serial interventions in the economy and nationalisations. Furthermore, despite the continued imposition of neoliberal demand, important steps are being taken in the South to reorganise the centre-periphery relationship.

We do not intend here to address directly the prospects of change within metropolitan states.[1] We focus instead on the various experiences of adjustment and resistance in the global South. Our purpose is to understand the internal character of peripheral states, particularly the structural changes that they have undergone over the last 30 years, in the hope that this will throw light on the possibilities of dealing with the current crisis – and advancing the national question.

We begin by offering some conceptual thoughts on sovereignty, the national question, and the changing relationship between centre and periphery. Such terms might seem passé. After all, among the various ideological claims of 'globalisation' were that the state, as the location of sovereignty, had been superseded by 'the market'; that capital exports would bring about material 'convergence' between centre and periphery, and that new information technologies would facilitate 'dialogue' and approximation between cultures. It claimed, in other words, that the market, convergence and dialogue would render the nationalist cause obsolete. Such views were not the property of conservative ideologues alone, but also the dominant currents of the left. But now, in the rubble of this false cosmopolitanism, we can see more clearly the enduring structures of international hierarchy and the relevance of the national question.

WHAT IS THE NATIONAL QUESTION?

The national question is a modern political and economic question which transformed sovereignty – or political authority. The two were not always coterminous – and they will not forever be. Pre-modern forms of sovereignty were mainly communal and tributary in character, with few cases of centralisation of economic, political and cultural life – the clearest examples of pre-modern nations being imperial China, ancient Egypt, and the Arab world in its apogee (Amin 1976). Later, centralisation became a generalised necessity in the North Atlantic birthplace of capitalism; but in its early absolutist form, it attributed sovereignty to the monarch, not the nation. The modern idea of the nation, that is, of a community with a common, earthly origin and a self-constructed destiny, transformed sovereignty by introducing the element of popular participation. The idea became a political doctrine, or *nationalism*, to posit that all human beings are national beings in essence, and deserving of their own centralised political home. In fact, so contagious was the idea – and so oppressive the imperialist system under which it incubated – that nationalism ran ahead of capitalism to demand the self-determination of peoples even in places where capitalism had not assumed its distinctive form.

Looking into the future, it might appear that nationalism and sovereignty are beginning to part ways. The change that can best be envisaged today is in a form of sovereignty beyond the nation-state, whereby states pool their sovereignties into 'regional unions', perhaps even with a federal character. But even so, to the extent that they advance, a *pan*-nationalist cause will most likely be built into them, whether of an imperialist or anti-imperialist nature. A 'global' form of sovereignty is harder to envisage; it is probable that, when it finally appears on the horizon, it will be pressed with the urgency to preserve the planet for future generations – an existential issue for human beings *as* human beings. Yet, it is certain that the national question will again be in the middle of it, given that the politics of climate change are primarily a centre-periphery affair.

For our present purposes, we may identify three key tendencies in the expansion of modern sovereignty: *within the state*, by the expansion of democracy and social rights; *beyond the centre*, by the dismantlement of empires; and *across the system*, by the development of the forces of production. These tendencies have been galvanised by nationalism, together with other modern *isms* (socialism, feminism), but they have not been the outcome of capitalist logic, abstractly understood; especially in the twentieth century, they have operated, in large part, against the immediate requirements of capital accumulation in its monopoly form. This explains the truncated nature of national sovereignty in the periphery today, as well as the erosion of democratic and social rights in the centre.

To clarify the historical trajectory of sovereignty, we must locate it in the three phases of modern imperialism: the rise and fall of *mercantile capitalism* (1500–1800), the rise of *industrial and monopoly capitalism* (1800–1945), and the recent phase of *systemic rivalry* between an evolved monopoly capitalism and the planned/autonomous modes of accumulation ushered in by socialist revolutions and national liberation struggles (1945–1990). The current crisis of sovereignty – and the rise of the fourth phase of the national question – is located in the epochal demise of planned and autonomous development, as well as in the decay of the capitalist system itself.[2]

Mercantile Capitalism

Mercantile capitalism constructed a new world economy in which the North Atlantic would rise above the Mediterranean world to expand outwards to the South and East to colonise new lands, establish a new division of labour, and erect a new hierarchy among peoples. The most lucrative market was the Atlantic triangle. Under the leadership of European merchants, Africa would export slaves to the Americas to supplement the enserfed indigenous workforce; the Americas would export bullion, sugar and cotton to Europe; and Europe would export manufactured goods, guns and ammunition to Africa and the Americas to keep the system working. Genocide on both sides of the Atlantic and enduring racial oppression was complemented by capital accumulation in Europe, erosion of feudal bonds, state-building and dynamic technological innovation. Economic and military prowess was further buttressed by a new view of history and civilisation in which the white Europeans were seen as the perennial masters of the darker races, the 'people without history'.

In the mid-eighteenth century, the stage was set for a breakthrough. The industrial revolution ignited the historical confluence of an assertive capitalist class and a pauperised peasantry in Europe, together with a self-confident class of American-born colonists (Creoles) and rebellious slaves and indigenous peoples in the Americas. The outcome was a cascade of revolutions, the American (1776), the French (1789) and the Haitian (1791), against absolutism, feudalism, colonialism and slavery. The Americans fired the first shot against colonialism and absolutism (by distributing state power among federal units), but not against slavery. The French followed with a much deeper transformation, a social revolution against feudalism and a political revolution against absolutism, but again not against slavery (with the brief exception of the Jacobins), or colonialism. The most radical of all for its time was the Haitian, a robust social and political revolution, waged in a decade-long guerrilla war by the slaves themselves, against both slavery and colonialism. They brought to a close the mercantile period, with the onward expansion of sovereignty within Europe, beyond Europe, and across the system.

Industrial and Monopoly Capitalism

The following century, until the outbreak of general war among imperialist states in 1914, was a long century of 'passive' revolutions. The industrial revolution led the way, by deepening the market across five continents, and even promoting new industrial centres, mainly in the United States and Germany, but also in Japan in the East. It was a 'peaceful' century among a quintet of European great powers, but not within them, and not between them and their peripheries. Anti-colonial struggles spread in the Americas leading to the independence of the white colonists, while slow and controlled reforms were made against forced labour and the slave system – for fear of the 'chaos' of another Haiti. British industrial capital played its part, requiring new producers and new consumers, as did US industrial capital in the northern states of the Union, which unwound its own slave system by internal war. In Europe, the conflict was also mainly internal and social, culminating in the failed revolutions of 1848, led by the new working classes and aspiring peasant nations in the intra-European periphery. The subsequent period in Europe was one of political and social reformism. In fact, never again would there be a successful revolution within the centres of the system. For the capitalist classes had learned their lesson from the 'chaos' of the French revolution that democracy had to be qualified and controlled. The new working classes were too weak to complete the task.

The historical forces were contradictory. As capital accumulation entered its monopoly phase at the turn of the century, it reversed the expansion of sovereignty beyond the centre, but boosted it unevenly across the system. Capital exports to locations considered 'secure' were accompanied by a new wave of colonial expansion, which had already crept upon South and North Africa and Asia, sweeping across Africa and large swathes of Asia and the Pacific. It also swept across the interior hinterlands of states, mainly in the United States, but also within Latin American states which resolved at this time to secure their 'whiteness' into the future by a policy of physical (European immigration) and ideological whitening. The states that survived the wave, such as China and the Ottomans, entered a period of decay and subordination to Western monopolies and banks. Thus, colonialism, internal colonialism and semi-colonialism were the necessary political parameters for the historical expansion, not of sovereignty, but monopoly capitalism. It had as its ally the white working classes nearly everywhere, which readily absorbed the Eurocentric culture of imperialist society.

The stage was now set for revolutionary breakthroughs in the peripheries of the system. But these would not be working class revolutions in the most part – even if, as in Russia, a small working class assumed the ideological leadership. They would be peasant revolutions against landlords, racial monopolies and imperial centres. The Mexican (1910) and Soviet (1917) revolutions, and the postwar dismemberment of the continental European and Ottoman empires, set into motion once again the onward march of sovereignty. Together with the further expansion of capitalism and the entry of ever-larger masses of dispossessed peasants into urban life, in both centres and peripheries, a second 'passive' revolution, of controlled democratic and social reforms, came into effect – once again to avoid revolutionary 'chaos'.

Pacts between capital and labour and the advance of workers' rights assumed different forms: Fordism and social democracy in the United States and Western Europe; fascism in Central and Southern Europe; and *mestiço* nationalism in Latin America, a populism which aggravated class relations but also invented the myth of racial equality and steered away from agrarian reform. All three in fact were populist in nature; mainly urban, with the exception of the rural wing of fascism; and racialised, with fascism and the Holocaust being a logical result of the same Eurocentric ideology. In the subsequent historical phase of the national question, the protagonists of the race and agrarian questions would be the national liberation movements of Asia and Africa.

Systemic Rivalry

The return to general war resolved the succession issue between imperialist powers and gave way to a 'collective imperialism', led by the United States (Amin 2003). New rounds of capital exports, by huge industrial monopolies looking to globalise their markets and production systems, spread from the United States to Western Europe and Japan, and on to East Asia and other strategically 'secure' locations in Latin America and Southern Africa. But the motive force of this expansion would not be the immediate accumulation drive of monopoly capital; it would be the need to secure strategically peripheral locations, especially in East Asia, against the rising tide of socialist and national liberation struggles. The geography of capital exports was expanded by third-world nationalism itself. Pressure from newly independent states, which joined together in the Non-Aligned Movement (NAM) under the leadership of national bourgeoisies, tilted further the relation of forces between centre and periphery. Indeed, the spectre of unity across the third world – to include countries as diverse as India, Egypt, Yugoslavia, Indonesia, Ghana, and many others – presented the threat of a nationalism all around, whether capitalist or not, which could break free of monopoly control and the strategic dominance of the Western alliance. The systemic rivalry which was born of the Bolshevik revolution 30 years earlier would thus mature in these years, and a 'Cold War' between superpowers would turn into a third general war, now between centres and peripheries (see Saull 2007).

The objective of the Western alliance was either to co-opt nationalism by economic means, or to undermine it by covert operations, or to defeat it outright by military interventions, or, in the last instance, to curb its potential via reforms in the countrysides, the matrix of liberation struggles. In most cases, including the many nationalist movements that came to power in Africa, as well as, eventually, the bourgeoisies of the NAM, a mixture of economic co-optation, covert operations and military intervention bore fruit. But in three key moments, the Western alliance lost control and was even obliged to carry out agrarian reforms – now to stop the 'domino' (Moyo and Yeros 2005). The Chinese revolutionary war compelled the United States to carry out deep, but controlled, agrarian reforms in Japan, South Korea and Taiwan, while elsewhere, other means were sufficient to flush out nationalist struggles or stem the tide, as in the nearby Philippines, or in Guatemala and Iran. The Cuban revolution initiated another wave of reforms in Latin America, which were first controlled and then suspended and replaced by support to military takeovers and their 'green revolutions'. Meanwhile, in the midst of escalating con-tradictions within the West and global economic crisis in the late 1960s, a series of radical nationalist struggles once again prevailed – from Vietnam to Yemen, Ethiopia, Mozambique, Angola, Guinea-Bissau, Zimbabwe, Nicaragua and Iran – and, moreover, lifted the struggles of others; especially in South Africa and Palestine, the remaining colonial questions.

The role of the Soviet Union in this global rivalry should not be overstated – as indeed it was by the Western alliance. The Soviet Union opened a space for manoeuvre by its mere existence as an alternative, planned system, but its structural impasse internally and its bureaucratic sclerosis rendered its foreign policy inconsistent at best, or outright intolerant of revolutionary internationalism. It was the nationalist struggles in the periphery of the system that would become the motive forces of systemic rivalry, not the Soviet Union. In the late 1950s, after a round of active engagement in the East Asian region, the Soviet Union reverted to a conservative role, in the policy of 'peaceful co-existence' with the West, while its last stand in the 1970s was itself contradictory: support for liberation movements gave way to the invasion of Afghanistan.

The further development of capitalism across the system in this third (and 'golden') age was led by the struggles for peasant land, independent statehood and autonomy from monopoly capital. They succeeded, at last, in globalising the states-system and in obtaining economic advances and social reforms, including in the countryside. They failed, however, to endow their new political homes with autonomy from monopoly capital; the latter not only expanded its reach to new sectors, most notably agribusiness, but also struck back in its financialised form to re-subordinate the periphery as a whole to its parasitic needs and to usher in a generation of 'structural adjustment'. The nationalist movement also failed to maintain its unity, not least because the onward development of capitalism advanced further in certain places than in others, giving way to a new differentiation to be exploited, now among peripheries and semi-peripheries.

By the 1990s, the collapse of the Soviet Union and the exuberance of finance capital managed the unthinkable: to take the national question off the global agenda. If the theory of 'modernisation' had previously adapted Eurocentric culture to the realities of a rising third world, the theory of 'globalisation' now proclaimed the end of the three worlds – in effect, the end of the national question! That ethnicised conflicts proliferated in the 1990s, or that large multinational states collapsed, did not impinge on the theory; these would be relegated to 'atavistic' or 'ancient' impulses, or localised 'identity politics'. It was no longer a national question of joining forces to confront monopoly capital, but of rushing to fall into its trap, one by one, in ever smaller and 'purer' nation-states.

Yet, just as the national question would lose its economic thrust and its political bearings, the deeper organic forces of social change and resistance would build back up against parasitic development, racism and militarism, to demand all the unresolved issues of the past, and more: participatory democracy, indigenous rights, racial equality, gender equality, agrarian reform, urban reform, employment, education, social security, amnesty for immigrants, sustainable development, control over natural resources, food sovereignty, and the freedom to develop the forces of production on the basis of internal needs. Questions of international reform would also return with urgency: from the abolition of the international financial institutions and reform of the United Nations, to the formation of regional unions for collective defence and economic autonomy. These are now the parameters of the new national question. While states may appear as the protagonists, the motive forces continue to be the semi-proletarianised peasants and rural workers, together with the unemployed and underemployed in the urban slums – still the wretched of the earth.

UNEQUAL DEVELOPMENT, THE STATE AND NATIONALISM

The logic of monopoly capitalism is not merely to 'develop the forces of production', but to secure monopoly profits and to ensure that the contradictions of accumulation can be shifted away from the centres of the system. Its systemic nemesis is not 'pure' socialism – although it serves ideological needs to present any progressive reform as 'socialist' – but a development path that threatens to become economically and strategically autonomous from the demands of the centre. And while monopoly capitalism may reproduce 'dependence' in the periphery by the mere operation of monopolies, it is the proactive political, economic and military instruments of metropolitan states, together with their class allies and supporting classes, which complete the task.

This 'really existing capitalism', as Amin points out (Chapter 15, this volume), is a system quite different from 'pure' notions of capitalism. It is a system that presents diverse *political* questions, which must be organised analytically – and strategically. It is clear to us that the centre-periphery relation imposes itself as a principal systemic contradiction, by the mere fact that capitalism today, more than ever before, requires centres and peripheries for its reproduction. As such, it is the advance of the national question that is most likely to facilitate the advance of other political questions.

This does not mean that nationalism, as a doctrine, is self-sufficient in advancing the national question: all too often it has lost its bearings and given way to reactionary causes. It also does not mean that the diverse contradictions of really existing capitalism cannot be fused or re-prioritised under specific conditions.

Before looking at the problems of nationalism more closely, it would be useful to map out the context of unequal development and the structural characteristics of peripheral states.

Paths to Unequal Development

The postwar phase of systemic rivalry and its immediate aftermath yielded a number of discernible paths to development and underdevelopment. In identifying these paths, it is important to throw light precisely on the *structural characteristics* of states and avoid facile dichotomies of 'democratic' versus 'totalitarian', 'market-led' versus 'state-led', or 'protectionist' versus 'export-oriented'. Peripheral states confront specific and enduring challenges of social and sectoral disarticulation – the historic result of monopoly capitalism – which have produced diverse domestic contradictions and political responses, and which continue to define the character of the national question. A key sub-set of the national question for all peripheral states has been the agrarian question, that is, how to organise the transition from agrarian to industrial society. The character of this transition has determined internal disequilibria, contradictions, and vulnerabilities to the external factor.

The most important paths to development and underdevelopment may be described as follows:

(a) Disarticulated accumulation: the dominant trajectory in Africa, Asia, and Latin America. This has been characterised by controlled agrarian reforms, uncontrolled urbanisation, stunted industrialisation, and export-dependence on primary agricultural and mineral commodities. A severe disjuncture between domestic production and consumption, as well as between economic sectors, is accompanied by extreme disequilibria between town and country and between domestic sub-regions. These are the cases of severe subordination to the world economy with chronic tendencies to national disintegration.

(b) Partially articulated accumulation *with* structural reform: the 'developmentalist' exceptions of deep agrarian reform, controlled urbanisation, class compromise, strategically protected industrialisation, and export-dependence on industrial commodities, namely in East Asia. The roots of this path are often attributed either to 'bureaucratic autonomy', or to 'positive rent-seeking' between bureaucrats and the business oligarchy, or to 'export-orientation'. The fact remains that the key questions of agrarian reform, together with technology transfer, strategic protection, and market access to metropolitan economies, created the structural possibilities of 'developmentalism'.

(c) Partially articulated accumulation *without* structural reform: the 'conservative modernisation' path, in such cases as Brazil, Argentina and India. This has involved controlled agrarian reforms, uncontrolled urbanisation and dependent industrialisation, based on elite domestic markets, along with export-dependence on primary commodities. In both cases, the absolute size of the elite domestic markets has been large enough to sustain industrialisation. This path has included smaller-scale variations, such as apartheid South Africa and Zimbabwe, based on much more limited domestic markets and without agrarian reform; and the Eastern Asian region in the 1980s and 1990s, but in this case with a new export-dependence on industrial commodities.

(d) Planned and articulated accumulation *from above*: the Soviet model of autonomous development, as established from the late 1920s onwards, and exported to the Soviet sphere of influence in Europe (but not outside). This involved top-down collectivisation, rural-urban inequality, industrialisation with domestic markets, and agro-industrial integration on a national basis, under centralised bureaucratic planning. Although the degree of autonomy of this model may be disputed, given its direct competition with the industrialisation patterns of the capitalist West, and although it reproduced rural-urban disequilibria common to capitalism and a new wage relation under a bureaucratised form, it cannot be considered as a mere expansion of monopoly capitalism within a centre-periphery relationship.

(e) Planned and articulated accumulation *from below*: experiences of autonomous development vying for independence from the Soviet model. The most prominent case is China, involving armed struggle (largely against Soviet directives), bottom-up collectivisation and balanced rural-urban development, leading to slower-paced industrialisation, but also integrated agro-industrial development. Variants of this bottom-up path which did not achieve 'model' status are Yugoslavia, involving independent armed struggle and experimentation with enterprise-level self-management, and Cuba, which similarly underwent independent armed struggle and collectivisation, but which did not avoid subordinate insertion into a new Soviet division of labour, with adverse consequences for national agro-industrial integration.

(f) Disarticulation of formerly autonomous development *without* state control: the reintegration of formerly planned economies into the world economy in the course of state disintegration, including the former Soviet bloc and Yugoslavia. Characteristic of this path is subordination to finance capital, decollectivisation, wholesale conversion to private property, stripping of public assets and deindustrialisation. While Russia would recover from the initial shock, it would reposition itself as an exporter of primary commodities, namely oil and gas, under state-led monopolies with a global agenda.

(g) Disarticulation of formerly autonomous development *with* state control: the case of China, where reintegration has been led by an integral state apparatus. This has maintained financial controls, retained rights to agricultural land (at least formally), negotiated the entry of foreign investment, and also embarked on its own capital-export drive, with state support. This path has led to rapid industrialisation and urbanisation, with a new class of domestic consumers, but also new rural-urban disequilibria and dependence on external markets.

(h) Enhanced disarticulation of partially articulated development: the prying open of partially articulated states, such as Brazil, India, South Africa and South Korea, under the leadership of finance capital. This has reinforced urban and rural poverty, as well as disequilibria between town and country, and led to both deindustrialisation and the formation of new monopolies, with state and foreign participation. The latter have obtained a new capacity to export capital and also to reinforce regionally the global demands of disarticulated accumulation.

The world economy has thus evolved dynamically, without abolishing the logic of the centre-periphery relationship. This relationship is reproduced internationally, but also nationally, between town and country and between sub-regions; the period of 'globalisation', especially, has enhanced the disarticulation of already disarticulated economies and disarticulated the formerly planned economies. The relationship is also reproduced in new forms, such as through the formation of politically significant semi-peripheries.

The national question has evolved accordingly. In all cases – even in the Chinese, which is now feeling the effects of internal disequilibria – international integration and national disintegration are two sides of the same coin.

The State in the Periphery

The expansion of the states-system in the period of systemic rivalry has required a new political relationship between centres and (semi) peripheries. The independent peripheral state would become a key location of political struggle between socio-political forces seeking either to perpetuate disarticulated accumulation or embark on re-articulation on a national basis.

It is thus ironic that, as the peripheral state would gain importance as a location of struggle, the theory of the state would not keep pace with analytical requirements. Indeed, after a period of intense debate in the 1960s and 1970s over the particular autonomy of the capitalist state and the character of revolutionary states, state theory would go into hibernation, together with the national question.[3] As Boron (Chapter 10, this volume) points out with respect to Latin America specifically, the theories that most incisively analysed the state were those of the Dependency School, which in turn was completely wiped in the 1980s, even as dependency was being *enhanced* by neoliberal policies. Once again, both left and right contributed to this. On both sides, a similar claim was made that the state had 'retreated' under the weight of the market (Strange 1996, Ohmae 1990), or withered away under a new 'imperial' sovereignty regime, above and beyond the nation-state (Hardt and Negri 2000). Programmatic conclusions were also drawn for social movements and calls were made to 'change the world without taking power' – that is, the state (Holloway 2002). So strong was this influence that it would even prevail in the World Social Forum.

But the climax of all this was the festival of state-labelling of the 1990s by the ideologues of the *belle époque*. Some states were now seen as 'emerging economies', others as 'failed', 'predatory' or 'patrimonial', yet others as 'weapons states' to be disarmed. What all these labels shared was a paternalistic construal of states to their political orientation to monopoly capital and the North Atlantic alliance, without any regard for their structural characteristics.

A notable attempt to redeem the state and 'bring it back in' was made in the mid 1980s (Evans et al. 1985). Its purpose was to demonstrate, against neoliberal wisdom, the existence of 'state autonomy' in particular situations and the potential to direct development in the periphery. Subsequently, East Asia emerged as an ideological battleground to explain its economic 'miracle'; even liberals began to speak of the state as an 'enabling' institution to be brought back in, against 'market failure' (North 1990, World Bank 1991, 1993). But it was only at the end of the century that the call was seriously heeded, especially after the East Asian financial crisis, and a more robust debate was undertaken on the 'developmental state' (Wade and Veneroso 1998, Johnson 1999, Mkandawire 2001). The current crisis will most certainly give more credibility to such thinking.

Suffice it to note here that, notwithstanding the innovative approaches of recent years, there is still much to be recuperated from previous debates. For there is a tendency today to find refuge in Weberian notions of the state as superimposed on society, a *deus ex machina* with self-referential 'autonomy'. The main victim here is the specific type of autonomy that inheres in the capitalist state, metropolitan or peripheral. To give one example, the Weberian approach was defended by one of its protagonists with the claim that unless the state is seen as acting independently of society, 'there is little need to talk about states as important actors' (Skocpol 1985: 9). But the problem was posed inadequately. The modern state both reflects capitalist society and is autonomous from the social classes which compose it. In other words, the state *is* an autonomous actor even as it reflects society. Moreover, it is not autonomous from all classes in equal measure. For its primordial historic function remains to organise the dominant classes, including domestic ruling classes and monopoly capital, *not* the oppressed.

Another tendency is to define 'developmentalism' formalistically, without specification of the structural characteristics of peripheral states and the particular historic challenges which they face. Thus, crucial and contentious political questions, such as land reform, balanced agro-industrial development, sustainability, and not least the external factor, give way to a new technocratic approach, whereby industrialisation for its own sake (that is, for elite consumption), liberal democracy and bureaucratised class pacts end up, once again, as the blueprint. Such 'developmentalism' is none other than a revived modernisation theory.

The questions thus remain: autonomy from whom? And for what purpose?

Nations and Nationalism

These are the questions that must guide the national question in its fourth historic phase. It entails the revival of the systemic confrontation of the postwar years, now in the absence of an alternative superpower and its ideological orthodoxy. And it requires the formation of new South-South alliances and collective self-reliance on economic and strategic matters. This does not, of course, mean that alliances with progressive forces in the North must not be sought: they are a crucial component of global transformation. But for obvious historic reasons, the initiative and leadership in the global confrontation with monopoly capital belongs to the peoples of the South.

Several issues must concern us regarding the type of nationalism that is necessary for the task. These issues are both conceptual and political and, moreover, they must be situated in the concrete realities of centre-periphery relations and the structural characteristics of peripheral states. It is not possible to speak of nationalism in a manner abstracted from the lived realities of the modern world.

Abstraction has been present in the definition of nationalism from the beginning. Objective criteria, such as language, or Stalin's infamous quartet of 'language, territory, economic cohesion and psychological make-up', cannot serve what is essentially a subjective phenomenon. Nationalism may attribute political significance to the above elements, but it is ultimately born of a common historical experience, including discrimination, oppression and struggle. Another form of abstraction has been to reify 'ethnic origins' and impute a pre-modern, even ancient, teleological need to modern nationalist claims (Smith 1986). More important have been the material transformations ushered in by modernity, together with the forms of oppression, *or modes of rule*, which incubate nationalist resistance in the course of capitalist expansion. Typically racialised, such modes of rule have yielded diverse institutional expressions to Eurocentric culture and its discrimination between 'citizens and subjects', or 'civil society' and the 'uncivil', and so on.[4]

In this regard, it is not sufficient to seek the emergence of nationalism in purely material conditions. It has been argued, for example, that industrialisation has been at the root cause of nationalism (Gellner 1983); or that the diffusion of 'print capitalism' transformed ways of 'imagining community', even in areas far away from the centres of industrial transformation (Anderson 1983). But such approaches have only tangentially addressed the emergence of nationalism in the peripheries of the world system. Not only did nationalism run far ahead of industrial capitalism, it also inspired peasant masses which were illiterate; mass political mobilisation has been achieved by dedicated political work and conscientisation *through struggle*, against specific modes of rule. Certainly, the 'black

Jacobins' of Haiti, the most committed of their time to the Rights of Man, did not require newspapers and novels to imagine their freedom from the colonial slave system (James 2001).

Thus, if we have generally overcome the definitional straightjacket of reified nations, we must still confront a set of similarly reified 'conditions' regarding when, where, and by what means nations should stake their claims. The attempt to address this sociologistic straightjacket has in recent years been led by post-structuralists, who have gone the other way, by abstracting identity from material conditions of any kind. And in this case, we are presented with a theory of 'identity politics', without any bearing on matters of politics. Even among the most sophisticated of statements in this vein (Chatterjee 1993) there is a conceptual abstraction of nationalism from contemporary imperialism: we are urged to consider the nation in its 'fragments', as if they cannot, or should not, be unified in reclaiming the nation; such unification, by definition, would do violence to the diversity of the oppressed.

We must be clear in what we mean by reclaiming the nation. For the nation has been invoked for the most reactionary of causes – and the cases abound, from ethnicised political conflict in the Balkans, Africa and Asia, to systematic discrimination in multi-ethnic states, to the military regimes in Latin America – so much so that there is, among many, automatic revulsion to this mode of mobilisation. But flight from the lived realities of imperialism and its racialised modes of rule also cannot provide an adequate alternative mode of mobilisation; often its refuge of choice is 'pure' notions of capitalism and socialism. What is required once again is a *critical engagement* with nationalism – that is, neither an *un*critical engagement, nor a critical *dis*engagement. This further requires that we distinguish between nationalisms 'from above' and 'from below' and, moreover, nationalisms that are imperialist and those that are anti-imperialist. One of the most astute of the early analysts of nationalism recognised these distinctions very clearly (Lenin 1964), in condemning the chauvinism of the decaying Second International *and* supporting the right of oppressed nations to separate statehood.

The national question today, in the aftermath of the globalisation of the states-system, presents new challenges to which such insights must be adapted. Separate statehood remains relevant in the most oppressive of cases, such as in contemporary Palestine, but even in this case it may legitimately be questioned whether a two-state solution, as opposed to a one-state solution, is capable of serving the aspirations of the Palestinian people (Hilal 2007 and Chapter

7, this volume). In the very similar case of South Africa, the historic option by the nationalist movement for a one-state solution was founded on the fact that separation, preferred by the apartheid regime itself, was a recipe for continued oppression. Many other classic examples may be cited: the success of the imperialists in weakening and ultimately eliminating Patrice Lumumba in the Congo by supporting breakaway regions; the more recent support for the unravelling of the multinational states of Eastern Europe and their flocking to the EU and NATO; and even more recently, the cantonisation of Iraq, or the attempts to weaken the Morales government in Bolivia by clandestine support to the 'autonomist' claims of a white oligarchy (a near repeat of the first Congo crisis).

If in the past the objective of imperialism was generally to deny separate statehood to oppressed nations, today it is to encourage it opportunistically. As Mkandawire argues (Chapter 2, this volume), the real challenge is how to reverse communal inequalities within existing states and, moreover, to ground sub-national and national identities in regional, *pan-nationalist* integration projects.[5] In confronting this challenge, it is important to heed not only separate identity claims (or endorse them for their own sake), but also the deeper questions related to the disarticulated material conditions in which such separate identities thrive. The relationship between nationalism and imperialism is, above all, dialectical, and irreducible to sociologistic or apolitical abstractions.

A final word is in order regarding the 'populism' of nationalism, not least because the recent resurgence of nationalism has been roundly accused of it, by both left and right. Populism is neither a 'rural' nor a 'petty bourgeois' phenomenon, nor a specific type of 'movement' or 'government', nor an essentially 'anti-elitist' discourse, nor coterminous with 'Bonapartism', a top-down, personalised form of politics. The liberal idea of 'the people' as individualised 'voters' is itself a populist ideological device which historically has claimed anti-elitism and which, moreover, has become institutionalised in multi-party parliamentary systems.

Thus, we may agree with Laclau (1977; see also 2005), that populism is a principle of articulation in modern class societies, which aggregates various classes and, therefore, lacks specific or 'pure' class content. Boratav (Chapter 5, this volume) makes a similar case regarding the populisms of the postwar years, which were, in effect, a mode of regulation of distributional dynamics. But, *pace* Laclau, it is not necessarily a phenomenon which emerges in crises of representation: it is a cohesive and enduring historical factor in the formation of the capitalist state, whether in crisis or not, and whether in the periphery or the centre (Poulantzas 1973, Losurdo 2004); just as it is, we might add, a factor in its disintegration. We may also agree that populism has a separate analytical status; it may appear indistinguishable from nationalism, but it is different in its moral referents: whereas nationalism is concerned with the origins and destiny of the nation, populism is more precisely concerned with its 'popular' traditions and virtues, the 'soul' of the nation, to which it attributes modern political significance. Thus, just like nationalism, populism is contested terrain, from above and from below, and capable of serving diverse social bases and political causes; indeed, there is no political movement, progressive or reactionary, which can turn its back on issues of cultural decay or renewal.

It is important, therefore, to distinguish not between a populist and a supposedly non-populist form of nationalism but between different forms of populism – be they rural-based or urban-biased, racialised or anti-racist, top-down or bottom-up – in short, progressive or reactionary. It is also important to recognise the limitations of populism. Like nationalism, it is a necessary but insufficient condition for the advancement of the national question: its undifferentiated view of the people may be a unifying force against a dominant power bloc, but it may also be a force of oppression.

FOUR TRAJECTORIES IN THE GLOBAL SOUTH

It remains for us to identify the recent trajectories among states in the global South, and to locate the contributions in this book. By identifying trajectories, we do not, in any way, imply 'ideal types' (in the Weberian sense), but tendencies which emerge from concrete contradictions, and whose course is subject to changes in accordance with the correlation of forces – nationally, regionally and globally. Moreover, we identify trajectories with reference to their political characteristics in the present conjuncture, but not in a way abstracted from the organic features inherent in (semi-) peripheral states, as outlined above. We must also add that, although there is general convergence among the contributors to this book on matters of method – with an interest in historical and structural processes – there is notable (and, we believe, healthy) difference in political conclusions. The trajectories identified may themselves be disputed; our main intention here is to provide a more organised basis for further debate.

There are four trajectories which we discern among (semi-) peripheral states in the closing year of neoliberalism, namely states that are *fractured, radicalised, stabilised* and *occupied*.

Fractured States

Among the most provocative terms in recent years is that of a 'failed' state. There are several problems with this term. First, the term is generally underpinned by inadequate theories of the state. Often a liberal notion is employed, whereby the main purpose of the state is to attend to the social and economic needs of its citizens and to uphold civil and political rights; where such 'public goods' are no longer served, the state is deemed to have failed. Alternatively, Weberian notions are invoked, whereby states are seen as territorial entities with a bureaucratic apparatus whose purpose it is to monopolise the legitimate means of violence within the borders of the state; where such monopoly and legitimacy are lost, as when armed groups assume control over swathes of territory within the state, the latter is similarly deemed to have failed. Second, the term is often overtaken by the ideological needs of metropolitan states, to label as 'failed' certain states that oppose the economic or strategic objectives of the Western alliance; thus, Colombia fails to be labelled a failed state, whereas Zimbabwe becomes its epitome.

Yet, the primary function of the capitalist state is neither to serve its citizens, nor merely to monopolise the means of violence for its own sake. It is to facilitate the reproduction of capitalism by overcoming fractional inter-capitalist conflicts and disorganising the working classes. When the state fails to provide 'public goods', as it typically does in the peripheries of the system, it is simply carrying out its primordial functions, in the absence of social forces capable to alter the character of state power. And when it fails to preserve control over its territory, it loses, more precisely, its capacity to overcome inter-capitalist conflicts, between domestic fractions of capital and/ or the hegemonic faction, which is monopoly capital. It is this which explains the periodic support for separatism by monopoly capital, which may find in state fracture a better possibility to preserve its interests – that is, through regionalised and ethnicised factions, especially in mineral rich areas, which vouch, without recourse to a centralised state, for the reproduction of monopoly profits.

For our purposes, fractured states are those peripheral states whose unequal development and internal contradictions have escalated to fractious and armed ethno-communal conflicts. These conflicts are largely rural, involving access to land, within the context of international strategic competition for access to energy resources and political influence. In this book, the experience of Sudan exemplifies the case of a fractured state. Mahmood Mamdani (Chapter 3, this volume) shows how the post-colonial state went through various attempts at nation-building, under successive Arabist, Sudanist, Islamist and Africanist ideologies, which ultimately failed to unite the political class, giving way to armed conflicts in the south and west.

Radicalised States

Other states which have at times been seen as 'failed' (or else 'weak' on the verge of failure) are those whose unequal development, economic crises, and intense socio-political conflict have given way to a process of radicalisation and polarisation. Such states typically have undergone classic revolutionary situations, which have not yielded revolutionary states. Cases in this volume which exemplify such radicalisation are those of Zimbabwe (Moyo and Yeros, Chapter 4), Nepal (Roka, Chapter 8), Bolivia (Aillón, Chapter 11) and Venezuela (Villa, Chapter 14). In these cases, the radicalisation of the state has involved a breach in the relations between monopoly capital and the domestic ruling classes, either by displacement of traditional, oligarchic ruling classes (Venezuela, Bolivia), or by compelling the post-colonial ruling class to break with monopoly capital or else risk being displaced (Zimbabwe). In the case of Nepal, the dispute of the state remains in progress.

In such cases, the correlation of forces around the state apparatus has been shifted by the mobilisation of popular classes, mainly in the rural areas, but also in the urban, on the basis of class and oppressed racial identities, above and beyond fractious communal identities. Typical of these radicalised states is a direct challenge to property rights and/or control over natural resources in the agrarian and extractive (minerals, oil and gas) sectors. Land reform, nationalisation of natural resources, rejection of basic dictates of neoliberalism, estrangement with reformist regional neighbours, and confrontation with metropolitan states have been some of the internal and external policy measures characteristic of radicalisation.

We must be clear that radicalised states are not revolutionary states, not least because the internal organisation of the state apparatus continues to reflect capitalist logic; in other words, the state has not been 'smashed' (Lenin 1992). Radicalisation in such cases has the potential of passing through uninterrupted phases of social transformation; or it may stall, unable to overcome its deep contradictions; or it may 'normalise' and reconstitute its relationship with monopoly capital. Radicalisation, in this sense, is an unstable category, which may retreat or advance.

The future potential of such societies that have been convulsed by revolutionary situations is disputed among the contributors to this volume. For example, Rafael Villa (Chapter 14) disputes the capacity of the Chavez government in Venezuela to carry through its proclaimed 'Socialism of the Twenty-First Century', given its personalised character; this is reflected internally, but also externally in its often contradictory policy with regional neighbours. Lorgio Orelana Aillón (Chapter 11) considers that the MAS government in Bolivia has already stalled and normalised its relations with monopoly capital. And Sam Moyo and Paris Yeros (Chapter 4) argue that the revolutionary situation in Zimbabwe was similarly interrupted, as the domestic bourgeoisie re-consolidated its control over the state apparatus. Yet, none has fully stabilised.

Stabilised States

We may affirm that the majority of states in the periphery, and especially in the semi-periphery, have neither fractured nor radicalised, even though they have not been spared of intense socio-political mobilisations. Some states, like Argentina (Vadell, Chapter 12, this volume), have themselves been convulsed by revolutionary situations; others, like India (Chachra, Chapter 6, this volume), Turkey (Somel, Chapter 9, this volume) and Brazil (Velasco and Moraes, Chapter 13, this volume), have also experienced significant socio-political mobilisations in the course of liberalisation – and, especially, as a direct result of financial crisis. But relations with monopoly capital have been administered without rupture; while in the specific case of Argentina, where there has been a hostile renegotiation of external debt, relations have been recomposed.

Overall, stabilised (or stabilising) states are those peripheral and semi-peripheral states whose unequal development and economic crises have led to socio-political conflict in different forms and degrees, both rural and urban, but which have suppressed, co-opted and contained conflict and polarisation. Such states have moderated their relations with monopoly capital and metropolitan states, refraining from explicit or sustained confrontation, and retaining the basic elements of neoliberalism.

Nonetheless, two caveats must be added. First, in many cases, most markedly in Latin America, the whole experience of crisis and mobilisation has undermined faith in the neoliberal model, even among the domestic ruling classes, and even if, in practice, neoliberalism remains in force. Especially in Latin America, there has been a strengthening of the economic and redistributive role of the state, such as in Brazil and Argentina, to the point of recuperating a discourse of 'neo-developmentalism'. There has also been a sustained (albeit still ambiguous and contradictory) effort to diversify economic and political relations away from metropolitan states and towards regional and South-South alliances. For example, issues of state-led investment in regional infrastructure, as well as collective security independently of metropolitan states, are back on the agenda.

Second, stabilisation should not be seen as a secular tendency, without the possibility of renewed mobilisation and contestation of the economic model and relations with metropolitan states. In the unfolding of the current systemic crisis, it is quite possible that intense socio-political mobilisation will be reignited. In peripheral states, such an eventuality may even lead to more fractured states, or more radicalised states. As for semi-peripheral states, it is unlikely that they will succumb to fractious forces, given the more organised nature of their domestic bourgeoisies, but the question remains whether they will enter a process of radicalisation.

Occupied Peoples

A final trajectory is of peoples that remain occupied/colonised, the principal case being that of Palestine (Hilal, Chapter 7, this volume), or states that have recently been occupied or penetrated militarily, such as Afghanistan, Iraq and Pakistan, or others that have succumbed to 'international administration' (Caplan 2005). These are states which have been subject, or have recently succumbed, to direct external political domination in the course of strategic competition for regional influence. This path is not necessarily and immediately linked to neoliberal reforms and internal unravelling; as Boratav argues (Chapter 5, this volume), it is direct military aggression that has undermined these societies. Their fate has been tied to the 'geopolitical' puzzle of how to maintain control over whole regions at a time in which the US/Western parasitic mode of accumulation has reached its ideological and material limits everywhere. Persistent support for settler-colonialism in Palestine and the re-militarisation of foreign policy in Western Asia have been the chosen strategies there (with certain parallels in Africa and Latin America).

In the Western Asian cases, the national question continues to revolve around sovereign statehood. And in these particular cases, the national liberation struggle has been overcome by a fundamentalist, backward-looking populism and inter-communal fracture. Guerrilla warfare, both internecine and against the occupation, has managed to bog down the invading forces, but it does not have the capacity to sustain a broad-based liberation project.

NOTES

1. For the Eurozone crisis specifically, see Lapavistas et al. (2010).
2. For an application of this argument to South America, see Yeros (2010).
3. See, among the leading theorists, Alavi (1972), Amin (1981), Bettelheim (1976), Cabral (1979), Cardoso and Faletto (1979), Fanon (2001), Marini (1974), Miliband (1969), Poulantzas (1973), Shivji (1976), and Therborn (1978).
4. For the application of this analysis to Africa specifically, see Mamdani (1996) and Moyo and Yeros (2007).
5. There is a useful historical precedent to this debate as well, as far back as the Second International, specifically in the work of Otto Bauer (2000); his concern was to recognise national aspirations while preventing the infinite fragmentation of the Austro-Hungarian state.

REFERENCES

Alavi, Hamza (1972), 'The State in Post-Colonial Societies: Pakistan and Bangladesh', *New Left Review*, 74 (July–August): 59–61.

Amin, Samir (1976), *Unequal Development*, trans. B. Pearce. London and New York: Monthly Review Press.

Amin, Samir (1981), *The Future of Maoism*, trans. N. Finkelstein. New York: Monthly Review Press.

Amin, Samir (2003), *Obsolescent Capitalism*, trans. P. Camiller. London and New York: Zed Books.

Anderson, Benedict (1983), *Imagined Communities*. London and New York: Verso.

Arrighi, Giovanni (2003), 'The Social and Political Economy of Global Turbulence', *New Left Review*, 2(20): 5-71.

Bauer, Otto (2000), *The Question of Nationalities and Social Democracy*, trans. J. O'Donnell, ed. E. Nimni. Minneapolis: University of Minnesota Press.

Bettelheim, Charles (1976), *Class Struggles in the USSR*, trans. B. Pearce. New York: Monthly Review Press.

Brenner, Robert (2006), *The Economics of Global Turbulence*. London and New York: Verso.

Cabral, Amilcar (1979), *Unity and Struggle*. New York: Monthly Review Press.

Caplan, Richard (2005), *International Governance of War-Torn Territories: Rule and Reconstruction*. Oxford: Oxford University Press.

Cardoso, Fernando Henrique, and Enzo Faletto (1979), *Dependency and Development in Latin America*, trans. M.M. Urquidi. Berkeley: University of California Press.

Chatterjee, Partha (1993), *The Nation and its Fragments*. Princeton, NJ: Princeton University Press.

Evans, Peter B., Dietrich Rueschemeyer and Theda Skocpol, eds (1985), *Bringing the State Back In*. Cambridge: Cambridge University Press.

Fanon, Frantz (2001), *The Wretched of the Earth*. London: Penguin Books.

Gellner, Ernest (1983), *Nations and Nationalism*. Oxford and Cambridge, MA: Blackwell Publishers.

Gowan, Peter (1999), *The Global Gamble*. London and New York: Verso.

Hardt, Michael, and Antonio Negri (2000), *Empire*. Cambridge, MA: Harvard University Press.

Harvey, David (2005), *The New Imperialism*. Oxford and New York: Oxford University Press.

Hilal, Jamil, ed. (2007), *Where Now for Palestine? The Demise of the Two-State Solution*. London and New York: Zed Books.

Holloway, John (2002), *Change the World Without Taking Power*. London and Sterling, VA: Pluto Press.

James, C.L.R. (2001), *The Black Jacobins*. London: Penguin Books.

Johnson, Chalmers (1999), 'The Developmental State: Odyssey of a Concept', in *The Developmental State*, ed. Meredith Woo-Cumings. London and Ithaca, NY: Cornell University Press.

Laclau, Ernesto (1977), *Politics and Ideology in Marxist Theory*. London: New Left Books.

Lalcau, Ernesto (2005), *On Populist Reason*. London and New York: Verso.

Lapavistas, Costas, et al. (2010), *Eurozone Crisis: Beggar Thyself and Thy Neigbour*, RMF Occasional Report, March, www.researchonmoneyandfinance.org.

Lenin, V.I. (1964), *Questions of National Policy and Proletarian Internationalism*. Moscow: Progress Publishers.

Lenin. V.I. (1992), *State and Revolution*, trans. R. Service. London: Penguin Books.

Losurdo, Domenico (2004), *Democracia ou Bonapartismo*, trans. L.S. Henriques. Rio de Janeiro: Editora UFRJ and Editora UNESP.

Mamdani, Mahmood (1996), *Citizen and Subject*. Princeton, NJ: Princeton University Press.

Marini, Ruy Mauro (1969), *Subdesarollo e Revolución*. Mexico, DF: Siglo XXI.

Moyo, Sam, and Paris Yeros (2005), 'The Resurgence of Rural Movements under Neoliberalism', in *Reclaiming the Land: The Resurgence of Rural Movements in Africa, Asia and Latin America*, ed. S. Moyo and P. Yeros. London, New York and Cape Town: Zed Books and David Philip.

Moyo, Sam, and Paris Yeros (2007), 'The Zimbabwe Question and the Two Lefts', *Historical Materialism*, 15(3): 171–204.

Miliband, Ralph (1969), *The State in Capitalist Society*, New York: Basic Books.

Mkandawire, Thandika (2001), 'Thinking about Developmental States in Africa', *Cambridge Journal of Economics*, 25: 289–313.

North, Douglass C. (1990), *Institutions, Institutional Change, and Economic Performance*. Cambridge: Cambridge University Press.

Ohmae, Kenichi (1990), *The Borderless World: Power and Strategy in the Interlinked Economy*. London: Collins.

Poulantzas, Nicos (1973), *Political Power and Social Classes*, trans. T. O'Hagen, London: New Left Books.

Saull, Richard (2007), *The Cold War and After: Capitalism, Revolution and Superpower Politics*. London and Ann Arbor, MI: Pluto Press.

Skocpol, Theda (1985), 'Bringing the State Back In: Strategies of Analysis in Current Research', in *Bringing the State Back In*, ed. P.B. Evans, D. Rueschemeyer and T. Skocpol. Cambridge: Cambridge University Press.

Shivji, Issa G. (1976), *Class Struggles in Tanzania*. London and New York: Monthly Review Press.

Smith, Anthony D. (1986), *The Ethnic Origins of Nations*. Oxford: Blackwell.

Strange, Susan (1996), *The Retreat of the State: The Diffusion of Power in the World Economy*. Cambridge: Cambridge University Press.

Therborn, Göran (1978), *What Does the Ruling Class Do When it Rules?* London: New Left Books.

Wade, Robert, and Frank Veneroso (1998), 'The Asian Crisis: The High Debt Model versus the Wall Street-Treasury-IMF Complex', *New Left Review*, 228: 3–22.

Wood, Ellen Meiksins (2002), 'Infinite War', *Historical Materialism*, 10(1): 7–27.

World Bank (1991), *World Development Report*. Oxford: Oxford University Press.

World Bank (1993), *The East Asian Miracle: Economic Growth and Public Policy*. Oxford: Oxford University Press.

Yeros, Paris (2010), 'Elos Fracos na América do Sul: As Duas Esquerdas Frente à Nova Questão Nacional', in *Os Novos Rumos do Regionalismo e as Alternativas Políticas na América do Sul*, ed. J.A. Vadell and T. Las Casas Campos. Belo Horizonte: Editora PUC Minas.

Part I
Africa

2
Rethinking Pan-Africanism, Nationalism and the New Regionalism

Thandika Mkandawire

INTRODUCTION

One of the major forms of globalisation has been regionalism, by which nations have sacrificed some of their sovereignty to regional supranational authorities in order to protect themselves from the assault on their sovereignty, social models and cultures.[1] The European Union is probably the most outstanding achievement in this respect, but there are many other regional initiatives and ideological expressions that indicate this response. In all these schemes, the regionalist ideologies and aspirations have to reconcile themselves to the nationalist aspirations, which remain a defining feature of the global order and, indeed, underpin much of the regional initiatives. It has often been argued that under the impetus of globalisation, the Westphalian project of 'nation-building' is passé, irrelevant and quixotic. For those of cosmopolitan inclinations, this is to be welcome: the nation-state became restrictive and exclusive; and in Africa, it provided a 'safe haven' for the practice of 'human wrongs', behind the veil of national sovereignty and non-interference. Transcending such an order in a world of diversity is thus celebrated. However, this celebration is premature, if only because it does not have much relevance for the life-world of human existence and political behaviour in much of Africa. And even among those whose horizons have been extended by globalisation, any mobility beyond that of the imagination is still severely restricted, as the developed countries close their borders and reinforce their regional identities.

For over a century, Pan-Africanism has been driven by different actors responding to a number of external pressures, of which globalisation is the most recent expression. From its origins as a movement for the assertion of the humanity of the people of African origin, it now appears as a movement both for collective self-reliance and the new regionalism. In its original form, Pan-Africanism was naturally borne by non-state actors, and it was deeply influenced by Africa's Diaspora and by the racism that pushed Africans together. Pan-Africanism was not simply a moment bringing together people of African origin; it was also an ideology that has left a deep imprint on African political thinking and sensitivities. It covered cultural, political and economic dimensions. Like all ideologies, Pan-African-ism articulated a vision of what is desirable; it set norms by which adherents were judged; it gave a semblance of cohesion to disparate interests. But like all ideologies, it has had its blind spots, some of which have threatened to subvert its central projects. And if it is to maintain its relevance and vitality, Pan-Africanism must be subjected to constant critical re-evaluation and refurbishing. It must be seen to speak to contemporary issues. The role of intellectuals is not simply to give coherence to a shared ideology, but to permanently critique the project, revealing its myths, falsifications and lacunae, reinforcing its strong points and identifying for it new sources of energy and new challenges.

The history of Pan-Africanism is characterised by seesaw-like shifts in emphasis, as continental or Diasporic issues have become dominant. This is not surprising, given the fact that the imaginary of exile is quite different from the nation-building project of the nationalist at home. In Africa, as elsewhere, Diasporas have played an important role in the reinvention and revitalisation of the identity of the 'home country'. And today, with the capacity to participate in the political life of their homelands, there can be no doubt that Diasporic groups will be even more immediate to the rethinking of a new Africa. In addition, Mamdani (1999) has noted the contributions to Pan-Africanism by the African intellectual work of the Creoles. The argument seems to be that their alienation has given them unique insight and driven their Pan-Africanism in a much more transcendental direction, which has been a source of its vitality and attraction. This is one of the reasons why, despite its poor record, Pan-Africanism has tenaciously held its grip on the minds of Africa's intelligentsia. When it seemed to have disappeared from serious official discourse, it persisted in popular cultural expressions and intellectual discourse partly because, unlike the prevailing forms of nationalism, it was freely adhered to and not imposed by the state.

However, there is another side to its transcendental character: it may also have detached Pan-Africanism from the day-to-day trials and tribulations of national actors and given it what has at times seemed to be an ethereal existence. This may also account for the extreme voluntarism surrounding it, so that failure in meeting its exigencies has often been attributed to wrong thought and much less to any objective conditions. Thus, it is asserted, Africa would have been better off if one form of identity had prevailed over another, or if one understanding of the national state (the Eurocentric one) had been rejected, or if only the ideas of the founding fathers had prevailed in their pristine form. Such voluntarism and concentration on the ideational may be understandable, given the intellectual foundations of Pan-Africanism and its self-conscious claims of an ideological status. And there can be no doubt that ideas will be decisive in the success or failure of the Pan-African project. But this one-sided focus on the ideational fails to come to terms with the objective conditions that gave birth to the bearers of the different ideas that are bemoaned and does not come to grips with the reality with which Pan-Africanism has had to contend in difference places and times. Agency divorced from structure has tended to pose the question in a rather utopian and voluntaristic manner.

One major task that Pan-Africanism set for itself – the complete liberation of the continent – has been achieved. However, on other items of the agenda that were expected to follow decolonisation, Pan-Africanism has not done well. The political unification and economic integration of the continent have thus far failed, at least when judged against the dreams of the key figures of the Pan-African movement. It has failed when judged against the well-articulated and widely shared understandings of the needs of the continent, as well as the declarations and rhetoric of African leadership and the documents and plans prepared at Pan-African conferences. It has also failed when judged against other projects of regional co-operation in other continents. I state these facts not to cast a diminishing light on the Pan-African vision writ large, and even less so to sow despondency among Pan-African ranks. Indeed, I believe that it is this Pan-Africanism that will ultimately make coherent the jigsaw puzzle of Africa's multiplicity of identities and interests and that will provide us with the real basis for addressing Africa's daunting problems and with a response to global pressures on our individual sovereignties.

NATIONAL PROJECTS AND PAN-AFRICANISM

While Pan-Africanism started as a 'stateless' and nationless movement over a century ago, since the Accra conference in 1958 it has had to reconcile its more transcendental agenda with the national agenda of new states and nations. And since then, the new agenda of Pan-Africanism has been much messier than its earlier variants, leading some nostalgically to long for the 'Golden Days' when the Pan-Africanist message, task and articulation were much more coherent and straightforward and with a moral sway that was unchallenged. The sheer size of the continent and the dispersion of peoples of African descent has meant that the Pan-Africanist project has had to come to terms with a wide range of identities, interests and concerns, which include gender, ethnicity, nationality, religion, race and geographical allocation, to name only some major ones. At times, the conflicts arising from some of these identities have put the Pan-African project under severe stress, such as the recent tragedy in Darfur (see Mamdani, Chapter 3, this volume).

Ethnicity, Nation and Pan-Africanism

Let me start with that most ubiquitous and most dreaded identity – ethnic identity. The projects of both nation-building and development presupposed a strong state governing a coherent nation. In this scheme of things, ethnicity was seen as inimical to both. It weakened the state by the conflicts it engendered, while the multiplicity of its claims simply denied the new countries a 'national image'. Nationalist movements saw recognition of this pluralism as succumbing to the 'divide and rule' tactics of the erstwhile colonialists and neocolonialist forces that were bent to deny Africans real independence, and wherever it was recognised, it was seen as emptying independence of any meaning by nursing the fissiparous potential that social pluralism always harboured. And so nationalism saw itself as being up in arms against imperialism and the retrograde forces of tribalism.

In the process, something else happened: in combating tribalism, nationalism denied ethnic identity and considered any political, or worse, economic claims based on such identities to be as diabolic as imperialism. Radicalisation of the nationalists, through armed struggle, was to banish ethnicity even further from any serious political consideration. In those states where an extremely reductionist 'Marxism' became the leading ideology, class analysis simply rode roughshod over any other social cleavages. Ethnic identities were seen as something 'invented' by the colonialists or the petty bourgeoisie locked in combat among themselves. It was part of 'false consciousness' that was bound to disappear through ideological struggle or as the development of capitalism made class consciousness more salient. This may eventually be the case, but 'false consciousness', while subjective in its origins, assumes an objective political presence that can only be dismissed at one's peril. The nationalist quest for identity was inadvertently transformed into a quest for uniformity. The consequence – and a dire one at that – was that otherwise anodyne expressions of ethnic identity and claims were turned into something lethal. It also produced a rather schizophrenic political culture in which leaders were nationalist by day and tribalist by night.

The nationalist can be excused for the conflation of tribalism and ethnic identity for, in many ways, the forces ranged against nationalism tended to abuse ethnic identity. The shock of Katanga[2] in the course of Congo's decolonisation, when Africa's worst enemies, imperialism and racism, championed tribalism against the central government, was to affect the nationalists' perception of ethnicity and regional claims so profoundly that 'Tshombes' and 'Katangas' were seen behind every movement challenging the authority of the central government. Part of the paranoia about ethnicity stemmed from a one-sided understanding of how colonialism affected African identities and how Africans themselves have responded to the colonialists strategy of 'divide and rule'. The usual view was that colonialism simply fragmented African society. But as Nnoli (1998) persuasively argues:

> despite the Machiavellian machinations of the colonial establishment in segmenting and fragmenting the colonized, the reality was that the socioeconomic upheavals unleashed by colonialism questioned people's erstwhile identities, and therefore led to the continuation of identity formation and boundary redefinition. This process of identity formation continued, even if its focus was not the Nigerian 'nation-state' in formation. The point, therefore, needs to be made that right through the colonial period, into the immediate post-colonial period, and now to the contemporary post-independence period, the processes of identity formation and boundary re-definition have continued, and an understanding of this process is just as important as comprehending the vicious 'divide-and-rule' machinations of British colonialism, or the political opportunism of the various fractions of the ruling classes of the post-colonial state. It is the totality of these pre-colonial, colonial, and post-colonial experiences and identities which form the substance of the 'National Question'.

The failure of African unity has not been because it has had to contend with primordial ties vying against its broader claims.

On the Artificial Problem of Artificial Borders

If nationalism made the error of believing that ethnic identity was incompatible with nation-building, Pan-Africanism has always run the risk of falsely assuming that national identity inherently undermines the Pan-African project. The usual observation is that African borders were artificially carved out at a conference in Berlin and that it is this artificiality that is the original sin. By accepting these boundaries, Africans had saddled themselves with the 'Black Man's Burden' (Davidson 1992). Not only were the borders artificial, but they also produced 'territorial absurdity' and wrong territorial shapes which could only be remedied by 'better boundaries' (Breytenbach 1999). Now, all borders are a social construct and therefore artificial – the results of treaties and conquest, human imagination of community, invented histories, and so on. It is also argued that the nation-building exercise has 'fostered a patriotic symbolism created by structures put in place by European imperialists at the beginning of the colonial encounter' and that 'identities left in place by departing colonial powers are glorified and sanctimoniously revered' (Prah 1998: 39). Such patriotism is often said to lead to the detachment of nationalism from its Pan-African moorings and thus to work against the Pan-African ideal. I believe, however, what was crucial was not so much that 'patriotism' undermined the Pan-African ideal, but that authoritarianism allowed only a very narrow brand of patriotism which often took on those attributes that made Samuel Johnson describe patriotism as 'the last refuge of a scoundrel' (Boswell 1900).

The nation-state in Africa was premised on the extension of the Westphalian privileges of nationhood to the decolonised states. Such an order was characterised by the primacy of the territorial state as a political actor at the global level, the centrality of international warfare, the autonomy of the sovereign state to govern affairs within recognised international boundaries, and the legitimacy of states that were ethnically diverse. Much has been written on whether post-colonial Africa ever attained any of these attributes of nationhood. There is, however, little doubt that the new states found these principles quite congenial. The respect of colonial borders assured a modicum of peace in Africa by minimising interstate conflicts; African nationalism, its paranoia notwithstanding, has been successful in creating national identities among its multi-ethnic countries. We should also recall that the Berlin Conference took place in 1884–85, and generations of Africans have lived within the present borders since then. National identity was not forged on the morrow of independence, but in the course of the struggle against colonialism. The identification with these 'artificial' spaces, therefore, did not emerge since independence, but is more than 100 years old – older than some European countries like Belgium. This, rather than complicating the Pan-African project may actually make it much easier. Nations that are assured of their territorial integrity and identity are more likely to reach out to others than those faced with serious internecine conflicts and external threats to their very existence.

Furthermore, it is arguable that precisely because colonial borders ignored much more 'natural' or primordial affinities, they undercut ethno-nationalism, a much more difficult nut to crack, as the case of the Balkans has demonstrated. Instead, we have multi-ethnic nationhood and an interlocking of multi-ethnic nations, which does not make regional unification emotionally anathema to large sections of the population. On the contrary, it makes it particularly difficult to mount political positions against one neighbour without dismembering oneself. It has also made secession an extremely unattractive option in Africa. We often ignore the fact that none of the major actors in the wars in Angola, Mozambique, Liberia and Sierra Leone has sought to dismember the nation-state. The acceptance of the nation-state and rejection of ethno-nationalism suggests that Africans are much more comfortable with, or at least resigned to, living in multi-ethnic states than many other cultures in other parts of the world.

Rather than continually harping on this obvious artificiality of African borders, we ought to work on rethinking the meaning of these borders and how they can be the basis of a new Pan-African identity which would be at ease with the African people's multiple identities. I do not believe that the failure of Pan-Africanism can be attributed to lack of identification with Africa by Africans chauvinistically mired in their diverse identities, as is often stated. Nor do I believe that the failure is due to the firm establishment of successful national identities by individual countries, which somehow militates against the Pan-African ideal. 'Africa' is probably the most emotionally evoked name of any continent. Its people sing about it, paint it, and sculpture it more than any continent. Its artists produce hundreds of icons of this much 'beloved continent'. Even national anthems often evoke Africa much more than individual names. If artificial boundaries, ethnic identities and nation-states are not the barrier to the Pan-African project, then what is the main problem?

LACK OF NATIONAL ANCHORING

One source of failure of regional integration in Africa has been its lack of national anchoring, due to divergence between Pan-African and nation-building projects. The politics of constitutive national entities are crucial to the success of the Pan-African project. Some of Africa's most prominent political actors have sought to develop an ideology and identity that would reconcile Pan-Africanism to the nationalist aspirations – Kwame Nkrumah's 'African Personality' (Ghana), Leopold Senghor's 'Negritude' (Senegal), Julius Nyerere's 'African Socialism' (Tanzania), Nnamdi Azikiwe's irredentism (Nigeria). These were attempts at giving intellectual and political expression to a deeply felt emotional identification with 'Africa' by individuals who were at the same time leaders of national movements. Yet, at the day-to-day political level, African regional integration has had, in political terms, an orphan-like existence. Not surprisingly, the emotional commitment to 'African Unity' has never translated into national political programmes and has no political resonance, except in the negative sense that one does not openly attack the idea of 'African Unity'. Despite the extremely high emotive force of Pan-Africanism and African Unity, neglect of their political and moral imperatives has never threatened the political position of any leader, let alone led to the overthrow of any government. On the contrary, leaders such as Nkrumah were accused of subsuming national interests under the Pan-African umbrella. National anchoring is crucial for African unity for the simple reason that quite a number of things that we all wish Pan-Africanism should have achieved – democratisation, social equality and development – are quintessentially national projects or premised on the nation-state. And in many parts of the world, these issues have been addressed rather successfully within the national context.

Authoritarian Rule and Pan-Africanism

Probably the single most important barrier to national anchoring of Pan-Africanism was authoritarianism, which only allowed the anchoring of anything to depend on one person and his (it was always his) coterie. It is this stifling political environment of authoritarian rule that accounts for the absence of a political correlate to our emotional commitment and that has made 'African

Unity' a matter for heads of states. It is this that explains why the preamble to the charter of the Organisation of African Unity (OAU) talks about 'We the heads of state' and not 'We the African people'. It is this that reduced the OAU into what Nyerere called a 'committee of dictators'. And so, even if African unity was emotionally accepted at the popular level, the authoritarian political rule of post-independence Africa meant that considerations to these emotions would really be at the whims and wiles of individual leaders. An important lesson of the last 30 years is that it was naïve to believe Africa's dictators could unite Africa. First, leaders that could ignore calls for such basic things as education and health could not be bothered with honouring such abstractions as the Lagos Plan of Action, the Economic Community of West African States (ECOWAS) and the Preferential Trade Area (PTA). Second, some have gone out of their way to foment ethnic conflict. A number of these dictators have been the source of the destabilising and divisive forces threatening national integration. Third, regional integration involves a partial surrender of national sovereignty. Accustomed to absolute power over the affairs of the nation, the notion of a higher political African instance was simply not acceptable. The tin-pot dictators that have thus far lorded it over the region tended to conflate national sovereignty with their own power and were most likely to view any diminution of national sovereignty as an attack on their person. They therefore tended to block any transfer of authority to a higher regional instance. Fourth, the OAU itself became irrelevant to the people's daily lives. Hamstrung by its absolutisation of national authority and its fear of offending member states, the OAU could not serve as a defender of African people against individual predatory or rogue states.

Worse was that this lack of accountability to national constituency rendered the official Pan-African gatherings the air of an extremely costly travelling circus. Not being accountable to anyone for the agreements they signed, given the lawlessness and impunity of authoritarian governance, such agreements had no force in law at both national and regional levels. The usual tradition was that heads of state, including heavily bemedalled generals, would meet at regular intervals to sign protocols of regional integration which were never debated, let alone approved at the national level. And so our dictators would solemnly sign a treaty on regional cooperation, while being fully aware that they would not raise a finger to have it implemented and knowing that this would not cost them anything politically. They could enter and exit any arrangement simply on the basis of the personal chemistry with the other members of the arrangement. Each government could renege on the agreements without any domestic political implications.

Such sense of irresponsibility and unaccountability partly explains the tantalising mosaic of regional schemes in Africa. Most African leaders have had no qualms in joining any of the arrangements even if it contradicts the demand of other regional accords to which they are signatories. Ever since Nkrumah's union government was defeated by the sub-regional approach articulated by Nyerere, Africa's integration has been understood in terms of a structure that has sub-regional entities as its building blocks. Nyerere's argument for beginning at the sub-regional level was essentially pragmatic, based largely on the prior existence of a number of regional schemes, especially the East African Common Market. However, what was gained in terms of pragmatism was lost in terms of coherence of regional initiatives, as well as of a standard against which to judge such efforts. It allowed a free-for-all view of regional co-operation.

If Africa is to unite, the spokesperson for the various political constitutive elements of the Pan-African project will have to obtain their authority from the people. It is necessary that the platform for unity be democratically derived. The popular will to unite can only be given expression by democratically elected governments. The argument here is not that democracy will automatically lead to Pan-African integration, but that it must be a central organising principle of Pan-Africanism. Democratisation can, in its initial phases, raise problems of national unity, an argument that enemies of democracy have repeated *ad nauseum*. Thus, by highlighting the rights of citizens, democracy can quite unintentionally lead to the questioning of the citizenship of others, producing such spectacles as the bizarre debates in Zambia and Côte d'Ivoire – where Kenneth Kaunda is suddenly a non-Zambian and Alassane Ouattara is no longer an Ivorian, despite the fact that both of them played distinguished and leading roles in their respective nations. The new spaces that democracy opens can also be abused to mobilise against the feeling for unity. All this said, it is still the case that a firm anchoring of Pan-Africanism will have to be based on democratic approval at all political levels in each member state. In any case, no lasting federal or regional scheme of which the composite members are dictators has ever held up. To transcend such positions, democrats will not only have to politicise regional integration, but also eschew or counsel against petty populism that exploits ethnicity and rejects the Pan-African ideal. In addition, democracy will only serve the Pan-African cause if it takes on the developmental dimension of Pan-Africanism. Thus far, however, democracy has eschewed substantive issues of material well-being and equity and focused on the more formal aspects of 'good governance', that is, free and fair elections, transparency, and so on. Only 'developmental democracies' will be responsive to the imperatives of 'Africa Must Unite' and to the institutional demands of regional integration.

One major weakness of Pan-Africanism and Africa's regional arrangements has been their failure to protect Africans from their home-made tyrants. Pan-Africanism has not been seen as reinforcing or guaranteeing people's rights as citizens of their respective nations. Solidarity in the name of Pan-Africanism has cast a pall of darkness on horrendous deeds by African dictators – from corruption to genocide. Pan-Africanism will have to be seen to reinforce national democratic order by providing a higher instance to which citizens can appeal against the predation of national authorities. The view that individual states had to be held to certain Pan-African standards has always been brought up in African politics. It was most dramatically raised by Nyerere when he questioned the morality of having a murderous Idi Amin as the chairman of the OAU. The silence by the rest of Africa over the invasion of Uganda by Tanzania (albeit in self-defence) marked the beginning of a tacit acceptance of change on the doctrine of non-intervention. The setting up of an African Commission on Human and People's Rights was also such a tacit acceptance.

One extremely important innovation in the new debates on African unity is self-monitoring. It is the final acceptance of the view that African states have a right to intervene in the affairs of its badly behaved neighbours. The current formulation of such mutual monitoring is the 'peer review' process, although it has the air of 'selling' Africa to the world, or collectively meeting the conditionalities of the G8. And, indeed, outsiders have already added compliance to the peer review mechanism to the long list of conditionalities to which Africans are already subject.

NEW POLITICAL ACTORS FOR PAN-AFRICANISM

Once the importance of democracy to Pan-Africanism is recognised, we then have to ask the following questions: what forces at the national level are pushing for African integration? Are there any groups at the national level for which regional integration may be worth expending effort on political mobilisation and lobbying?

What are the ideological trajectories of the old and new social movements? Which of these are likely to enhance, contradict, undermine or complicate the Pan-African project? Can their agenda be made to dovetail with the Pan-African project? These questions are rarely raised in debates on integration in Africa. Let me just briefly mention three types of interests or social groups that one might wish to consider in such an exercise: political parties and social movements, the African capitalist class, and intellectuals.

Political Parties and Social Movements

During the last two decades, we have seen the resurgence of political parties and social movements. While there is growing literature on the effects of such social and political organisations on democratisation, its quality and sustainability, there is little discussion on their relationship with Pan-Africanism. Much has been said about the ideology among political parties, their personalisation, their ethnic basis and their paternalism. But what does all this entail for the political grounding of Pan-Africanism in these countries? And how do these parties actually respond to the Pan-African agenda?

Similar questions arise with respect to both 'old' and 'new' social movements. Most of the 'new social movements', especially those referred to as non-governmental organisations (NGOs), do not seem to pay much attention to regional issues. With their minds focused on 'projects', they usually do not spend much time thinking of national macro-issues, let alone regional ones. Many of them are involved in vertical global alliances and do not engage actively in South-South or horizontal Pan-African networks. While for some the vertical links are reflection of ideological affinities, in all too many cases it is the funding that steers their search for allies.

The Special Case of the African Capitalist Class

Most policy-makers have resigned to the fact that, whatever integration takes places in Africa, it will largely be of capitalist economies. This immediately raises the question of the capacity of African capitalism and the specific interests of such a capitalist class. There have been few well-articulated or well-organised national economic interests seeking large markets that are collectively protected against extra-regional competition. This is not surprising, especially if one looks closely at the structure of ownership of industry in the region. Are there any groups at the national level for whom regional integration may be worth expending effort? If regional integration is to have political anchoring at the national level, key political actors at that level must embrace it. Thus, one will have to identify the key actors at the national level and their real and perceived economic interests.

For a whole range of historical reasons, African states have played an active role in the setting up of rudimentary industrial structures in Africa. Most of what are nationally-owned industries have been public. Many publicly or jointly-owned industries in Africa were characterised by excess capacity, and one would have assumed that they would have supported regional integration, that is, that the widening of the market would have been beneficial. One would, therefore, have expected the managers of parastatals and joint ventures to be a force for regional integration. This, however, was not the case. The managers of these enterprises preferred the easy life of a proverbial big fish in a small pond. Heavily protected by high tariff barriers, quantitative import restrictions, and overvalued currencies, and also confronted with soft budget constraints, they felt no compulsion towards the search for external markets. Indeed, to the extent that the market was protected, the managers preferred such a leisurely existence to the demands of competitive markets that regional integration might have brought along. The excess capacity induced by their large-scale operations within small markets was viewed as 'reserves' that could be used to increase output as demand went up and not as cause for widening the market. One could meet additional demand at a leisurely pace by simply harnessing existing capacity without major new investments. Our 'captains of industry' were not keen on new markets, let alone competition. It should be pointed out that such a view of things was, more often than not, shared by the workers who preferred the job security guaranteed by the monopoly situation to whatever gains regional competition might bring them as consumers. And it was the managers of such enterprises that often went through the motions of negotiating regional co-operation. The point here is that one could not expect much pressure from the bureaucracy in the parastatals and organised labour in favour of regional integration.

In addition, there have been few well-articulated or well-organised national economic interests seeking large markets that are collectively protected against extra-regional competition. This in a way is not surprising, when one looks closely at the structure of ownership of industry in the region. The private sector, which was also largely foreign, had been attracted to individual countries by specific incentives. Foreign investors, too, were often content with the fragmentation of the African market. As for the indigenous capitalists, there has been an ideological sea-change in Africa. There is much greater acceptance of the private sector and markets than there was in the in the 1960s and 1970s. But what is not yet clear are the interests of this emergent class in the Pan-African project and its capacities to exploit the enlarged economic space. Embracing the private sector does not necessarily mean the private sector will respond favourably; it also does not mean it will share the Pan-African vision – definitely not if it is simply subservient to global corporate interests. The process of 'compradorisation' that came along with structural adjustment, whereby mercantile activities became more important than production, militates against the emergence of a national bourgeoisie for which production for a consolidated regional market might be of interest.

Intellectuals, Technocracy and Pan-Africanism

I would be remiss if I did not say something about the role of intellectuals in rethinking Pan-Africanism. Among African intellectuals, Pan-Africanism has historically reigned supreme. I have argued elsewhere that one weakness of the nation-building in Africa was its failure to link up or produce an 'organic intellectual' (Mkandawire 2002). These arguments may hold, by extension, to the Pan-African project. The point here is that we need a better understanding of what thinking is going on in intellectual circles about Pan-Africanism and what capacities exist for reflection and analysis. And given the importance of Africa's Diaspora, similar questions are pertinent to it as well. What is the political clout of Africa's Diasporas and how do they link that up to Africa? And what do they expect of their counterparts in Africa and how do they relate to each other?

Such an analysis must go beyond academics and artists, to whom we often confine the term 'intellectual' and take on other elements of the intelligentsia. Gramsci's understanding of 'organic intellectuals' included professionals and technicians. In the case of Europe, the role of such elements (the 'Eurocrats') in the building of the European Union has been widely recognised. This was an intelligentsia, shaken by the carnage of many European wars, which dreamed of a new Europe and used their technical and administrative skills to build the foundations of a new Europe. What is lacking in Africa are such organic intellectuals – that is, 'Afrocrats' imbued with the spirit of Pan-Africanism, aware of the political imperatives driving individual member states and Diasporas, and respectful of the democratic authority of the people. African regional schemes have not only lacked political bases but have also been dismally managed. The African intelligentsia have fallen out of the loop of decision-making. Partly because of the weaknesses of Africa's own regional institutions, considerable initiative on Pan-African affairs has been left to international and regional bureaucracies with no organisational links to their national counterparts. One consequence is that the argument for integration has always been pitched only at a continental level. It has rarely demonstrated how each country, let alone each social group, would benefit from that continental project. The commitment of these bureaucracies to Pan-African ideals has been very much dependent on the leadership of their respective organisations.

ECONOMIC DEVELOPMENT AND INTEGRATION

The founding fathers of Pan-Africanism were always acutely aware that one of the functions of Pan-Africanism was to develop the economies and the technological capacity of the continent. The best articulation of this task was made by Nkrumah in many of his pronouncements, but most eloquently in his *Africa Must Unite* (1965). Over the years, the developmentalist agenda of Pan-Africanism and individual states has been watered down by both ideological shifts and the vicissitudes of adjustment during the 'lost decades' (Mkandawire 1999, 2001). With most of our economies tethered to the Washington Consensus, the interventionism of the developmental projects and the developmentalist thrust of thinking on regionalism, as demonstrated in the setting up of the African Development Bank and the Lagos Plan of Action, lost their resonance. The New Partnership for Africa's Development (NEPAD) is in a way a reminder of the centrality of development to Pan-Africanism.

What National Economies?

If regional cooperation is to succeed, it is important to have a fairly accurate view of the constituent economies. Perhaps the most damning flaw in past experiments was the assumption that member states were somehow 'planned' economies, when in fact they were market economies. One says all this despite the ubiquity of development plans, despite the *dirigisme* so vocally decried by the Bretton Woods Institutions, and despite the anti-capitalist ideologies of some of the constituent regimes. It is true that the market system had not been fully developed and there were many 'missing' markets, but the fact remains that the constituent members were highly open-market economies. Structural Adjustment Programmes (SAPs) have made my argument otiose. The view that one was dealing with planned economies led to a fatal misunderstanding of the nature of the economies of constituent members and had serious repercussions on the thinking about and functioning of the whole. Such an approach automatically led to greater emphasis on complementarities and planned and concerted allocation of economic activities, and less on competition within a protected market and compensation of losers in the process. As a result, regional integration in Africa has been of the 'plan mode', whereby efforts at integration have focused on deciding how to allocate what were conceived as essentially complementary activities in order to exploit economies of scale, rather than in creating an internally competitive market which is 'governed' in such a way as to encourage regional industrialisation while preparing local industry for eventual competition in the global market.

Such an approach has proved difficult to sustain. The first problem is that the efficiency of the particular allocation of industry in terms of the development of the entity and its components are not easily measurable. And so given the uncertainty about outcomes of any investment, satisfaction or dissatisfaction with a particular allocation will be based on largely subjective reasons. The second problem is that of compliance: the absence of enforcement mechanisms for decisions taken by regional entities is often compounded by the lack of respect for the administrative allocation of economic activities by member states. Such 'slippage' could depend on a whole number of factors. The state may never have fully accepted its lot in the particular allocation of industries. In addition, member states may never have enjoyed full control of investment decisions in their respective countries. Where the logic of the administrative allocation of industrial activities collided with the global investment strategies of transnational corporations (TNCs), most states complied with the exigencies of the latter.

One major argument for regional integration is the size of the market. Underlying arguments for regional integration was a strategy for 'deepening' import substitution, whose 'easy' phase of production of consumption foods had been brought to a grinding halt by the limitations of the Lilliputian markets of African economies. Such markets did not allow for the production of intermediate and capital goods for domestic markets, because they relied on the economies of specialisation and scales. Regional integration would provide the requisite markets for 'deepening' the industrial process within a large but protected market. The argument is a strong one as far as it goes. However, it is important to stress that the case is often stated in such a manner as to suggest that size alone will do the trick. This is not as obviously true as it seems. For one, size has not helped much in Africa. A simple regression shows no relationship between growth and size. Nigeria is a huge market and it is not obvious what good it would do Nigeria, under its current policy regime, to expand its market by another 10, 20 or 30 million West Africans. Economies of scale must be exploited deliberately if size is to matter. And that immediately calls for a strategy that spells out areas of co-operation and competition. It also calls for a specific set of institutions. Regional integration involves, in one form or another, a preferential treatment of constituent members. It means that individual producers within these states enjoy the advantages of a protected market. Such a privileged position must be reciprocated by the subjection of individual firms to the rigours of competition within this unit. And this for two reasons: the regional market should not serve as the *chasse gardé* of monopolies, but a training ground to give regional industries a competitive edge in the global market. As the 'new regionalisim' in other regions of the world suggests, globalisation might make this particular role of regional cooperation even more imperative. In such a situation, a major task of the central authorities of integration schemes will be to regulate markets both to stimulate the dynamism of competition and to attenuate the inequalities that markets can spawn.

NEPAD started off with a different assumption about member states. It started with the assumption and hope that its member states are market economies, in the mode of the Washington Consensus, each pursuing export-oriented strategies and desperately seeking foreign investment. If earlier arguments for regional integration were premised on the quite reasonable assumption that further import-substitution would be facilitated by widening this market, the NEPAD argument is premised on the implausible assumption that failed neoliberalism will be sustained by regionalism. Neoliberalism has no interest in genuine regionalism, one which would assume some form of protectionism and preferential treatment. Indeed, neoliberalism and regionalism are fundamentally in contradiction. This SAP reform agenda was fundamentally opposed to regional integration and simply advised each country to open its markets to the world economy.

Both the African Union and NEPAD were born at a time of much greater external control of African economies by outsiders than at any time since independence. This was a period after two 'lost decades', during which many African countries were subjected to economic reforms guided by the Washington Consensus. There is today a heightened tension between the assertions of collective self-reliance and the appeals for financial dependence. NEPAD is quite unusual in that there has been extraordinary interest in NEPAD by many non-state actors, including aid donors, private companies and NGOs. The enthusiasm and alacrity with which NEPAD has been embraced by the outside world, even before it has been adequately debated by Africans and clearly fleshed out in its goals, strategies and resource needs, should be cause for reflection.

Concern with economic growth and appeals to outsiders for help has characterised quite a number of initiatives in the past. In the 1980s, the African states simultaneously adopted the Lagos Plan of Action while appealing to the World Bank to help them prepare a strategy for development. The latter led to the Accelerated Development in Sub-Saharan Africa, popularly known as the 'Berg Report', which completely overwhelmed the Lagos Plan of Action, as structural adjustment began to drive policies in individual member states. For many years, African governments collectively have sworn by the Lagos Plan of Action, while individually swearing by the neoliberal Berg Report. What may be new about NEPAD is that the conflict between the more structural continental vision and the neoliberal, 'market-friendly' Washington Consensus has been settled in favour of the latter. In a sense, NEPAD was the final collective admission of the new paradigm of policy-making to which individual members had already succumbed. Historically, while Africans have been forced to accept impositions at the national level, they have articulated at the collective level more assertive positions about Africa's sovereignty, collective self-reliance and repositioning in the world order.

GLOBALISATION AND REGIONALISM

Pan-Africanism has always had to engage the global order of the day. First, the Diaspora that gave birth to Pan-Africanism was the product of the peculiar integration of Africa into the global order through plunder, slavery, and later colonialism. The agenda of regional cooperation has always involved providing a collective shield against forms of globalisation that were inimical to African interests, more specifically imperialism. The recourse to regionalism in the face of a globalisation that has been weakening individual states is, of course, not peculiar to Africa. In contemporary trade negotiations, regional trading groups have become extremely important. However, so far only the European Union negotiates as a bloc. One common response to globalisation has been the intensification of regional efforts. Indeed, there is ample evidence suggesting that in the more successful countries, increase in trade within regional blocs has played a much more important role than globalisation (Chortareas and Pelagidis 2004). Indeed, 'globalisers' such as African and Latin American countries have performed less well than 'regionalisers' such as European and Asian economies. Pan-Africanism must still seek to improve Africa's standing in a global world where many players individually, nationally, or regionally pursue interests that are all too often in contradiction with ours. Regionalism has always implied the preferential treatment of member states (or, as in the European case, 'community preference'), while the rhetoric of globalisation insists on 'level playing fields' and 'non-discriminatory' behaviour towards all countries party to the new global order.

There is tension between extra-African and intra-African relations. This is an old story. Ever since independence, attempts at regional co-operation have been bedevilled by the special link that individual African countries have maintained with the outside world, especially their erstwhile colonial masters. Pan-Africanism has had to respond to the individual dependence of member states on their erstwhile colonial masters and to new structures of global power. And even today, the special relations that individual countries maintain with the outside world do not always serve intra-African relations well.

Historically, the Bretton Wood Institutions have shown little interest in regional collaboration. The main reason is that, in general, regional integration has led to the collective adoption of import-substitution industrialisation, a strategy of economic development that these institutions strongly condemn and have sought to reverse with the structural adjustment programmes. In addition, these institutions believe that the economies should be 'open' to the entire world – buying from the cheapest supplier and selling to the best buyer, neither of which need be immediate neighbours with whom one seeks to integrate. This undermines preferential treatment of member states over non-members, which is an inherent part of regional co-operation. And so the adjustment programmes that individual member states have signed insist on non-discriminatory 'opening up' to the world that often undermines whatever agreements Africans states may have reached among themselves. The supine position that individual nations have adopted vis-à-vis foreign powers is not compatible with the bold image of Pan-Africanism.

Africa's relations with the rest of the world remain fraught with unresolved contradictions and mutual recriminations. Although a number of donors have signed on to NEPAD as the basis for a new partnership, it should be recalled that, notwithstanding the goodwill of individual states, many of these same donors are structurally imbricated in regional and global arrangements that militate against African interests, or place their own regional interests above African interests. This is part of the incoherence of investment, trade and aid policies of individual states, which has been extensively debated among the donors themselves (Forster and Stokke 1999). A Pan-Africanism premised on a benign world ready to underwrite our Pan-Africanist dreams involves a leap of faith and unilateral disarmament that is irresponsible, to say the least.

CONCLUSION

The problems that nation-states have created for Pan-Africanism are not the consequences of nations taking their national project seriously to the neglect of the Pan-African project. Something else has made the national project appear so hostile. Rather, it is that nation-states did not take their national projects seriously enough to see that their consummation required the collective self-reliance which was so central to Pan-Africanism.

The great source of incoherence of the national projects arose from the failure to reconcile what were obviously socially pluralistic arrangements with political and economic arrangements that were monolithic and highly centralised. While the counterfactual can underscore the elements of choice in the historical process, contemporary political actors have to act on the basis of where the path chosen has led them. The new thinking about Pan-Africanism will have to start with such givens as Africa's rich tapestry of criss-crossing identities, as well as the nation-state. Whatever missed opportunities have produced so many states in Africa, it is politically significant that these states will constitute the building blocks of Pan-Africanism. The identities they reflect are no more imaginary than those of any other nation-states. Important concerns of the citizens – human rights, democracy, equality, citizenship and social inclusion

– are now being raised within the context of the nation-state, even when the solution may eventually transcend the confines of the nation-state. Pan-Africanism must demonstrate that it is relevant to these concerns and that it provides both ideological and spatial contexts within which these issues can be adequately addressed. The vision that Pan-Africanism puts forward must be built not on the path not taken, but on the lived histories of the continent and its people in both Africa and the Diaspora, and on the constellation of social forces in the various spaces that constitute Africa.

Pan-Africanism also runs the danger of failing because it has misinterpreted its foundations and the basic units upon which it will eventually will be built. It is probably the case that had Africa taken another path, we would be somewhere else. But like all counterfactuals, such a conjecture does not help us much. We must take as our point of departure what we have. If regional integration is to have any political anchoring at the national level, it must be embraced by key political actors at that level. And more significantly, if Pan-Africanism is to have resonance among the new generation, it must align itself with struggles for democracy and social justice in post-colonial Africa. It must extend itself to protect Africans not only from the ravages of imperialism but also from that of its own predators. It must therefore pay greater attentions to the new emerging voices.

The African Union stands a better chance. It was born at a time of increased demand for democratisation and the end to authoritarian rule. The total decolonisation of Africa and the end of the scourge of apartheid have dramatically changed the African political landscape and African priorities. For one, we no longer see bemedalled clowns like Idi Amin or Jean-Bedel Bokassa at OAU meetings, strutting their stuff at Pan-African fora. The liberation of South Africa has brought onto the African scene a new vibrancy with regards to debates on democracy, and also permitted a shift away from problems of decolonisation and 'collective rights' towards those of development, democracy and human rights. We can no longer justify the violation of human rights in the name of 'collective rights'. The democratisation of the region may, therefore, augur well for regional integration, as the new democracies take economic development seriously and see regional integration as a useful tool, and as the new regimes share a number of values which make them more willing to accept collectively a higher regional authority on a number of issues. It will also bring a more open and collective debate on the future of Africa. Already, we see how, unlike past continental documents on Africa's integration, NEPAD has been heavily contested and more openly debated. This is not necessarily because it is any worse than its predecessors, but because it has been born in a much freer political environment.

While Pan-Africanism is the most emotionally resonant continental ideology, it has had little political success in its project of unifying Africa. I have argued that much of this can be attributed to authoritarian rule that did not constrict our imagination but considered regional cooperation as inimical to national interests because it might diminish the authority of our local potentates. A more democratic and developmentalist project in which self-reliance is the guiding principle would lead ineluctably to the realisation that the pan-African vision not only resonates well with the African people's identities, but also provides both the ideological scaffolding and the resource base for individual and collective progress. If one takes the national agenda seriously, one is led to Nkrumah's injunction: 'Africa Must Unite'. This is because our history and current situation leaves us with no other credible or viable option other than collective self-reliance.

If my analysis is correct, the new Pan-Africanism will have to take on a more democratic and more participatory process in which the Pan-Africanist project will be an aggregation, albeit not an arithmetical one, of the concerns of new social movements for which Pan-Africanism provides a new framework for addressing their local or national agenda. Obviously, in such a situation, Pan-Africanism will have to reflect the synergies and contradictions among the many social and political agendas. And the role of the intellectuals will be to contribute to the imagination of a new democratic Pan-Africanism that will enhance the capacity of the continent to mobilise its vast human resources (Diasporic and continental) and its natural wealth, for laying to rest, once and for all, the sources of poverty and disease that have haunted Africa for so long and for weaving one, inclusive tapestry out its great cultural diversity.

NOTES

1. A version of this chapter was first presented at the Conference of Intellectuals from Africa and the Diaspora (CIAD), 7–9 October 2004, Dakar, Senegal.
2. In the immediate aftermath of Congolese independence in 1960, the nationalist government of Prime Minister Patrice Lumumba was undermined by an alliance between Western forces and Moise Tshombe in the southern Katanga region, which seceded from the rest of Congo.

REFERENCES

Boswell, James (1900), *The Life of Samuel Johnson – Including a Journal of a Tour to the Hebrides*. London: Sands & Co.

Breytenbach, Willie (1999), 'The History and Destiny of National Minorities in the African Renaissance: The Case for Better Boundaries', in *African Renaissance: The New Struggle*, ed. M.W. Makgoba. Cape Town: Mafube Publishing.

Chortareas, Georgios E., and Theodore Pelagidis (2004), 'Trade Flows: A Facet of Regionalism or Globalisation?', *Cambridge Journal of Economics*, 28(2): 253–71.

Davidson, Basil (1992), *The Black Man's Burden*. London: James Currey.

Escobar, Arturo (2004), 'Beyond the Third World: Imperial Globality, Global Coloniality and Anti-globalisation Social Movements', *Third World Quarterly*, 25(1): 207–30.

Forster, Jacques, and Olav Stokke (1999), *Policy Coherence in Development Cooperation*. London: Frank Cass.

Mamdani, Mahmood (1999), 'There Can Be No African Renaissance without an African-focused Intelligentsia', in *African Renaissance: The New Struggle*, ed. M.W. Makgoba. Cape Town: Mafube Publishing.

Mkandawire, Thandika (1999), 'Shifting Commitments and National Cohesion in African Countries', in *Common Security and Civil Society in Africa*, eds L. Wohlegemuth, S. Gibson, S. Klasen and E. Rothchild. Uppsala: Nordiska Afrikainstitutet.

Mkandawire, Thandika (2001), 'Thinking About Developmental States in Africa', *Cambridge Journal of Economics*, 25(3): 289–313.

Mkandawire, Thandika (2002), 'African Intellectuals, Political Culture and Development', *Journal für Entwicklungspolititik*, 18(1): 31–47.

Nkrumah, Kwame (1895[1965]), *Africa Must Unite*. London: Panaf Books.

Nnoli, Okwudiba (1998). *Ethnic Conflicts in Africa*. Dakar: CODESRIA.

Prah, Kwesi (1998), *Beyond the Colour Line*. Trenton, NJ: African World Press.

3
Nation-Building and State Fracture in Sudan

Mahmood Mamdani

INTRODUCTION

The chronic tendencies to political fragmentation in post-colonial Sudan can be understood by tracing nation-building through the various national visions which have vied for supremacy.[1] These visions have defined citizenship in various ways, not least by establishing different systems of local governance over rural land and natural resources. The politics of access to land and natural resources has been at the heart of social conflict throughout this time, while nationalism has failed to provide a democratic alternative to the colonial inheritance, specifically the distinction between 'tradition' and 'modernity' in rural governance. This chapter will analyse the various national visions which have disputed power at local and national levels, including Arabism, Sudanism, Islamism and Africanism.

The colonial system reversed the earlier introduction of individual access to land alongside communal access, as well as the corresponding shift away from tribal leaders towards a political and administrative class of state officials. A process of re-tribalisation was thus set into motion (Mamdani 1996), whereby land was defined exclusively as a composite of different *dars*, each *dar* the homeland of a designated tribe. The result was that participation in public affairs was no longer the right of all those who lived on the land; instead, it became the exclusive preserve of those who were said to possess land as their *dar*. The colonial state claimed that re-tribalisation was faithful to the 'traditional' system.

The nationalist movement that emerged under colonialism fully accepted this claim. 'Tradition' was said to be defended by forces that organised around the identity of tribe and religion: in particular, chiefs in the native authority system and religious leaders in the *sufi tariqas* provided urban politicians with a rural base. As an elite movement of the educated class, nationalism depended for its success on the mass movement of religious sects. This led to an early split in the political class, resulting in the formation of sectarian parties, the National Unionist Party (NUP, later renamed the Democratic Unionist Party, DUP) and the Umma Party, in the electoral politics that followed independence.

Nonetheless, it is the rivalry between the defenders of 'tradition' and the champions of 'modernity', and not the electoral contest between the two mass parties, that drove the seesaw of Sudanese politics between civilian parliamentary politics and a series of military-led coups. The civilian parliamentary governments were inevitably led by one of the two main sectarian parties, NUP or Umma, championing 'tradition', whereas military factions were invariably allied with one or another group of modernist intellectuals. The most ambitious attempt to introduce 'modern' institutions in Sudan followed the coup of 1969 and it was ushered in by the Jaafer Nimeiry regime. The clash between 'modern' reforms and 'traditional' institutions is key to understanding the current conflict in Darfur.

ARABISM

The consequence of colonial policy was to create two Sudans – north and south – within a single state. In a first stage, Britain followed a policy of joint development of the south and the north. But because they feared the Mahdist sentiment among northerners, the British staffed the colonial army with troops recruited in the south. The decision to separate the north from the south was triggered by the onset of the Egyptian anti-British revolution of 1919. In 1924, the Governor-General of Sudan was assassinated by Egyptian nationalists in Cairo. When Britain withdrew Egyptian troops from Sudan in retaliation, Sudanese troops – southerners included – demonstrated in solidarity and refused to obey British officers. The revolt was put down mercilessly and southern troops were withdrawn from the Sudanese army. A strategic decision was taken to separate the development of the south from the north, so much so that it was resolved that the south would henceforth 'progress on African and Negroid lines' (Deng 1995).

A single piece of legislation, the Closed Districts Ordinance of 1922, criminalised movement between the south and the north. The 1922 Passport and Permits Ordinance declared the south 'a closed district'. Emigration from the south to the north was declared illegal, subject to jail or fine. A pass was needed for movement of persons in and out of the south. In short, the north and south were run as two different countries meant to have two different and contrasting destinies. The overall objective was eventually to link the south to a settler-dominated federation of East African territories.

All hues of nationalists in northern Sudan saw Britain's Southern Policy as an attempt to thwart the development of the Sudanese nation and were united in opposition to it. For Britain, however, a separate 'Southern Policy' was part of a larger project. That project included linking Sudan to Egypt in a comprehensive effort to contain the development of nationalist consciousness and organisation. But the project fell apart with the resurgence of Egyptian nationalism in the period that followed the Second World War. It was now clear that the link with Egypt was more likely to fuel than to contain the growth of nationalism in Sudan. It is this realisation that made Britain reverse course in the 1940s. By acceding to the nationalist demand that the south be integrated into Sudan, Britain hoped to wean Sudanese nationalism away from an Egyptian orientation.

The termination of the Southern Policy was a great victory for northern Sudanese nationalists who had been unanimously opposed to it. But the end of the Southern Policy did not mean an end to its effects. By the late 1940s, major structural inequalities were already visible. A cumulative outcome was the development of two parallel elites in the country: a missionary-educated Christian elite in the south and a riverine Muslim elite in the North. Whereas the latter inherited the colonial state at independence, the former felt so cut off from access to the state that it took recourse to armed struggle.

Northern writers would speak of the Southern Policy as a colonial aberration which had created a Christian and non-Arab elite in the south. But the fact was that the Southern Policy was simply the flip-side of Britain's 'Northern Policy' which had coddled a tribal and sectarian (Muslim) elite in the north. Together, the two policies had nurtured two wings of the nationalist movement in the country. If northern nationalists saw themselves as Arab, then southern nationalists saw their common feature as being not-Arab. To this extent, both were products of colonial policy. The difference, however, was that whereas the southern elite saw itself as both non-Arab and southern, the northern elite saw itself as Arab and national, that is, Sudanese.

This is why nationalism turned out to be a fig leaf for the domination of the riverine Arab elite from the north. This became clear as two key safeguards in the transitional process – the Sudanisation and Constitutional Committees, meant to create a national civil service and a national political framework, respectively – were subverted by this very elite. The Sudanisation Committee was set up in agreement with the British, to include one British, one Egyptian and three northern Sudanese members. It concluded that Sudanisation would proceed on the basis of a combination of seniority and merit. With no room for affirmative action, all senior posts were allocated to northerners. Only six of 800 vacated posts went to southerners. The Constitutional Committee was appointed by the National Assembly; only three of its 46 members were southerners. All three called for federalism. When the Committee refused to even discuss the question of federalism, its three southern members boycotted it. Marginalised in both Committees, the southern political class withdrew from the process.

The withdrawal of the southern elite led to the first major political schism in the coalition government created at independence. The Umma Party, with its main base of support in the west, joined the southern parties at a conference in Juba in 1954. The Juba Conference called for a federal status for the south. The DUP, with its main base in the riverine north, resolved to oppose a federal project so as to keep the country united. With the southern political class paralysed following independence in 1954, the response came from southern units in the army. Their mutiny at Torit in 1955 turned into a revolt and ushered in the first phase of the southern armed struggle.

The declaration by the government that the only appropriate response to an armed revolt would be armed repression laid the ground for a military coup pledged to pursue 'Arabisation' with maximum vigor. The coup of 1958 brought General Ibrahim Abboud to power. The response of the DUP government, and the 1958 junta that followed it, was a top-down nation-building project: Arabisation. The junta pronounced that there must be 'a single language and a single religion for a single country'. At the most elementary level, state-sponsored Arabisation simply turned Britain's southern policy upside down. Arabic became the official language in government offices and schools, and Friday replaced Sunday as the official public holiday. All religious gatherings outside churches were banned in 1961, and all foreign missionaries were expelled in 1962. State funds were advanced to build mosques and Islamic religious schools, and there were pressures on chiefs to convert to Islam.

The effect of state-sponsored Arabisation was not only to reinforce a self-consciously Arab power at the centre but also to broaden resistance from the south to other marginal areas in northern Sudan, particularly the east and the west. When civil organisations in the capital launched civil action against the 1958 junta, Darfur joined the national cause enthusiastically. The agitation was finally successful in 1964, when the military junta invited the population to demonstrate in the streets in favour of national unity and an end to the war in the south. The civilian population did pour into the streets of Khartoum and Omdurman in their thousands, but when they unfurled their banners, their target was the junta in Khartoum and not the insurgency in the south. When soldiers refused to fire at demonstrators, the junta tottered. Its overthrow came to be known as the October Revolution. It was the first time the educated class and the young graduates outside of the sectarian and traditional political parties found an opportunity to participate in the national political process. And it would not be the last.

The opposition to Arabisation was strong. We shall trace the main contours of this development in relation to Darfur where students led the opposition to state-sponsored Arabisation. Darfuri students held a conference at El Fasher in 1956, its object being to promote development and progress in the province. The student initiative followed in the wake of a long history of activism around this question. As early as 1938, Dr Adam Ahdam had founded an organisation called Black Block, with the stated aim of representing non-Arab Sudanese in Anglo-Egyptian Sudan. After independence, the successor to the Black Block was the Darfur Development Front (DDF), formed in 1964 on the heels of similar regional initiatives. The initiative to establish the DDF came from the educated class.

The status quo in Darfur was supported by both traditional sectarian parties. The Umma Party had strong support among both the Fur and the Baqqara of Darfur. If the Umma treated Darfur as its traditional reservoir, a kind of a closed region, the NUP was content with its support among riverine traders in the region – the Jellaba – and did little to upset this arrangement. The DDF began by questioning the conventional practice of bringing Khartoum politicians of the Umma and the NUP to work in Darfur – where they were known as 'exported members' – regardless of whether or not they knew anything about the circumstances of the people they alleged to represent. The DDF began by mediating several inter-tribal disputes in Darfur; success in this endeavour made its claim to the leadership of the region sound real.

The DDF soon linked up with two clandestine groups in the province that had been at the centre of the discontent before the

October Revolution. The first group was named al-Lahib al-ahmar, literally the 'Red Flame'. Its main activity was to distribute leaflets threatening action against the Jellaba in the main trading centres of Darfur. But it is the second group which was taken more seriously by the government, mainly because it recruited from rank and file members in the army. This group organised in 1963 as an underground and clandestine group, calling itself Soony, after the name of a place just below Jebel Marra. Although its origins are subject to debate, its claim to the mantle of Darfuri nationalism was based on its pledge to fight the Jellaba for the benefit of Darfuris. It is as a result of the work of Soony and the Red Flame that an internal debate began among the now growing body of educated Darfuris on the merits of having an overt organisation that would wage an open and legal battle for a legitimate goal: to advance the interests of Darfur within Sudan. This discussion led to the launching of the Darfur Development Front in Khartoum in 1964.

The Umma Party both wooed the DDF leadership and tried to isolate it. During the 1968 elections, leading factions within the ruling Umma Party, alternately appealed to sedentary peoples by blaming the region's underdevelopment on Arabs, and to the Baqqara semi-nomads by calling on them to support their fellow Nile Arabs. At the same time, both sectarian political parties waged a heavy war against the Front. Unionist supporters, many of them riverine merchants, accused the DDF of mobilising the people on ethnic and demagogic lines. As pressure mounted from established parties, the leadership of the DDF found it increasingly difficult to maintain their autonomy. Members of the DDF leadership joined the Umma Party, thus making limited and individual gains. When Ahmed Ibrahim Draige became a minister in the government and then emerged as a leader of the Umma parliamentary opposition in 1968, the DDF was swallowed up by the Umma Party and lost its popular base. It was revived in 1986 as an autonomous organisation, but it could no longer claim to be fully representative of all sections of the Darfuri population (Harir 1994: 156–7).

NIMEIRY AND SUDANISM

The 1964 October Revolution brought down the Abboud military dictatorship. There followed a caretaker regime which excluded the two sectarian parties and whose express agenda was to 'solve the Southern problem'. A Roundtable Conference of all northern and southern parties (and exiles) was called for March 1965. When the conference failed, the coalition of left parties fell, the traditional parties returned to power and the war resumed.

The second parliamentary regime was dominated as before by the sectarian political parties. The parliamentary regime was overthrown by a second military coup, led by Jaafer Nimeiry. The Nimeiry regime provided a Sudanese version of militant nationalism in post-colonial Africa. Uncompromisingly modernist, the regime was determined to chart a course free of the sectarian parties. Its efforts took the regime through three different alliances: the first with the Communist Party (CP), the second with the southern rebel movement, and the third with the National Islamic Front. It was a journey that spanned the entire political spectrum. To many observers, the passage from one alliance to another seemed to make for a bewildering – and opportunistic – set of twists and turns. Yet, there was a consistency to these shifts. There was one thing in common between its choices of allies: all championed a modernist agenda, and all were pledged to fight the legacy of sectarian politics. By the time the regime was overthrown in 1983, it had exhausted the entire list of organised political forces with a modernist agenda.

The Nimeiry regime has two achievements to its credit: the Addis Ababa Agreement of 1972 which ended the war in the south, and the fundamental reform of the local government system inherited from colonial times. Through these reforms, the regime tried to lay the basis for a modern state and citizenship rights. Neither reform, however, proved sustainable in the long run. To understand why this was so, we need to grasp the political dynamics that deepened the crisis of a military regime that tried to build popular reforms on the political foundation of an autocracy.

The Nimeiry regime immediately faced organised opposition from sectarian parties. The coup leadership responded by banning all existing political organisations and creating a single state party. The list of banned organisations included the Umma Party, and the DDF which had become a part of it. Henceforth, the only way for a political group to organise was to wage factional struggles within the ruling party, the Sudan Socialist Union (SSU). Throughout 1969 and the spring of 1970, Nimeiry's principal opposition came from the Ansar brotherhood and the Umma Party, with their political and military strongholds in Kordofan and Darfur. A violent conflict ensued in March 1970, when Nimeiry confronted the Ansar. In a fierce engagement, the Sudanese army of the Free Officers, presumably representing the modern and progressive future against a traditional and conservative past, killed the Imam al-Hadi and 12,000 of his followers.

In this opening phase, the Nimeiry regime was allied with the CP. The party saw the alliance with nationalist officers as a tactical rather than a strategic measure, as an opportunity to build its presence within the state and tighten its grip on the levers of power. The sad fact was that every self-confessedly modernist political force in contemporary Sudan – from the CP to its mirror image on the political right, the National Islamic Front – was locked into this kind of top-down putschist power-grabbing strategy. For the CP, the dilemma was a direct result of its analysis of Sudanese society and the avenues of action open to it. The party analysed Sudanese society through the binary of 'modern' and 'traditional', whereby the modern represented the technically advanced sectors of the economy, such as industry, education, communication and the state apparatus, and the traditional the technologically backward sectors, agriculture, pastoralism and crafts, all bonded by religious and ethnic sentiment. The result of such an analysis was an inevitable dilemma: since the modern sector was a minority and the traditional sector a majority, the party could not possibly hope to come to power with the support of the majority. Its only hope was to usurp power through a conspiracy, which is why it spent so much effort in building up alliances within the army, hatching an effective conspiracy, and executing it successfully.

With the coup of 1969, the party seemed to have its first opportunity to put its theory into practice. But since the makers of the coup were not communist officers under the party's discipline but nationalist officers with whom the party was allied, 1969 represented only the first step in its political strategy. The second step would be to overthrow the nationalist officers and take direct control. This step was indeed taken when communist army officers staged a coup in July 1971. They briefly captured Nimeiry, but he escaped and went on to rally his supporters and stage a comeback with the support of Egyptian troops and the dramatic intervention of Muammar Qaddafi of Libya. When two of the principal communist leaders who had been away in London flew to Khartoum to participate in the formation of the revolutionary government, Qaddafi ordered his mirage fighters to intercept and force BOAC, Britain's state-owned airliner, to land at Benghazi airport. It was a flagrant act of air piracy, but it worked. The coup collapsed, its two communist leaders were arrested and sent to Sudan where they were promptly executed.

The end of the alliance with the CP both freed the regime of its ideological straightjacket and opened the way to realising its most important political victory on the domestic front, negotiating an end to the war in the south. While both the CP and the nationalist officers had agreed that the civil war would only end through peaceful means, they were disagreed on the key to reform in the south. The CP's programme for the south called for 'development', not 'democracy'. From the party's point of view, the south needed preferential access to resources so it could 'develop', but in return it would have to accede to a national programme implemented by a national leadership. Autonomy would be the price the south would have to pay for development. When the leadership of the southern rebel movement disagreed with this quid pro quo, the party saw no option but to continue with armed repression. But once the CP was out of power, a new coalition of nationalist non-communist officers converged around Nimeiry and began to explore a different array of political reforms, including regionalisation. It is the willingness of the military to agree to regional autonomy that cleared the way for the Addis Ababa agreement of 1972, thereby settling the southern problem.

The irony was that while the agreement moved towards reforming the structure of power in the south, it did not set in motion a similar process in the north. The post-Addis Ababa regime was Janus-faced: it combined reform in the south with repression in the north. In time, the regime gained popularity in the south as it lost support in the north. The process resulted in a curious anomaly whereby the regime increasingly came to depend on the armed power of southern rebels to maintain its hold over Khartoum, so much so that a time came when Nimeiry's presidential guard came from the south. In contrast, popular opinion in the north, in both the riverine centre and in the fringe areas to the west and east, seethed with discontent.

The gains of the Addis Ababa agreement were summed up in the Regional Autonomy Act of 1972. In 1980, the May regime decided to extend this Act to all the other regions of Sudan. The implementation of the Act led to the appointment of a governor for Darfur. But the appointment of a non-Darfuri as governor triggered popular opposition, known by the Darfuris as the *Intifadha* (upheaval). The *Intifadha* led to clashes with the police and casualties among demonstrators. Soon, the central government gave in and appointed Ahmed Draige, the first chairman of the DDF, to the post. Thus was appointed the first Darfuri to govern the province since independence – a milestone that, according to Harir (1994: 158), marked the end of internal colonialism.

However, success also had an unintended consequence: it unleashed internal political competition in Darfur and opened the gates to the ethnicisation of politics in the region. As long as the administration of the region was controlled by members of the riverine group, the movement against control from outside and for internal autonomy could appeal to all Darfuris and indeed claim to represent them all. But the granting of internal autonomy in 1981 began to erode the unity of the region, which, on the face of it, was united between North and South Darfur. There were already signs of an impending division during the *Intifadha*. On one side were those who participated in the upheaval through demonstrations and, on the other, those who tried to sabotage the upheaval whenever possible. When a smaller group of inhabitants of El Fasher staged a night-time demonstration against the Commissioner of Northern Darfur Province, the majority labelled them 'dogs of the night' – a label for anyone seen to be against the call for Darfur to be governed by an ethnic Darfuri.

The events before and after the 1981 *Intifadha* divided the Darfuri public, especially in urban areas, into two opposing groups. The tension arose from either an ongoing competition for natural resources (mainly pasture and water) or mutual raiding for livestock, and it was exacerbated by the devolution of power. In the past, such conflicts were relatively easily settled by government-supported tribal reconciliation conferences, for the government was an external force whose main interest was in the maintenance of law and order. The original DDF had also proved a successful arbiter of differences. Mainly because its ambition was to unite all ethnic groups in Darfur, it was able to intervene in ethnic conflicts as a supra-ethnic force and settle them through mediation. Whether from the outside or from within, the mediating authority could only have a chance of success if it was seen as non-partisan by both parties to a conflict.

It is this condition that ceased to obtain in 1982, for the new regional authority was born in the midst of tensions between ethnic groups, and was not considered bipartisan by any side. As soon as the regional cabinet was formed and began to function, two opposing political alliances crystallised and cut through the cabinet and the population it claimed to represent. One side was identified with an alliance of all nomadic groups (the Zaghawa, and the Arab nomads) and the doctrinaire Muslim Brothers. On the other side were the major sedentary groups, mainly the Fur and the Tunjur, alongside elements of urban Darfur elites.

These alignments provided the building blocks for the alliances that fought the 1986 election, in which the Islamists defeated the Front for the Resistance of Darfur (FRD), which included many former DDF stalwarts. The Islamist victory was the result of two factors. First, Islamists had the support of Darfuri graduates who had shifted from the 'Arabist' to the 'Islamist' camp following the October Revolution. Strongly supported by the graduate constituency, the National Islamic Front (NIF) won two geographical and four graduate seats. By contrast, the FRD did not win a single seat. The dismal performance put up by the FRD was testimony that many in the population had not forgotten that the DDF had formed a coalition government with the sectarian Umma Party after the 1965 elections and that many of its members had occupied leading positions in the Umma Party. Popular support for the Islamists expressed popular opposition to sectarian parties. Islamist support clearly went beyond the boundaries of ethnic Zaghawa and the Arab tribes: many Darfuris thought the NIF capable of a trans-ethnic endeavour, indeed duplicating DDF's achievement before 1965.

If provincial autonomy was the first prong in the reform of local government, the second was a reform of laws that defined landholding and the system of local governance. Throughout the colonial period, and for over a decade after independence, all rural land had de facto been held as tribal land. The Registered Land Act of 1970 had declared all unregistered land the property of the government of Sudan. Its legal consequence was to turn tribal into state property. Initially, the Act had introduced an ambiguity in the legal status of land, because many families did not formally own the land they cultivated. This ambiguity was removed in 1984 with the passage of the Civil Transactions Act (CTA), which confirmed occupation (use) rights alongside ownership (exchange) rights. With this revision, the state achieved a dual objective: declaring most land (99 per cent) as state-owned, while recognising the rights of actual cultivators and users of the land (Morton 2005).

The reform of local governance was the object of the People's Local Government Act of 1971. This Act abolished the native authority system and replaced it by twenty-two rural councils. This attempt to reform the colonial state failed over the long run mainly because it lacked a viable democratic orientation. Like all modernists, the Nimeiry regime saw electoral democracy as a means of reproducing the hold of sectarian religiously-based parties, an arrangement it replaced with the rule of a single party. The 1971 Act had two important consequences. The first was the proliferation of a bureaucracy, staffed by insensitive officials from the Nile, and directed by the single party, the SSU. This single party bureaucracy began by infuriating traditional authorities, and ended up by intruding upon the historic independence of villagers and nomads in the west. The 1971 Act also repudiated the reform in the colonial ordinance of 1951, which had introduced separation of powers into the native authority system, thereby fusing rule-making and rule-enforcing (legislative and executive) powers in the hands of the new single party bureaucracy. Ironically, the very Act that claimed to end the decentralised despotism of colonial administration laid the institutional basis for a centralised despotism.

Many think that the internal dynamic set in motion by the post-1981 devolution of regional power was responsible for the intensification of internal conflicts within Darfur, particularly the ones that tended to stretch over years, such as the Arab-Fur conflicts of 1982–89 and the Arab-Masalit conflict of 1996–99. Their argument is that the appointment of a Fur governor politicised the civil service, and led to Fur dominance in the new regional government. From the point of view of many an Arab tribe, this indicated a trend which could spell a return to the days of the British-supported Sultanate of Ali Dinar and Fur to dominance of Darfur mainly by the settled Fur.

It is not surprising that the abrogation of the tribal character of land should have had the trigger effect of bringing to life all dormant inter-ethnic land disputes. On that basis alone, many commentators have held the 1971 reform responsible for accelerating ethnic conflict in the province (Ateem 1999). To adopt such an attitude, however, would be to focus on the destabilising effect of every reform, no matter its overall consequence. We need to evaluate the May regime of 1969 not simply in light of its actual results but also in light of its strategic perspective, its promise and ambitions, even if it did not succeed in fulfilling these. On at least one count, the May political regime appeared different from all others that had preceded it. It was the source of many new political ideas which penetrated even the most remote parts of the country. The first among these was the opposition of the regime to the involvement of chiefs and chief-like sectarian notables in politics. This alone began to undermine the sacrosanct authority of those who had hitherto been canonised as 'traditional' leaders. Land reform was a second important factor. According to the policy of the new regime, land belonged to the state; individuals or groups could no longer claim exclusive rights to land, only rights that were explicitly protected by law and registration. Alongside these changes was a third, perhaps the most important: the liquidation of native authorities as a major agency for maintaining law and order in the rural areas.

Those who blamed the Nimeiry reforms for growing ethnic conflict in Darfur were not entirely wrong. Their mistake was to trace this influence to the introduction of reform, rather than to the failure to sustain it. The colonial order had a dual impact in the countryside, both negative and positive. The negative side of chiefly authority was that it became an instrument for the perpetuation of stagnation in rural areas. On the positive side, chiefly authority ensured order at a reasonably low cost, especially in areas where no basic changes had been introduced in economic and social structures. The powers of the chiefs rested upon their customary sanctions by which they could keep the balance between different interests and ensure harmony between tribes. This discussion shows why it is important to distinguish between two different needs in the countryside: on the one hand, to maintain traditional law and order and, on the other, to galvanise forces capable of ushering development in the region.

Though they failed, the Nimeiry reforms placed an important question on the agenda of reform: how to reform indirect rule. The argument for replacing native chiefs by modern bureaucracies rested on the need to combine the maintenance of law and order with creative administrative duties that normally go under the rubric 'development'. If the role of the state in the countryside is confined to maintaining law and order, then there is little doubt that this role can be performed both more efficiently and with less expense by chiefs. But if the point of state intervention is to break the cycle of stagnation that has gripped Darfur over the past several decades, then the case for a modern bureaucracy to replace chiefly rule will be that much stronger. For those convinced that chiefly rule must give way to administration by a modern bureaucracy, the reform also raised a second question, one having to do with accountability at all levels of governance.

ISLAMISM

There was more than just a passing resemblance between the CP and the NIF. Both were modernist to a fault. Both thought in universal terms and believed themselves to be free of parochial

alignments, whether of locality, or ethnicity, or sect. Their organisational efforts focused on the modern sector and both competed to
organise the same urban constituencies: educated youth and women,
graduates and professionals (doctors, lawyers, teachers, professors,
engineers), and salaried workers. They combined open agitation
with clandestine cadre-based organisation. Most importantly,
neither believed they could come to power through a democratic
struggle; both prepared actively for a clandestine and conspiratorial
politics. With that in mind, both organised within the army. Like the
Nimeiry/CP coup of 1969, the NIF-backed 1989 coup of General
Omar al-Bashir also proclaimed itself in revolutionary terms, as a
'revolution of national salvation', dissolved political parties and
trade unions under emergency laws, and ruled by decrees issued
by the Revolutionary Command Council (RCC).

The NIF had a strong base among students. Its cells in Khartoum
University were dominated by students from Darfur. Following
the introduction of regional government in 1983, they returned to
Darfur on instruction from the party leadership and held prominent
positions in the regional government. When 15 army officers of the
RCC led by General al-Bashir overthrew the civilian government of
Sadiq el Mahdi in June 1989, the army, civil service, and police force
were reorganised, and positions filled with members of the NIF. In
addition, a parallel armed organisation called the Popular Defence
Force was established. The NIF coup of 1989 also created the first
opportunity since independence for many of Darfur's educated
political elite to enter national politics as part of the Turabi faction
within the NIF. If the first few Darfuris to enter national political
leadership had done so under the patronage of the Umma Party in
1968, the second round of Darfuris did so under the wing of the
NIF in the early 1990s.

When fresh elections were held in 1986, the year after Nimeiry
was overthrown, Islamists won 54 seats, emerging as the third
largest bloc, ahead of the CP and its allies. It was the first time an
ideological political movement had succeeded in finding a place
alongside the mass-based sectarian parties. Hassan Turabi, the head
of the NIF, provided a double critique, theoretical and practical, of
the traditional parties and their sectarian religious orientation. An
uncompromising modernist, he reminded his audience of the deeply
historical nature of Islam and its law:

Muslims have failed to absorb and understand their history.
They are not able to renew their movement because they do not

understand the ever-changing movement of history. They have assumed that human thought, or the body of achievement of Islamic *ijtihad*, is not connected in any way to time and place. They have stripped the application of *shari'ah* from its practical and realistic aspects, and turned it into abstract concepts existing outside the time-pace framework. (Turabi quoted in Hamdi 1998: 13).

Asked whether Muslim groups which claim 'a monopoly of sacred truth' would not 'impose their ideas and beliefs on others by force' if they were to come to power, he responded that the interpretation of religious truths in light of time and place (*ijtihad*) was a right of every Muslim, and not just of specialists: 'I respect the sufi tradition but I do not pay allegiance to a sheikh. I also respect the *mujtahideen* [interpreters of *fiqh*, jurisprudence] but do not believe that they have a monopoly of *ijtihad* ... I believe that *ijtihad* is open to every Muslim, no matter how ignorant or illiterate he or she might be' (ibid.: 45). When it comes to knowledge, he argued, there can be no absolute authority: '[k]nowledge is a common commodity and people attain various degrees of it, and can exercise *ijtihad* at various levels' (ibid.: 89). Which is why there could neither be an official church nor a canonised truth:

> I am not in favor of sitting somewhere and issuing a fatwa and forcing people to accept it. Nor am I by any means a believer in a church that monopolizes the truth and separates man from God. I regret to say that the Muslims have been affected by the Western malaise, and they have developed pseudo-churches where '*ulama* and sheikhs pontificate and issue sacred edicts. (ibid.: 46)

This translated into a warning against sectarian Islam, for it had confused the general principles of the religion with values and practices prevalent in specific places at particular times. This is why Islam in Iran could come packaged in 'Iranian chauvinism' (ibid.: 87), and in Pakistan bundled with a legacy of the Indian caste system:

> I fear that it [*Jama'at-e-Islami*] might have been influenced by some of the traditions of the Indian culture. That culture is based on a caste system dividing society into Brahmins, middle caste, and the deprived classes that carry no weight in society at all. The *Jama'at* at times looks as if it has this division within its

own structure ... Women are totally separated from men, which of course has nothing to do with Islam, and a religion that is for men only is a deformed religion. (ibid.: 91)

Closer to home, Turabi warned of the need to distinguish Islamic principles from their particular cultural wrapping, Arabism.

Many have emphasised Turabi's opportunism in practical politics, but it is not his practical opportunism but his theoretical arguments that set him apart from other politicians. It is what he said and not what he did that galvanised non-Arab Islamists, and explain his long-term impact on Sudanese politics. Turabi's volcanic impact on Sudanese politics derived from the distinction he made between the universalism of Islamic principles and the parochialism of Arabic cultural practices, and the need to free the former from the latter. Islamism presented itself as a worthy successor to Arabism precisely because it could claim that, unlike Arabs, who were a minority in Sudan, Muslims were in the majority – and the making of a Sudanese nation would have to be a majority project if it was going to be successful. It is the NIF's insistence on distinguishing between Arabism and Islamism that explained why Darfuri Islamists poured into the ranks of the NIF at an early stage. Finally, it is the collapse of this distinction once the Islamists were in power that explains both the split among Islamists and the retreat of Darfuri Islamists to a separate organisation.

Islamists implemented a new set of reforms in the countryside. If Communists and allied officers tried to change the very structure of local government, Islamists took the broad structure for granted and attempted to carry out reforms within these parameters. The point of these reforms was to give 'justice' to the *dar*less tribes. This, at least, was the rationale behind the local government reforms of 1991 and 1995. The Islamist regime began by appointing a military governor for Darfur in August 1991. This was the infamous al-Tayeb Mohamed Kheir, known as 'al-Sikha', the 'Iron Bar', a reference to the actual iron bar he carried and applied with enthusiasm during street riots in Khartoum. The reform began in February 1994 by splitting Darfur into three separate states, North, West, and South. Supporters of the reform explained it as a skilful way of balancing a Fur majority in one state with non-Fur majorities in other states, but opponents decried it as an equally skilful way of dividing the Fur, the largest ethnic group in Darfur, into so many minorities spread over different states. A second reform took land from some of the settled tribes with officially designated *dars* and created *dars* for hitherto *dar*less tribes. The result was a fragmentation of the territory hitherto demarcated as Dar Masalit. With the creation of a new Native Administration, the authority of the Masalit Sultan was also demoted. Furthermore, Dar Erenga and Dar Jebel in Kulbus Province became two different administrative entities outside Dar Masalit Sultanate. If the division of Darfur into three separate provinces alienated the Fur, the granting of land to *dar*less tribes mainly alienated the Masalit. When the Masalit protested, the regime's response was to replace the civilian governor with a military one. The new governor immediately took to imprisoning and torturing prominent leaders of the protest. This was the background to the raging conflicts between the Masalit and the Arab tribes in the late 1990s.

When they began in 1995, these were still local conflicts, fought around local power, tribal territory, and access to natural resources. The central government made things worse by a patently partisan reform that made no claim to be reforming the system as a whole and yet seemed to tilt in favour of Arab tribes of the region at the expense of the Masalit and the Fur. As the existing system of admin-istration came undone, traditional mechanisms of conflict resolution began to come apart. Three separate reconciliation conferences in 1995–96 came to naught. The more the government became party to a hitherto local conflict, the more the conflict spiralled into an officially recognised State of Emergency. This is the time different ethnic groups established, trained, and armed militia groups which would provide the basis for the recruitment of forces in the war that followed ten years later. They began by remobilising traditional village militia structures, *warnang* among the Fur and *ornang* among the Masalit, both historically used to organise hunting parties, communal work in the fields, and feasts (Fadul and Tanner 2007). The Masalit drifted into a guerrilla war until January 1999, when government troops, helicopters and Arab militias crushed the Masalit insurgents, killing over 2,000 and displacing 100,000, of whom 40,000 were said to have fled to Chad (Johnson 2003: 140–1, Prunier 2007: 75, Flint & de Waal 2005: 57–61). If the Nimeiry regime fused the rule-making and rule-enforcing powers of local authorities, the Islamists not only revived colonial-style native authorities, but also militarised them by broadening their duties to include preparation of youth for counter-insurgency (dubbed *jihad*), touted as part of the duty of an official who it was said must lead his people in both prayer and war.

A split in the Islamist elite ensued at two levels, the national and the provincial. Whereas the national crisis split the ruling party, the provincial crisis ignited rebellion in Darfur. The first indicator that all was not well within the Islamist political project came before the Bashir coup of 1989: two parliamentarians, both from Darfur, resigned from the NIF block during the 1986–89 democratic period. The division between settled and nomadic factions within Darfur had national implications. If the Fur-dominated DDF had earlier evolved into a pro-cultivator lobby, the Fur felt the National Salvation government was tilting too much in favour of nomads. This led to further splits and a Masalit revolt against the central government. The government responded predictably, mobilising Arab nomads, most of them recent immigrants from Chad. These militia, which came to be known as the Janjaweed, began to operate in the lands of both the Fur in Jebel Merra and the Masalit to the west.

The second indicator was the development of factional conflict which split the Islamic Front into two ethnically polarised groups: the Quraish as the symbol for Arab tribes and the Black Book as the symbol for African tribes. The leadership split between Bashir and Turabi, ultimately crystallising into an organisational divide with the emergence of two parties from the Front, the ruling National Congress Party (NCP) and the opposing Popular National Congress (PNC) led by Turabi in 1999. For many, Turabi symbolised the interests of those from Darfur, in contrast to the NCP which was taken to stand for riverine Arabs. The claim of the Turabi faction to represent the people of Darfur was the presence of a prominent Darfuri in its ranks, Dr Khalil Ibrahim, who had been the Minister of Health in the Sudanese government before the Bashir-Turabi split, and would frequently become the leader of one of the two main rebel movements, the Justice and Equality Movement (JEM). Even after he left for Europe to build foundations for JEM, Khalil Ibrahim sided with the PNC in 2002. In March 2004, the government arrested ten middle-ranking officers, all from Darfur and the neighbouring Kordofan, on suspicion of plotting a coup. Days later, it detained Turabi, along with six top PNC political figures, accusing them of inciting regionalism and tribalism in Darfur.

AFRICANISM

When the Sudanese political class coalesced around an Arabisation project on the morrow of independence, it built on deep-seated assumptions that had driven intellectual pursuits throughout the colonial period. The key assumption was that civilisation in Sudan had been mainly an exogenous affair, narrowly a product of 'Arab' emigration and inter-marriage and broadly an outcome of Arabisation of the indigenous population of Sudan.

There were two responses to Arabism as a state-imposed national project: Islamism and Africanism. Both claimed that the Arabist project was caught in a dilemma of its own making: since 'Arabs' were a minority in Sudan, the Arabist project would have to be an imposition on the non-Arab majority. Both claimed to stand for a majoritarian project. Instead of a state imposition on the majority in society, such a project would refashion the state in the image of a majority in society.

Neither, however, was in a mood to think through the contradictions of the majoritarian position. There were at least two. The first and more obvious question concerned rights of a minority in a democracy. How could a state designed in the image of the majority still claim the legitimate right to govern all the people of Sudan? The second was a more complex question, one that concerned the definition of the majority. As the very contention between Islamist and Africanist projects showed, there was no single, self-evident and permanent majority in society which could be obtained through simple arithmetic calculations. Because people had multiple cultural identities, even cultural majorities were multiple and overlapping. In this case, the overlapping ground was occupied by African Muslims who belonged simultaneously to two majorities, African and Muslim. Their particular political identification would determine which cultural identity would translate into a political majority at a given point in time. Finally, the nature of a majority project, Islamist or Africanist, was not self-evident at all. As the Islamist period demonstrated clearly, there were rival notions of Islamism, presenting alternatives that were inclusive or exclusive, with radically different consequences for democratic politics. Similar questions would arise when it came to the debate on how state and society in Sudan should be reorganised in line with Africanist conceptions.

Africanism in Sudan had deep intellectual and political roots in all parts of the country. A recent history of artistic and political expression in Sudan traces the Africanist assertion to debates inside the Sudanese Union Society, the first literary society formed by young graduates in 1920 'to strengthen the nationalist consciousness of Sudanese, partly though literary activities and partly through directly disseminating views critical of the Condominium government' (Abusabib 2004: 62–3). It is the split in the Union Society that led to the formation of the first explicitly political organisation, the White Flag League of 1923. That split turned on a debate as to which dedication would be the most appropriate to a collection of religious poems: 'to a noble Arabic nation' or 'to a noble Sudanese nation' (ibid.: 97). The division has come to reflect a running ideological chasm in Sudanese politics between two sides, one championing Arabic nationalism and 'the Unity of the Nile Valley' and the other a Sudanese nationalism calling for 'Sudan for the Sudanese' (ibid.: 72–3).

Sudanism and Africanism became the terms of two different critiques of Arabism in the artistic and literary world, the first more multicultural in its conception than the second. Both currents found expression in northern Sudan in the 1960s. Quite often, these currents drew inspiration from the historical example of Sinnar, the capital in the kingdom of Funj. The visual artist Zein al-'Abdin coined the term *Sudanawiyya* (Sudanism). In the words of Mohamed Abusabib (2004), it 'defines the cultural basis of a pioneering and influential trend in modern Sudanese visual art' and refers to 'artists who derive inspiration from local heritages with the aim of creating an "authentic Sudanese" art'. Poets Bubakar and al-Hai similarly sought a reconciliation of Arabic-Islamic and indigenous elements. The rise of Sinnar brings together a multiple heritage, from the south (the jungle), from Arabic and Islamic Sufism (the desert) and from Nubia, and it creates 'a new tongue, history and homeland' for the Sudanese. In the 1970s, Nuba intellectuals began to speak of Nuba as an 'African' area, marginalised under the rule of an 'Arabist' central government.

The political roots of Africanism lay in the struggles of southern peoples. As independence approached, members of parliament and the educated class from the south called for a form of government that would give them the right to choose their own state system; most demanded a federal form of government. No sooner had the Sudan become an independent state than an armed insurgency began raging in the south. That insurgency has been like an undertow shaping the history of independent Sudan, either directly by its own impact or indirectly by inspiring movements in peripheral regions. The southern insurgency went through three different phases: the 1955 insurrection was followed by an armed struggle that unfolded in two phases, the first from 1963 to 1972, and the second from 1983 to 2003. Two major political shifts occurred during these periods.

The first was in the method of struggle, which moved from the armed insurrection of 1955 in Torit, to a protracted armed uprising that unfolded in different phases, from 1963 to 1972. The second was a shift in perspective. Both the insurrection of 1955 and the guerrilla struggle that began in 1963 looked for a specifically southern solution to a problem it defined as southern in its manifestation. A radical change in perspective came after 1983, with the formation of the Sudan Peoples Liberation Army (SPLA). Unlike its predecessors, the SPLA refused to be confined within the borders of South Sudan. It demonstrated an ability to mobilise beyond sacrosanct ethnic boundaries, first beyond its supposedly Nilotic heartland to Eastern Equatoria, and then beyond the old North-Sudan border to the Nuba Hills in Southern Kordofan and the Southern Blue Nile. The SPLA presence in the Southern Blue Nile Province appeared in late 1985, when armed SPLA units began passing through it, as they moved between Ethiopia and the White Nile. The SPLA put forth an all-Sudan demand, one that called for the reorganisation of Sudanese state and society around the recognition that Sudan was an African country. The key question was: who is an African?

John Garang tackled this question in his statement to the historic Koka Dam conference, a preliminary dialogue held in March 1986 between the SPLM (Sudan Peoples Liberation Movement)/SPLA and the northern Sudan-based opposition coalition, the National Alliance for National Salvation:

> I present to this historic conference that our major problem is that the Sudan has been looking for its soul, for its true identity. Failing to find it (because they do not look inside the Sudan, they look outside), some take refuge in Arabism, and failing in this, they find refuge in Islam as a uniting factor. Others get frustrated as they failed to discover how they can become Arabs when their creator thought otherwise. And they take refuge in separation. (Garang 1992: 127)

Next he distinguished between Arabism as a political project and Arabic culture (ibid.: 55):

> We are a product of historical development. Arabic (though I am poor in it – I should learn it fast) must be the national language

in a new Sudan, and therefore we must learn it. Arabic cannot be said to be the language of the Arabs. No, it is the language of the Sudan. English is the language of the Americans, but that country is America, not England. Spanish is the language of Argentina, Bolivia, Cuba and they are those countries, not Spain. Therefore I take Arabic on scientific grounds as the language of the Sudan and I must learn it. So, next time, I will address you in Arabic if Daniel Kodi, my Arabic teacher, does his job well, and if I am a good student ... We are serious about the formation of a new Sudan, a new civilization that will contribute to the Arab world and to the African world and to the human civilization. Civilization is nobody's property. Cross-fertilization of civilization has happened historically and we are not going to separate whose civilization this and this is, it may be inseparable.

The problem of the Sudan was that of political power, not cultural diversity (Garang 1989a: 258):

I believe that the central question, the basic problem of the Sudan is that since independence in 1956, the various regimes that have come and gone in Khartoum and have to provide a commonality, a paradigm, a basis for the Sudan as a state; that is, there has been no conscious evolution of that common Sudanese identity and destiny to which we all pay undivided allegiance, irrespective of our backgrounds, irrespective of our tribes, irrespective of race, irrespective of religious belief.

And the way to solve this problem is to address the question of how power is organised (Garang 1989b: 214, 205):

The method which we have chosen in order to achieve the objective of a united Sudan, is to struggle to restructure power in the center so that questions as to what does John Garang want do not arise, so that questions as to what does the South want do not arise ... I totally disagree with this concept of sharing power, for it is not something in a 'siniya' (food tray). I use the words restructuring of political power in Khartoum rather than power sharing because the latter brings to mind immediately the question, who is sharing power with whom? And the answer is usually North and South, Arabs and Africans, Christians and Muslims. It has the connotation of the old paradigm.

John Garang died prematurely, barely a year after he assumed the position of First Vice President in Sudan. Even the day of arrival suggested the guerrilla struggle may have ended, but its impact on civilian politics was just beginning. The very composition of the million supporters that gathered to welcome him, the very fact that they cut across all conventional political divisions, had the hint of something new.

It may be that, as with Turabi, so with Garang, what he said had a much greater effect than what he did. Even then, the effect of what they said could be read in the actions of others who took those words seriously. This much is clear from developments in Darfur, particularly the mushrooming of two rebel movements, the Sudan Liberation Army (SLA) and JEM, one inspired by the African secularism of Garang and the other by the African Islamism of Turabi.

NOTE

1. This chapter is adapted from 'Building Nation and State in Independent Sudan', *Saviors and Survivors* (New York: Pantheon Books, 2009), ch. 6, and reprinted with permission.

REFERENCES

Abusabib, Mohamed (2004), *Art, Politics and Cultural Identification in Sudan*. Uppsala: Uppsala University.

Ateem, E.S.M. (1999), 'Tribal Conflicts in Darfur: Causes and Solutions', Paper presented at the conference on *The Political Problems of the Sudan*, 9–11 July. Germany: Vlotho/NRW.

Deng, Francis (1995), *War of Visions: Conflict of Identities in the Sudan*. Washington, DC: Brookings Institution.

Fadul, Abdul Jabbar, and Victor Tanner (2007), 'Darfur After Abuja: A View from the Ground', in *War in Darfur and the Search for Peace*, ed. A. de Waal. Cambridge, MA: Harvard University Press.

Flint, Julie, and Alex de Waal (2005), *Darfur: A Short History of a Long War*. London and New York: Zed Books.

Garang, John (1992), *The Call for Democracy in Sudan*, ed. M. Khalid. London and New York: Paul Kegan International.

Garang, John (1989a), *First Statement to the Sudanese People*, 10 August.

Garang, John (1989b), *Speech to the Media and the Sudanese Community in London*, June.

Hamdi, Mohamed Elhachmi (1998), *Conversations with Hassan al-Turabi*. Boulder, CO: Westview Press.

Harir, Sharif (1994), 'Arab Belt vs. African Belt: Ethno-Political Conflict in Darfur and the Regional Political Factors' and 'Re-Cycling the Past in the Sudan: An

Overview of Political Decay', in *Short-Cut to Decay: The Case of the Sudan*, ed. S. Harir and T. Tvedt. Uppsala: Nordiska Afrikainstitutet.

Johnson, Douglas H. (2003), *The Root Causes of Sudan's Civil Wars*. Bloomington: Indiana University Press.

Mamdani, Mahmood (1996), *Citizen and Subject: Contemporary Africa and the Legacy of Late Colonialism*. Princeton, NJ: Princeton University Press.

Morton, J. (2005), 'The History and Origins of the Current Conflict in Darfur', in *Darfur: Livelihoods under Siege*, ed. H. Young, A. Monim, O.Y. Aklilu, R. Dale, B. Badri and A.J. Fadul. Medford, MA: Tufts University Press.

Prunier, Gerard (2007), Letter to the Editor, *London Review of Books*, 27 April.

4
After Zimbabwe: State, Nation and Region in Africa

Sam Moyo and Paris Yeros

INTRODUCTION

It has become clear that the Zimbabwean state has exercised a degree of autonomy in a way that no other state has in Africa for well over a generation. While the generalised implementation of neoliberal policies continues to subordinate the continent to the requirements of finance capital, Zimbabwe set out on a different path at the turn of the century, which has only recently begun to falter, under the new inclusive government. This makes contemporary Zimbabwe worthy of attention in its own right, but also for the impact it is having on political developments in Africa.

The impact of Zimbabwe on politics remains poorly acknowledged. In South Africa, for example, it forms the backdrop to the country's enhanced post-2001 black empowerment strategy; in the region, it has broken the settler-donor consensus over the land question and has even led to the formation of a mutual defence pact against US/Western intervention; on the continent, it has emboldened resistance to the World Trade Organisation (WTO) and United Nations (UN) reformism. But the impact on academic debate has generally lagged behind: many commentators have either been hesitant on Zimbabwe or in deep denial. It is curious, for example, that a debate has been conducted on the possibility of a 'democratic developmental state' in Africa without taking direct interest in the questions raised by Zimbabwe. This has much to do with a narrow human rights perspective that has prevailed in public discourse. The emerging consensus seems to be that development requires autonomy, and autonomy requires a new conciliatory foundation, a 'people's contract', together with effective planning bureaucracies (Edigheji 2006). It would appear that Zimbabwe's polarisation, social conflict, anti-bureaucratic struggles and international stand-off have nothing interesting to tell us about autonomy and development: Zimbabwe is the case gone 'wrong', perhaps more proximate to a 'failed' state.

The problem was there from the beginning. Initial reactions to Zimbabwe's radicalisation failed to see this as an exercise in state autonomy, seeing it as its exact opposite, 'state destruction' (Hammar et al. 2003). Other conservative commentators inclined in the same direction, seeing Zimbabwe as a 'weak' state, on the verge of 'failure', or a 'dangerous place' to be tamed (Rotberg 2002a, 2002b, Collier 2009). Meanwhile, surveys of 'progressive' trends on the continent have noticed nothing at all in Zimbabwe (Seddon and Zeilig 2005), or just 'violence and demagogy' (Saul 2003: 197). Only one observer inadvertently recognised the exercise of autonomy, via the concept of 'Bonapartism' (Moore 2004), but the concept was misapplied (Moyo and Yeros 2007b). It was only in late 2008 that a wider debate erupted, occasioned by Mahmood Mamdani's (2008) recognition of a progressive rupture in the neocolonial state, as well as the subsequent signing of an open letter by 200 African intellectuals against the militarisation of the Zimbabwe question, as threatened by the West.

In all, what has been distinct about the denialist perspective, of both left and right, is the ideological suppression of the neocolonial character of the transition to independence in Southern Africa. Beyond the negotiated settlements in Zimbabwe, Namibia and South Africa, the transition has also included a trade-off between, on the one hand, the ending of externally instigated wars, in Mozambique, Angola and the Democratic Republic of Congo (DRC), and on the other, submission to the neoliberal straightjacket. Overall, the transition has been based on a certain 'pact': the ceding of formal independence and peace, in return for the preservation of the economic status quo. This is the context of a persistent and internationalised settler politics against overt and less visible forms of resentment and resistance that continue to demand closure on the national question. Was it really a 'deviation', or mere 'demagogy', that such issues as the land question, economic empowerment and sovereignty, equitable development, and regional defence would become once again the basis of social and political struggle?

We intend here to focus on the impact of these struggles on the character of the state in Zimbabwe, by tracing its continuous transformation, from its consolidation after independence, to its neoliberal shift in the 1990s, and to its radicalisation and tentative normalisation in the 2000s. We will also return to the debates on state theory, whose prior climax was in the 1970s, as well as to the debates on nationalism and regionalism. For it is our view that, after Zimbabwe, a whole gamut of questions has re-emerged not only about the state, but also about nationalism as an ideological force and regionalism as a framework for autonomous development.

STATE, NATION AND REGION IN PERSPECTIVE

A recurrent question concerns the *potential* and *limits* of the capitalist state in implementing progressive structural reforms. This question requires us to look more systematically into the structure of the state apparatus, its material and ideological basis, and the class contradictions which endow it with power. In Africa, this same question imposed itself in the course of decolonisation, as the euphoria of independence gave way to the realities of the international settlement by which sovereignty had been bequeathed. Kwame Nkrumah famously spoke of 'neocolonialism' to refer to the limits imposed on Africa by its subordinate insertion into the world economy. His solution was partly introverted, requiring nationalisation of the economy, and partly outward-looking, calling for the political unification of the continent. The concept of neo-colonialism later gained analytical rigour in the hands of Frantz Fanon (1967) and Amílcar Cabral (1978). They both defended continental unification, but also looked to the internal mechanisms by which neocolonialism was sustained. They pointed to the pitfalls of nationalism, an ideology which was both a mobilising force for national liberation/unification *and* a mystifying force in the service of neocolonialism and fragmentation. However, Fanon and Cabral tended to diverge on the potential and limits of the state in carrying forward the national democratic revolution. Whereas Fanon seemed to view cooptation of the new petty-bourgeois ruling class as a foregone conclusion, Cabral held out the possibility of 'class suicide' by the petty bourgeoisie in the interest of the popular classes.

These questions reverberated around the continent. They re-imposed themselves on Tanzania in the aftermath of the Arusha Declaration, when the ruling petty bourgeoisie forged ahead with nationalisations and villagisation. The positions again diverged: John Saul (1974) held out the possibility of a socialist future led by a vanguard state, evident in the collectivist, as opposed to private, accumulation strategies of the ruling party; Issa Shivji (1976) ruled this out, pointing out that the same collectivist solutions masked the emergence of a 'bureaucratic bourgeoisie' whose purpose it was to reproduce the capitalist mode of appropriation within a collectivised economy.[1] The debate clearly felt the influence of the Cultural Revolution in China, and synergised also with the reinvigorated debates of post-1968 Europe, where similar positions were taken up: Nicos Poulantzas (1968) attributed to the capitalist state inherently capitalist functions, while Ralph Miliband (1969) construed the state to the class origins/affiliations of its functionaries.

Is it possible for a bureaucracy with popular class origins and/or radical nationalist ideology to redirect the capitalist state towards popular and Pan-Africanist ends? Or does it remain necessary to 'smash' the state, as Lenin had advocated? Can such a state survive without the escalation of its contradictions, towards its final reckoning (or 'normalisation')? Can it survive without the diffusion of its radicalism throughout the system, or at least the region?

The questions may seem passé, but they are precisely the questions that imposed themselves at the millennium, this time on Zimbabwe. The country was convulsed by a revolutionary situation, driven by a militant land occupation movement and escalating socio-political conflict. The result was a rare phenomenon: the bureaucracy was both suspended *and* mobilised into a social force with a radical nationalist ideology. The dynamics and contradictions of this process will be reviewed below. For our immediate purposes, it is necessary to make a few conceptual points regarding the capitalist state, nationalism and regionalism in Africa.

The Autonomy of the Capitalist State

Following Poulantzas (1968), the capitalist state is a distinct type of state which both separates economic from political power and unifies the latter at the territorial level. In the capitalist state, the dominant class, the bourgeoisie or its fractions, need not rule directly: it may cede political functions to other classes (for example, the petty bourgeoisie), while the fractions of the bourgeoisie continue to look to the same state apparatus to achieve their own political unity. It is the basic logic of the capitalist state to provide a cohesive force for the functioning of the economic system as a whole. It does so by organising and reconciling the political interests of the bourgeois fractions, while disorganising and reconciling the interests of the popular classes to those of the bourgeoisie, not least via the ideologies of nationalism, universal suffrage and reformism. The separation of the economic from the political, and the aggregation of power in an ensemble of overarching institutions, is what bestows upon the state its relative autonomy. This autonomy is intrinsic to the capitalist state; it does not emerge merely in 'Bonapartist' conjunctures.

Furthermore, 'state apparatus' and 'state power' are analytically distinct. The state apparatus does not have a self-referential power of its own – as neo-Weberians would have it (Callaghy 1988, Hyden and Bratton 1992). The state apparatus exercises state power, which in turn consists in the correlation of class forces at any given time. But neither is the state apparatus reducible to state power, nor vice versa (Therborn 1978). For the internal, inherently capitalist, character of the state apparatus conditions the exercise of state power; and the content of state power, which finds expression in state policies, may reinforce a shifting correlation of class forces to such an extent as to create chronic disjunctures between the state apparatus and state power. In other words, an emphasis on the state apparatus at the expense of state power may not capture the contradictions and possible 'hybridity' of the state. This is the quintessential case of revolutionary societies (expressed, for example, in the notion of the 'dictatorship of the proletariat'), but also of Zimbabwe in the course of its radicalisation.

The branches of the state apparatus may also be in conflict. Poulantzas may not have unpacked the state apparatus sufficiently, but he made the important distinction between bureaucracy as a *social category* and bureaucracy as a *system of organisation*, or 'bureaucratism'. Bureaucratism is the ideology that unifies the diverse class elements of the bureaucracy (as a social category) and makes them function coherently (as a system of organisation); it determines the administrative division of labour, its hierarchy, impersonality and formal rule application. But the state apparatus is not an entirely homogeneous unit (Therborn 1978), as we will also see in the case of Zimbabwe. It includes various branches and functions, namely of coercion (military and police), rule-making (executive, legislature), rule-application (public administration, including local government) and rule-adjudication (judiciary). The very ideology of bureaucratism is diversely applied among the branches (for example, it is less expressive in the legislature than the military), and the class character or affiliation of the branches may also vary (for example, the personnel of the military may be different from that of the line ministries). It is noteworthy that, in African states, local government in the countryside includes subordinate 'customary' structures, staffed by 'hereditary bureaucrats' with certain powers of rule-making and rule-adjudication, especially over land. This bureaucratic 'bifurcation' (Mamdani 1996) is an important feature of most states in Africa, although in our view it is not the defining feature. As we will see, Zimbabwe's recent radicalisation entailed a struggle against bureaucracy, as well as between branches of the bureaucracy.

One final comment will serve to qualify the nature of the state. The superstructure of the capitalist system is not in fact the state, as is so often argued, but the *states-system*, a territorially fragmented group of competing states, each with its own relative autonomy from monopoly capital. This political system is both *hierarchical* and *heterogeneous* in its state-society relations, such that the cohesive function of the state is obtained in some places, namely the periphery, less from material and ideological sources ('hegemony', in the Gramscian sense) and more from coercion (Moyo and Yeros 2007b). One effect is the creation of a series of unstable 'weak links' throughout the system, as the case of Zimbabwe has once again demonstrated. Another is that the state apparatus in the periphery is deprived of self-sustaining capacity: over time, cohesion is obtained, destroyed or restored by external support and/or intervention. This is a point which became clear in earlier debates, where John Saul's application of the concept of the 'overdeveloped state' attributed to the African state an exaggerated, self-contained coercive capacity (Saul 1974; see the critique by Colin Leys 1976).

Nationalism and Regionalism

We consider nationalism to be a historically progressive force (see Moyo and Yeros, Chapter 1, this volume), which in the twentieth century succeeded in altering the global balance of forces to expand the states-system and establish the principle of self-determination as a universal right. This basic balance of forces continues to hold; despite setbacks and reversals, it continues to sustain the collective existence and relative autonomy of peripheral capitalist states.

As we have argued, the relationship of nationalism to imperialism is essentially dialectical, such that its resurgence must ultimately be judged by its political orientation to imperialism. In practice, today, with decolonisation behind us, it means that self-determination is more clearly a question of economic sovereignty; and that separate identity claims within states are more clearly a question of reversing unequal development within existing states. In the past, radical nationalists fully recognised the material requirements of genuine self-determination – as Cabral would say, 'the objective of national liberation is ... the liberation of the process of development of the national productive forces' (1978: 208; our translation) – and they were rightly cautious of ethnic claims, even though their routine dismissal of them as 'petty bourgeois' gave insufficient recognition to the real grievances on which they thrived.

With the onset of neoliberalism, the very submergence of the national question as an economic project has had as its corollary the reinforcement of unequal development and proliferation of social conflict. Today, as in the past, this has assumed various ethnic or religious expressions; and it continues to reflect not only unequal development, but also the degeneration of political organisation among both capitalist and working classes which, inevitably, gives expression to petty accumulation strategies. The ethnicised violence which broke out in Kenya in 2008/09 is a case in point. Yet, this is not the only trend, as the counter-case of Zimbabwe has shown. Here, radical nationalism has once again sidelined ethnicised politics and reclaimed the national question as an economic project. It has shown that radical nationalism remains the necessary, even if not sufficient, ideological force against imperialism.

The neoliberal submergence of the national question has also impacted adversely on regional integration. It is true that Pan-Africanism has always competed with the established state nationalisms, as well as with dissident ethno-nationalisms; these three currents have never been reconciled in a compatible way (see Mkandawire, Chapter 2, this volume). Yet, over the last three decades, there has been a deepening contradiction in the logic of integration. For the proposed principle of integration has been that of the market, serving to integrate African states *not* among themselves on the basis of political and social criteria, but into the global market on the requirements of the latter.

This raises the question as to the means by which integration, whether continental or sub-continental, is to be achieved. There is no consensus on the matter, but two basic points have become clear. First, there are two distinct paths to integration, the functionalist and the federalist. The functionalist, represented by an idealised European model, seeks the gradual integration of economic sectors on the basis of market criteria, on the assumption that economic integration 'spills over' into political integration. But there are two key drawbacks to this ideology: the logic of the monopolistic market reinforces asymmetries between and within member states and sows the seeds of its own paralysis (Europe being the prime example), and it excludes the competitive security component, which in Europe was resolved by subordination to an external force.

The federalist path seeks to establish a collectively agreed distribution of political power (as opposed to market power) between member states, via a federal constitution, so as to protect the weak against the strong and strengthen the whole over the long term. Today, such a project is necessarily anti-imperialist and no doubt requires a solid mutual defence pact. Above all, it requires ideological convergence around a popular Pan-Africanism (essentially, a change in the correlation of forces on a regional level), for it is this which will enable member states to submit their territorial sovereignty to regional planning. To be sure, such a radical consensus is still missing. But it is of great importance that Southern African states have arrived at a historic mutual defence pact, in which Zimbabwe has been, in large part, both subject and object. Unless this is bolstered by federal thinking and regional planning, autonomous regional development will remain a pipe dream.

THE AUTONOMY OF THE ZIMBABWEAN STATE

Our inquiry into the Zimbabwean state is guided by one basic question: *from what* and *for whom* has autonomy been exercised? We are concerned mainly with the various branches and functions of the bureaucracy in the process of its consolidation, radicalisation and recent normalisation.

The Consolidation of the State

The white-settler state of Southern Rhodesia was the form of state that corresponded to the stage of colonial primitive accumulation. The Rhodesian state gradually obtained some elements of relative autonomy from monopoly capital, as expressed most clearly in its Unilateral Declaration of Independence in 1965. Such autonomy was deepened by its subsequent *dirigiste* economic strategy. However, its autonomy from the black population was contradicted by the onset of armed struggle in the countryside; the liberation forces eventually assumed control of the state apparatus by negotiated settlement at Lancaster House in 1979. The settlement did not consist in outright victory by the liberation forces; nor did it have the same meaning among the parties to the agreement; nor, for that matter, among the various elements that constituted the liberation forces. For the imperialists, it was a means to pacify the exploitation of black labour; for the liberation forces it was either a matter of strategy (an end in itself), or tactics (a stepping-stone to more meaningful liberation). It is important to recall this trifurcation to understand the general context of the subsequent re-radicalisation.

This unstable neocolonial pact was a precursor to the pact sealed in South Africa a decade later, but there are significant differences. The correlation of forces that brought the liberation forces to power in Zimbabwe was in some respects similar to that of Mozambique, Angola and Namibia, all of which obtained control of the state through protracted armed struggle. In Zimbabwe, the immediate task of the liberation movement, led by the Zimbabwe African National Union – Patriotic Front (ZANU-PF), was to consolidate its position in the state apparatus by rapid indigenisation of the bureaucracy, especially the military; defend against the destabilisation strategy of apartheid South Africa; and also employ state force against dissident elements among the liberation forces in Matabeleland. What would be left untouched, as per the terms of Lancaster House, was the economic structure, that is, the position of monopoly capital and the white bourgeoisie.

In effect, the political struggles within the nationalist movement would be channelled, by force of the settlement, towards the control of the state apparatus. Thus, whether a tactical or strategic instrument, the state would become the main source of power in the new order, especially for a leadership that already adhered to a petty bourgeois perspective, even if dosed with radicalism. Importantly, all these factors – the neocolonial pact, external destabilisation and internal opportunism – go far to explain both the Matabeleland dissidence and the brutality of state repression, which so tragically marked Zimbabwe in this first stage of state consolidation.

The most crucial component of the subsequent indigenisation process was the military. As in the similar cases above, the military in Zimbabwe was constructed on the back of a non-colonial army, developed outside and against the settler-colonial state. The consolidation of power in the military apparatus was achieved rapidly by integrating the various armies under the leadership of guerrilla commanders, who in turn adhered to a radical petty bourgeois nationalism. These factors enabled Zimbabwe, inter alia, to secure the state from South African destabilisation and external military subversion, as well as to undertake the defence of neighbouring countries, first in Mozambique and much later in the DRC (significantly, with the support of Angola and Namibia, but not South Africa). Nonetheless, the contradiction between the nature of the liberation army and the bureaucratic requirements of the neocolonial state remained to be resolved. On the one hand, the military apparatus fell into line with these requirements, being increasingly deployed against the demands of workers and peasants; indeed, in due course, even the higher ranks of the military bureaucracy would follow the path of private accumulation. On the other hand, the contradiction was never fully resolved, given that their radical nationalist ideals were never entirely abandoned; this was the case especially among the lower echelons of the bureaucracy and a large number of unaccommodated war veterans, many of them workers and peasants, who retained stronger commitments to national liberation.

The liberation movement also took control of central bureaucracy, using externally educated, nationalist cadres. The indigenisation process was again rapid, taking hold by the mid 1980s in most branches of the state apparatus, excluding the legislature (which retained disproportional constitutional safeguards for whites until 1987) and the judiciary, which lagged far behind. In due course, alongside the expansion of the education system and the bureaucracy itself, a new generation of university graduates became absorbed into the system; these were largely of rural origins but without direct experience in the liberation struggle. While some moved up through the system to positions of relative privilege, the whole of the bureaucracy typically gained an interest in the relative economic stability that public service offered; even those among the higher ranks who converted privilege into private profit continued to face constraints in the white-dominated economy. Thus, public servants, including teachers and health workers, swore their allegiance to the state and the ruling party, and in fact did not affiliate to the Zimbabwe Congress of Trade Unions (ZCTU), which covers the private sector, until the events of the late 1990s.

In the countryside, a complex system of local government evolved at provincial and district levels under the highly centralised control of policy and budgets by line ministries and parastatals. Local staff and resources came to be co-ordinated at the lower tiers by the Ministry of Local Government through District Administrators, while district level structures became the pivot of rural policy implementation. The coordination process at district level included an unelected District Administrator and various committees involving local representatives of various ministries and the security apparatus, plus elected councillors and an elaborate unelected traditional leadership structure, including chiefs and village heads – the 'customary' sub-branch of the local government bureaucracy. Alongside these structures, relatively well-organised ruling party structures came to oversee and often influence the local administration process. The complexity of this system reflected, once again, the requirements and contradictions of the neocolonial state. After independence, government sought to establish democratic, secular and non-racist channels for popular participation to replace chiefdom and racially segregated local government structures. The latter obtained, but the state soon proceeded to *re*-subordinate local to central government, by marginalising the new democratic structures and reducing them to policy-implementing agencies; even chiefdom was partly resurrected, to regain control over rule-making and rule-adjudication over peasant land (Alexander 1993).

At the same time, the state succeeded in corporatising black farming interests, specifically the small-scale commercial and communal area farmers, united in 1991 into the Zimbabwe Farmers' Union (ZFU). A parallel process of corporatisation was pursued in relation to workers, who were organised from above, through the newly-created ZCTU, until 1987, when the trade union centre sought an independent political footing. Nonetheless, as we have argued elsewhere (Moyo and Yeros 2005), the whole of society came to be 'civilised' to the requirements of monopoly capital in the neocolonial state, either by the state itself, via corporatisation and repression, or by external donor agencies, including international trade unions, which systematically co-opted trade unions and proliferating non-governmental organisations (NGOs) into workerist, welfarist and, ultimately, 'good governance' agendas. The two organisations that were left untouched were those of white capital, the Commercial Farmers' Union and the Confederation of Zimbabwe Industries – the vanguards of domestic 'civilised' politics.

Finally, the state expanded rather than diminished its foothold in the economy – though always within the limits of monopoly capitalism – by maintaining the parastatals inherited from the settler state and increasing its control over agricultural markets, mineral marketing and mining, and a few industries. Major advances were made in the expansion and integration of rural markets, social services and infrastructure, by diverting resources from the white farming sector to the peasant sector by means of the marketing parastatals. At this stage, rural co-operativism was also promoted, though it foundered on the top-down, corporatist tactics of the neocolonial state.

The underlying dynamics of the consolidation of bureaucracy are to be found in the horizontal (intra-class) and vertical (inter-class) conflicts that unfolded in the post-white-settler colonial state. On the one hand, the civilisation of society rendered the working class organisationally weak, divided between town and country, and prone to co-optation and reformism. On the other hand, the unity of the capitalist class was stitched together by initiative of the black petty bourgeoisie – the *ruling* fraction, without roots of its own in the economy – under the watchful eye of established settler capital and foreign capital – the *hegemonic* fraction. The main inter-capitalist conflict of the 1980s revolved around the pattern of accumulation, this being a contest between introversion and extraversion. However, all capitals – international, domestic, financial, commercial, agrarian, and industrial – were soon to abandon the *dirigiste* mentality of the previous settler state and adopt an extraverted orientation, given that they no longer enjoyed undisputed control over the state apparatus; industrial capital held out the longest, until its cooptation by the World Bank in the late 1980s. For its part, the black petty bourgeoisie in the state apparatus, which still lacked an economic footing of its own, abandoned both the spirit and the letter of the Leadership Code of the ruling party, prohibiting private accumulation; by the late 1980s, embourgeoisement and compradorisation were well underway.

Alongside this, new black business lobbies began to make vocal demands to shift the indigenisation project to the private sector, which had hitherto remained untouched, via affirmative action by the state in finance and agricultural land. Nonetheless, at the turn of the decade, and in step with the global political and economic transformations, all fractions of the bourgeoisie, black and white, lined up behind the structural adjustment programme promoted by the World Bank. The programme was implemented faithfully, the state apparatus being rolled back from all sectors of the economy, but not from politics. The prime losers of the programme were the workers and peasants, but also certain fractions of capital, especially white industrial capital and the black petty bourgeoisie, neither of which was able to compete in the monopolistic 'free' market.

The Radicalisation of the State

This set the stage for the main inter-capitalist conflict of the 1990s: a racial competition over the spoils of structural adjustment, pitting a large section of the aspiring black bourgeoisie against a united white bourgeoisie, led by its agrarian and foreign fractions. Meanwhile, vertical contradictions escalated in both town and country, marked by serial strike action by the ZCTU, its successful incorporation of public servants, a rising tide of land occupations in the countryside, and all-around state repression. When, by 1997, the war veterans association, and especially its lower ranks, resolved to make a stand against the degeneration of national liberation and the land reform agenda, the contradictions of neocolonialism were to move from the streets into the state apparatus itself. They also spilled over into the region, especially from 1998 onwards, as Zimbabwe mobilised Angola and Namibia to intervene in the DRC against the US-sponsored invasion by Rwandan and Ugandan forces. The re-radicalisation of nationalism in the region was thus a 'geopolitical' problem for more reasons than one. The United States and the West had already lost their solid strategic footholds in Southern and Central Africa; now the economic power of their settler allies was coming under threat.

The radicalisation of both the ruling party and the state ensued, whose policy focus turned once again to the rural areas, where the liberation war had been fought, and to radical land reform specifically, a key demand of the liberation struggle. Radicalisation escalated dialectically with the onset of imperialist sanctions and with the formation of the Movement for Democratic Change (MDC) in 1999, a political party led by the ZCTU but funded by white domestic capital and Western governments and agencies. In 2000, the political situation reached boiling point, when the war veterans association moved decisively to organise the hitherto disparate land occupations into a country-wide mass land occupation movement (Moyo 2001, Sadomba 2008). Thus, by the turn of the millennium, the political alliances had polarised into two blocs: on one side, the aspiring black bourgeoisie and the rural landless organised by the war veterans, all under a ZANU-PF banner, and propounding a radical nationalism; on the other, international capital, all sectors of the white bourgeoisie, a small section of the nascent black bourgeoisie, plus NGOs and workers led by the ZCTU, under an MDC banner, all advocating a liberal 'human rights' and 'regime change' agenda.

It is clear that, as long as the ruling petty bourgeoisie toed the line of international capital, neocolonialism remained secure; thus, it is no surprise that the sudden rebellion of the ruling fraction would cause a power struggle over control of the state apparatus. This was not a mere factional fight, however. As we have argued elsewhere (Moyo and Yeros 2007a), the political crisis of 2000 amounted to a *revolutionary situation*, in which diverse social forces became highly mobilised, and in which property rights became contested in a *fundamentally progressive way*. Importantly, the ruling fraction itself struggled to maintain control of the state apparatus. For the mass land occupation movement that emerged was not 'orchestrated from above', as is so often argued, but was organised by a militant war veterans' association which maintained unique organic links to the countryside, as well as to the state apparatus, especially the military and the police. In the event, the top brass of the security forces faced an unsavoury dilemma: either to use force against the land occupation movement and fellow war veterans, or against the imperialist alliance. Both options were high risk, but the first option may have been the riskier, given the extent and influence of the rebellion among the security forces; the second option had history on its side.

What transpired after 2000 continues to require careful analysis. For the bureaucracy was both suspended *and* mobilised into a social force. Its purpose was to adopt *and* co-opt the land occupation movement into a petty bourgeois land reform programme. Adoption entailed suspension of bureaucracy; co-optation, mobilisation into a social force.

What do we mean by suspension of bureaucracy? Suspension involved the sidelining of functionaries normally responsible for land allocation, together with the inclusion of elements which did not previously comprise of the bureaucracy as a social category; suspension also entailed the abrogation of technocracy and established top-down procedures – or bureaucratism – by including popular forces directly into the policy process. Since 1996, the state had introduced 'land committees' into the local level to determine the allocation of land and its use, committees which at best remained inoperative, or at worst vehicles for 'squatter control' (Yeros 2002). In 2000, both the form and content of land committees were transformed, to include not only local ministry officials and traditional leaders, but also ruling party representatives, security organs and war veterans – 15–30 persons in all; the purpose of the committees now was to serve fast-track land reform, regardless of technocratic criteria. In this process, the authority of established local state structures was sidelined (the process of bureaucratic suspension) while land committees were made to report to similarly constituted provincial land committees and the Ministry of Local government (the source of co-optation).

At the same time, the war veterans constituted themselves into 'base camps' represented by 'committees of seven', whose purpose it was to co-ordinate the identification of land for acquisition and its beneficiaries, using pre-existing communal area waiting lists and war veterans' lists, as well as to coordinate new settlers and war veterans and oversee farmworkers, new occupiers and criminals. The base camps took the form of an embryonic power centre, armed and independent of the state apparatus. They were, in fact, the potential source of that feared 'second state', so common in revolutionary situations, whereby a 'dual power' structure emerges to pit popular power against the state apparatus.

At the height of the revolutionary situation in 2000–03, a broad-based nationalist alliance was stitched together through the multi-class war veterans' association, whereby two processes were set into motion. First, the land occupation movement spread to all provinces, from Masvingo to Mashonaland, and then at a slower pace to Matabeleland. In due course, the occupations would also spread to peri-urban areas, to incorporate urban poor and petty bourgeois elements, led in large part by the war veterans. Like their rural counterparts, these urban land occupiers organised themselves into housing cooperatives and other associations, and proceeded to establish residential structures outside the urban planning framework. A broad rural-urban movement thus began to take shape, with substantial independence from the bureaucracy and the higher ranks of the ruling party.

However, the second tendency set into motion was by initiative of the bureaucracy, with the purpose of co-opting the landless movement and making room for the aspiring black bourgeoisie as well. Thus, several moves were rapidly made to remove procedural impediments to land acquisition, to protect occupiers from eviction, to broaden the categories of land to be acquired, but also to formulate a fast-track land reform policy that would deliver land to diverse categories, mainly landless peasants and the black petty bourgeoisie. Alongside this, the security apparatus was mobilised for two specific reasons: on the one hand, to control violence on the farms and to prevent any attempt by white farmers to take up arms; on the other, to repress the urban mobilisation under ZCTU/MDC leadership, which continued to seek the reversal of the land reform and removal of the ruling party from the state. And while the security forces were mobilised in the defence of a multi-class land reform, the judiciary held out in the defence of property rights and white privilege. This led to an intra-bureaucratic struggle to remove/retire reactionary judges. The rest of the bureaucracy also felt the pressure to conform to the requirements of fast-track land reform, or be dismissed. As the dialectic of radicalisation and sanctions unravelled, a number of strategic positions in the state apparatus, and especially in the revived parastatals, were to pass into the hands of retired and/or reliable military personnel.

The immediate results of these processes were the following: the acquisition and redistribution of 80 per cent of agricultural land, essentially without compensation; the liquidation of settler politics and entrenched racial privilege; the broadening of the ownership base in the agricultural sector; the bifurcation of the land reform programme into competing peasant and small-to-medium capitalist sectors; the cooptation of the rural land movement, but not yet the urban; and the disorganisation of the political opposition. But in this process, the revolutionary situation would itself be laid to rest. The final nail in the coffin would be driven two years later by Operation Restore Order, a military-style urban eviction policy. Its objective was two-fold: to liquidate the remaining challenge of the urban land occupations and its rebellious war veterans, and to stabilise the economy in accordance with the longer-term accumulation requirements of the new black capitalist class – given that a large part of business activity was being informalised through the peri-urban areas (Moyo and Yeros 2007a).

We have argued that the war veterans did not go far enough, either within the state, to guarantee the momentum and working-class character of the revolutionary situation, or outside it, to prepare the ground for a sustained struggle against the reassertion of the black bourgeoisie (Moyo and Yeros 2005: 193). The first option may indeed have been impossible, if we accept the thesis regarding the limits of the capitalist state – the inability of the petty bourgeoisie to commit class suicide. The second option did not materialise due to the petty bourgeois limitations of the war veterans' movement itself. Despite its radicalism and organic links to the countryside, and despite even socialist elements within it, it did not advance to a proletarian ideology and strategy. The movement limited itself to a 'single issue' platform – land repossession – and instead of establishing a durable, democratic rural movement and a solid rural-urban alliance – which was a real possibility under the escalating contradictions – it opted effectively for the abandonment of radical politics and its re-subordination to the ruling party. Under the circumstances, the reassertion of the black bourgeoisie, now with a footing of its own in the economy, and the re-consolidation of the bureaucracy, were a matter of time.

Two concluding points may be made. First, it is clear that, despite its radicalism, the bureaucracy in Zimbabwe did not opt for collectivist solutions. Autonomy was exercised from international capital and its white domestic allies, and, ultimately, *for the black bourgeoisie*, given the eventual cooptation and defeat of the rural and urban semi-proletariat. Yet, in the indeterminacy of the situation, there *was* a clear disjuncture between the capitalist state apparatus and state power, expressed in the mobilisation of the state apparatus in defence of the landless movement and a radical land reform.

Did this alter the position of class forces in a progressive way? The revolutionary situation did not result in a revolution. But the political economy of Zimbabwe has now made a progressive lateral shift from a 'Junker' path of settler capitalism to a new capitalist path that combines elements of the 'peasant' and 'merchant' paths (Moyo and Yeros 2005). This has broadened the ownership base of the economy and has set the stage for a broad-based accumulation strategy – together with new class contradictions (Moyo et al. 2010, Chambati 2009). At the same time, it has clarified the class struggle by removing the source of racialised class struggle, the settler element; thus, the black bourgeoisie will henceforth find it ever more difficult to cloak its particular interests in a universalist nationalism. Finally, there has also been a marked change of attitudes in relation to property rights, and especially in relation to the role of international capital. Until 2009, the state was obliged to intervene directly in the regulation of the economy and to control credit, distribution, and even production, in a new *dirigiste* strategy.

Nonetheless, the shortcomings of the new strategy were also painfully evident, in a record-setting hyperinflation and, consequently, in the inability of the state to jump-start the economy. Indeed, it is the failure to implement a collectivist and democratic strategy from the beginning that has undermined the ability of the state to withstand sanctions and to bring the economy under control, given that it is impossible to control an economy whose strategic production decisions remain in private hands. Unavoidably, this popular democratic deficit has had as its corollary the shift to an economic policy-making process characterised by a series of 'operations', each with its own code name (see below).

The final point concerns the persisting rift between monopoly capital and the new black bourgeoisie: why has monopoly capital kept the sanctions regime in place, instead of making peace with the ruling black bourgeoisie? After all, it is the black bourgeoisie that saved Zimbabwe from an uninterrupted revolution! The answer is simple: under really existing capitalism, the nemesis of monopoly capital is *autonomous* development, even of the capitalist variety, outside the geostrategic control of the monopolies. And Zimbabwe's radicalised state has indeed been in a stubborn conflict with monopoly capital, not only on the land question but also on the DRC war (which it entered against US geostrategic designs), WTO negotiations, UN reformism, and the New Partnership for Africa's Development (NEPAD). More threatening still has been the potential of a generalised nationalist resurgence in Southern Africa, led by a South Africa which remains the most consequential 'weak link' on the continent.

The Normalisation of the State

Despite the economic warfare waged by Western governments and capital, the black bourgeoisie has sought to re-establish capitalist order domestically. As we have argued, the basic *internal* contradiction has been to promote a new order on the terms of private accumulation (Moyo and Yeros 2009). Of course, it is significant that the state responded to the external siege by intervening heavily in the economy, across all sectors, and by nationalising land, reasserting control over natural resources and imposing majority control over the mining industry. But in the absence of direct control of strategic sectors, including the banking system, the heterodox strategy opened the way to the financialisation and informalisation of business activity, the entrenchment of speculative and profiteering interests and the excessive printing of money, all too often applied in the interest of the larger capitalists. The strategy was both insufficient and incoherent: instead of redirecting credit towards rural co-operatives and urban housing – that is, the popular classes – the strategy permitted the flourishing of financial opportunism and hyperinflation.

This type of heterodoxy has not been a problem of 'bad governance', but emblematic of the changing balance of class forces. If in the earlier stages of radicalisation (2000–03) the state apparatus had been used in the interest of the landless, from 2003 onwards the enlarged black capitalist class repositioned itself within the ruling party to impose its own version of 'order'. This led to a series of tragedies between 2005 and 2008, especially as economic hardship deepened. The earlier tactics of popular mobilisation gave way to quick-fix, military-style operations: first against 'illegal' urban dwellers (2005), destroying the new urban settlements that had emerged during the land occupation; then against 'illegal' rural miners (2006–08), who had resorted to smuggling for their livelihood; then against profiteers (2007), in a price control blitz whose effect was to expand the parallel market; and finally, during the presidential contest of 2008, against those who could no longer be convinced of the 'vanguard' claims of the ruling party, even in the countryside. This culminated in a deep and tense electoral polarisation, with the opposition taking the lead for the first time, which could only be diffused through negotiations over power-sharing. Thus, a Government of National Unity (GNU) was installed in February 2009.

The agreement over GNU created a dual executive structure, whereby President Mugabe retained his post and the newly-created post of Prime Minister was assigned to Morgan Tsvangirai, the head of the MDC-T (MDC-Tsvangirai). Cabinet posts were also redistributed among the two parties: most importantly, the Ministry of Finance was assigned to the MDC-T, while the security forces remained with ZANU-PF. The result has been a return to peaceful politics generally, but also to intense political struggles among the branches of the bureaucracy. This is most clear at the level of central government, where the state apparatus has now been penetrated by the West through its direct funding of MDC ministries against those held by ZANU-PF. But there are also less visible transformations at the local level: despite the formal extension of customary authority to newly-resettled areas, the emergence of grassroots co-operativism has tended to erode customary authority further (Murisa 2010).

On the economic front, normalisation has been equally significant and turbulent. The MDC-T has refused to confront sanctions outright, even though, once in power, it has recognised the existence of 'restrictive measures'. But the main turnaround has been in the fight against inflation, by means of the extinction of the Zimbabwe dollar and the adoption of a multi-currency system. Implemented by ZANU-PF just before GNU, the surrender of monetary policy was seen as a better alternative to a full-fledged return to IMF tutelage. Beyond this, agricultural markets have been decontrolled; the privatisation of state enterprises, such as the iron and steel company, are under negotiation; the capital account has been loosened; and trade liberalisation has returned, especially via the Southern African Development Community (SADC) and the Common Market for Eastern and Southern Africa (COMESA) agreements. Yet, the struggle continues over the control of the mining sector, this being the main foreign-exchange earner: ZANU-PF, in control of the ministry, has insisted on majority control by indigenous capital. Another battleground is again the land question, where the unresolved issues over tenure and compensation are being reorganised in the course of constitutional reform: the bourgeois fractions, straddling both parties, and supported by NGOs and Western agencies, are regrouping around freehold tenure; while compensation is not in the interest of the black bourgeoisie, but it is kept on the table by the West and the settler politics of the region.

TOWARDS THE AUTONOMY OF THE REGION?

To understand Zimbabwe's interrupted revolution it is not enough to establish 'what happened' but also 'what did not happen'. In order for a revolution to escalate without interruption, it is necessary that two conditions hold: internally, that popular mobilisation obtains a proletarian perspective; externally, that its radicalism spreads to other states and is defended collectively. These two conditions interact in that they affect the internal and external balance of class forces at any given time.

This is what did not happen in Southern Africa. Instead of a regional convergence around a national-popular project, Zimbabwe's radical nationalism stopped short at its borders, impinging on the internal relations of neighbouring Southern African states only in a controlled manner. And although the states of the region, led by South Africa, have provided diplomatic cover for Zimbabwe, this has fallen far short of what was required to sustain its progressive momentum. It is important, therefore, to examine briefly the regional contradictions and their implications for autonomous regional development.

Southern Africa is the most economically integrated region in Africa, an integration whose origins lie in the mineral revolution in South Africa at the end of the nineteenth century. The economic expansion of South Africa became the hub of a profoundly asymmetrical regional economy, integrated by a chronic migration of labour from the neighbouring hinterlands. In the latter half of the twentieth century, the region became embroiled in a series of protracted liberation struggles against colonialism and entrenched white power. The epicentre of this struggle inevitably was South Africa, which, with the assistance of the West, exercised dispro-portional influence on the course of the liberation struggles in the region, especially through its military doctrine of 'destabilisation'. With the end of the Cold War and the transition to majority rule in the new Republic of South Africa (RSA), the latter rolled back the militarism of the past, but retained and even expanded its economic position, now on pacific terrain.

The South African state has been transformed, but not sufficiently (Yeros 2010). In fact, it has integrated itself ever-more intimately with finance capital, at the same time as it has been charged with the task of exercising relative autonomy in the interest of the popular classes. The black ruling class which now occupies the state must not only serve imperialism, but also its black citizenry, as well as its neighbours, who together defeated apartheid. So it was a matter of time before post-apartheid South Africa would be thrust back into crisis, for it thrives on the super-exploitation of domestic and regional labour at the same time as it claims an 'exceptional' role in the service of Pan-Africanism.

The asymmetries born of settler colonialism persist and, indeed, are expanding at a rapid pace. The RSA runs a trade surplus with the region at the tune of 9:1, this having *tripled* since the end of apartheid (Pallotti 2004, Daniel et al. 2004). The RSA also is the largest source of, or conduit for, foreign investment in the SADC, having *quadrupled* in recent years. Although South African firms are not entirely 'South African' – they include Western capital and many, in any case, now maintain their financial headquarters in London – estimates show that total 'RSA' foreign direct investment on the continent exceeds the combined value of foreign direct investment (FDI) exported directly from the US and Britain, while 90 per cent of the RSA's investments are now concentrated in the SADC (Pallotti 2004, Daniel et al. 2004). It is important to note that the large majority of these investments are concentrated in capital-intensive production for export; 77 per cent is in the minerals-energy complex alone (Pallotti 2004). In other words, South African capitalism reproduces the disarticulated pattern of accumulation entrenched on the continent, while at the same time avoids reinvestment at home and the related socio-political reordering that this would entail.

The foreign policy of the RSA parted ways with destabilisation to settle into a policy of 'stabilisation', proclaiming 'security and development' as its goal (Alden and Le Pere 2004), but defined on the basis of neoliberal criteria. This has been a 'pragmatic' foreign policy insofar as it has sought to defend the economic and political status quo by non-coercive means. Thus, in the DRC conflict, South Africa promoted a peace-building process, but one that accorded with its own interests and those of the West. In the SADC, it has promoted a policy of regional integration based on trade liberalisation, together with protections built in for South African industry and labour, while, at the same time, it has resisted a regional industrial policy based on political criteria (Pallotti 2004).

And on the continent, it has promoted NEPAD, a neoliberal policy framework for continental underdevelopment. We might say that the new, non-coercive South Africa relies on economic power and diplomacy to depoliticise peace, integration and development.

This is the context in which the Zimbabwe question emerged to challenge both imperialism and South African capitalism. Zimbabwe's dispute with the RSA was already underway in the 1990s, when the two sparred over trade liberalisation and the security policy of the SADC with regards to the DRC. When, in 2000, Zimbabwe lurched ahead with an autonomous land reform programme, the economic and security order of the region was confronted with a robust challenge. Had this challenge been mounted during the Cold War, we would certainly have expected a militarised response by the West and its South African proxy. However, under the new conditions, South Africa has been torn between the requirements of stabilisation and the revitalised ideals of national liberation. These ideals have strongly reverberated within South Africa, given that its own class/race contradictions have been subject to a new (and much more timid) bourgeois indigenisation policy. In fact, both countries today pursue the same objectives – the creation of a black bourgeoisie by means of affirmative action – with the exception that Zimbabwe's contradictions have escalated to a radical policy on property and to a confrontation with the geostrategic ambitions of both South Africa and the West.

South Africa's policy on Zimbabwe has taken the form of 'quiet diplomacy'. It has amounted to a balancing act, proclaiming non-interference in the internal affairs of Zimbabwe, in accordance with the egalitarian ideals of Pan-Africanism, while seeking to defend the status quo by guiding Zimbabwe back to neoliberal 'stability'. It has indeed been a deeply contradictory situation, whose indeterminacies and inconsistencies have not been fully acknowledged; this has partly to do with a common recourse to rationalist or reductionist approaches. Thus, South African foreign policy has been construed either as a zealous defence of the economic interests of its emergent black bourgeoisie (McKinley 2004) or as a reluctant defence of the interests of white corporate capital (Uzodike and Naidoo n.d.); or as a pragmatic defence of its regional security interests (Landsberg n.d.); or as a faithful defence of the geostrategic interests of the West (Bond 2004). Obviously, elements of all these approaches are somehow at play. But how do they fit together?

We cannot escape the requirement of state theory. South Africa is a relatively autonomous, semi-peripheral capitalist state balancing between conflicting internal and external forces, whose relations can tilt in one direction or another in accordance with ongoing horizontal and vertical conflicts. Insofar as the state serves as a cohesive factor internally, it cannot serve the exclusive interests of a seemingly 'all-powerful' black ruling class, or the white hegemonic fraction for that matter. And its external security interests cannot but reflect its profoundly extroverted business interests. The result is that the black ruling class in South Africa has managed to control the diffusion of Zimbabwe's resurgent nationalism, not least by renewing the momentum of its own bourgeois indigenisation programme and by taking care not to offend the ideals of national liberation, to which black South Africans, and the region as a whole, remain sensitive. The result has also been the extension, in 2003, of the mutual defence pact reached in 1998 by Zimbabwe, Angola and Namibia. This has effectively shielded Zimbabwe from the repeated attempts by the West to control the course of inter-party negotiations. Indeed, thanks to Zimbabwe, larger room for manoeuvre now exists in Southern Africa vis-à-vis international capital.

CONCLUSION

It is clear to us that autonomous development can only be sustained by a regional convergence around a popular nationalism and the formation of a new, federated state that can overcome fragmentation, entrenched asymmetries, and beggar-thy-neighbour policies. It is pointless to speak of regional autonomy in any other way. In this regard, it is also clear that the black bourgeoisie in the racially divided societies of Southern Africa can be enlisted in such a project, but it cannot be assigned a leadership role, for it is axiomatic that its accumulation needs will prevail tomorrow over whatever patriotism it might feel today. Left to its own devices, it will seek the easy road of compradorisation, neocolonialism and regional dispute. After Zimbabwe, the congruence of state, nation and region has once again become an imperative, but one whose agent is still missing.

NOTE

1. Yet others circumvented the issue, by refuting the existence of a 'local ruling class' as distinct from monopoly capital, effectively claiming that neocolonialism entailed a 'change of government', not the birth of a relatively autonomous state (Nabudere 1982, Tandon 1982).

REFERENCES

Alexander, Jocelyn (1993), 'The State, Agrarian Policy and Rural Politics in Zimbabwe: Case Studies of Insiza and Chimanimani Districts, 1940–90', DPhil. thesis, Oxford University.

Alden, Chris, and Garth le Pere (2004), 'South Africa's Post-Apartheid Foreign Policy: From Reconciliation to Ambiguity?', *Review of African Political Economy*, 100: 283–97.

Bond, Patrick (2004), 'The ANC's "Left Turn" and South African Sub-imperialism', *Review of African Political Economy*, 102: 599–616.

Cabral, Amílcar (1978), *A Arma da Teoria: Unidade e Luta I*, second edition, Seara Nova.

Callaghy, Thomas M. (1988), 'The State and the Development of Capitalism in Africa: Theoretical, Historical, and Comparative Reflections', in *The Precarious Balance: State and Society in Africa*, ed. D. Rothchild and N. Chazan. London and Boulder, CO: Westview Press.

Chambati, Walter (2009), *Land Reform and Changing Agrarian Labour Process in Zimbabwe*, Master of Management (Public and Development Management) dissertation, University of Witwatersrand.

Collier, Paul (2009), *Wars, Guns and Votes: Democracy in Dangerous Places*. London: Bodley Head.

Daniel, John, Jessica Lutchman and Sanusha Naidu (2004), 'Post-apartheid South Africa's Corporate Expansion into Africa', *Review of African Political Economy*, 100: 343–8.

Edigheji, Omano (2006), 'The Emerging South African Democratic Developmental State and the People's Contract', Centre for Policy Studies, mimeo.

Fanon, Frantz (1967), *The Wretched of the Earth*, trans. C. Farrington. London: Penguin Books.

Hammar, Amanda, Brian Raftopoulos and Stig Jensen, eds (2003), *Zimbabwe's Unfinished Business*. Harare: Weaver Press.

Hyden, Göran, and Michael Bratton, eds (1992), *Governance and Politics in Africa*, London and Boulder, CO: Lynne Rienner.

Landsberg, Chris (n.d.), 'The Diplomacy of Appeasement? South Africa's Quiet Diplomacy Strategy vis-à-vis Zimbabwe', Centre for Policy Studies, mimeo.

Leys, Colin (1976), 'The "Overdeveloped" Post Colonial State: A Re-evaluation', *Review of African Political Economy*, 3(5): 39–48.

Mamdani, Mahmood (1996), *Citizen and Subject*. Princeton, NJ: Princeton University Press.

Mamdani, Mahmood (2008), 'Lessons of Zimbabwe', *London Review of Books*, 30(23): 17–21.

McKinley, Dale T. (2004), 'South African Foreign Policy Towards Zimbabwe under Mbeki', *Review of African Political Economy*, 100: 357–64.

Miliband, Ralph (1969), *The State in Capitalist Society*. London: Weidenfeld & Nicolson.

Moore, David (2004), 'Marxism and Marxist Intellectuals in Schizophrenic Zimbabwe: How Many Rights for Zimbabwe's Left? A Comment', *Historical Materialism*, 12(4): 405–25.

Moyo, Sam (2001), 'The Land Occupation Movement in Zimbabwe: Contradictions of Neoliberalism', *Millennium*, 30(2): 311–30.

Moyo, Sam, Walter Chambati, Tendai Murisa, Dumisani Siziba, Charity Dangwa, Kingstone Mujeyi and Ndabezinhle Nyoni (2010), *Fast Track Land Reform Baseline Survey in Zimbabwe: Trends and Tendencies, 2005/06*. Harare: AIAS Monograph.

Moyo, Sam, and Paris Yeros (2005), 'Land Occupations and Land Reform in Zimbabwe: Towards the National Democratic Revolution', in *Reclaiming the Land: The Resurgence of Rural Movements in Africa, Asia and Latin America*, ed. S. Moyo and P. Yeros. London: Zed Books.

Moyo, Sam, and Paris Yeros (2007a), 'The Radicalised State: Zimbabwe's Interrupted Revolution', *Review of African Political Economy*, 111: 103–21.

Moyo, Sam, and Paris Yeros (2007b), 'The Zimbabwe Question and the Two Lefts', *Historical Materialism*, 15(3): 171–204.

Moyo, Sam, and Paris Yeros (2009), 'Zimbabwe Ten Years On: Results and Prospects', *MRzine*, 10 February, http://mrzine.monthlyreview.org/2009/my100209.html.

Nabudere, Dan W. (1982), 'Imperialism, State, Class and Race', in *University of Dar es Salaam Debate on Class, State and Imperialism*, ed. T. Tandon. Dar es Salaam: Tanzania Publishing House.

Murisa, Tendai (2010), *An Analysis of Emerging Forms of Social Organisation and Agency in the Aftermath of 'Fast Track' Land Reform in Zimbabwe*, PhD thesis, Rhodes University.

Pallotti, Arrigo (2004), 'SADC: A Development Community without a Development Policy?', *Review of African Political Economy*, 100: 513–31.

Poulantzas, Nicos (1968), *Political Power and Social Classes*, trans. T. O'Hagan. London: Verso.

Rotberg, Robert I. (2002a), 'The New Nature of Nation-State Failure', *The Washington Quarterly*, 25(3): 85–96.

Rotberg, Robert I. (2002b), 'Failed States in a World of Terror', *Foreign Affairs*, 81(4): 127–40.

Sadomba, Wilbert Z. (2008), *War Veterans in Zimbabwe's Land Occupations*, PhD thesis, Wageningen University.

Saul, John (1974), 'The State in Postcolonial Societies: Tanzania', in *The Socialist Register*, ed. R. Miliband and J. Saville. New York: Monthly Review Press.

Saul, John (2003), 'Africa: The Next Liberation Struggle?', *Review of African Political Economy*, 96: 187–202.

Seddon, David, and Leo Zeilig (2005), 'Class and Protest in Africa: New Waves', *Review of African Political Economy*, 103: 9–27.

Shivji, Issa G. (1976), *Class Struggles in Tanzania*. New York and London: Monthly Review Press.

Tandon, Yash (1982), 'Whose Capital and Whose State?', in *University of Dar es Salaam Debate on Class, State and Imperialism*, ed. T. Tandon. Dar es Salaam: Tanzania Publishing House.

Therborn, Göran (1978), *What Does the Ruling Class Do When it Rules?* London: New Left Books.

Uzodike, Ufo Okeke, and Varusha Naidoo (n.d.), 'The Quest for Partnership in Southern Africa: South Africa's Foreign Policy Dilemma', Political Studies, University of Natal, mimeo.

Yeros, Paris (2002), *The Political Economy of Civilisation: Peasant-Workers in Zimbabwe and the Neo-colonial World*, PhD thesis, University of London.

Yeros, Paris (2010), 'Rescrambling for Africa: What Kind of Imperialism?', paper presented at the AIAS Agrarian Summer School, Dar es Salaam, January, mimeo.

Part II
Asia

5
Peripheral States in Asia under Neoliberalism and After

Korkut Boratav

NEOLIBERALISM: THE COMPREHENSIVE ASSAULT ON CAPITAL

The neoliberal mode of regulation has been dominating the world economy during the past three decades. The electoral victories of Thatcher and Reagan, representing a radical shift in economic philosophy, and the appointment of Paul Volcker to the Chair of the Federal Reserve, representing the move toward monetarism, all in 1979, are events which can be considered as the starting point of the neoliberal era.

'Neoliberalism' is a neutral term, used by social scientists, particularly economists of differing persuasions, focusing on changing modes of economic regulation. An alternative characterisation on the basis of a shifting balance of forces between social classes would be *a systematic and comprehensive assault of capital* against the past social and economic acquisitions of working people in both North and South. A second and closely-related 'assault' has been aimed at undermining the modest degrees of economic independence realised through national liberation struggles and the subsequent attempts for autonomous development. During the 1970s, at a crucial phase of the 'golden age' of capitalism, those developments had led to the questioning of power relations within the world economy, culminating in the campaign for 'a new international economic order' called by various third world organisations.

Three dimensions were involved. The first targeted the ultimate dismantling of the welfare state in the North, facilitated by a policy of deregulation of the labour market. The second undermined the peripheral state as a productive and investing agent and dismantled elements of domestic regulation of market processes. In a number of third world countries, those features had previously resulted in generating favourable conditions to labour, due to development processes based on domestic markets. The third targeted the elimination of barriers to international trade and capital movements at the periphery, seriously undermining protected, state-led developmental states.

The collapse of the Soviet Union and the incorporation of the former socialist countries of Europe into the periphery of the imperialist system facilitated the pace of change. Change was unidirectional and, consequently, all countries, almost without exception, were affected. Nevertheless, the pace of progress was not uniform in terms of regional and national incidence, and full realisation of strategic objectives was not attained everywhere.

In terms of sequencing at the periphery, three phases can be distinguished: (i) liberalisation and deregulation of domestic commodity, financial and (albeit in erratic fashion) labour markets; (ii) liberalisation of international trade, that is, moving into a free trade regime; and (iii) full liberalisation of capital movements into and out of the national economies. All phases were also accompanied by the so-called structural adjustment policies, or (in the terminology of the World Bank) 'market-friendly reforms', in most cases incorporating comprehensive institutional and legal transformations. Elimination and liquidation of state ownership in the means of production was an essential component thereof.

Peripheral Asia was no exception to the foregoing transformations. But national experiences were much more dispersed around the overall trend than other regions. Imperialist aggression seriously undermined economies and societies in the Middle East, Afghanistan and Pakistan. Reluctance and resistance to certain components of the neoliberal agenda (for example, comprehensive privatisation and capital account liberalisation) was more effective in parts of Asia (for example, in China, India, and, at least, for certain phases in some East Asian countries) than elsewhere. However, the mainstream neoliberal agenda was the unifying framework.

TRADITIONAL POPULISM AND ITS AFTERMATH

The domestic component of the neoliberal project on peripheral countries can be summarised as *deregulation and privatisation at the level of the national economy*. The consequences and implications are closely related to the erosion and dismantlement of the 'populist' mode of regulating distributional dynamics prevailing in many nation-states in the South. Persistence with that mode was starting to threaten vital interests of dominant classes by the late 1970s. Some cautious generalisations on common features of populism before they were undermined and, at times, destroyed by neoliberal transformations will be helpful at this stage.

The distributional and policy-related dimensions of populism refer to a de facto modus vivendi betweeen two classes, or class coalitions, confronting each other in a peripheral economy. *Economically dominant classes* are capable of controlling the state apparatus, but *popular classes*, due to their numerical size, have to be co-opted into accepting this control in return for a set of economic advantages extended to them. Under the authoritarian version of populism, popular classes have transmitted their demands by means of the 'power of the street'. Under parliamentary populism, the ballot box emerged as the transmission channel.

Under the parliamentarian version, the working class and the peasantry have been either legally prevented or effectively discouraged from organising politically with their class-based (for example, socialist, communist, or even social-democratic) programmes as alternatives to those parties essentially representing the interests of the economically dominant classes (or certain factions thereof). This signifies the exclusion of class-based politics. But, as voters outnumber dominant interest groups, their economic and social demands have had to be taken into consideration by competing bourgeois parties, at times during the pre-election phase of the political cycle, although, in many cases, they have carried more permanent features which, gradually, have become part of the economic and social structure.

In understanding traditional populism, it may be useful to recall a well-known Turkish saying: 'Giving without taking is the privilege of Allah'. Parliamentary populism has historically been a continual attempt by governments to find ways and means of violating this common wisdom, that is, how to accommodate distributional demands by 'giving to the poor without taking from the rich'. Such policies included agricultural support; legislation on industrial relations and social security, based, somewhat, on Western patterns; 'loose' employment policies by state-owned enterprises (SOEs) and by the public sector at large; extension of municipal services to the urban poor, and subsidies on basic necessities. All these policies were essential components of traditional populism, not only in Asia, but elsewhere in the South. Together with the continued provision of free education and health, populism became, in some respects, reminiscent of European social policy systems; but it was never explicitly built on a rights-based approach.

Budgetary and/or external deficits were the inevitable outcomes – the former covered by monetary expansion and the latter by soft credits from abroad, as international Keynesianism was facilitating 'soft' external funding. As emphasised by Cem Somel for the Turkish experience (Chapter 9, this volume), it was, moreover, a functional model based on an expanding domestic market and in which pressures on international competitiveness could be disregarded. Most of the distributive 'corrections' were class-specific, but they took place within a framework in which explicit class-based politics were excluded.

It was inevitable that the changing rules of the game in the imperialist system, starting with the external debt crises in Latin America, Turkey, and elsewhere at the beginning of the neoliberal period would, sooner or later, push the populist model into an impasse. There were cases when externally-imposed change was resisted by governments and temporary concessions to neoliberal recipes were followed with a partial return to conventional policies. Other cases were observed when domestic business interests campaigned fanatically – sometimes under military regimes, Turkey being the typical model (see Somel, Chapter 9, this volume) – to realise a total break with the old model. There were also countries where a sense of urgency for a radical break with the past was absent, because a gradual and smooth transition out of the conventional mode of regulation was already taking place.

These variations were due to differences in national circumstances. During the 1980s and after, foreign exchange crises forced some reluctant governments to comply with International Monetary Fund (IMF)-based programmes. However, a consensus was developing within the ranks of the business circles that persistence with the conventional populist model would be too costly for their immediate and medium-term interests, and that the new, market-based reform had much to recommend itself, due to its potential contribution in alleviating distributional conflicts. The pre-crisis periods in these countries were also phases when strong pro-labour pressures were building in the economy and were considered unsustainable by powerful business interests. This was the typical Latin American pattern, but it was also observed in Turkey, as well as in the Middle East and North Africa (MENA) region (including Egypt and the Maghreb).[1]

A 'mature' transition from populism into a European model in response to the external shocks of the post-1980 period would have been to share the incidence of the burden of adjustment by 'taking from the rich' as well. This would have been an orientation toward an explicit class-based bargaining process which would have also involved concessions from popular classes.[2] However, institutional 'reforms' led by the Bretton Woods Institutions (BWIs) excluded this option. Interventions with distributive objectives (that is, 'giving without taking') were to be totally scrapped and inter-class distribution was to be determined predominantly through market mechanisms. This transition implied 'neither giving, nor taking'. Public policy with social objectives was to be limited to poverty-alleviation, targeting vulnerable segments of the population, plus public expenditures on *basic* education and health (that is, primary education and preventive health). This reorientation implies that the traditional social policy objective of *strengthening dependent, exploited social groups against market forces* would gradually be eliminated and replaced by a new task of *compensating extreme market outcomes for the excluded, the vulnerable and the poor*. Vulnerability and poverty are not, per se, class attributes; in other words, targeted populations cut across classes and social strata. Hence, the conventional populist distributional mechanisms built upon the economic/social attributes of specific groups (as market-oriented farmer/peasants, as wage-earners, as self-employed urban producers and small to medium-sized enterprises (SMEs)), that is, class-based social policies, were to be ultimately scrapped. Market interventions to affect distributional outcomes were strictly off limits. The targeted populations for social transfers were now to be sought within the *déclassé* elements of the society (for example, the pauper), regardless of the diverse economic conditions that generate the particular conditions of poverty.

A number of anti-populist shock treatments were effectively implemented by BWIs during the 1980s in countries which were incapable of coping with the changing conditions in the world economy and had run into external bottlenecks. Elsewhere in Asia, most countries were immune to the first phase of BWI-imposed distributional adjustments. But a gradual path toward the same outcome was being followed. 'Market-friendly' reforms were taking place at a relatively slower pace before the 1997–98 crises, but, also contributing to them. East Asian economies had moved into open trade regimes based on exports of manufactures much earlier than elsewhere in the developing world and did not experience foreign exchange bottlenecks. On the other hand, the neoliberal discourse on the long-term beneficial effects of open capital accounts found willing converts in East Asian governments.[3] The boom in capital inflows of all kinds pushed investment rates above national savings, but also generated pre-conditions of subsequent crises: difficulties in external debt-servicing by domestic borrowers who had invested in non-tradable activities, 'sudden stops' of external flows which followed, and the contagion facilitated by 'herd behaviour' of finance capital contributed to the series of crises in the South, starting from Thailand in 1997 and ending in 2002 with Argentina. Hence, the active involvement of BWIs in the neoliberal reform agenda in East Asia took place much later than other developing regions. A rigid and relentless programme imposed on most crisis-ridden economies after 1997 seriously undermined economic sovereignty. Later criticism of this programme contributed much to the erosion of the reputation of the IMF in the developing world.

India and China, on the other hand, followed different trajectories. Both countries rejected full opening of the capital account. While 'greenfield' foreign direct investment was encouraged into non-strategic activities, liberalisation of resident outflows and arbitrage-seeking ('hot') inflows were restricted. It was, essentially, thanks to these limitations that the Asian financial crisis skipped these two economies. On the other hand, India had been gradually adopting selected components of the neoliberal agenda since the mid 1970s. As for China, a labour market without social safety nets was generated during the 1990s, and the consequent decline of labour costs contributed to the explosive growth of exports.

Regardless of the external or domestic political circumstances of their implementation – that is, under authoritarian or military regimes, or through pressure from BWIs under crisis conditions, or voluntary and slow-paced progress toward a more open and deregulated regime – the overall impact of the neoliberal reform package was two-fold. First, domestic inter-class relations shifted dramatically in favour of the bourgeoisies and, therefore, the new orientation was advocated strongly, and welcomed enthusiastically, by domestic business interests. Secondly, liberalisation of international trade and capital movements created the preconditions for formally equalising market conditions between international and domestic capital. Integration of local business with international partners was an ongoing phenomenon which had contributed to domestic support for the externally-oriented liberalisation agenda.

However, unexpected outcomes occurred which have to be discussed separately.

METROPOLITAN CAPITAL SEEKING COMPLETE CONTROL

As discussed earlier, elimination of barriers established by peripheral nation-states during the preceding eras was one of the components of the neoliberal reform package, and this was closely linked to a strategic objective: expanding the degree of freedom of metropolitan capital in its endeavours to establish a unified globe without effective economic barriers. Provided that they were accompanied by comprehensive 'market-friendly' reforms at the domestic level, the foregoing strategic objective was expected to follow.

However, it soon became clear that rent-generation, rent-appropriation, and corruption in favour of domestic business groups were rising to unprecedented levels during the neoliberal era. Before the comprehensive neoliberal packages were launched, one of the basic functions of the traditional economic bureaucracies, sometimes inherited from the colonial regime (India) or established during the early phases of the new nation-state (Turkey), was to control the mechanisms of appropriation of 'rents of protection and intervention'. The objective was not the elimination or restriction of rent-generation; but, rather, the creation of equal conditions for competing claims from business groups on existing or emerging rents. Some degree of autonomy from the political layer of the state apparatus, a certain ideological commitment 'to protect the interests of the state and of the public coffer', and a relatively advantageous pay scale compared with other segments of public administration were helpful in fulfilling their functions.

Reforms of public administrations resulted in the gradual paralysis and, by degrees, the atrophy of these bureaucracies. In any case, conventional bureaucrats raised and trained under planned, interventionist, 'mixed economy' regimes were incapable of coping with the neoliberal period. The campaign for 'less government' implied scrapping regulations and controls on business-government linkages. The ideological atmosphere which made fetishes of 'free markets and profit-seeking' conflicted with the traditional, ethical norms of civil service. In time, and in many countries, financial experts with MBA degrees from abroad replaced the former bureaucrats.[4] This happened contemporaneously with the emergence of new areas of rent-generation under the neoliberal mode of regulation, for example, in the areas of privatisation, financial systems and government tenders. Domestic business groups intimately linked with the political layers of the state apparatus were capable of adapting to the new atmosphere and developed methods of benefiting from it.

Metropolitan capital and BWIs soon realised that 'market-friendly' reforms accompanied by free trade and capital account liberalisation were necessary but not sufficient to eliminate practices which favoured local business and, additionally, politically privileged business groups therein. A new terminology, such as 'crony capitalism' and 'capture of the state by powerful interest groups',[5] was invented to depict the class character of states (for example, in East Asia and Russia during transition) which had been loyal followers of neoliberal recipes and 'shock treatments'. The apparently paradoxical phenomenon of corruption under fully liberalised market regimes suddenly emerged right in front of unbelieving observers.

This was the background to the later moves by the BWIs to make the elimination of corruption an important policy agenda. It was exclusively an intra-class issue of the bourgeoisies. The establishment of neutrality between different (for example, domestic and external) business groups was the strategic priority. Public administrations, having already gotten rid of their 'excess employment', were now to be organised toward flexibility and performance-based, contractual pay systems. The vague slogan of 'governance' emerged as another priority area, and agencies autonomous from government control (hence, non-accountable to the electorate) were advocated to prevent 'state capture' by domestic interests. Comprehensive, unlimited control by international capital was, thus, to be realised.

DEMOCRACY UNDER NEOLIBERALISM

Historically, and in the value systems of broad segments of Asian peoples, the state was obliged to 'provide for its Children'. Even today, in a typical marketplace in the Middle East, the housewife reacts to rising prices for basic commodities by inquiring: 'Where is the state?' 'Food riots' in the Maghreb and Egypt from the 1980s onward, in response to IMF prescriptions on the elimination of urban subsidies, led in many cases to total or partial repeal of price adjustments. In the Middle East, consumer subsidies are usually regarded as part of a social contract between the state and the people. Even an anonymous IMF official, after a long battle with the Egyptian government over consumer subsidies, has been forced to concede that 'the financial awards of an agreement with IMF are not worth the risk of pushing disadvantaged Egyptians over the brink of forbearance into insurrection'.[6]

These are observations on authoritarian/paternalistic populism, where 'the street' reacts against a state which violates the basic premises of its 'social contract' with the people. Under parliamentary populism, compliance with the modus vivendi between the popular and dominant classes, as discussed earlier, provides the legitimacy of representative democracy. It is based on the regulation of the distributive process by state interventions on a broad spectrum of markets (involving labour, agricultural products and inputs, basic necessities, and credit), whereas the neoliberal agenda aims at the total depoliticisation of the distributional process.

'What does the state provide to me?' This is the question on which the legitimacy of representative democracy within the ranks of popular classes rests. If current trends continue, and the distributive functions of the political authority – borrowing from Pierre Bourdieu (1998: 2–5), 'the left hand of the state' – withers away, the state apparatus will gradually transform itself into an institution merely endowed with repressive functions, that is, 'the right hand of the state'. Alienation, social exclusion, political indifference, and withdrawal into individualised survival strategies are the likely outcomes for the majority of the population. This is fertile ground for the emergence of obscurantist, fundamentalist, reactionary, ultra-nationalistic ideologies and violence.

DIFFERENT ADJUSTMENT PATTERNS DURING THE PRE-CRISIS PERIOD

The capitalist world system is passing through the most serious crisis since the Great Depression. The comprehensive assault of capital, depicted earlier, has run into a bottleneck. It is not clear whether the failure will be temporary or permanent. Everything depends on possible shifts on the balance of class forces in national economies or at the international level. The reorganisation of popular classes against imperialism and capitalism has revived radical politics and contributed to the leftward shift in Latin America, with similar (though more contained) tendencies in Asia, especially in Nepal (see Roka, Chapter 8, this volume), as well as in Africa (see Moyo and Yeros, Chapter 4, this volume). This was realised during the boom period of the world economy before the current crisis. Asia did not pass through a similar route, and it is too early to predict the societal impact of the crisis here. It is, however, clear that the super-optimistic globalisation discourse is bankrupt and capitalism is facing a legitimacy crisis.

The near future for peripheral Asian economies is closely linked with the trajectories followed during the 2002–07 boom phase of the world economy and the defensive reactions being developed against the crisis since 2008.

Once again, non-identical paths and adjustment patterns are observed. A typical one incorporates East Asia, which was dramatically affected by the preceding (1997–98) crisis. The path toward that crisis was characterised by high levels of capital inflows, rising external indebtedness and current account deficits. The bitter experience with IMF and international capital during 1998 was the factor which pushed these countries to move into current account surpluses later, through declining investment and rising (or preserving the already high) savings rates. Reserve accumulation and 'improvement' of current account balances were transformed almost into policy targets which facilitated servicing the external debt during the following years. Growth rates declined substantially compared with the preceding period. Between 1989–97 and 1998–2007, the unweighted average growth rates in the four large crisis-ridden economies of East Asia (Indonesia, South Korea, Malaysia and Thailand) declined from 8.1 per cent to 4.4 per cent. Even during the 'boom' of 2002–07, the average growth performance of these four countries, at 5.4 per cent, was significantly below their 1989–97 average.

These countries are confronting the current crisis with current account surpluses and moderate, manageable external indebtedness. This is why dominant circles of the international system, the G8 and the IMF, are recommending expansionary macro-eonomic policies to their governments. The realised (2008) and estimated (2009) average growth rate of this group is marginally positive, at 1 per cent (IMF 2009: Table A4). In one sense, these countries are now reaping the 'benefits' of their cautious policies during the immediate pre-crisis period by being spared from enforced contractionary policies now. Hence, despite the relative stagnation to which these economies had drifted during the past decade, their ruling classes are currently in a more secure position than those in vulnerable economies.

Vulnerability to the current crisis refers to those economies which passively accommodated to the dramatic rise in capital inflows during the 2002–07 boom by sustaining, or even raising, their current deficits and drifting into rising levels and rates of external debt. A determining feature of this period was the astronomic current account deficits of the United States. Hence, peripheral economies with high and rising external deficits were the exception. This was typically a Central and Eastern European (CEE) phenomenon, with limited Asian examples. Turkey and Pakistan fall into the same pattern, and these were the only Asian countries which had to negotiate and sign stand-by agreements with IMF since late 2008. The remaining 'IMF clients' during the crisis have been almost exclusively from the CEE region.

The growth estimates of the IMF for 2009, covering all developing and emerging economies in Asia, Europe, and Latin America (excluding oil exporters), place Turkey in the fourth place in terms of contraction, at –5.1 per cent, after three Baltic countries and Ukraine. Contractionary neoliberal recipes are on the agenda for vulnerable economies. This was to be expected since finance capital, the initial and major victim of the crisis, is in urgent need of the full and uninterrupted servicing of the external obligations of peripheral countries, particularly those with high and risky external debt positions, such that expansionary policies feeding into rising current account deficits should be off limits to those countries.

During the pre-crisis 2002–07 years, Asian economies with combined high growth rates and current surpluses (or roughly balanced current accounts) were China, India and (thanks to the rise in crude oil prices) the oil exporters of the Middle East. The significant cases are China and India. Well-known factors positively affecting competitiveness, that is, very low labour costs and respectable productivity levels, are reinforced by the targeting of real exchange rates, thanks to relatively controlled capital accounts. China has also attained historical records on rates of capital accumulation and growth. The recommendation of imperialist centres for these economies in the current crisis conditions has been to implement expansionary macro-economic policies which, in turn, are expected to spill over into higher import demand and restrain the downturn of output in the metropolitan states. China quickly moved into a fiscal stimulus and investment programme for 2009 and 2010, approaching US$600 billion, and a number of social measures benefiting the retired, the unemployed, the rural and the urban poor. Rising public spending on education and health is also envisaged. The Congress government in India followed suit immediately before the May 2009 elections and reaped the fruits by an electoral victory.

Compared with elsewhere in the South, China and India appear to be facing the current international crisis in more secure positions. Average growth rates for the two crisis years, that is, 2008 (realised) and 2009 (forecast), for China and India are 7.8 per cent and 5.9 per cent, respectively (IMF 2009: Table A4). Such growth performance under crisis condition exceeds the growth rates of most major emerging economies during the boom period.

The responses of these two large peripheral economies to the crisis of capitalism is crucial not only for the peoples of China and India, but also for the future of the balance of social forces in the world economy. Whether 'acts of resistance' to the comprehensive assault of capital flourishes from these countries, or from elsewhere in Asia, must be discussed briefly.

ASIAN PROSPECTS: POPULISM, RADICAL POLITICS, FUNDAMENTALISM

As observed earlier, India and China had rejected full capitulation to the comprehensive assault of capital during the past decades. However, this was a partial resistance. In India, neoliberal reforms had been making gradual but permanent inroads into the structural features of the developmental state; as depicted by Sandeep Chachra (Chapter 6, this volume), the inroads involved anti-labour legislation under the 'emergency rule' of the mid 1970s, 'a mild trend toward deregulation' since the early 1980s, and a new wave of 'romance with neoliberalism' in the early 1990s. China commodified labour extensively, through the elimination of major components of socialist relations of distribution (that is, the 'iron bowl' system of employment protection, social services extended by state enterprises, free provision of education and health); and dramatically reduced labour costs and managed to integrate itself completely to the new division of labour of the imperialist system. However, full liberalisation of the capital account was rejected and, hence, policy tools under the control of the Chinese state were considerable and more effective than most other peripheral economies.

India's traditional populism was under further attack under the fundamentalist Hindu government of the Bharatiya Janata Party (BJP), also fully committed to neoliberalism. The decade following 1994 was a period of modest growth (5.7 per cent) accompanied by rising unemployment and rural immiseration due to hunger, indebtedness, and unemployment, leading to high numbers of peasant suicides (Chachra, Chapter 6, this volume). However, there are strong elements of resistance in Indian society which prevent full capitulation to the rule of capital. Populism is almost a permanent feature of traditional Congress politics. There is, moreover, another tradition of class-based politics in India reflected by three states ruled by communist parties. The joint impact of these traditions was effective in the electoral defeat of BJP in 2004, followed by a Congress Party government supported by the left. The alliance of the secular populism of Congress with the class-based politics of communist parties was accompanied by a very impressive growth performance, approaching a gross domestic product (GDP) growth rate of 9 per cent in 2005–08. Rising growth and the pro-labour, pro-poor peasant policy measures, realised thanks to pressures from the parliamentary left – for example, the 'Right to Food' campaign and the National Rural Employment Generation Programme (Chachra, Chapter 6, this volume) – contributed to the second electoral victory of Congress in five years; this time, however, accompanied by regression of the left.

It is significant that immediately after the victory of Congress in 2009, international financial circles started an apparently co-ordinated campaign calling on India to engage in 'reforms', now that the blackmail of communist parties was lifted. This is a call for full liberalisation of the capital account, extensive and limitless privatisation, and total elimination of labour market rigidities. This recipe violates economic common sense. On the contrary, there is a strong case for arguing that the successful recent performance of the Indian economy owes a great deal to the absence, or slowness, of a 'reform movement' advocated by domestic business lobbies and international capital. It is equally striking that the call for deregulation and financial opening-up in India is coming at a moment when metropolitan capital is paying an extremely heavy price for similar recipes.

China's combination of double-digit growth with high and rising current account surpluses can be characterised as a 'positive/ dynamic' pattern of adjustment to the growing imbalances in the world economy of the past decade.[7] The capacity of adaptation of China to crisis conditions and a possible modification of her preceding linkages to the world economy is now being tested. It should have been clear to the pragmatic Chinese leadership that the export-led growth pattern could not be a permanent feature, and their past experience with strategic planning based on sectoral priorities must have prepared them to the conditions of collapsing export demand. The current and coming years will show whether the past two decades of double-digit growth have created the fundamentals of a qualitative leap in productive forces to carry the Chinese economy to a sustained and long-term dynamic progress.

On the other hand, a critical assessment of the social costs of the impressive Chinese growth is called for. It should be emphasised that the Chinese economy transferred US$1.1 trillion abroad, about 6 per cent of her cumulative national income, from 1998 onwards.[8] This was possible thanks to extremely high savings per GDP ratios in China, a historical record, realised, at least to some degree, by extremely low consumption levels of Chinese households, combined with their enforced adaptation to the previous dismantlement of *socialist* safety nets of workers and peasants. This was part of the 'commodification' of labour (incorporating measures to 'commodify' parts of the medical/educational services and social security) in China during market-based 'reforms'. The Chinese premier, Wen Jiabao, in an interview given to the *Financial Times* in Davos on 2 February 2008, made the following comments:

> About 12m migrant workers have chosen to return to the countryside because of the financial crisis. As this is a floating population, it is easy to understand that they will come to cities when there are job opportunities there and they will choose to return to the countryside when there aren't. When they have returned to the countryside you can see that, for most of them, they still have their piece of land in the rural areas. I think land provides the most important safeguard for the lives of those farmers in China. We should thank those Chinese migrant workers because they made an enormous contribution to China's modernisation drive and, in times of this financial crisis, they have also become a big reservoir of the labour force.

This is an implicit admission of the almost 'primitive' character of accumulation in China. But primitive accumulation resembling a totally specific case: the depiction of peasant farming at the countryside as a 'safeguard' for the livelihood of low-wage urban workers is reminiscent of the 'Bantustan' system of exploitation under apartheid in South Africa.

On the other hand, it is not easy to characterise the regression from socialist relations of distribution through the commodification of labour as a full transition to capitalism. A significant part of the surplus generated in China ultimately accrues to the state; sometimes directly by means of the still important SOEs and surpluses of the public sector; but more importantly through indirect channels. Astronomical reserves accumulated during the past decade are owned by the Chinese state. This phenomenon provides the Chinese state with considerable freedom of economic manoeuvre, something which is absent for capitalist ruling classes in other peripheral societies. A transition from socialism toward state capitalism is one interpretation of recent changes. On the other hand, commodification of labour was accompanied by double-digit growth rates and impressive increases in employment and household incomes. Private domestic capital played a secondary role in this development pattern.

Giovanni Arrighi (2009: 84, 92), in an interview in *New Left Review* shortly before his death, observed that 'looking at present day China, one can say, maybe it's capitalism, maybe not … Assuming that it is capitalism, it's not the same as that of the previous periods.' Arrighi noted that the leadership had resisted in moving too far into this 'transition toward this peculiar form of capitalism [state capitalism]': '[i]n the 1990s, it was certainly headed in the direction of making workers compete for the benefit of capital and profit … Now there is a reversal, one which … takes into account not only the tradition of the Revolution and the Mao period, but also of the welfare aspects of late-imperial China.' These somewhat asymmetrical pendulum-like swings in relations of distribution can, perhaps, be characterised as *transitions between socialist and populist distributional dynamics*. However, the background of 'populism' here is not identical with the duality of economically dominant and popular classes in peripheral capitalism. In state-capitalist China, one of the essential preoccupations of the leadership of the Chinese Communist Party (CCP) aims at preventing and controlling social unrest. High growth rates leading to rising employment and income levels was the mechanism to attain 'social peace' during the pre-crisis decade. Nowadays, it seems that some elements of the preceding welfare arrangements are on the agenda.

Why this sensitivity to social unrest in China? Arrighi adds that a determining factor behind the 'reversal' is the fact that 'Chinese peasants and workers have a millennial tradition of unrest that has no parallel anywhere else in the world'. He concludes that 'if rebellions of the Chinese subordinate classes materialize in a new form of welfare state, that will influence the pattern of international relations over the next twenty, thirty years' (Arrighi 2009: 79–80, 84, 92). It remains to be seen how far the CCP leadership will use the current crisis as an opportunity to take the first steps toward the re-establishment of socialist relations of distribution. This requires going beyond the palliative and apparently temporary measures for the rural and urban poor as part of expansionary policies. The outcome depends on whether the balance of social forces in China shifts toward workers and peasants; or in other words, whether class-based politics makes a comeback.[9]

Somewhat different issues and choices confront popular classes in the Muslim world. A crucial difference from other Asian regions is the presence and threat of military aggression by imperialism. Palestine, Iraq and Afghanistan are occupied. Lebanon shared the same tragedy in the recent past. Iran, Syria and Pakistan are and have been under threat. The 'war on terror' launched by the United States has been expressed explicitly as a crusade by George W. Bush and interpreted as such against Islam by wide segments of Muslim populations.

Popular classes in the Middle East and elsewhere in Asia with predominantly Muslim populations have thus been under heavy pressure from both the neoliberal assault and imperialist aggression. The end result has been a massive penetration of political and fundamentalist Islam in its different variants within the ranks of popular classes.

The contribution of US imperialism and its allies in the Muslim world, such as Saudi Arabia and Pakistan, to the flourishing of radical political Islam through the organisation and support of Afghan resistance to Soviet occupation,[10] as well as Israel's early toleration and implicit support extended to Hamas and the Muslim Brotherhood, are well-known facts (see Jamil Hilal, Chapter 7, this volume). Observers have emphasised that the original and long-lasting strategic targets of fundamentalist Islam in the Middle East have been the annihilation of communism and of secular nationalism in its anti-imperialist and reformist versions (see Ahmad 2007, Bayat 2007, Achcar 2007).

There is nowadays a widespread conviction that secular politics and socialist movements are historically and sociologically alien to societies with predominantly Muslim populations. This viewpoint disregards the fact that the country with the largest Communist Party membership outside the socialist bloc was Indonesia until the 1965 massacre, following the Suharto coup. Communist parties in the Middle East, particularly in Iraq had wide mass bases (Alnasseri 2007: 82–4). In Turkey, socialist and communist movements had established strong roots within the working classes and the urban poor during the 1965–80 period before being decimated after the military coup of 1980. Radical-secular nationalism represented by Gamal Abdel Nasser or early leaderships of liberation struggles in the Maghreb had also benefited from genuine support from popular classes.

The presence and influence of secular (socialistic or nationalist) political movements within the ranks of Muslim working classes and peasantry during these periods are related to the sociological particularities of 'people's' (or 'popular') Islam. Islam was practised in different forms and shaped by non-uniform cultural and historical factors in a geography extending from the Pacific to the Atlantic Oceans. Under these variations, popular Islam adapted itself to differing political forms and established de facto modi vivendi with political authorities and at times participated actively in progressive politics and secular liberation movements.

It was this de facto secular version of Islam which fundamentalist movements, including Vahhabi, Muslim Brotherhood, and their Shiite versions, rejected and targeted to eliminate and replace with their own interpretations. 'Alien' value systems, ideological and political movements which had penetrated Muslim masses, had to be eliminated. Hence, the early battle against Marxism, communism, socialism in its Western and 'Arab' variants and against secular-nationalist radicalisms. At critical junctures, this battle joined ranks with imperialism against their 'common enemies'. Political movements based on secular origins gradually lost their mass bases and ultimately became marginalised in many countries.

This new, fundamentalist version of Islam within the ranks of popular classes provides the social base of opposition to governments in the MENA region which have not yet been taken over. Opposition to 'Western imperialism' is one of the battle cries. Since subservience by corrupt regimes to the neoliberal assault has also been widespread in these countries (for example, Egypt, the Maghreb and Pakistan), opposition to IMF recipes becomes part of the same battle cry. However, this opposition is not aimed at the capitalist mode of production both at the centre and the periphery, which provides the base upon which imperialism and subservience to neoliberalism is built, but rather on lifestyles, value systems and appearances imported from the Western world (Bayat 2007). These symbols of degeneration are considered to be the natural and inevitable outcomes of secular systems. An opposition to the capitalist system per se and to the domestic class roots of imperialism and neoliberalism, that is, capitalists and landlords, is absent.

Moreover, active collaboration of Islamist regimes with imperialism in the Arabic Peninsula is well known. There, resistance to the penetration of 'Western' lifestyles and values is a strategic part of official ideology and policies which have not prevented long-lasting linkages with US imperialism. A more recent transformation on the same lines has been realised in Turkey, where the de facto Islamist and anti-secular AKP (Justice and Development Party) has followed neoliberal recipes faithfully; renewed standby agreements with the IMF, even when there was no economic necessity; accepted most external demands on full membership negotiations with the European Union; supported the US occupation of Iraq;[11] and continued with the military agreements with Israel. No massive protest movements from Islamist circles took place. This unusual and implicit submission of popular classes to the pro-business, pro-imperialist policies of the AKP has been realised, in part, thanks to the decimation of left-wing socialist movements rooted within the ranks of popular classes during and after the 1980 military coup and their replacement by Islamist sects, *jemaats*, communities, and '*tarikat*' within urban slums and villages. Supportive of the AKP, these Islamist groups disseminated a fundamentalist version of Islam targeting the elimination of traditional/popular practices of Islam. Secular ideologies and value-systems were equally targeted.

The shift away from moderate class-based opposition of centre-left parties facilitated the process. The current opposition of these parties is directed against creeping Islamisation of society and the gradual invasion of public administration by Islamist cadres. This narrow agenda contributes to their further isolation from popular classes. At the end of the first decade of the new century, Islamism dominates the popular classes whose traditional class reflexes appear to be paralysed.[12] On the other hand, the pro-imperialist, pro-EU and neoliberal orientation of AKP governments are fully supported by all (secular, Islamist, metropolitan, Anatolian, industrial, trade-oriented and financial) segments of the bourgeoisie. This is a situation in which domination by capital in its 'corrupt' version prevails in Turkey with occasional (within the context of current anti-crisis measures) shifts into populism.[13] Hence, unless a dramatic economic collapse occurs during the current crisis, Turkish politics will be dominated by the AKP-version of Islamism in the foreseeable future.

There is an essential difference between Islamist movements and the well-known 'liberation theology' of the Catholic Church in Latin America. The former's ultimate target is the establishment of an Islamic state according to the original recipes formulated in the holy Koran and by the Prophet's teaching (the Hadith). A just and equitable society is expected to be the natural outcome. This is, by definition, a utopia with a regressive, backward-looking character. By contrast, followers of liberation theology directly target the elimination of exploitation, oppression observed in the actual world and, hence, can and do collaborate with all anti-systemic movements in their own countries. With Islamism as the dominating ideology, no other anti-systemic oppositional movement is to be allowed to survive (Bayat 2007: 47, Achcar 2007: 47, 66–72). There, and in other peripheral countries of the non-Muslim world, the reactionary role of religion is played by evangelical churches originating from North America and 'exported' to urban slums (Ahmad 2007: 10, 20, Bayat 2007: 47–9, Achcar 2007: 60–7).

CONCLUSION

As the capitalist world system is entering a legitimacy crisis, many countries in Asia are currently at, or moving toward, a crossroads, in terms of inter-class relations and their incidence on nation-states: *regression from populism toward full submission to capital*, or *superseding populism gradually by moving toward class-based politics*. Or, perhaps, in response to the heavy burden of the current crisis on popular classes, *skipping the 'populist' phase and taking a shortcut from comprehensive domination by capital and imperialism toward class-based politics*. The third alternative implies a more radical, quasi-revolutionary path corresponding to some Latin American experiences; but it is the least probable one in Asia, considering current conditions there – with the exception of Nepal, where control of the state remains in dispute.

The international economic crisis occurred at a moment when, as a result of three decades of comprehensive assault by capital, the imperialist system had changed radically. A gradual evolution toward the establishment of a single labour market, in a world where international labour movements are negligible, had been affecting class relations. Whereas for most of the twentieth century the industrial working class was concentrated in the centres of the imperialist system, at the end of the past three decades, industrial workers in the third world have grown by more than two-fold. Capital account liberalisation has, in most cases, paralysed the manipulation of the exchange rate, and competitiveness on the basis of labour costs has become the key to successful performance. As the new international accumulation dynamic shifts from a policy of 'beggar thy neighbour' to 'beggar thy worker', the destinies and interests of working classes everywhere are becoming more and more opposed to each other.[14] Asia has played a determining role in this transformation.

On the other hand, lifestyles, ideologies and interests between the bourgeoisies of the North and South have been converging. 'National' and increasingly nationalistic working classes are currently confronting the 'International of Capital'. The class map and solidarities of the nineteenth and early twentieth centuries are thus transformed into their opposites (Boratav et al. 2001: 36).

At this stage, it is too early to predict whether the incidence of the crisis on nation-states on peripheral economies and on the inter-class balance of forces will initiate a process to 'correct' what has happened during the recent decades in Asia and elsewhere.

NOTES

1. For a comparative quantitative analysis of Asian and Latin American economies in terms of distributional (that is, real wage and labour productivity) movements immediately before, during and after economic crises, see UNCTAD (2000: 61–8 and Tables 4.3 and 4.4). For Turkey and the Maghreb during the 1980s, see Boratav (1993).
2. Slavoj Žižek (2008: 285, 304) expresses this duality as 'populism versus class struggle' and later clarifies it thus: '[t]he ultimate difference between the radical-emancipatory politics and populist politics is that authentic radical politics is active, imposing, enforcing its vision, while populism is fundamentally *reactive*'. 'Radical' politics here is, clearly, 'class-based' politics.
3. Full capital account liberalisation was undertaken by South Korea because it was seen, or actually demanded, as a precondition of Organisation for Economic Co-operation and Development (OECD) membership.
4. On the Turkish experience specifically, see Somel (Chapter 9, this volume).
5. A cursory observation of the emergence and management of the current financial crisis shows that the same terminology is much more appropriate for depicting linkages between the state and business groups in the West, particularly in the United States.
6. In the somewhat clumsy expression of an Egyptian observer, 'bread is not an economic commodity, it is a social and political commodity'; see Boratav (1993: 40–1).
7. Between 1997 and 2006, the US current account deficit had risen from US$140 to US$812 billion, creating the inevitable conditions for the rest of the world economy to generate conditions for an equal move in the opposite direction. Chinese current surpluses rose from US$37 to US$250 billion, hence 'covering' nearly one-third of rising US surpluses (IMF, *World Economic Outlook Database*, various dates, www.imf.org). This 'contribution' was accompanied by rising growth rates, unlike elsewhere in East Asia.
8. For details and method of calculation, see Boratav (2009).
9. It should be noted that there is, still, a hard core within the CCP, labelled

'leftists' or 'conservatives' by 'reformists', which carries out a rearguard struggle against the erosion of socialist relations. On new legislation related to private property and reactions, see the article by Lee Datong (2007) and news items in the *Independent*, 9 March 2007, and the *New York Times*, 16 March 2007. For an assessment from a Marxist-Maoist perspective, see Minqi Li (2008, Preface and chs 3 and 7).

10. In an interview with *Le Nouvel Observateur* (15–21 January 1998), Zbigniew Brzezinski said: 'The day that the Soviets officially crossed the border, I wrote to President Carter. We now have the opportunity of giving to the USSR its Vietnam war ... What is most important to the history of the world? The Taliban or the collapse of the Soviet Empire? Some stirred-up Moslems or the liberation of Central Europe?' Quoted in Ahmad (2007: 37).

11. The parliament rejected an *AKP* government motion to accept US demands on using Turkey as a base for the US invasion. Despite this temporary setback, AKP governments supported the US occupation of Iraq and helped US operations in various guises later on.

12. In a meeting of a teachers' trade union where I was present, a social sciences teacher of a high school in one of Ankara's slums told the following incident: 'In class I made the observation that in Turkey poor people were much more religious than others. A student responded by thanking to Allah that his family was poor'. *See also Yıldız Atasoy* (2007).

13. This is reflected by the resistance of the AKP government to conclude the negotiations for a stand-by agreement with the IMF which had started soon after the first wave of international crisis arrived in Turkey. On the other hand, corruption under neoliberalism generates discontents among the 'excluded and politically non-priviledged' segments of the business community. However, these difficulties are not crucial enough to overcome the overall support which almost all sub-groups of the bourgeoisie extend to the neoliberal model.

14. See *Communique of the Symposium* on *Acts of Resistance Against Globalisation from the South*, 5–7 September 2005, Turkish Social Science Association, Ankara.

REFERENCES

Achcar, Gilbert (2007), 'Religion and Politics Today from a Marxist Perspective', in *Global Flashpoints: Reactions to Imperialism and Neoliberalism*, Socialist Register 2008, ed. L. Panitch and C. Leys. London: Merlin Press.

Ahmad, Aijaz (2007), 'Islam, Islamisms and the West', in *Global Flashpoints: Reactions to Imperialism and Neoliberalism*, Socialist Register 2008, ed. L. Panitch and C. Leys. London: Merlin Press.

Alnasseri, Sabah (2007), 'Understanding Iraq', in *Global Flashpoints: Reactions to Imperialism and Neoliberalism*, Socialist Register 2008, ed. L. Panitch and C. Leys. London: Merlin Press.

Arrighi, Giovanni (2007), *Adam Smith in Beijing*. London and New York: Verso.

Arrighi, Giovanni (2009), 'The Winding Paths of Capital: Interview by David Harvey', *New Left Review*, 56 (March–April): 61–94.

Atasoy, Yildiz (2007), 'The Islamic Ethic and the Spirit of Turkish Capitalism Today', in *Global Flashpoints: Reactions to Imperialism and Neoliberalism*, Socialist Register 2008, ed. L. Panitch and C. Leys. London: Merlin Press.

Bayat, Asef (2007), 'Islamism and Empire: The Incongruous Nature of Islamist Anti-Imperialism', in *Global Flashpoints: Reactions to Imperialism and Neoliberalism*, Socialist Register 2008, ed. L. Panitch and C. Leys. London: Merlin Press.

Boratav, Korkut (1993), *Public Sector, Public Intervention and Economic Development: The Impact of Changing Perspectives and Policies During the 1980s*, UNCTAD Discussion Paper No. 61. Geneva: UNCTAD.

Boratav, Korkut (2009), 'A Comparison of Two Cycles in the World Economy: 1989–2007', Featured Article, IDEAS, April, www.networkideas.org.

Boratav, Korkut, A.H. Köse and E. Yeldan (2001), 'Turkey: Globalization, Distribution and Social Policy', in *External Liberalization, Economic Performance and Social Policy*, ed. Lance Taylor. Oxford and New York: Oxford University Press.

Bourdieu, Pierre (1998), *Acts of Resistance: Against the Tyranny of the Market*. New York: The New Press.

Datong, Lee (2007), 'The Next Land Revolution?', *Open Democracy*, 8 August, www.opendemocracy.net/article/democracy_power/china_inside/land_revolution.

IMF (2009), *World Economic Outlook*, April. Washington, DC: IMF.

Li, Minqi (2008), *The Rise of China and the Demise of the Capitalist World-Economy*. London: Pluto Press.

UNCTAD (2000), *Trade and Development Report 2000*. Geneva and New York: United Nations.

Žižek, Slavoj (2008), *In Defense of Lost-Causes*. London and New York: Verso.

6
The National Question in India

Sandeep Chachra

INTRODUCTION

It is often said that the Indian state has had an autonomous development trajectory and that it is one of few states in the periphery – and one of few in Asia – which have progressed on this path since decolonisation. Civilisational continuity, whose foundations predate by millennia that of the dominant capitalist centres, and a more recent post-colonial autonomous nation-building project, are deemed to be the foundational blocks in the resurgence of India, celebrated and amplified by its growth successes and 'emergence' into the global clubs of power.

It is said that India and China will be the new global powers, with China already one of the 'G2' today. Imperial centres, alarmed by the spectre of losing dominance and seeking to maintain it, justify the economic growth and growing influence of the two continent-countries as a demonstration of the supremacy of the neoliberal path to development, finding in it several reasons to commemorate the success of their eventual emergence. To them, China and India are living examples that socialism has been mortally wounded, injured as it was with the fall of Soviet Russia and the isolation of Cuba.

In the case of the Indian state, such a trajectory of growth and development has enabled it to wear with some respect, the fabric of liberal democracy. Backed by the opiate of high economic growth rates and its success in opening up, the Indian state propounds the vision of a 'Shining India' to its own people and to the world, a vision where the high tide of growth would lift the boats of Indian masses out of poverty and deprivation.

Whether India will shine for its people or whether its promises to the masses rust would be determined by the turn India takes in the first decades of the twenty-first century. It would be determined by who decides on what constitutes the national question for India today.

The national development and progress of India needs to be reviewed with a rear-view mirror. While the democratic struggle against imperialism brought together diverse forces into a nationalist ideology oriented towards popular nation-building ends, the failure of the Indian state in the last six decades to expand the economic and social bases for sovereignty, and its tryst with neoliberalism since the 1990s, throws up several issues of a foundational and functional nature. Several decades after committing to a sovereign socialist secular democratic republic, the Indian state stands at a crossroads once again.

The choice India made in 'opening up' in the 1990s takes it to a different phase of development, one which could open up India's national autocentric development to a new level of consolidation or lead it to catapult its accrued gains in a further search for accumulation. While it was not a choice determined by the masses and, in itself, does not constitute a route for popular development in India, this chapter argues that the choice of opening up to a more intensive phase of accumulation was a no-choice. It was made in a state where nationalist ideology was captured by the elites and subsumed to their class interests; and where, therefore, incomplete projects of agrarian, industrial and democratic transformation necessitated 'catching up' and nurturing external solidarities.

Popular progress and radicalisation of the Indian state now also requires the resurrection of struggle. The fabric of democracy that India wears is faded and in need of recolouring and reshaping by the people of India, for which sustained struggle is the only path to redirect the state towards popular ends.

CONSOLIDATION OF THE INDIAN STATE

An important foundational issue to analyse while examining the progress and autonomy of the Indian state is whether, and to what depth, the bourgeois revolution (that is, the anti-imperialist national struggle) has cleared a path for substantive democratic progress and social development. If the revolution did arouse conditions for a change in the balance of power, then how can the progressive conservatism of the Indian state be explained? Is it a stage in the making before the radicalisation of the Indian state through praxis? Answers to such questions help explain the anatomy of the state as it consolidates its existence and its relationships with the super-structure of the capitalist system – a system of loosely-cohering competing states.

At the time of the anti-imperialist struggle, there existed for India, as well as other peripheries where revolutions came to fruition (Russia, China, Cuba, Tanzania, Vietnam, and more recently Nepal), the following opportunities to advance emancipatory pathways of development on a long transition to socialism:

- the transformation of agrarian relations and socialisation of the agrarian economy;
- the development, control and centralisation of industry and the nationalisation of banks, industry, and trade;
- the control over the army and bureaucracy and its ideological transformation in accordance with radical nationalism;
- the genesis/transformation of democracy into a people's democracy linked to social progress which, unlike the other two socialisations, could only be put into effect gradually and through the intervention of both the self-organisation of the popular classes and the state.

The way in which the seizure of power and ensuing construction of society was handled by the revolutionary forces, whether bourgeois democratic or socialist, is reflected today in the strength of economic, social, and political bases constructed during that period of post-colonial nation-building. Whether these social bases have been able to tie the masses to revolutionary ideals of social progress in the longer term also determines the nature and autonomy of the state which has thus evolved. Experience in this regard varies. In some instances, attempts were made to elaborate a full programme of construction of socialism (agrarian relations, industry, people's army, and democracy with social progress), but in most other instances these stopped short of full elaboration, and progressed, whether by design or mistakes, as humbler truncated versions in opening a path for the long transition towards socialism.

In the case of Russia, as a measure to fortify the proletarian government, Lenin and the Bolsheviks promoted the nationalisation of land and the development of heavy industry, along with the nationalisation of industry, banks and trade. The emphasis on industrialisation witnessed huge investments in heavy industry, laying the foundations for the later predominance of the Soviet Union in the arenas of heavy industry and technology. On the front of agrarian reform, the Decree on Land (1917) abolished all private property, and land was confiscated by peasants directly, under the slogan 'go and take the land for yourself'. Such a step led to the conversion of large landownership into peasant landownership, without real nationalisation of land – a fundamental necessity for large-scale production and its union with industry. The separation between the rural economy and industry continued, in part promoted by a powerful layer of peasants in the countryside who opposed socialist land reform. Later attempts to develop rural communes mostly out of urban unemployed proletarians were met by stiff resistance and antagonism, and a divide between peasants and urban workers continued, in part being exacerbated by an additional emphasis on urban industrial and military development for a privileged techno-bureaucracy.

While planning a revolutionary advance on the national economy front, the model of democratic centralism informed how the Bolsheviks would deal with developing a democratic programme of action. With the exception of promoting the right of self-determination for the peoples of other nationalities (Finland, Ukraine, for example) – that, too, for tactical reasons – the Bolsheviks displayed disregard for a gamut of democratic liberties, such as the constituent assembly, universal suffrage and freedom of the press.

Maoist China dealt with the immediate tasks of building the new nation with state control over property, development of industry, centralisation of the economy, planning and decision-making, and suppression of any kind of autonomous decision-making by basic units. Centralised planning in the case of China served as a base for redistributing income among workers and peasants, unlike in Russia where the rural masses were bled to the benefit of urban industrial development. Such a strategy propelled China into reducing inequalities rapidly through egalitarian policies and the pursuit of social solidarity. Collectivisation of land and the transformation of agrarian relations with fundamental reform, in the first instance upon seizure of power, ensured that the peasantry would be immediately and organically tied up with the revolutionary advance, unlike in Soviet Russia where early policies created a divide between urban workers and peasants. Whilst not equal to the emphasis on heavy industry, in China considerable attention was centred on agriculture which occupied four-fifths of the rural population, ensuring rapid increase in food production between the years 1952 and 1978 where agrarian reforms through commune organisation saw food production increase by 75 per cent. Similarly, the Chinese also placed heavy emphasis on industrialisation as a necessary and important step towards establishing a base in pursuit of catching up, as it did in the case of the army, with the formation of the Red Army imbued with revolutionary fervour.

However, it was in the area of securing bases for democratisation that the Chinese advance did not progress far. In subsuming the autonomous decision-making of the basic units (which was perhaps considered important given the class character of who would have used the power to exercise control, seeing the example of Russia), the system weakened the agency and aspirations of the labouring classes. Such an approach prevented the emergence of real democratisation, adopting as it did a hierarchical organisation of work and culture, stifling opportunities for struggles to manifest themselves in matters of developing and determining the national question.

Learning from the experience of China that building socialism is a long-term process, where each step would have to be negotiated, each river crossed by feeling the stones, a radical advance promised by the Maoists in Nepal now bases itself on gradually putting in place a people's democracy wedded to social development, with step-by-step advances in social rights, which the Constituent Assembly formulates.

In other countries and regimes that arose from other national liberation struggles in Africa and Asia, the understanding of socialism was quite different and incomplete. The socialist element in the national planning of several of these newly independent countries presented itself as an eclectic model of democratic forms of exercise of state control, which was expected to distribute social justice on its own. In most cases, the national bourgeoisie had gained ascendancy in the nation-building processes of the post-colonial phase, and had thereby subverted the institutions of the state to its own interests. Socialist promises of liberation and freedom in these states remained a distant slogan for workers and peasants, whose aspirations for emancipation rested on a fundamental transformation of economic, social and political relationships.

In India, the anti-imperialist struggle was led by the bourgeoisie, the landowners and the professionally educated, while the foot-soldiers were the peasants and the working classes. Thus, while the national democratic struggle against imperialism brought together diverse forces into a nationalist ideology orientated towards popular and emancipatory ends, it was the upper classes of India, which came into power at the end of a long struggle for independence, which were to become the protagonists in setting the foundations of the Indian state. The Indian national struggle, therefore, could be classified as a bourgeois democratic movement, with socialist influence.

The construction of the foundations of the Indian state followed a mixed approach, reflecting the character of the Indian National Congress which took upon itself the leadership mantle. Congress contained both conservative and progressive elements – inspired in large measure by the ideas of bourgeois republicanism and in smaller measure by the Bolshevik ideas of socialism. It is in the early contestation of ideas between the two, which gradually led to the former taking control, that the work of the Constituent Assembly and the resulting constitution can be understood, resolving to constitute India into a Sovereign, Socialist, Secular, Democratic Republic.

In line with its mixed approach, in the first phase of national development and reconstruction, the state 'talked' of fundamental agrarian reforms and transformation of agriculture, but without a socialist content of radically changing the nature of agrarian relations embedded in India's feudal history. Land reform, as the first of independent India's planning instruments noted (the First Five-Year Plan), was a fundamental task ahead.

Two questions guided the Indian agrarian reform programme in the early years of independence. The first was to change the nature of exploitative agrarian relations, and the second was to enhance food production so as to achieve self-sufficiency and promote the base for national sovereignty. The programme of land reform was designed to promote economic growth and food production by removing rentier intermediaries, as well as to eradicate rural inequities by giving ownership to the peasant tiller. The reform programme particularly targeted the Zamindari system (and its collaboration with the colonial administration in extracting and transferring surplus out of India), aimed at abolishing intermediaries, inducing tenancy reforms and fixing a ceiling on ownership of agricultural land, with the idea of introducing structural change in rural India. As distinct from the socialist experiment of nearby China, the Indian land reform programme, elaborated early on in the central planning instruments, promoted private ownership of land without any attempt to nationalise property. Given the nature of the national movement, the land reform programme did not challenge capitalist property (except in imposing ceilings, which in any case were not implemented effectively) while promoting private peasant property. The idea of nationalisation of property, where required by national interest, was promoted.

Ownership and tenurial reforms, based on the premise of unleashing the private engine of agricultural growth, were successful to the extent that with the passage of the Zamindari abolition act and its implementation in the states by 1972, 20 million farmers had come in direct contact with the state. Similarly, with the lowering of land ceilings, nearly three-fifths of the declared surplus land was redistributed. To the extent that 92 per cent of the holdings were wholly owned and self-operated towards the end of the programme, there was progress on the declared policy front, but land reform measures thus introduced did not manage to change the nature of class ownership. One of the major negative features of agrarian transition in India is the continued concentration of land in the hands of the upper strata of rural society. This has not undergone any significant change in the past six decades, despite the reforms. In fact, land leasing by affluent farmers is commonplace, without jeopardising the interests of the large landowners. As the Planning Commission of India itself admitted in the Sixth Five-Year Plan (1980–85), if progress on land reforms has been less than satisfactory, it has not been due to a flaw in policy but rather to indifferent implementation. Often the necessary determination has been lacking to undertake effective action, particularly in the matter of the implementation of ceiling laws and consolidation of holdings, and in failing vigorously to pursue concealed tenancies and transform them into tenancy/occupancy rights as enjoined under the law.

The land reform agenda took a back seat (eventually going off the radar in early 1990s), when the land question was overtaken by agricultural production worries in the 1960s, induced by famines in the eastern states of the country. It was at this time that the World Bank also decided to intervene in Indian agriculture for the first time; 1964 was the year when the Bell Mission came to India to advise on capital and chemical-intensive agriculture, devaluation of the currency and liberalisation of trade.

These were defining years for the decisive shift on the agrarian question, from the early ideas of changes in agrarian relations (through limited land reforms) to the promotion of capital-intensive agriculture and the genesis of the 'green revolution' in the 1970s.

On the food production and availability front, India's post-colonial record is positive until the onset of neoliberal reforms in 1990s. While there is a considerable debate on the contribution of land reform (and peasant landownership) versus technological innovation in augmenting agricultural production, the fact remains that in the four decades after independence, food grain production increased nearly four-fold, building a strong foundation for national food self-sufficiency and security. Per capita availability of food increased

from 134.8 kg in 1946 to 172.7 kg in 1990, declining thereafter to
155.2 kg in 2002 with the onset of neoliberal reforms.

In a broader sense, agrarian reform succeeded in bringing to India
an assured security of food production, but it did not manage to
change the basic structure of inequality in the countryside, nor did
it manage to liberate the peasants and seek their agency for fuller
progress. That the number of landless labourers has increased, and
the top 10 per cent of India's landowning classes occupy more land
than they did in 1951, only indicates that the inequalities have
increased and the task of socialisation of the agrarian economy
remains unfinished. A recent survey by the National Sample Survey
Organisation (NSSO 2003) on landownership patterns also shows
extremely skewed landholding patterns. At the all-India level,
marginal and small landowners constituted 90 per cent of the
total number of owners. But they owned only 43 per cent of land,
whereas medium and large farmers who constituted only 10 per
cent of landowners owned as much as 56 per cent of land. The
divide between the capitalist farmers and peasantry, and between
the rural and the urban, is wider to bridge.

Another key prerequisite which the nationalist revolution
considered was to build an industrial infrastructure as a base for
economic self-sufficiency, as a nationalist response to centuries
of colonial bleeding. The Nehruvian development paradigm
emphasised the building of heavy industries as 'temples of modern
India', which was considered a basic necessity for India's advance
towards achieving socialism. Centralised planning was of essence
if the country was to industrialise rapidly. As a foundation of self-
sufficiency, an imposing structure of industrial and technological
development was set up as a strong and dependent lever of
development under state control. The Industries (Development and
Regulation) Act of 1951 laid the foundations for this administrative
national control over industrial capacity.

Nationalised industries included electric power, steel, machine-
building, metals and minerals, defence, chemicals, transportation,
life insurance, portions of the coal and textile industries, and
banking. To promote industrial development, high tariffs and import
restrictions were put in place, along with subsidies for nationalised
firms. Investment funds were directed to nationalised industries,
along with control of land use and prices. With support from the
Soviet Union, and also some other countries, through technology
transfer agreements, new technology was hoped to be absorbed (by
the famous reverse engineering) and new skills promoted.

Industrial emphasis posted rich returns for Indian self-sufficiency. In the first five decades of independence, for instance, steel production increased from 1.25 million tons to 53 million tons and coal production from 30 million tons to 299 million tons, while the commissioned capacity for power generation experienced nearly a 100-fold increase.

In the phase of national development till the end of the 1980s, serious emphasis was given to establishing what could be called 'temples' of national sovereignty. Public enterprises controlled a fifth of the gross domestic product (GDP) by the 1970s. This strategy (similar to that of the Chinese) was in sharp contrast to that followed by other East Asian countries, which chose to use state intervention to build private sector industries, or the South Asian neighbours who chose not to follow the path of import-substitution, thereby stifling the potential growth of their industry, whether nationalised or not.

Two contradictions emerged on this path, both of which laid the foundation for India's later transition to economic pragmatism and neoliberalism, beginning with a shift towards export promotion and greater integration into the global economy.

First of all, believing the potential of agriculture to be limited, the Indian government taxed agriculture by skewing the terms of trade against it and emphasising import-substitution, thus giving priority to heavy industry. Agrarian relations were not transformed and the separation of industry and agriculture continued, as the planning for agricultural and industrial development did not happen under a unified point of view (agriculture remained in private hands, while heavy industry was progressively nationalised). The early planning hope that rapid industrialisation would draw away surplus labour from agriculture was mistaken; at the end of the Tenth Five-Year Plan, almost 60 per cent of India's labour force is still engaged in the primary sector, contributing around 21 per cent to the country's GDP, while industry employs 17 per cent of the labour force, producing 27 per cent of GDP. The strategy of development at that stage had failed to create better options for the rural poor, to allow them to develop productive assets, or to obtain gainful employment, or to significantly improve their quality of life and time for creative human pursuits. This strategy did not go far enough (in relation to other steps of agrarian transformation) and was therefore unable to address the divide between the city and the countryside.

Second, the state heavily subsidised the growth of a national bourgeoisie – with cheap credit, energy and infrastructure, and other indirect and direct subsidies – in activities of an intermediary nature, oriented to trade and small enterprise. Thus, apart from a few large industries in India – the Tatas and Birlas – the subsidies opened the way for the blossoming of a parasitic private sector on the hard work of the public sector. Such growth could not possibly have overcome the divide between the city and the countryside, since it thrived on it. It was a policy which could not have led the country to the eventual socialisation of intermediary gains.

While emphasis was placed on economic development, human development suffered in the first five decades of development planning. These defining decades left a poor record with respect to developing a strong human base. The promise of universal education and health care did not see the light of day, six decades after it was first held out. The result is that, today, 40 per cent of Indian children are undernourished, six in 100 die at birth, and illiteracy rates among women and men are at 44 per cent and 25 per cent, respectively. Public spending on education and health, until recently, remained well below the minimum norm, let alone a progressive one. Moreover, both education and health programmes have suffered from inadequacy in quality and equity.

The promise to root out social discrimination was held out to millions of *dalits* and *adivasis* (indigenous people). The constitution provided for measures of positive discrimination for the lower castes and indigenous people (activated through reservations, for instance). Yet, it did not provide for substantive mechanisms for their fulfilment, or where they were provided much later, they were not implemented properly. Thus, bonded labour was abolished in India only in 1976; manual scavenging, one of the worst forms of human denigration, was officially prohibited only in 1993, though the practice continues today, along with various forms of untouchability. A recent study, of which this author was part, revealed 130 different forms of discrimination in India, despite its official prohibition in 1955 (Shah et al. 2006).

One of the weakest links in the consolidation of the Indian state, therefore, was on the human development front, crashing one of the fundamental engines for transforming class relations. The goal of full development of the human potential for free development of a creative life remains a path crying out to be pursued. However, what the national promises did was to awaken the democratic aspirations of the people for a better life, fuelling prospects for emancipation and social progress (as we will see in a later section).

CONSERVATISM OF THE INDIAN STATE: A CHOICE OR A NECESSITY?

By the mid 1970s, the limits of the Indian model were becoming visible. Widespread discontent had begun to surface in India, with large sections of the populace coming out to demonstrate against unemployment, commodity shortages, rising prices, corruption and an unaccountable administration. Rural unrest was rising rapidly; popularly called Naxalism, it was voicing powerfully the discontent of the peasantry on the progress of agrarian reform.

Contradictions were also beginning to surface. Land reforms and minimum wages remained empty rhetoric for the peasantry. Village landlords held ceiling lands illegally, continuing to exploit rural labour, under bondage and extremely low wages. Unable to absorb even urban unemployed youth, industry was not able to provide basic security to workers, who were increasingly resorting to strikes and boycott actions, at the risk of losing their jobs. By 1975, the numbers of registered jobseekers (only a fraction of the jobless) climbed to 4.1 million; 24 per cent of the urban youth remained unemployed. The slogan '*Garibi Hatao*' ('Remove Poverty') and the 20-point programme which it elaborated was not able to address the manifest problems, and came to be popularly referred to as the '*Garib Hatao*' ('Remove the Poor') programme.

The state response to the public outcry was to promote greater investment in agriculture through credit, subsidies and green revolution. Worried that the green revolution would turn into a 'red revolution', the government announced concessions by introducing tenancy reforms and the reduction of land ceilings. State control over every aspect of the economy was tightened. Banks were nationalised, trade was increasingly restricted, price controls were imposed on a wide range of products, and foreign investment was squeezed. By 1973, dealings in foreign exchanges as well as foreign investment came to be regulated by the Foreign Exchange and Regulation Act (FERA).

Citing threats to internal security, and the opposition of the rich to the progressive pro-poor programmes of the government, emergency rule was imposed in India in 1975, which suspended fundamental civil and political rights (such as free speech) and imposed censorship on the media. For the workers, new controls were established – emergency provisions denied the right to strike, and were backed by several anti-worker ordinances. The Indian private sector, which had been nurtured by state subsidies since independence, welcomed the industrial policies of emergency rule, while the World Bank applauded the emergency measures with increased aid flows from the Aid India consortium.

It became clear that central planning, and the choice of economy associated with it, would need reform as it had reached its social limits. A new phase of development was needed. By the early 1980s, a mild trend towards deregulation began. Economic reforms were introduced, and initial steps to liberalise trade, industrial and financial policies were initiated, while subsidies, tax concessions and depreciation of the currency improved export incentives. These measures helped economic growth to accelerate to 5.2 per cent annually during the 1980s, compared to 3.5 per cent during the 1970s, spurring a forward movement towards further fundamental liberal reform.

Choices for India were limited at that stage. Continuing on a mixed-economy path by maintaining the system and 'managing the rubble' was no longer a choice. The choice was either to accelerate 'development' and move into a more aggressive phase of accumulation, or to promote a more intense form of socialisation of the economy. The nature of class relations in India – the existing character of consolidated social blocs – made the latter choice unreal in the short term. The version of democracy which India exercised, which did not defend social-economic rights and privileged the private domain over the public, while providing space for reinventing itself, limited the choice further. Moreover, a rhetorical understanding of the failures of socialism and the setbacks to its credibility in the 1990s provided popular justification for the ruling classes of India to decisively attempt to move towards a more aggressive phase of accumulation.

In the early 1990s, India 'opened up' and commenced its romance with neoliberalism. The economy was opened up to foreign capital and trade. The liberalisation of the economy, which gave primacy to exports, the entry of multinationals, and structural adjustment loans, promised high growth and integration into the world economy.

A certain amount of opening and catching up was necessary in the sphere of obtaining technology and capital, and for claiming space in global economic and political governance (after a loss of that space by the Non-Aligned Movement (NAM)). The choice of strategy was to establish the base for opening up using the comparative advantage of labour, reflected also in the external policy to promote a 'Group of 15' within the NAM to negotiate with the developed countries. The scope of this strategy encompassed liberalisation, deregulation and privatisation.

The Indian strategy for a more intense form of accumulation and the establishment of a new space in the global economy is, therefore, a choice based on the development of light industry and services, construed on the advantage of cheap labour power. It is further based on the principle of the market trumping the state, where gradual withdrawal of the state from the economic and developmental arena is supported by filling up this vacant space with global capital.

The trouble with this model is that it is an exclusive social model which benefits less than a quarter of the population and condemns the remaining, the masses, to stagnation and long-term impoverishment. This strategy in no way allows for optimising development and progress in the long term, but rather promotes a renewed basis for social and regional divide. The last two decades of India's embrace of this choice are testimony to its exploitative potential of ruthless, pitiless, uncaring 'jobless' growth, of pauperisation, immiseration, displacement and chauvinism.

Indian development statistics are replete with data regarding growing inequalities on the social and economic aspects, including on the most basic aspects of food availability and employment. Between 1993/94 and 2004, the unemployment rate increased sharply in rural India, from 5.6 per cent to 9 per cent for men and from 5.3 per cent to 9.3 per cent for women; as well as in urban India, from 6.7 per cent to 8.1 per cent for men and from 10.5 per cent to 11.7 per cent for women. What is being witnessed is a squeezing out of regular employment and the increasing casualisation and feminisation of jobs in the organised sector. Employment in the public and private sectors dropped over the first 13 years of reform by 300,000. It is no surprise that India reports an astonishingly high number of workers in the self-employed category (45 per cent), indicating a problem in the laws guiding employer-worker relations, especially in the private sector. During this period, per capita food availability decreased from 172.7 kg in 1990 to 155.2 kg in 2002, when agriculture witnessed declining growth and the dwindling of the share of agriculture in the economy, from 34 per cent in 1990–91 to 18.5 per cent in 2006–07.

The vacuum created by a dehumanised package of liberalisation is a breeding ground for chauvinistic forces and versions of political Hinduism and political Islam, which offer to the populace a rudder to assert their identity and space. As we well know, the history of capitalism is not about catching up based on comparative advantage ... it is a history of exploitation of the periphery on the basis of comparative advantage!

The other trouble with the model is the seductive nature of the growth that it offers, especially to the middle and professional classes. It is in this seduction that the invasive potential of this model resides, which leads to the fragmentation of a social bloc which would defend emancipatory advance. The seduction of market fundamentalism has been elaborated by scriptwriters of popular narratives who have (finally) managed to transform the Indian image of a land of poverty into that of 'Shining India', a story of success and resurgence of power (due in no small measure to the collaboration of neoliberal interests which see the potential to exploit India's huge market). India's migration from a 'Hindu rate of growth' to one around double digits forms the backbone of this narrative, celebrated in the circles of popular news magazines, films and newspapers as heralding the arrival of India on the global scene. The exclusivist nature of this path and the inequities it creates is reflected in the schizophrenic nature of a state promoting a conjunction of two nations, connected only by corridors of exploitation: one nation which promises speedy reforms and further progress on the road to capitalism for those living in 'India', and another which pledges to deliver development to those living in 'Bharat', its country-cousin counterpart.

The issue is not about opening up and moving on to a new stage of reforms, since it was a historical necessity given the level of development of the social and productive forces, but the choice is about knowing how to manage relations (externally and internally) and when/where to dissociate in order to advance from this phase of development in securing an autonomous path.

But that choice will be determined by struggle and the level of development of authentic democracy. It was never a free choice; not when it was first made and not when it will be remade, when the falsehoods of neoliberalism are forcefully exposed and a million mutinies resonate with voices for liberation from within the state and from within the states-system.

NATIONAL AUTONOMY IN INTERNATIONAL AND REGIONAL PERSPECTIVE

To understand the trajectory of India's experience with autonomy and its conservatism, it is pertinent to analyse its relationship with the wider states-system. History provides evidence that capitalist accumulation conditions a highly asymmetric global system, in that colonies/peripheries are outward-looking to the extent of servicing capitalism's hunger, while capitalist centres have the luxury of following an autocentric path, only looking outwards to the extent of shaping and directing the system. Accumulation promoted through an asymmetric integration of states was foundational for colonialism, and continues to form the basis of political economy in the current world order. Messages reiterating the need for global economic integration are continually propagated, whether through wars or through the varied engines of liberal ideology. As recently as the onset of the food and financial crises of 2008, such rhetoric was holding forth on why developing countries should not follow protectionism and autocentrism.

For the peripheries proposing to embark on autocentric paths, it is not only enough that the proletariat is wedded to goals of socialist progress. Alongside internal nationalisation, democratisation and socialisation, 'projects' to secure external solidarities assume critical importance in the overall progress of national autonomy and its popular elaboration. The current experience of Zimbabwe under ZANU-PF (see Moyo and Yeros, Chapter 4, this volume), and the current struggle of Maoists in Nepal (see Roka, Chapter 8, this volume) illustrate the difficulties of redirecting the state to radical ends without external solidarity and internal politicisation and consolidation. In fact, the modern history of states in the South which embarked on national reconstruction along autonomous routes resonates with Marx's comments that 'islands of socialism cannot exist in a sea of capitalism'.

With enclave socialism impossible to sustain, the task becomes two-fold. To develop the popular bases for promoting autonomy internally, while defending such progress externally by means of solidarity and progressive alliances. No doubt, the need to catch up externally creates contradictions, as it promotes class interests which jettison the gains of internal autonomy. To what extent has progress in India contributed to, and sought support from, external solidarities in strengthening its autonomy? Has the Indian self-centred development trajectory succeeded in consolidating a progressive alliance regionally and internationally, especially since its opening up in the 1990s?

In the early post-colonial period, India sought to build solidarity against the hegemony of imperial powers. Through the political instrument of the NAM, formed in the aftermath of the Bandung meeting of 1955, a socialist-inspired India sought to build a base for collective progress and technological development. The progress of NAM over nearly five decades explains the difficulties but also underlines the necessity of securing external alliances for the South. While Bandung (and later NAM) nurtured the formation of a new political bloc and promoted broader co-operation among countries in the South, it could not resolve the question of economic co-operation (including industrial and technological development) on any significant scale. Therefore, almost all of the NAM countries had to import technology from the centres and submit to the conditionalities associated with it. In addition, in response to the needs of technological catching-up, there emerged within the NAM a Group of 15 (G15), led by India, which sought collaboration with the West to facilitate dialogue on economic development.

India's approach to NAM has undergone a considerable shift since the 1970s. At that time, the question of developing India was how to secure technological progress and economic co-operation, together with securing a progressive political base with a Southern alliance. While there is no doubt that the NAM platform and India's early leadership provided an opportunity for India to enhance its global political influence beyond its contested regional one, as well as enabling it to obtain political support for self-centred progress, the role of NAM was quite limited on the front of economic and technological development. By the 1970s, India's internal contradictions had necessitated an urgent need for technological catching-up and a revival of a second phase of industrial development (alongside the land question). Unable to do so at the collective NAM platform of the 1960s and 1970s, India secured technological co-operation through bilateral routes, that is, through minor technological co-operation agreements with the imperial centres and a more substantive one with Soviet Russia through the 1971 Treaty of Peace, Friendship and Co-operation. The latter was not without its limitations, especially since the level of technological progress in Soviet Russia began its decline in the 1980s. By this time India, together with a few other countries, was beginning to push the NAM to consider partnership with the West on technological and economic co-operation.

Strong internal contradictions in the 1970s, gradual liberalisation in the 1980s and opening up in the 1990s had further propelled a new consolidation of upper-class interests in India to seek new alliances with the Triad (the US, the EU and Japan), as well as co-operation to help resolve its internal and external contradictions. The shift is evident in the Indian influence on the decision-making of NAM and its increasingly moderating and conservative influence. Thus, in 1979, it opposed the Cuban proposal of a linkage of NAM with its natural ally, socialism; in 1989, it was the leader in the formation of the G15 for co-operation on economic development with the West; in 1992, it opposed the Malaysian proposal to boycott the West over the international economy; and in 2007 it negotiated a nuclear treaty with the United States, issued a joint statement on the relevance of NAM, entered the G20, and later agreed with the G20 measures in response to the financial crisis.

Despite the conservatism of some of its members and their foreign policy assessments on the relevance of NAM in the current world order, membership of NAM has continued to grow, to become the largest platform outside of the United Nations, with 116 members. Recent shifts in the NAM proposals on its role and strategy in the new world order open up distinct possibilities for the renewal of a Southern front. Its condemnation of the imperialist strategy of the United States at the Kuala Lumpur meeting and the subsequent gravitation of NAM around a need for alternative economic development thinking (at the Cuba meeting) could be seen as steps towards non-alignment with the US strategy as well as with neoliberalism, particularly in the context of the economic crisis. These could be positive signs for the re-emergence of NAM on a stronger footing, which could now propel a positive agenda for renewal of South-South solidarity. The resurgence of the role of the state in the wake of the finance crisis, socialist progress in Latin America, the formation of ALBA (Bolivarian Alliance for the Americas), the wider economic and political space that exists for Southern countries which are not fully integrated into the global financial system, together with the renewal of NAM, could now have the potential to advance the South as a collective platform to promote national and regional autonomy.

India's role in promoting a new form of regional co-operation, though currently beset with contradictions and difficulties, would be critical in South Asia and the wider Asian continent. The colonial division of the Indian subcontinent, culminating in the formation of Pakistan on the basis of political Islam, Bengali nationalism, the subsequent division of Pakistan, and Indian sub-imperialism in the region, particularly with regard to smaller countries, has not enabled the South Asian region to converge around progressive projects of nation-building and regional co-operation. Early on in its nation-building phase, the state of Pakistan, while following a capitalist path of development, sought an alliance with the West through two treaty agreements, as a counterpoint to the Indian proximity with the Soviet Union. Following the Arab-Israeli conflict and the oil shock of 1973, Pakistan's emergent centrality at the Organisation of the Islamic Conference (OIC), its recent positioning in the World Trade Organisation (WTO), and the rise of the Taliban, have interwoven regional convergence with conservative and capitalist interests – inasmuch as the expanded economic position of India, the rise of political Hinduism and Sinhala nationalism perpetuate the asymmetric relationships and fragmenting possibilities for a fundamental reordering of South Asian Association for Regional Co-operation (SAARC) relations. Therefore, despite calls for a progressive, people-centred SAARC, South Asia has largely remained immune to the question of regional autonomy, as much as Southeast and East Asia, in the form of the Association of Southeast Asian Nations (ASEAN) platform, remain wedded to the neoliberal pathways of development (albeit with notable exceptions).

Recent developments in Nepal have the potential of politicising development in the sub-region and could serve as a starting point for a more fundamental reordering, which would be possible if India and China realigned on the question of Asian autonomy and on revitalising the alliance of Southern countries. For as long as India and China see each other as 'counter-forces' and not 'co-forces' in Asia, and as long as this question is determined by the ruling classes of India without a challenge from popular classes, India will continue to move closer to full integration with the centre and into the logic of the G20, perpetuating deeper asymmetries within the region.

THE RESURRECTION OF STRUGGLE AND THE RADICALISATION OF THE INDIAN STATE

We must realise that India, while following an autonomous development path, has done so increasingly on the road of capitalism and, moreover, has exercised this choice without being part of a strong Southern platform, except in the middle decades of the last century in the context of NAM. The problem, however, lies in the further advance in this direction and in the choice of route for that progression. The success of this strategy of accumulation (though it is highly exploitative and can only be justified in the short run on account of catching up) is pursued at the cost of strengthening social progress and solidarity internally. Efforts at autonomy would therefore necessitate a strong reconsolidation of social forces, since it will not be the internationally-aligned national bourgeoisie which will carry it forward, or lead the transformation in any manner. Furthermore, it will need crucial support from other states, collective defence and further progress in this direction.

What will lead India to the path of radicalisation will be an exercise of popular contestation and autonomy in the service of popular classes. Therefore, the key question on the radicalisation of the state is: for whom and for what is autonomy exercised?

The exercise of the autonomy of the state lies in the liberation of the masses in India and a realignment of social blocs for overcoming exploitative relations which have not been deconstructed over the last six decades. In the case of India, such a prospect resides in the consolidation of its democratic trajectory. Below we will examine some of these avenues.

The early constitutional promises and foundations of a functioning (albeit low-intensity) democracy opened up opportunities for authentic democratisation and social progress. Such spaces have set up a foundation for the self-determination of social actors, in the process of being and becoming. The version of representative democracy which India adopted at the culmination of the independence struggle, and one which has survived the test of time – through a written constitution, a parliamentary system, a multi-party framework, a bicameral legislature at central and federal levels, the separation of powers, and routine elections – offers to the Indian citizens, at least in theory, an opportunity for expression, participation and shaping the progress of the nation. Even though, in practice, the possibility of changing national trajectories is limited in low-intensity democracies, in the actual progression of Indian democracy such a system has enabled the development of contradictions and the prospect for development of continuous struggle. Where social relations are far from being at peace, a sustained struggle can be the locomotive for the radicalisation of society and the state.

The most important opportunity for building participatory democracy exists in nurturing the cradles of democracy, the local governments of India. After decades of neglect of local governments (aside from their brief ascendancy in the 1960s in limited form as instruments of the developmental apparatus of the state) the emergence of the *Panchayati Raj* system as a platform of self-government illustrates the potential of a democratic local base in reinventing itself and in expanding its social base through continuous struggle.

While the origin and existence of the *Panchayats*, or units of local democracy, can be traced back through centuries, these bases were plagued with imperfections and were relegated into sideshows of the mainstream of India's political history. Treated as lesser governments through much of their recent history, the *Panchayati Raj* and municipal governance bodies have been partly resurrected through the 73rd and 74th constitutional amendments of 1993, giving *Panchayati Raj* Institutions (PRIs) a constitutional status, the agency of regular elections and a 'right to live'.

The resurrection of PRIs has been an outcome of a long struggle among the political parties and bureaucracy that have actively sought to set aside these democratic bases, given the potential of the PRIs to change the nature of democracy. At the time of the independence movement, Mahatma Gandhi's idea of local government as one which would elect provincial and national governments was largely ignored in the framework of the governance system which evolved post-1947. The *Panchayati Raj* system only received a reluctant mention in the Directive Principles of State Policy in the Constitution of India,[1] in the non-justifiable and non-enforceable part of the constitution, before its rescue through the constitutional amendment of 1993. During the intervening decades, PRIs were converted into implementation instruments for the development apparatuses of the state and their self-government status was emasculated through irregular elections and an emphasis on their functional, rather than foundational, roles. In the cities, beginning with the Calcutta Corporation in 1947, urban area municipalities and corporations were ignored, and for nearly three decades urban local governments were superseded by every single Indian government (the Chennai Corporation was superseded from 1970–92), as municipal functions for development and provision of public services were shifted to the newly established development authorities and parastatals.

The rising aspirations of people, failures of development programming and inadequacy of the system of democratic representation pushed a reform-minded Rajiv Gandhi (more than his Congress Party) to widen the funnel of democratic representation and use PRIs as potential platforms for expanded participation. In pursuance of this reform, the Indian constitution was amended through the parliamentary majority, and PRIs were offered constitutional status and regularity of elections in 1993.

Panchayats and municipal bodies are now a political reality; two rounds of elections have been held in most states, and three in some. In the short span of a decade and half, the base of representation has been expanded dramatically. More than 3 million elected representative from PRIs and municipalities (to represent over 1 billion people) have emerged as defenders of democracy.

The essence of this change is not merely in numbers. It is a change in the substantive nature of democracy. With the right to live, the urban and rural local bodies have the potential to undertake the transformation of the society and the economy, as the Kerala example of radicalisation of local governments shows.

Using the amended constitutional framework of PRIs as its antecedent, the first democratically elected Communist government in the world, the government in the southern Indian state of Kerala, developed the potential of local government while undertaking a radical experiment in developing democracy. With the backing of the 73rd and 74th amendment acts, a People's Planning Campaign (PPC) was initiated to promote the people's own developmental planning in 1996 when the left government took power. It remains one of the most innovative models in strengthening grassroots democracy. In 1996, the left government in Kerala declared the decision to devolve 35–40 per cent of the Annual Development Plan fund to local governments and initiated a set of programmes to prepare annual plans at the local level. From there on began the PPC, which, in its amplest development in Kerala, led to the participation of 2 million people in 1996, along with the training of more than 130,000 people. What such a process did was to widen quickly and exponentially the logic of participation and solidarity, while putting pressure on the development administration for an accountable performance. Participatory planning actions stimulated people's assemblies, or *gram sabhas*; gave stronger forums for neighbourhood groups; built bases for solidarity, and promoted local leadership while holding development works accountable and forcing bureaucracy to maintain contact with people. It promoted a rejuvenation of local democracy in which people feel stimulated to contribute time and resources while advancing social and economic development. While in the last decade the campaign has become a fulcrum of changing state politics (the People's Planning Campaign was renamed the Kerala Development Plan in 2001), it is also true that, despite changes, governments were not able to reverse the basic advance of people's planning in Kerala.

Like the evolution of local governance, there are two other democratic advances which propel prospects for the radicalisation of the Indian state. The first is the struggle for the right to information, and the second, the struggle for the right to food and work.

The Right to Information (RTI) struggle creates spaces for substantive participation and empowerment of people at their workplaces and in the geographical spaces where they live by creating a necessary foundation for the transformation of power. The RTI struggle developed on the basis of workers' and peasants' experience (the *Mazdoor Kisan Shakti Sangathana*) of the large deficits of accountability and transparency in the functioning of Indian democracy. The struggle is rooted in the belief that people can participate effectively in democratic processes only when they have access to sufficient and truthful information. Hegemonic control thrives on the control of the content and dissemination of information, making it more difficult for working classes to question, challenge and change power relationships. Beginning with a local base and the slogan '*Hamara paisa, hamara hisab!*' ('Our money, our account, account for us!') in the western state of Rajasthan, and using innovative methods of social auditing and public hearings, the movement developed an India-wide consolidation of social and political forces for information as a right. The passage of the Right to Information legislation after long years of resistance has been a victory for mass movements and progressive elements in civil society. However, RTI still faces considerable challenges. There is the ever present danger of minimising its potential during implementation and in the formulation of laws defining domains – what is within the purview of RTI and what is not, what constitutes sensitive information, what will be the mechanisms for ensuring accountability, and so forth. There is therefore no substitute for continued struggle for further gains and a vigilant guarding of what has been achieved.

At the same time, the opportunity of securing social, economic and cultural rights lies in the radicalisation of the agenda of social development. The resurgence of a number of people's movements in the last decade, through campaigns on forest and land rights, *dalit* rights, agricultural workers' rights, labour rights and the rights of women, provides a social basis for fundamental advance. One such struggle has been the Right to Food (RTF) campaign. Born in 2001 around demands for access to food, and its availability and affordability for all citizens of India, RTF blossomed into a movement responding to the grave situation of distress and unemployment which the rural and urban impoverished face. The RTF struggle, located within the constitutional promises and methodologies of peaceful protest, has shaped the National Rural Employment Generation Programme (NREGA), one of the largest employment programmes in the world, which guarantees 100 days of employment above the minimum wage. NREGA presents another opportunity for deepening the struggle and solidarity of a workers' and peasants' alliance. Its potential in rural transformation is evident in the popular vote it generated for the recent electoral victory of the Congress Party, under whose government it was passed and financed.

The emergence of the above movements in India raises several issues on the nature of development of new solidarities of struggle. Several of these movements are based on identity and other sectoral silos, in contrast to 'older' class movements of working classes and peasants. The critical issue for the transformation of the Indian state is whether these solidarities constitute a sufficient basis for mobilisation at a time when the state is retreating, or whether these promote further fragmentation through the politics of identity. What is needed is a new form of political expression and a medium which is able to defeat powerful forces that oppose the transformation of power. In this regard, the experience of political parties in India opens up lessons on the need for renewal of the prime political instrument, that is, the political parties, and possibly their interface with social movements.

Six decades of multi-party politics have allowed the parties critical spaces for experimentation, introspection, action and renewal. During this time, political parties have succeeded in promoting the representation of different interests and regional and social identities, as well as nurturing a tendency for argumentation and discussion. Without a doubt, this political space has encouraged the development of a stronger national project, and it is within this space that the seeds of transformation reside. Yet, we have also witnessed a growing centralisation of politics among major political parties. Political parties in India have shown a greater tendency to gravitate towards centrist politics; even amongst some of the numerous left formations in India, we have seen a softer stand and warming up to neoliberalism, a trend displaying what some authors have called the global emergence of a 'neoliberalised left'.

A growing tendency to use fascist methods to curb dissent and maintain power is also emerging on the Indian political terrain, with its causal links to finance capital being clearly visible. The invocation of exclusionary ideologies, the recourse to chauvinistic nationalism, the rise of political Hinduism and Islam, and the use of muscle-power and arms to coerce voters and capture positions of political power, while displaying all the theatrics of an active democracy, also painfully underscore the need for the re-orientation of the political instrument towards mass interests.

After the electoral debacle in the 2009 elections, the left has begun seriously to reflect on this tendency. However, it is not the left alone which needs to reflect on its trajectory over the past decades. As political instruments which promised liberation for the poor and excluded masses, other progressive political parties in India also need to reflect seriously on their promise of liberation. They need to re-examine their agendas, functioning and relationship with the masses on several fronts, including the relevance of their programmes to the masses, their increasing confinement to parliamentary politics, their internal democratic organisation and their ability to renew themselves in the interest of alternative forms of progress.

Renewal of the political instrument is a mechanism for bringing together the various emancipatory forces. The more recent movements and campaigns in India, such as Action 2007 (against neoliberalism) or Janadesh 2007 (on land rights), have reaffirmed that a new consolidation of forces is needed for the formation of a broad social bloc. The current economic crisis offers the progressive forces in India an important opportunity to elaborate a full programme and a platform for the accumulation of forces. Its role needs to be to unite all those affected historically and now being marginalised further. Even sections of the middle class radicalised by this crisis, for which the crisis has removed the mask of benevolence from the face of capitalism, are allies in progress. This kind of broad platform would allow the building of new alliances and the formation of a large oppositional social bloc, committed to building authentic democracy on the long road to socialism.

NOTE

1. As per Article 40, 'The state shall take steps to organise village *Panchayats* and endow them with such powers and authority as may be necessary to enable them to function as units of self government.'

REFERENCES

National Sample Survey Organisation (NSSO) (2003), Ministry of Statistics and Programme Implementation, New Delhi.
Shah, Ghanshyam, Harsh Mander, Sukhdeo Thorat, Satish Deshpande and Amita Baviskar (2006), *Untouchability in Rural India*. New Delhi, Thousand Oaks, CA, and London: Sage Publications.

7
The Palestinian National Question: Settler-Colonialism and the International Power Regime

Jamil Hilal

INTRODUCTION

The emergence of the Palestinian national question needs to be situated in its international and historical context. This was constituted, in the first instance, by four factors: European colonialism; the emergence of Zionism as a colonial-settler ideology aimed at ethnic cleansing and the creation of an exclusive Jewish state in Palestine; the collapse of the Ottoman Empire under European pressure; and the Sykes-Picot agreement which divided the Arab world into territorial states under British and French colonialism. Since the establishment of Israel in 1948 and the end of European colonialism, the Palestinian national question has been subject to the changing forces in international relations, marked by the emergence of the United States as the dominant Western power, its competition with the Soviet Union, and its strategic alliance with Israel, the latter serving as a sub-imperialist state in the region.

Under these conditions, the Palestinian national question has been shaped by Israel's monopoly over military nuclear capability in the region and its constant aggression against national movements and neighbouring states, including wars and invasion of their territories: in 1948, 1956 (Suez); June 1967; October 1973 (although this was initiated by Egypt and Syria in order to capture their occupied land); 1982 (the invasion of Lebanon and the besiegement of the Palestine Liberation Organisation (PLO)); the first Palestinian *Intifada* of 1987–92; the second *Intifada* of 2000–06; the war against Lebanon in the summer of 2006; and against Gaza in December 2008 and January 2009. The Palestinian national question has also been shaped by further changes in international forces in the closing years of the Cold War, including: the collapse of the Soviet bloc itself; the

Gulf wars – first between Iraq and Iran, then by the United States and allies against Iraq in 1991 and in 2003; the Iranian revolution in 1979, and the rise of political Islam in recent decades.

More recently, the deployment of the discourse of 'reform' and 'democracy' has also been relevant to the Palestinian national question. This discourse has served as an ideological tool to facilitate global hegemonic structures (with a neoliberal agenda), led by the United States. With the establishment of the Palestinian Authority, following the Oslo Accords in 1993, the discourse of democracy, transparency, human rights and good governance has been geared to limit the powers of the nation-state in confronting hegemonic structures and to marginalise and besiege movements for emancipation.

This chapter will trace the changing character of the Palestinian national question, from its origins under colonialism to the post-Cold War neoliberal period, seeking to clarify the nature of settler-colonialism and the predicament in which the Palestinian national movement now finds itself.

CONSULTING HISTORY: THE ETHNIC CLEANSING OF PALESTINIANS

The Palestinian demand for an independent state began to be articulated at the time of the collapse of the Ottoman Empire and the rise of Turkish nationalism, following the First World War. Nationalist demands gathered force with the entrenchment of colonial rule through the British Mandate, as well as with the arbitrary division of the Middle East among the main imperialist powers, Britain and France, into territorial allotments with a view to becoming separate states. Britain, as the dominant world power at the time, issued the Balfour Declaration in 1917, which committed itself to the establishment of a 'Jewish homeland' in Palestine, regardless of the fact that Palestine had its own indigenous people that, like other peoples, possessed the right to self-determination.

Such a right was expressed, first, in the preference to be part of a unified Arab state for the Arab nation. Subsequently, when this was obstructed by Britain and France, the Palestinian national movement demanded a democratic state in Palestine, with Muslims, Christians and Jews living as equal citizens, as an expression of the right to self-determination and as the only means to thwart the aims of Zionist project (see Khalidi 1997, Porath 1974). Indeed, a sovereign Palestinian state was the rationale behind the Palestinian struggle against British colonialism, Zionist colonisation and the partition of the country into an Arab and a Jewish state, as proposed by the Partition Plan of 1947, and rejected by the Palestinian leadership of the time.

It is important to bear in mind that religious pluralism, which was an integral feature of Palestinian life, was not the cause of the conflict between Palestinians (who include Muslims, Christians with different denominations, Druze, Jews, and other faiths) and Zionists. The people of Palestine co-existed, albeit not as equal citizens in a modern nation-state, but as communities that respected religious differences and had, generally, workable neighbourly relations and common traditions. The conflict was consequent upon the arrival of European colonial-settlers with an exclusivist (ethno-religious) state-building project in Palestine that was sponsored and protected by British imperial power.

The Palestinian Arabs, who constituted the majority of the population in Palestine,[1] waged, when everything else failed, armed struggle against both the British military occupation and Zionist settler-colonialism. However, unlike in other cases, liberation struggles were defeated by the combined forces of British and Zionist colonialism. The well-organised and well-armed European Zionist movement was able, with British support, to defeat the predominantly peasant Palestinian society – although undergoing rapid changes as a result of industrialisation, urbanisation and the spread of education – with its badly organised national movement, led by the semi-feudal notable families (see Kimmerling and Migdal 2003). In 1948, neighbouring Arab states, still under British and French imperial rule, sent military contingents to the aid of the Palestinians, but these were highly disorganised, badly armed and easily defeated by Zionist forces. Thus, the Zionist leadership forcibly established the state of Israel on 78 per cent of Palestine, much more than the 51 per cent allotted to it by the United Nations Partition Plan of 1947. The remaining 22 per cent of the territory – compromising what came to be known as the West Bank and Gaza Strip – came under Jordanian and Egyptian rule, respectively. Only a fraction of Palestinians (some 150,000) remained in the areas on which Israel was established to become a minority in their homeland (but not acknowledged as a *national* minority by the Israeli state or allotted equal citizenship to Jewish Israelis), comprising nearly 20 per cent of Israel's population in 2007. Since 1948, the maintenance, expansion and strengthening of Israel depended heavily on the political, military and economic support of the dominant imperial power, first Britain and then the United States.

The majority of Palestinians, as new Israeli historians have come to acknowledge decades later (for example, Morris 1987, Pappe 1994), were driven out by force and through methods that amounted to systematic ethnic cleansing (Pappe 2006). Palestinians living in Israel today are denied the same rights as Jewish Israeli citizens. This is consistent with the self-definition of Israel as a Jewish state, and as a democratic one at the same time (Rouhana 1997), and of confining full democratic rights to Israeli Jews only.[2]

THE ECLIPSE OF THE VISION OF A DEMOCRATIC STATE IN ALL OF PALESTINE

The construction of a democratic independent state (regardless of religion, sect, ethnicity or national origin) over Mandate Palestine was the vision that inspired the Palestinian national movement, once the ambition to be part of a pan-Arab state receded with the imperialist division of the region into a number of territorial states. In 1947, the Palestinian national movement rejected the partition of Palestinian into a Jewish and an Arab state and insisted on having one state for all of the inhabitants of the country. This notion of a unified Palestinian state for all its citizens, irrespective of religion or ethnicity, was revived again in the late 1960s and early 1970s by the PLO, only to be replaced in 1974, following the Israeli-Arab war of October 1973, by the idea of establishing, as an interim measure, a Palestinian state over Palestinian land to be evacuated by Israel. This position – that is, dividing Palestine into two states: one Palestinian, one Israeli – was formalised by the PLO in November 1988, in the midst of the first *Intifada*.

But it was the international, regional and internal changes that drove the PLO to enter the US-sponsored negotiations with Israel on an unequal footing, with no clear agenda and with no real empowerment of the PLO in the international setting. It was clear that the dismantling of the Soviet Union (as the main international ally of the PLO), the first Gulf war in 1990, following Iraq's invasion of Kuwait, which left the PLO isolated, and the *Intifada* in the Palestinian territories occupied in 1967, all influenced the PLO to accept the heavily imbalanced terms of the Oslo Accords.

The Oslo Accords signed by Israel and the PLO in 1993 amounted to a commitment by Israel to enter into negotiations with the PLO without a commitment to respect the Palestinian right to create an independent Palestinian state, even on the 22 per cent of historic Palestine (which is what the area of the West Bank and Gaza Strip amounts to), or to acknowledge its responsibility towards the 5 million Palestinian refugees, or to respect their right of return, recognised by UN Resolution 194. The Oslo Accords did not even clearly oblige Israel to stop building or expanding colonies. Negotiations on borders, refugees, Jerusalem, water and colonies were left to final status negotiations which were to begin five years after the establishment of the Palestinian Authority.

When final status negotiations began at Camp David in July 2000, it was already clear to Palestinians that the Israeli leadership was using negotiations as a stalling tactic to gain time to chew as much as it could of the Palestinian land it had occupied in 1967, while making sure that the area annexed had as few Palestinians as possible. Israel has been extremely careful to circumvent the emergence of a binational state. Israel as an ethnic state is an ideological imperative of Zionism, which has necessitated the cleansing of Palestine and the walling of Palestinians in ethnic enclaves to guard against the growing Palestinian minority that threatens the 'Jewish' character of the Israeli state.

In the interest of constructing and reconstructing its 'Jewish' character since the June war of 1967, Israel has busied itself with the task of confiscating land, building colonies, underdeveloping the Palestinian economy, controlling natural resources (land, water tables and Dead Sea resources) and Judaising East Jerusalem and its environs.

AN APARTHEID COLONIAL STATE: WALLING IN PALESTINIANS

The failure of the Camp David negotiations, led by Yasser Arafat, Ehud Barak and Bill Clinton, to reach agreement on the final status issues, particularly Jerusalem, refugees and settlements, led to the outbreak of the second *Intifada* in September 2000, which was sparked by the provocative visit by Ariel Sharon at al-Aqsa Mosque.

Israel's leadership was quick to respond to the second Palestinian *Intifada* by a series of military, security, economic, and administrative measures to weaken the institutions of the Palestinian Authority, fragment its territory and dehumanise the Palestinian national movement as 'terrorist' (Arafat was classified as Israel's 'Bin Laden' and, accordingly, was besieged in his headquarters in Ramallah), as well as to dismiss the existing Palestinian leadership as incapable of being a partner in negotiations. More than 4,000 Palestinians were killed during the first seven years of the *Intifada*, many more were injured, and some 60,000 were detained for varying periods of time. Well over 9,000 political prisoners were held in Israel in mid 2007.[3]

In 2003, under the same excuse – that is, fighting the 'terrorism' of suicide bombers (usually in response to Israeli killings of leaders, militants, and civilians) – Israel began to build the Separation or Segregation Wall around Palestinian towns and villages – what Palestinians term the 'apartheid wall' and the Israeli military, the 'security fence' – and to ensure that its colonies are within its own side of the wall. The Segregation Wall, some 790 kilometres long when finished,[4] annexes Jerusalem and the environs, including major colonial settlement blocks; and by means of fences, checkpoints and road blocks, it establishes control over the Jordan valley, where the best agricultural land is found, and thereby ensures also the food dependency of Palestinian towns and villages on Israel.

The death of Arafat in November 2004, and the election of Mahmoud Abbas (Abu Mazen) to replace Arafat in January 2005, did not alter substantively the discourse of the Israeli leadership, although the new Palestinian leader was explicit in his opposition to the *Intifada* and his commitment to negotiations as the only viable strategy for the Palestinians. He was required to disarm and disempower Hamas, which grew in strength and credibility during the second *Intifada*, but also to rein in the al-Aqsa Martyrs' Brigades, the armed wing of Fatah (the ruling party at the time). Because he could not do this, he was considered weak and therefore still unqualified to be a partner for negotiations. All this facilitated the continuation of unilateral Israeli action in the West Bank and Gaza Strip without having to sit at a negotiating table.

Sharon's 'disengagement' plan and Ehud Olmert's subsequent 'convergence' plan were not novel ideas.[5] In an interview in *Haaretz*, published on 15 November 2003, Olmert explained the reasons for the impending 'disengagement' from the Gaza Strip. He argued that Israel faces the problem of how to prevent Palestinians – who will become a numerical majority in the near future – from launching a struggle similar to the one against apartheid waged by black South Africans. Olmert was concerned that if Palestinians renounced violence and started to struggle for one man, one vote, Israel would be faced by 'a much cleaner struggle, a much more popular struggle – and ultimately a much more powerful one'. Such a Palestinian objective had to be pre-empted. The rationale of the unilateral solution behind 'disengagement' in Gaza carried out in August 2005, together with 'convergence' in the West Bank, has been 'to maximize the size of land annexed but with the minimum number of Palestinians to ensure a permanent majority of Jews; to minimize the number of Palestinians'. Or, as Olmert put it in early May 2006, '[dividing] the land, with the goal of ensuring a Jewish majority, is Zionism's lifeline' (Cook 2006a).

Disengagement or convergence, or any Israeli unilateral measure, is not a response to the Palestinian *Intifada* or suicide bombing, as Israeli propagandists have maintained. It is on record that the Israeli military and political establishment was pushing for 'unilateral separation' since the early 1990s. This failed to make it into official policy until 2005, because the main two parties in Israel at the time, Labour and Likud, were not in a hurry to impose an end to the conflict, which would be implicit in a separation imposed by Israel. In fact, unilateral action has been the policy used by Israel since its occupation of the West Bank and Gaza Strip. It is the strategy of *fait accompli* that has guided Israeli action, and before that, Zionist actions, since the beginning.

Israel's new borders were being demarcated from at least the early 1990s, when the policy of closure and checkpoints became the norm. Israeli colonialist measures were considered by Israeli leaders as a means of consolidating an apartheid existence for Palestinians who remained on the parts of the West Bank and Gaza evacuated by the Israelis. Statements and actions by the US and EU governments did not hide their stance, as they applauded Israeli unilateral measures while simultaneously penalising Palestinians for exercising their democratic right of electing a legislative council and government that would not be inclined to implement Israeli and American commands unquestioningly.

It is fairly well known that Yitzhak Rabin believed that he could achieve effective separation from the Palestinians by generating consent among Palestinian leaders and by establishing a client regime headed by Yasser Arafat. Rabin was assassinated by a right-wing Jewish fundamentalist Israeli in 1995, and Arafat resisted the Israeli Labour Party idea of turning the Palestinian Authority into a client rump-state, providing Israel with cheap labour and a captive market and policing its borders. However, Rabin did think he would need to fall back on a dividing wall to enforce a separation between the Jewish and Palestinian inhabitants. It is reported that, before his assassination, he began to contemplate the building of a wall, in order to contain the 'demographic threat' posed by Israel's continuing occupation of the West Bank and Gaza Strip.[6]

THE ISRAELI CONCOCTION OF PALESTINIAN 'STATEHOOD'

Sharon and Binyamin Netanyahu of the Likud Party rejected throughout the 1990s the idea of separating from the Palestinians in the West Bank, as it would thwart the project of 'Greater Israel' – the whole of Palestine as the land of Israel – to include all of the 1967 Occupied Territories, but particularly the West Bank, which Israeli schoolbooks refer to as Judea and Samaria. In 1998, Sharon exhorted his followers to 'go grab the hilltops' in the West Bank, expressing his utter disregard for the Oslo Accords, and continuing the tradition of settler-colonialism that the Oslo Accords did not, in any way, slow down. In fact, in the decade following the Oslo agreement, the population of Israeli Jewish colonial settlements in the West Bank doubled. The route of the separation wall demonstrates Israel's intention to annex large slices of the West Bank that are not populated, or sparsely so.

In short, Israeli measures and policies have been geared, right from the beginning, towards ensuring that no sovereign Palestinian state could emerge or maintain itself. As Regis Debray (2007) rightly concludes:

> The years since the Oslo accords demonstrated to Palestinians that Israel has its own definition of what a Jewish right to self-determination should mean including the right of all Jews in the world to return to Israel and to become immediately citizens. But this definition does not apply to Palestinians who are expected to accept to stay in exile, or accept a stateless status, or live in client 'Bantustans' that they could call a state. Israel has no objection to calling the Palestinian areas that it separates from (about 12% of historic Palestine), a state as long as these areas remain under its territory military control (from land, air and sea), under its economic grip, and its security surveillance.

In early 2003, Sharon mentioned Palestinian statehood for the first time. By May 2003, he told a meeting of his party: '[t]he idea that it is possible to continue keeping 3.5 million Palestinians under occupation – yes, it is occupation, you might not like the word, but what is happening is occupation – is bad for Israel, and bad for the Palestinians, and bad for the Israeli economy. Controlling 3.5 million Palestinians cannot go on forever' (Blecher 2006). The change came once Sharon realised that the 'demographic threat' facing Israel as a Jewish state is real. Ruling over a majority of

Palestinians means the existence of a classic apartheid situation, and that would invite the end of the legitimacy of the Jewish state. The Roadmap, supported by the United States and the other three members of the Quartet (the EU, Russia and the UN), appeared in late 2002 and referred to the emergence of a Palestinian state as the outcome of the 'peace' process. In response, Sharon and his advisers had to devise a plan to ensure that such a state would be so only in name. It was not long afterwards that the 'disengagement' plan was born as a stage in the unilateral separation scheme. And once 'disengagement' took place in the Gaza Strip, Sharon aides repeatedly said that 'disengagements' from the West Bank would come next, to serve the same end (that is, to prevent the emergence of a binational state).

Sharon's creation of the Kadima Party came as a result of his realisation that he could not persuade the 'Greater Israel' old guards and the mainstream leaders of the Likud Party, represented by Binyamin Netanyahu. Kadima was presented as a new 'centrist' party that attracted figures from both Labour and Likud. It represented a move to come to terms with the realisation that Palestinians would never give up their dream of independence and statehood, but to combine it with a strategy of forced separation that renders, so Kadima leaders believed, Palestinians powerless to resist it.

Israel has been imposing facts on the ground on the Palestinians unilaterally with US and European support. The Separation Wall, which is meant as Israel's permanent 'demographic border', slices 46 per cent of the West Bank, including the major colonies, leaving out the Palestinian population centres.[7] It slices the West Bank into disconnected and impoverished 'reserves', linked only by tunnels, bridges and roads controlled by Israel. It robs the West Bank of its best agricultural land and leaves Israel with the control of all Palestinian water.[8] The separation plan also removes Greater Jerusalem from the central part of the West Bank, thereby cutting the economic, cultural, religious and historic heart out of any Palestinian state. It squeezes Palestinians between the Separation Wall and another Israeli 'security' fence, the Jordan Valley, which means that what is left of the West Bank will fall between Israel's two eastern borders. Any movement of Palestinians and their commodities will thus remain completely under Israel's control. In addition, Israel insists on retaining control over Palestinian air space, the electromagnetic sphere, and insists that any future Palestinian state would not possess an army or any weapons that can threaten Israel, and would not be allowed to enter into defence pacts with other states without Israel's approval.

THE OPEN COMPLICITY OF INTERNATIONAL POWERS

What has been striking is the support that these colonial and racist policies have received from the governments of the United States (which have been subsidising the Israeli military and defence for decades), the EU and Russia, as well as the acquiescence of nearly all the Arab states. There are differences in the stances of the latter powers (that is, the EU and Russia), but these have never been allowed to develop into policies or strategies independent from the United States. The so-called Roadmap that was proposed by the Bush administration in 2003, and adopted by Russia and Europe, does not demand from Israel the unconditional end of its occupation of the territories taken over by military force in June 1967, or the unconditional and unequivocal dismantling of its racist colonies – all illegal according to UN resolutions. We have not seen from these powers demands to bring down the apartheid wall, as specified by the ruling of the International Court of Justice (ICJ) in 2005. There has never been a call to use sanctions to oblige Israel to end its illegal annexation of Jerusalem, nor to make it take steps to implement the right of return for Palestinian refugees in accordance with relevant UN resolutions, particularly Resolution 194.

In fact, the Roadmap, as well as the Annapolis agreement read out by US president George W. Bush in November 2007, without specifying borders or the fate of refugees, or colonial settlements, or Jerusalem, makes the establishment of a Palestinian state contingent on the 'democratic' reforms carried out by the Palestinian Authority. These amount to changing its leadership to one that is amenable to American-Israeli diktat, as well as to the demolition of the 'infrastructure' of resistance and the renouncing and banning of its discourse (termed 'terrorist'), before any conditions are put on Israel, as an occupying power, with regards to the national rights of Palestinians.[9] This became too clear in January 2006, when the Palestinian Authority did institute free and fair elections, and Hamas won the majority of seats in the Legislative Council. Israel and the Quartet immediately instituted sanctions against the Hamas government, demanding immediate change in its policies and strategies.

What transpires from the above outline is the contingent and arbitrary nature of international relations, in each conjuncture, in defining national sovereignty within regional systems. So, while the Quartet grants Israel a wide range of powers in its exercise of sovereignty, allowing it to continue to violate UN and Security Council resolutions and ICJ rulings, and to possess nuclear weapons without inspections or sanctions, other states in the Middle East are invaded, bombed and occupied under false pretexts (Iraq), others are not allowed to develop their nuclear energy for fear of acquiring nuclear weapons (Iran), and the Palestinian Authority is presented with multiple conditions to prevent it acquiring any state-like powers, making it impossible to have a viable independent Palestinian state in the foreseeable future.

'Separation', given its apartheid underpinnings, does not mean the end of Israeli colonial domination, as the situation of the Gaza Strip after 'disengagement' demonstrates. It has been turned into a prison camp where Israel controls water and electricity, imports and exports, and sea, air and land space. Israel has given itself the right to determine what sort of security forces and army the Palestinians can possess, which roads, tunnels and border crossings they can use, and how much water they are allowed.

Israel's war on the besieged Gaza Strip in December 2008 and January 2009 killed more than 1,400 Palestinians (mostly civilians) and injured more than 5,000. This has raised the issue of war crimes and crimes against humanity to be added to that of ethnic cleansing. It was clear right from the start that the aim of the war was not simply to stop Hamas firing rockets into Israel. Indeed, Hamas and other Palestinian factions had observed a strict truce with Israel, brokered by Egypt, for six months (from mid June 2008 to mid December 2008) – a truce that Israel, in fact, did not honour: it neither ceased its assassinations of Palestinian militants in the Gaza Strip and their arrest in the West Bank, nor lifted the blockade (an act of aggression by any definition) on Gaza that had been imposed on the Strip 18 months earlier. And it is for this reason that Hamas and other Palestinian factions agreed not to renew the truce as long as Israel continued to break it, leading to the slow starvation of the people of Gaza. The tunnels under the border between Egypt and Gaza were the only means the Gazans possessed of alleviating the strangulating effects of the siege imposed on them by land, sea and air.

That the real aim of the war is not just to stop the rockets of Hamas is clear from the fact, disclosed by Israeli sources, that the Israeli Defence Minister had planned the war as early as June 2008, that is, at the time the truce was agreed. The rationale behind

Operation Cast Iron is similar to that behind Operation Defense Shield, when Israeli tanks rolled into the West Bank and put Arafat under house arrest in March 2002. Then it was because Arafat had rejected the Bantustan state offered the Palestinians by Barak and Clinton – a 'state' which excluded the Palestinian capital of Jerusalem, and which would have had hardly any real sovereignty, with no right of return for Palestinian refugees.

The war on Gaza is the latest attempt by Israel to weaken and dishearten the Palestinian national movement, to the point where it is no longer capable of opposing Israel's imposition of political arrangement that would remove the 'demographic threat' posed by the Palestinians, by creating Bantusans, or reserves, in the West Bank encircled by colonial settlements, bypass roads, checkpoints and the Separation Wall, thus safeguarding the 'purity' of the Jewish State while colonising as much as it can of the geography of Palestine (that is, land). The fact that Israel failed to achieve its objective of crushing or weakening Hamas could mean that another war will be planned. The February 2009 Israeli Parliamentary elections have shown a further drift of Israeli politics towards the right, with the upper hand gained by the extreme, belligerent, nationalist right (exemplified by Lieberman, the leader of Yisrael Beiteinu, and Netanyahu, leader of the Likud Party). This raises more dangers and new challenges for the Palestinian national movement.

THE PREDICAMENT OF THE PALESTINIAN NATIONAL MOVEMENT

In the existing regional and international structures of power, the predicament of the Palestinian national movement is apparent in numerous ways. It is apparent in the failure of the Palestinian Authority to transform itself into anything that resembles an independent or a possibly viable state, after more than 16 years since the Oslo Accords. The clear objective of Israel has been to create a client and dependent 'rump state': one that is made up of the bits Israel does not want, because they are densely-populated by Palestinians; that revolves completely in Israel's orbit; and that is established on a fraction of Mandate Palestine, without Jerusalem, without control over borders, skies and underground water resources, and without an acknowledgement of the right of return to Palestinian refugees. The ongoing process of creating such a political entity amounts, in effect, to ethnic cleansing, since the results that are already present in high unemployment, poverty, economic stagnation and the total siege conditions will drive many Palestinians to emigrate.[10]

The Palestinian national movement, which lost many of its features as a liberation movement once it accepted to become a national authority without the minimum conditions of sovereignty, has become a dangerously polarised movement. It has become polarised between two major political factions, one populist nationalist, represented by Fatah, and one populist Islamist, represented by Hamas. The secular nationalist orientation of the PLO began to be challenged by political Islam during the first *Intifada* in the late 1980s, as radical Islamist influence in the region grew, following the Iranian Revolution in 1979, and as Arab secular nationalist states failed to deliver politically (democracy and civil rights), economically (sustained economic development) and culturally (as culture fell under the control of the central state). But one needs to add the huge sums of dollars invested by the Saudi regime and the Gulf states in supporting Islamist fundamentalist movements in the area.

The collapse of the Soviet Union and the socialist countries in Eastern and Central Europe impacted negatively on the secular left. At the same time, the financial expansion of the oil-producing states in the region – particularly Saudi Arabia, which is governed by a fundamentalist religious ideology (*wahabism*), other Gulf states, and Iran with its radical form of Islamism – was invested in gaining political influence, both in the region and in the West, and in promoting conservative, right-wing ideology and advocacy by utilising mosques, mass media and charity networks against secular pan-Arab nationalism and left-wing movements and progressive aspirations.

The organising of military resistance against the Soviet occupation of Afghanistan, which was financed by Saudi money under American instruction and strategy, provided training, networking, and further indoctrination in fundamentalist Islam in the Arab world. However, Hamas and Islamic Jihad owe their formation to the Muslim Brotherhood movement that was active in Egypt and Jordan. The Muslim Brotherhood was not repressed by the Israel military occupation, but was left to operate as a counter-force to the PLO.[11] As an offshoot of the Muslim Brotherhood, Hamas could easily adopt the same pragmatic and conciliatory outlook as the branches of the Muslim Brotherhood in Egypt and Jordan, or for that matter, Turkey.[12] It seems that this is what the United States, Europe and the Arab states are wagering on, by means of financial and diplomatic pressures, as well as Israel, by security and military repression. Islam, like other religions, provides ideological cover for various types of political and social formations.

FORMAL DEMOCRACY AND THE REINFORCEMENT OF DUAL AUTHORITY

The results of the elections for the Palestinian Legislative Council in January 2006, signalled significant changes in the political field that have been taking place since the late 1980s. In an unexpected electoral win, Hamas replaced Fatah, which had dominated Palestinian politics since the late 1960s. This heralded a transformation in the largely secular political culture of Palestinian politics and announced the ascent of an agenda seeking the Islamisation of state and society. At first glance, this could mean a switch from a paradigm seeking the establishment of a national state and its attendant institutions (executive, legislative and judicial) to a paradigm that promotes the idea of an *umma*, or community of believers, ruled by one ultimate religious authority. In this case, politics would focus more on religious identity, or rather defining national identity as an expression of a religious identity, which can be defined in essentialist terms. This would marginalise the vision of a modern state as a community of equal citizens regardless of religion; and it could restrict the freedom of expression and thought by imposing a culture that emphasises uniformity (in behaviour, customs, ideas, dress and identities) and conformity to codes of behaviour that are defined by those who claim the right to interpret sacred texts. However, the picture is more complex than this, given that Hamas has tended to adopt some of the vocabulary of the Palestinian nationalist ideology and has allowed the language of democracy and human rights to permeate its own language (see Hilal 2007). Meanwhile, religious language has crept into the discourse of Fatah. The outcome of the conflict between the two movements will largely be determined by the actions of the Israeli military and colonial occupation, the demise of the two-state solution, and the regional and international pressures and contradictions.

In any case, the significance of the ascent of Hamas in Palestinian politics should be understood within the context of the Israeli colonial occupation and the sustained frustration of the Palestinian national project of statehood, independence and self-determination. Moreover, it should be understood within the context of the general elections that have recently been held under foreign domination in the wider region – including Iraq, Lebanon and Afghanistan – and which have produced an extreme political polarisation that threatens the survival of states and the integration of their societies. Such general elections tend not only to reduce democracy to formal and periodic procedures, but are applied in situations where national institutions and options are either non-existent or extremely weak, or controlled, or suppressed by foreign powers.

The classification of Hamas by the United States and the EU as a 'terrorist' organisation and the imposition of financial and political sanctions on the Hamas government, which has amounted to a collective punishment of Palestinians, seems incongruent with the simplest ideas of fairness and impartiality. Israel has never been subjected to any kind of sanctions by the Western powers, despite its ethnic cleansing, longest occupation in modern history, and its constant violations of UN resolutions on Palestinian issues. Israel, encouraged by such actions by the West, imposed its own embargo on Palestinians and intensified its repressive and apartheid measures. Arab and international banks with branches in the West Bank and Gaza were threatened with persecution for aiding 'terrorism', should they make dealings with the Palestinian government, including the payment of salaries of government employees who form a quarter of the active labour force there. This measure came on the heels of Israel's closure of its labour markets to Palestinian workers, who formed another quarter of the Palestinian labour force.

The sanctions have aimed at forcing Hamas to recognise Israel (without specifying the borders of Israel), without Israel recognising right of Palestinians to self-determination, as well as pressuring Hamas into renouncing 'violence' and dismantling its armed wing before Israel ends its occupation, or ceasing its targeted assassinations of militants. The message sent to Hamas by the Quartet – which represents the contemporary centres of the global power system – was clear enough: these centres will do all they can to bring down Hamas and its government, knowing that the probable result would be the plunging of the Palestinian areas into political chaos and further territorial fragmentation.

The capacity of Israel, as a regional power, to determine the outcome of its conflict with the Palestinians (and the Arab states) is due in no small part to its past and present location in the international political and economic regime, particularly its strategic relationship with the United States, as well as the absence of a clear and unified Arab strategy regarding the conflict and its resolution. This conflict is determined, to a great extent, by the balance of forces (economic, military, technological and political) that have evolved in the region and internationally over the last century. Within this evolving international system, Israel was formed and developed, and has come to conceive of itself, as part of the Western world. It sees itself not as regional power but as an extension of the West, and acts as a sub-imperialist power relying on its own military power and on the unrelenting support of the United States.

Israel presents itself as an ethnocracy that is defined a state for the Jews anywhere in the world. The Separation Wall is there to isolate itself not only from the Palestinians but also from the region as a whole. By imposing an apartheid system on the Palestinians it is creating a ghetto around itself, and that signals its political illegitimacy and moral bankruptcy. Some Israeli intellectuals, concerned with the future of Israel and its role in the area, have been arguing that Israel was able to pursue its colonial and apartheid policies because of its willingness to serve Western (mainly US) imperial interests, including acting as a galvanising centre for global neoconservative forces.[13]

It is now obvious that the formation of a viable and sovereign Palestinian state is not on the agenda of Israel, the United States or Europe, despite all the talk about a two-state solution and the vision of President G.W. Bush. The Palestinian national project before 1948, and from 1964, when the PLO was instituted, until 1974, revolved around the establishment of an independent state over Mandate Palestine that accorded equal rights to its citizens irrespective of religion, ethnicity, or gender. In 1974, under the impact of the Arab-Israeli war in October 1973, and under pressure from the PLO's international supporters, particularly the Soviet Union, the PLO started to ponder seriously the idea of a Palestinian state on any part of Palestine that is liberated, or from which Israel withdraws. The most likely part from which Israel could withdraw through international and regional pressure was the area known as the West Bank and Gaza Strip (22 per cent of Palestine). It was (and still is) assumed that Israel will have to evacuate or dismantle the colonies it has built there, as well as rescind its annexation of East Jerusalem, accept its responsibility for the Palestinian refugee problem, and also accept a solution in accordance with UN General Assembly Resolution 194, which clearly acknowledges the right of return of Palestinian refugees.

The collapse in July 2000 of the Camp David negotiations on the political future of the West Bank and Gaza Strip made it clear that the political elite in Israel does not have on its agenda the creation of a viable and independent Palestinian state. This realisation is what ignited the second *Intifada* in September 2000. It coincided with the US invasions of Afghanistan and Iraq. For its part, Israel used the events of 9/11 to label all Palestinian resistance to its colonial occupation and the struggle for self-determination as 'terrorist'. The dehumanisation of Palestinians and their struggle found enthusiastic support from the United States, as well as the complicity of Europe.

If the first *Intifada* saw the birth of Hamas, the second *Intifada* saw Hamas grow into a mass force capable of challenging the Fatah movement, and in fact defeating it in the Palestinian Legislative Council (PLC) elections in January of 2006. This fact led to the institutionalisation of a dual Palestinian Authority system given the presidential-parliamentary system of the Palestinian Authority, with both wings of that authority (Fatah and Hamas) possessing armed organisations. This dualism, compounded by international and regional economic and political pressure, exploded into armed conflict between the two factions, the last round being in June 2007, that split the Palestinian movement not only politically, but also territorially, with Hamas taking control over the Gaza Strip and Fatah maintaining control over the West Bank.

REMAKING A LIBERATION MOVEMENT

It can no longer be taken for granted that the Palestinian Authority is worth keeping, as it has not been able to stop the colonisation project, let alone establish the Palestinian state for which the Oslo process gave hope. With its division between Gaza and the West Bank, the Authority's role has been reduced to little more than a municipal authority, that cannot even guarantee paying the salaries of its civil servants, or provide the minimum security for its citizens, let alone transform itself into a full-fledged independent state able to pursue the interests and aspirations of Palestinians nominally under its rule.

What is needed is a refashioned Palestinian liberation movement that reunites the Palestinians in the various communities in the Diaspora (refugees and non-refugees in Lebanon, Syria, Jordan, the Gulf states, Europe, the Americas, and so on) with those in Palestine, and those in the Gaza Strip with those in the West Bank, and these two communities with Palestinians in areas occupied by Israel in 1948. The vision of a single state in Mandate Palestine is best suited to providing the unifying aspiration of Palestinians everywhere, while a rump state on parts of the West Bank and Gaza Strip will be a source of division of Palestinians, and will not address the rights and suffering of the refugees. What is needed is a reorganisation of the Palestinian national movement around the theme of liberation and emancipation, not pseudo-state-building that can produce no more than a client and dependent entity for Israel's sub-imperialist role in the region. The existing balance of power is not a permanent feature of the current situation; in fact, there are many signs that it is changing, and such change could accelerate towards altering the existing international and regional balance of forces, which in turn would allow us to prepare for a just resolution of the Israeli-Palestinian problem, and with it an emancipated region from US and European control.

One major sign of change is the backfiring of the Israeli-American policy of reliance on military power, as shown in Iraq, Afghanistan, Lebanon and the Gaza Strip. This gradual change in the balance of power in the region and internationally raises the possibility of the re-emergence of a multi-polar world system, one which would support a strategy of a new Palestinian liberation movement with a vision of a democratic, secular, progressive Palestinian state over all of Mandate Palestine, where both Palestinian Arabs and Jews could co-exist as equal citizens in a unified multi-ethnic and multicultural democratic state.[14]

NOTES

1. According to Ottoman records, in 1878 there were 462,465 inhabitants in the Jerusalem, Nablus and Acre districts, that is, of what constituted the larger part of Palestine. These included 403,795 Muslims (including Druze), 43,659 Christians and 15,011 Jews. In addition, there were some 10,000 Jews with foreign citizenship (recent immigrants to the country) and several thousand Muslim Arab nomads who were not counted as Ottoman subjects. Jews in Palestine, before the Zionist colonisation began, were considered part of the religious mosaic of indigenous populations, like the different sects of Christians and Muslims, and shared a common culture. By the outbreak of the First World War, the population of Jews in Palestine had risen to about 60,000, some 33,000 of whom were recent settlers. The Arab Palestinian population in 1914 was approximately 683,000. Jews remained a minority in Palestine on the eve of the creation of Israel in May 1948, despite the backing that Zionist immigration into Palestine received from Britain.
2. The decision by the Israeli High Court of Justice on 14 May 2006 to uphold a law which explicitly denies family rights on the basis of ethnicity or national origins is a step further in the institutionalisation of the apartheid system in Israel. The Citizenship and Entry into Israel Law bars family reunification for Israelis married to Palestinians from the 1967 Occupied Territories. It specifically targets Israeli Palestinians who make up a fifth of Israel's population, as well as

Palestinian Jerusalemites, for it is they who marry Palestinians from the West Bank and the Gaza Strip. This discriminatory law forces Israeli Palestinians married to Palestinians living in the West Bank or Gaza Strip to leave the country or to be separated from their spouses and children.

3. See B'Tselem (the Israeli human rights organisation), 'Statistics on Palestinians in Custody of the Israeli Security Forces', www.btselem.org.

4. See the report by Amos Harel in the Israeli newspaper *Haaretz*, www.haaretz. com, 17 May 2006. The report was based on Israeli army estimates and expected its completion within one year.

5. 'Convergence' or 'realignment', as an Israeli strategy for managing the conflict with the Palestinians, was advocated by Olmert's Kadima Party in the Knesset election campaign in March 2006. According to the plan, Israel would move its soldiers and settlers from parts of the West Bank to behind a unilaterally fixed 'eastern border' for the Israeli state. The idea of 'convergence' was initially popular, but more and more Israelis became sceptical during the first half of 2006. Public support for withdrawals in the West Bank declined to just over 30 per cent in June 2006, and some Kadima leaders began to express reservations, thereby putting the Israeli government under pressure to demonstrate the wisdom of its plan. Some analysts saw in Israel's two-front war in June and July 2006, in Gaza and Lebanon, an attempt by the Israeli government to prove emphatically that 'disengagement' was not a mistake (Blecher 2006).

6. According to Cook (2006a), who is a journalist living in Nazareth, Israel, and a writer for the *Al'Ahram Weekly*, Rabin entrusted the Wall project to a committee headed by his public security minister, Moshe Shahal. The scheme was dropped by his two successors, Shimon Peres and Binyamin Netanyahu, but returned with Ehud Barak, a long-time Oslo sceptic, who advocated unilateral separation. In May 2000, he put his ideas into practice by unilaterally withdrawing troops from Israel's 'security zone' in south Lebanon. A fortnight before departing for talks at Camp David, he is reported as saying: 'Israel will insist upon a physical separation between itself and the independent Palestinian entity to be formed as a result of the settlement. I am convinced that a separation of this sort is necessary for both sides.' Cook also adds: 'In one typical commentary in June 2002, some 18 months before Sharon's own proposals for unilateral "disengagement" were revealed, Barak wrote: "The disengagement would be implemented gradually over several years. The fence should include the seven big settlement blocs that spread over 12 or 13 percent of the area and contain 80 percent of the settlers. Israel will also need a security zone along the Jordan River and some early warning sites, which combined will cover another 12 percent, adding up to 25 percent of the West Bank … In Jerusalem, there would have to be two physical fences. The first would delineate the political boundary and be placed around the Greater City, including the settlement blocs adjacent to Jerusalem. The second would be a security-dictated barrier, with controlled gates and passes, to separate most of the Palestinian neighborhoods from the Jewish ones and the Holy Basin, including the Old City"' (ibid.. See also Cook (2006b).

7. See www.nad-plo.org/news-updates/wallmapoct07.pdf, accessed 9 October 2007.

8. The West Bank aquifers provide Israel with half a billion cubic metres annually of the best-quality water, a third of Israel's present supply. It is difficult to imagine Israel willingly handing these aquifers to Palestinians in the near future,

or even after it has built the planned, expensive desalination plants. Israel allocates 10 per cent of West Bank water to Palestinians, a fraction of what the Palestinian population needs.

9. Following the electoral victory of Hamas in January 2006, and its formation of a government in March of that year, Israel and the Quartet added the requirement that Hamas should accept agreements previously signed by Palestinian representatives, including the Oslo Accords, and demanded that Hamas recognise Israel 'as a Jewish state' and reject the use of 'violence'.

10. Surveys conducted in late 2007 showed that more than a quarter of the adult population in the West Bank and Gaza Strip were considering permanent emigration, due to the conditions described above; see, for example, Palestinian Centre for Policy and Survey Research (Ramallah), Public Opinion Poll No. 26, 11–16 December 2007, www.pcpsr.org/survey/polls/2007/p26e1.html.

11. The Palestinian Muslim Brotherhood remained on the sidelines, as the secular PLO waged its struggles with surrounding Arab states and its armed resistance against Israel in the 1960s, 1970s and most of the 1980s. Hamas, which emerged in early 1988, soon after the eruption of the first *Intifada*, continued to wear the cloak of Islam, but adopted an increasingly nationalist discourse.

12. In March 2005, Hamas joined its main secular rival, Fatah, and eleven other Palestinian organisations in endorsing what came to be known as the Cairo Declaration, whereby it agreed to halt attacks on Israel for the rest of the year, to participate in the impending Palestinian parliamentary elections, and to commence discussions about joining the PLO. For a discussion of Hamas' political pragmatism, see Usher (2005). In January 2006, Hamas participated in parliamentary elections and won most seats.

13. See, for example, Halper (2005).

14. On the one-state solution, see Virginia Tilley (2005), as well as the critical examination of this proposal by an Israeli writer, Yoav Peled (2006), and Tilley's reply (2006). See also the debate in *New Left Review* (2001) by Perry Anderson, Guy Mandron, Gabriel Piterberg and Yitzhak Laor.

REFERENCES

Anderson, Perry (2001), 'Scurrying towards Bethlehem', *New Left Review*, 10 (July– August): 5–30.

Blecher, Robert (2006), 'Converging Upon War', *Middle East Report Online*, www.merip.org/mero/mero.html, July.

Cook, Jonathan (2006a), 'Olmert's Old Rose', *Al'Ahram Weekly*, No. 794, 11–17 May.

Cook, Jonathan (2006b), *Blood and Religion: The Unmasking of the Jewish and Democratic State*. London: Pluto Press.

Debray, Regis (2007), 'How the World Backed Itself into a Corner: Palestine, a Policy of Deliberate Blindness', *Le Monde Diplomatique*, http://mondediplo.com, August.

Halper, Jeff (2005), 'Israel as an Extension of American Empire', *Counterpunch*, www.counterpunch.org, 7 November.

Hilal, Jamil (2006), 'Hamas's Rise as Charted in the Polls, 1994–2005', *Journal of Palestine Studies*, 35(3): 6–19.

Hilal, Jamil (2007), *Where Now for Palestine? The Demise of the Two-State Solution*. London and New York: Zed Books.

Kimmerling, Baruch, and Joel S. Migdal (2003), *The Palestinian People: A History*. London and Cambridge, MA: Cambridge University Press.

Khalidi, Rashid (1997), *Palestinian Identity: The Construction of Modern National Consciousness*. New York: Columbia University Press.

Laor, Yitzhak (2001), 'Tears of Zion', *New Left Review*, 10 (July–August): 47–60.

Mandron, Guy (2001), 'Re-dividing Palestine?', *New Left Review*, 10 (July–August): 61–9.Morris, Benny (1987), *The Birth of the Palestinian Refugee Problem, 1947–1949*. Cambridge: Cambridge University Press.

Pappe, Ilan (1994), *The Making of the Arab-Israeli Conflict, 1947–1951*. London: I.B. Tauris.

Pappe, Ilan (2006), *The Ethnic Cleansing of Palestine*. Oxford: Oneworld Publications.

Peled, Yoav (2006), 'Zionist Realities', *New Left Review*, 38 (March–April): 21–36.

Piterberg, Gabriel (2001), 'Erasing the Palestinians', *New Left Review*, 10 (July–August): 31–46.

Porath, Yehoshusa (1974), *The Emergence of The Palestinian Arab Movement, 1919–1929*. London: Frank Cass.

Rouhana, Nadim N. (1997), *Palestinian Citizens in an Ethnic Jewish State: Identities in Conflict*. New Haven, CT: Yale University Press.

Tilley, Virginia (2005a), *The One-State Solution: A Breakthrough for Peace in the Israeli-Palestinian Deadlock*. Ann Arbor: University of Michigan Press.

Tilley, Virginia (2005b), 'From "Jewish State and Arab State" to "Israel and Palestine"? International Norms, Ethnocracy and the Two-State Solution', *The Arab World Geographer*, 8(3): 140–6.

Tilley, Virginia (2006), 'The Secular Solution: Debating Israel-Palestine', *New Left Review*, 38 (March–April): 37–57.

Usher, Graham (2005), 'The New Hamas: Between Resistance and Participation', *Middle East Report Online*, www.merip.org/mero/mero.html, August.

8
The National Question and the Unfinished Revolution in Nepal

Hari Roka

INTRODUCTION

Every revolution has its own uniqueness, which develops as certain challenges and possibilities appear in the revolutionary process. In Nepal, the national democratic revolution has been developing since the 1950s and has confronted various challenges, at times tilting in a rightist direction, other times turning left; sometimes advancing very slowly, other times very rapidly. In the 1990s, against the background of fake democracies in the South Asian region, the national democratic revolution in Nepal advanced to a new kind of struggle, aiming to establish genuine and sustainable democracy. At this time, the Communist Party of Nepal (CPN) (Maoist), commenced its People's War, which advanced the revolutionary process very rapidly and expanded it quickly throughout the nation. Within a short period of ten years, the People's War overcame the various problems of previous social movements and unified all contradictions – those of class, identity, region and gender – behind a programme for structural change of the state and society. Thereafter, the People's Uprising of April 2006 carried forward the agenda of the People's War and achieved a Comprehensive Peace Agreement. This entailed the election of a Constituent Assembly, the abolition of the monarchy, which had ruled for centuries, and the establishment of a democratic republic, all of which furthered the restructuring of the state and society.

However, like every revolution, the Nepali revolution has had to confront various complexities and, not least, the challenge of counter-revolution. The replacement of the Maoist-led government in 2009 was part of such a counter-revolutionary move. Rightist forces, with the help of imperialist and regional hegemonic powers, sought to stifle the progressive agenda of state restructuring. Yet, the contradictions have been sharpening ever since the announcement of the Republic of Nepal, culminating in a deep polarisation between progressive and rightist forces. This is accompanied by growing class struggle within the reactionary forces as well, while most of the centrist parties are now on the brink of collapse. The task of the revolution now is to consolidate workers, peasants, racially discriminated indigenous people, Dalits, and women into a force capable of completing the restructuring of the state and society.

HISTORICAL FORMATION OF THE NEPALI STATE

At the time of the American and French revolutions, Nepal was struggling to build a nation from among the several vassal states under Gorkhali King Prithivi Narayan Shah, himself king of a small state, Gorkha. He wanted to constitute this state as a distinctly Hindu state, Asali Hindustan, different from Mugal India where Muslims were in power. He was highly influenced by the dominant social and political group which was settling the mid-hill regions of the country, where the high-caste Hindus from India had taken refuge centuries earlier. This elite group dominated politics everywhere they settled in the region. Their language was *parbate* (a branch of Sanskrit) and their religion Hindu. Moreover, they were subdivided among the Brahman and Kshatriya castes, the latter being the king's caste (Rose and Fisher 1970).

At that time, the Mugals were losing power, as British imperial power was gradually occupying the whole of the Indian territory. After Prithivi Narayan, the Shah's dynasty sought to expand Nepali territory from the eastern to the western hills and mountains. But in the war with the British imperialists in 1814–16, Nepal would lose its newly conquered western and southern parts, which thereafter obstructed its expansionist ambition. Thus, Nepal was contained within a fixed territory, to become a satellite state of British India.

Nepal was composed of a heterogeneous society, which was multilingual, multi-racial, multicultural and multi-religious. Indeed, most of society did not have a historic association with the state that was being created, nor was there an enduring cultural elite. Therefore, the conquering elite ruled brutally without any form of consensus from the dominated groups. State formation was a process entailing the establishment of feudal relations, instead of a system of ethnic- and community-based rule.

After the war, two contradictions evolved within Nepali society. First, there was a contradiction between centrally imposed authorities and the dominated communities. The noble class, which was formed in the period of the unification of the kingdom, began to quarrel over the control of the central state. After the reign of Prithivi Narayan Shah, conflicts emerged among the members of his own family, which realigned into different royal groups. In this context, the king intervened to replace nobles, in accordance with the apparent loyalties among his administrators and armed forces. The result of these intrigues was the elimination of many nobles and generals, during the 30 years following the war with the British. The political system in this period was characterised by a highly segmented, pyramidal structure dominated by a handful of Kshatriya nobles with the support and advice of a number of prominent Brahman families. But in 1846, the Rana family, among the class of nobles, prevailed and seized all political power from the king. Thus, the king became a titular Head of State, while the Rana families became the actual rulers of the state until 1950.

The Rana regime (1846–1950) was a very gloomy period in the history of Nepal, during which the Nepali people were treated practically as slaves, as a source of cheap labour for British India and mercenaries for the British colonial army. The regime was highly dependent on British India, rendering services to the latter to maintain their own rule. For instance, the struggle of the Indian people against British rule in 1858 was brutally suppressed by the Nepali army to gain the confidence of the British. During this time, all natural resources and most of the source of revenue of the state were collected and monopolised by the ruling class. The regime did not develop educational institutions and health care facilities, or construct any modern infrastructure to transform the old state into a modern nation-state: there were no hydro-electric projects, no highways or railways or any means of transportation. The Rana regime remained a puppet of the British Colonial Empire.

The Indian salvation movement geared up in the second decade of the twentieth century under the leadership of the All India National Congress. The British Empire realised at this time that sooner or later it would have to leave India. By its own initiative, therefore, the British recognised Nepal as a sovereign nation in 1923, through the 'Treaty of Friendship'. After this achievement, the government of Nepal proceeded to hand over the ownership of agricultural land to the landlord class. This enabled the landlords to buy and sell the land as they deemed fit, as well as to do business with their Indian neighbours, with whom they had a close socio-economic, linguistic and cultural relationship. The landlord class in Nepal also sent its children to Indian educational institutions (Stiller 1993).

In such circumstances, it was obvious that the Indian people's struggle against British rule would highly impress the emergent Nepali middle class. Most of the students and youth participated in that long Indian struggle. And they believed that without Indian independence they would not achieve freedom from the autocratic rule of the Rana family. After 1946, when most of the Nepali prisoners who had participated in the Indian freedom movement were released from Indian jails, they organised the masses for armed struggle against the Rana regime, under the banner of the Nepali Congress Party. As an ally of the British, the Rana regime was fully opposed to the movement led by the Indian National Congress, with its modernist, democratic and 'anti-feudal' proclivities (Rose 1971).

Before 1947, Britain's strategic interests and responsibilities included all of India's neighbours – Afghanistan, Tibet, Nepal, Sikkim, Bhutan, and Sri Lanka – in an extended security framework. India inherited this policy after independence, but in a different scenario, given that, around 1950, only three states, Nepal, Bhutan and Sikkim, remained in its defence perimeter. The first Prime Minister of India, Jawaharlal Nehru, skilfully tried to put pressure on the autocratic Rana regime to liberalise the political system. In one occasion, Nehru said: 'much as we stand for the independence of Nepal, we can not allow anything to go wrong there ... because that would be a risk to our own security' (Rose 1971).

A further dimension of the region's politics evolved in relation to China. Nepal is located between India and China, however, at that time, road, rail and air access to Nepal was exclusively through India. Thus, the Indian government eschewed any kind of influence over Nepal by China. During most of the 1950s, India further strengthened its influence over Nepal, using commercial as well as political treaties as an instrument of control. Due to this reason, in the so-called Nepalese revolution of 1950, a new kind of parliamentary democracy was installed, but the monarchy once again consolidated its grip on power and dissolved the popularly elected parliament and government. This revolution did not result in any structural changes in society. Again, the Nepali state remained semi-colonial, semi-feudal, and under Indian economic and political hegemony.

In the 1960s and 1970s, Nepal experimented with an independent foreign policy in the context of wars between India and China and India and Pakistan, as well as the creation of Bangladesh. At this time, another factor also intensified as the United States and the Soviet Union increased their interference in the socio-economic and political affairs of the region. Thus, the Indian monopoly over Nepal somehow receded. It was an appropriate time for the king to try to assert an independent foreign policy. However, it was not in favour of the majority of the people.

CONFLICT AND COMPROMISE

From 1960 to the 1990s, in several occasions powerful movements emerged against the feudal monarchical system, but without success. This is because the Nepalese monarchy maintained a vertical structure of kinship and feudal relations all the way down to the grassroots, which enjoyed Indian and US support. They all shared a similar agenda, which was to keep the Nepali people out of the political and ideological influence of the Chinese Revolution. In this context, the supra-feudal,[1] small to middle feudal, and comprador business classes in Nepal closed ranks with the absolutist monarchy. Major movements in Nepal have thus always ended in compromise, despite decades of struggle for social and political transformation. However, in the 1990s, when the people's movement tilted the balance of forces towards the comprador bourgeoisie, the monarchy came to accept the division of power, and both forces agreed to an elected parliament with a constitutional monarchy.

Yet, this was also a time of neoliberal policies, which reinforced the structures of discrimination in Nepali society. As in many countries of the third world, the state in Nepal has been born of the systematic discrimination against certain castes, religious groups, indigenous people, and even within the family, against women and children. And as in other countries, the state has typically allocated its budget to the towns, cities, and especially the capital city, at the expense of the countryside. With the adoption of neoliberal economic policies in the second half of the 1980s, this type of fiscal and budgetary discrimination became further entrenched.

This pre-existing inequality in income distribution served to deliver the benefits of liberalisation to the wealthy, on account of their privileged access to the state and their powerful connections to the international arena. Neoliberal theorists argued that the overall economic and social development of the country depended on the free movement of global financial capital and investments. Employment generation, the building of infrastructure, industrialisation and modernisation, all became collaborative activities between the wealthy local class and their international allies. Thus, all national assets and enterprises were privatised, tariffs were lowered and trade liberalised, the financial sector was deregulated, and the whole of the national economy was integrated into global markets. However, the major chunk of trade and industry remained unconnected to the largest domestic sector, that is, agriculture; therefore, the majority of the people remained excluded from the major economic activities. Moreover, the social expenditures of the state were cut down, the public distribution system collapsed, and the accumulation of capital at the national level gradually concentrated in the hands of a few rich business people. The outcome of this policy was clear: the gap between rich and poor widened immensely.

The implementation of the second phase of the neoliberal programme after 1992 created even greater inequalities. The Gini coefficient in Table 8.1 traces the growing inequality over two decades.

Table 8.1   Gini coefficient for income distribution, 1984–2004

Survey	Rural	Urban	Nepal
1984/85[a]	0.23	0.26	0.24
1995/96[b]	0.31	0.43	0.34
2003/04[b]	0.35	0.44	0.41
% change 1995/96–2003/04	13	2	21

[a] Multi-purpose Household Budget Survey.
[b] National Living Standard Survey.

Sources: NESAC (1998), CBS (2004).

The contradiction between rich and poor ripened in the same proportion, not least because the establishment of new democratic rights in 1990s sharpened the political awareness of the Nepali people. Within a short period of time, people started to raise their demands from various corners, especially for the restructuring of the state. But for the ruling elites, neither did they have any dream of restructuring the state, nor did they have any ready-made solutions to fulfil the demands of the people. When the ruling parties in various names engaged in their own political benefit, the people gradually took the initiative in their own hands.

In February 1996, the CPN (Maoist) declared a People's War against the system. At first, its influence was less impressive. However, within three years of armed struggle, the polarisation sharpened. And as the armed struggle gained force, the three major contradictions in Nepali society became clear: first, between the capital city, Kathmandu, and the countryside; second, among the racial, linguistic and regional identities and hierarchies; and third, the overall class contradiction. In a very short period of time, the armed struggle became popular among the youth and the economically deprived, those discriminated on the basis of caste, religion, gender and region, and who joined the struggle in large numbers. The popularity of the People's Liberation Army (PLA) was evident not least in that 40 per cent of its recruits were young women. Within six years of its commencement, the People's War spread all over Nepal, and the government lost the capacity to govern on approximately 80 per cent of the territory.

A decade of armed struggle created a new balance of forces between (1) the monarchy and the Royal Nepal Army (later Nepal Army); (2) the existing political parties, such as the Nepali Congress (NC), the Communist Party of Nepal (UML) and another five small parties; and (3) the CPN (Maoist). A sharp contradiction surfaced among the political elites, their organisations and institutions. This led to a royal massacre in the Narayan Hiti palace in May 2001, where King Birendra and his family were killed. Then, the largest political party of the bourgeoisies, the NC, split into two. Thereafter, in September 2003, the new king, Gyanendra, took state power into his own hands, dismissing the elected government of the NC. This unconstitutional coup provoked the political parties, which converged in the Seven Political Party Alliance (SPA) and joined with CPN (Maoist) within the framework of a twelve-point understanding in New Delhi in November 2005.

This new alliance positioned itself against the monarchy, whose legitimacy had already loosened after the royal massacre. The large majority of the people believed that there was a certain involvement of King Gyanendra in the massacre. In the process, the Maoists and the SPA achieved unprecedented political support from among the grassroots. They obtained the full support of the political class, intellectuals and the vast majority of people in India, as well as people all over the world. It was a unique political circumstance which created the ground for the People's Uprising of April 2006. In 19 days of struggle, more than 10 million people, out of a population of 24 million, came out into the streets without fear of tear gas, batons and water cannon, or the possibility of exile and long-term imprisonment.

The People's Uprising stood not just for a change of government; the people joined the struggle for the fundamental restructuring of the state. The People's Uprising stood against neoliberalism, individualism, and the accumulation of super-profits by the elites and their corporate allies. It stood against the unequal distribution of wealth and all forms of social, political, economic, cultural, linguistic and regional discrimination. The prior People's War (1996–2006) had already been setting the agenda of change. The CPN (Maoist) had already popularised the demand for the free and fair election of a Constituent Assembly, the elimination of all remnants of feudal relations, the re-distribution of wealth, popular joint government by means of alliances, and popular participation in all levels of federal and state institutions. Thus, at the time of the People's Uprising, the CPN (Maoist) advanced a proposal for a minimum forward-looking political solution towards the completion of the bourgeois democratic revolution through peaceful negotiation (Bhattarai 2008). But after the restoration of the old parliament, the SPA headed by the Nepali Congress sought to derail this agenda and downplay the influential role of the People's War. The SPA thus began to prevaricate on the restructuring of the state.

However, after several meetings, consultations, and tough bargaining, the government of the SPA accepted a Comprehensive Peace Agreement, which was signed in November 2006, under the supervision of the United Nations Mission in Nepal (UNMIN), eight months after the People's Uprising. An agreement was also reached in January 2007 on a new interim constitution to form a new legislative house of parliament with 329 members, in which the same old parliamentarians retained their seats along with 87 new members nominated by the Maoists. After three months, the Maoists also joined the government. But the popular demand for a 'federal structure' had not yet been included in the interim constitution. It was only after a major section of Nepali society, the Madheshi, from Terai in southern Nepal, came to constitute the fourth largest party in the Constituent Assembly that the government submitted to the demand of including a future federal structure in the interim constitution.[2]

Between May 2007 and January 2008, there appeared several points of tension between the Maoists and the old SPA. The Nepali Congress and the CPN (UML) were not ready for a new kind of structural change. There were three major differences between them. The first concerned the future of the monarchy, as the largest party, the Nepali Congress, refused the call for its abolition. The NC feared a possible future alliance between the two major left parties in the election of the Constituent Assembly under a common minimum programme (CMP). In its estimation, the NC ran the risk of being routed in several constituencies, which would prevent it from blocking a radical agenda. For this reason, the NC showed a willingness to retain a cordial relationship with the monarchy, which still had under its influence the top brass of the army.

Second, there was a difference over the election model and procedure. The Maoists demanded a full-fledged proportional representation system (PRS) which, in their estimation, would enable a larger number of representatives from among the discriminated groups to become involved in the constitution-making process. But the NC and the CPN (UML) were not ready for this. They preferred to retain the Westminster 'first past the post' model, as this, in their view, would favour the elite personalities with money and muscle.

The third major difference concerned the integration of the PLA and the Nepali army. For the Maoists, this was a very important issue, given that their real power lay in their army of 20,000 fighters. Without assurance of real integration, it was not possible to secure the personal future of those who had dedicated their lives to the creation of the new republic. Nor was it possible to defend the democratic achievements of the People's Uprising of April 2006 against the counter-revolution. But other political parties were not in favour of integration. They believed that the integration of the politically motivated and trained PLA fighters would enable the Maoists to impose their 'communist autocratic rule'. The SPA obstructed integration before the elections for the Constituent Assembly; the elections were not held in June 2007, and thus became uncertain.

In January 2008, the SPA and Maoists reached a new agreement and scheduled the date of the elections for April 2008. They agreed that the first meeting of the Constituent Assembly would pronounce the nation, unconditionally, as a Federal Republic. In the meantime, it became clear that neither would a wider left alliance be possible in the elections, nor the integration of the two armies before the election. The NC and the CPN (UML) were hoping that the Maoists would be defeated in the election and that these two major issues would be diluted. Moreover, they counted on the support of the mainstream media in the aftermath of the election. Simultaneously, various pre-election surveys were predicting the supremacy of the NC and the UML, and that the Maoists would get thin popular support. It was under the influence of this enthusiasm that the mainstream political parties accepted to hold the elections in April.

In the event, the Maoists emerged as the largest party in the Constituent Assembly elections, clinching 120 out of 241 seats in the first-past-the-post system and 30 per cent of the vote in the PRS.

The NC came second, with 37 seats in the first-post-the-post system and around 20 per cent of the vote in the PRS. The CPN (UML) came third, with 32 seats and 18 per cent of the vote, respectively. Out of a total of 601 seats, 229 went to the Maoists, 115 to the NC, and 108 to the UML. The newly-formed MJF emerged as the fourth force in the Constituent Assembly, with a total of 52 representatives.

This was a shocking result not only for the NC and the UML, but the international community too. The latter opposed radical change and vigorously supported the old parties with financial and moral support. However, the first meeting of the Constituent Assembly announced the Federal Republic and the abolition of the monarchy. The institution which had ruled the country, directly and indirectly, for 240 years was abolished. This was a great achievement of the people. The event was peaceful and had no immediate chance of counter-revolution, for two reasons. First, all political representatives elected by popular vote had promised a federal republic in their election manifestos; they could not betray the people immediately. Second, there was a strong presence by the PLA, which watched carefully for any kind of movement towards a military coup. Therefore, all political forces accepted the outcome.

But the interim government led by Girija Prasad Koirala and his party, the NC, which had performed badly in the Constituent Assembly election, were not ready to hand over the post of prime minister to the largest party, the CPN (Maoist), until the latter accepted the amendment in the interim constitution for the simple majority system.[3] This was part of their strategy to continue with the Westminster model and resist any kind of fundamental change in the existing state structure.

THE CONTRADICTIONS

We have already seen that three major contradictions surfaced in Nepali society: between the capital city, Kathmandu, and the countryside; among identities and nationalities; and the overall class contradiction. These three contradictions matured in the 1990s.

We have also seen that social inequalities grew tremendously over the last 25 years, as reflected in the Gini coefficient. The agricultural sector was especially hard hit by neoliberal policies and cuts in subsidies. This sector employs 74 per cent of the workforce above the age of 15, which means that agriculture is the source of livelihood for about 85 per cent of the population. Yet, the contribution of agriculture to gross domestic product (GDP) declined from 60 per cent in 1984 to 32 per cent in 2008. Access to land has also been precarious: 24 per cent of rural households (with an average size of 5.6 members) do not own land, while nearly 45 per cent of households which own less than half a hectare of land account for only 11 per cent of cultivated land; the latter cannot sustain their members with the grains they produce for more than three months. According to the Central Bureau of Statistics (CBS), 46.93 per cent of the households, the poorest, owned only 12.32 per cent of total cultivated land, less than half a hectare each; while 2.88 per cent of households, the richest, owned 17.29 per cent of total cultivated land, more than 6.3 hectares on average (CBS 2006: 74).

The uneven distribution of land has consequences for poverty, which in turn has certain regional differences. As Table 8.2 shows, in the Hill and Mountain regions, 62 per cent of households are below the poverty line, while in Tarai region the figure is almost half that, at 32 per cent.

Table 8.2   Regional distribution of poor and non-poor households by farm category

Region	Status	Landless	Small	Med./Large	Total
Terai	Poor	476 (40%)	320 (30%)	97 (18%)	893 (32%)
	Non-poor	723 (60%)	759 (70%)	441 (82%)	1923 (68%)
Hill	Poor	877 (70%)	1138 (60%)	162 (43%)	3177 (62%)
	Non-poor	371 (30%)	766 (40%)	211 (57%)	1348 (38%)
Mountain	Poor	296 (77%)	300 (58%)	24 (24%)	620 (62%)
	Non-poor	87 (23%)	214 (42%)	74 (76%)	375 (38%)

Source: Sharma (2003).

The above findings suggest that farm size alone does not determine the status of each household with respect to poverty, whose incomes might vary within each farm category, but they do suggest an inverse relationship between farm size and poverty. However, the Nepali Congress, the CPN (UML), and the Madhesh-based parties do not support radical land reform. They argue that the state should provide compensation at market prices to landowners, even when they are above the ceiling defined by the state. But it would not be possible for the state to give such compensation. Thus, the CPN (Maoist) is in favour of land redistribution without compensation and demands the confiscation of land in the case of absentee landlordism on the basis of 'one man, one profession'.

It is also notable that differential access to education has further exacerbated inequality. In 1996–2004, aggregate per capita consumption increased by 42 per cent, yet the consumption of the educated strata increased by 76 pe rcent (Sharma 2009: 3–4). It is such social inequalities that led to the emergence of a movement from below, as well as to the People's War which further raised the consciousness of the masses.

The rural-urban divide also became more clearly a political issue. Kathmandu had emerged in the late eighteenth century, after the defeat in the war with Britain, as a city-state with a periphery, guarded against foreign invasion. The nature of the state did not change after the recognition of independence in 1923. In the 1950s, the elite classes of the nation migrated continuously to Kathmandu, for several reasons. Kathmandu valley has a very good climate with fertile land, well-maintained physical infrastructure, educational and health facilities, and other services, as well as an industrial structure with employment opportunities. More than half of the wealth of the nation is concentrated in Kathmandu valley, including 70 per cent of financial institutions, 80 per cent of technical education institutions, and 80 per cent of hospital beds. Even to travel abroad for employment purposes it is necessary to visit Kathmandu for the passport and visa services located there. The nation's only international airport is also located in Kathmandu. This means that the majority of the population of the countryside is highly dependent on Kathmandu for education, health, employment, and all other facilities. It is for this reason that equal development among all regions is necessary and that the federal structure is important for the resolution of the Kathmandu-countryside contradiction. Yet, elites of different political parties and a segment of the business class are still not in favour of actual decentralisation of state power.

Nepal is a country of linguistic, racial, cultural, and religious minorities. As mentioned earlier, the rulers of the country set their minds on the Hinduisation of the nation. Immediately after unification, they adopted a one-language policy based on *parbate* (the ruler's mother tongue), which is known today as 'Nepali'. When the ruler decreed Nepali as the national language and Hinduism as the national religion, obviously the other national languages were discriminated against, and the religion and culture of other communities could not flourish. The process of such discrimination directly and indirectly impacted on the political, economic and social power of all other nationalities. Thus, the hill-mountain Khas-Brahmin community continued to dominate state power, even after the 1950s. Their privileged access to education, government services, employment, economic resources, and political power necessary marginalised the other communities. The long-established hegemony of this group has created deep economic and social contradictions within the whole of society.

In the 1990s, the first democratic movement restored parliamentary institutions. After that, two major issues, language and religion, came to the forefront. However, they remained abstract, for they were not directly associated to the distribution of wealth. There were two basic reasons for this. First, the question of class was on the defensive, due to the collapse of the Soviet Union and East European socialism. Second, the logic of neoliberalism was spreading so fast that the so-called social democrats and communists were themselves speedily adjusting to neoliberal political economy. When the consequences of neoliberalism began to be felt, especially in the countryside, cultural issues gained an economic dimension. Thus, untouchables (Dalits), indigenous people (Adibasi), women and Madheshi were directly affected. The problem required not only cultural recognition, but redistribution of wealth and socio-economic transformation. Yet, the existing political parties did not have any ideas or programmes for such transformation. When their ideology failed to address the plight of the discriminated communities, political organisations themselves raised the question of racial, linguistic and religious inequalities under new light.

The last two contradictions relate to class, directly or indirectly. It is true that even the majority of the Chhetri and Brahmin communities are not so wealthy and powerful. Certainly, a few privileged persons have disproportionate access to wealth and power. In fact, more than half of the Chhetri households are themselves living below the poverty line. Therefore, the resolution of the overall class contradiction requires a search for an equilibrium point at which all the contradictions may be addressed in the right measure.

THE EXTERNAL BALANCE OF FORCES

A small landlocked country, such as Nepal, surrounded by powerful neighbours is presented with a series of problems, but also certain opportunities. Nepal's hegemonic neighbour, India, has sought to keep Nepal within its sphere of influence by expanding political, economic, social, and cultural ties. Ever since the downfall of the Rana regime, India has maintained a strong influence in Nepal and has played a key role in every transformation, be it in strengthening absolutism or in forming a democratic republic. In this context, India has not hesitated to use strategic, political or other means to interrupt the revolutionary upsurges in Nepal when these have threatened to contradict India's national interest. This implies that the stability and development of the Nepalese revolution depends significantly on the role of India.

To understand India's policy towards Nepal, it is important to look more closely at the nature of the Indian ruling class and the political and economic structures that influence it. It is obvious that working people in India occupy no significant place at the political level. Thus, although nearly 60 per cent of the total working population of India continues to depend on agriculture, the latter sector has been in decline. At the same time, the service sector (approaching 40 per cent of GDP) and the industrial sector have expanded under the leadership of private capital. Ever since independence in 1947, India has gone through different developmental phases, from the mixed economy and welfare state of the earlier decades to the neoliberal reforms of the 1990s. And although the political parties remain the same, their priorities and principles have undergone profound change. India's interest in Nepal has followed suit, changing from a more sentimental to a commercial approach, mainly inclined towards the extraction of natural resources. Throughout this time, India has also perceived China as its competitor and has sought to weaken the latter's growing influence in the region. India's deepening relationship with the United States after 1990 is an example of this.

Even though Nepal accounts for only 1 per cent of India's foreign trade, its economic dependence on India is increasing by the day. Nepal's trade deficit with India has grown from US$267 million in 2000 to US$1.3 billion in 2008. Meanwhile, in 2002–08, Nepal's growth rate remained at only 3.8 per cent of GDP, with its industrial production nearly stagnating, at a growth rate of 1.6 per cent (Taneja and Choudhury 2009). It is imperative for Nepal to realise a complete structural change and develop its own independent economy – by means of industrialisation, establishment of agro-industries and the export of raw materials – in order to reduce its dependence on India. But opposed to this process is the alliance between Nepali and Indian industrialists, who have already embraced globalisation and privatisation. The Indian transnational firms, under the protection of imperialist economic and political forces, not only influence Indian politics but also have become a medium through which the status quo is defended in Nepal. They have played an active role against revolution and structural change in Nepal.

Nepal has to make a leap. It cannot persist as a politically unstable, economically unsuccessful nation, when its large neighbour, India, has been undergoing rapid economic growth, at an average rate of 7 per cent annually over the past two decades. Today, with the rise in political consciousness, progressive Nepalese social forces need to expand and strengthen their relationship with progressive forces in India. The Nepalese revolution can be sustained only if such a political relationship prevails over the Indian bureaucracy, which is guided by the interests of transnational firms.

A further dimension of the external balance of forces is the competitive relationship between India and China. Although the volume of trade between India and China has grown exponentially over the last decade, from US$1 billion in 2001 to US$50 billion in 2007, territorial tensions and the struggle for regional dominance has intensified. India is suspicious about China's economic and political encroachment, in the midst of a growing territorial dispute in India's north-east, Arunachal Pradesh, as well as disputes over the import and export of certain goods. Similarly, China is suspicious that India gives shelter to US interests, especially in support of separatist movements in Xinjiang province and Tibet. Although every Nepalese government officially pledges not to let Nepal become a ground for either anti-China or anti-India activities, Nepal has not been able fully to assure both of its neighbours. Indeed, it will be difficult to maintain peace and stability in the whole Asian region if smooth relations between India and China are not developed. Nepal, especially, would have to bear the brunt if there continues to be unhealthy conflict between the two countries over trade and industry, or use and production of weaponry. The progressive changes taking place within Nepal can only be advanced if Nepal is able to assist in co-ordinating and broadening the relationship between India and China. A policy of using one neighbour against the other will never prove fruitful for Nepal.

India's economic and political influence on Nepal is greater than that of any other country. However, as an independent nation-state, Nepal has to reclaim itself from its heavy dependence on India. How can Nepal ensure its existence in between the world's two most populous and increasingly powerful states, without undergoing structural change? This is the fundamental question that confronts Nepal today.

THE NATIONAL QUESTIONS

The People's Uprising of April 2006 was a great event in the history of Nepal. This abolished the feudal monarchy. But the partnership between right-wing and left political parties always stumbles on the issue of transformation. The hung parliament, the opportunism of small and medium-sized parties, the extreme right-wingers and the hunger for power by the leadership of the old political parties – all continue to obstruct the smooth transformation of the nation. At present, there are a number of issues at stake, which were brought to the fore by the People's Uprising, the Madhesh movement, and the Comprehensive Peace Accord.[4] The issues include: (1) the conversion of the unitary state into federal structure; (2) political and social transformation; (3) the management of armies and arms; (4) the ceasefire provisions and measures for normalisation; and (5) the election of a Constituent Assembly. These five issues constituted the agenda of the CPN (Maoist) at first. The SPA later accepted them in principle, because the people's movement compelled them to do so. Among these five points, the last one, the election of the Constituent Assembly, has been completed. Points (3) and (4) are in progress and will be completed with the announcement of the new constitution. Thus, here we will only discuss points (1) and (2).

The conversion of the unitary state into a federal structure was the demand of the Maoists, but it was not included in the compromise with the SPA in the process of the Comprehensive Peace Accord. The Madheshi movement brought it back and, since then, it has become a crucial issue in Nepal, obliging all classes and most of the political parties to deal with the nationalities question as a matter of practical politics. But the leaders of the NC and the CPN (UML) have not accepted the federal structure wholeheartedly. They argue that rights based on language, religion and culture will divide the country. They prefer a geographical division into federal units without any provision of special rights to the indigenous people, Dalits, and women. However, all segments of Nepali society, except the Chhetri and Brahmin leaders of the NC and CPN (UML), are ready to accept the proposals of the most marginalised.

On this issue, the CPN (Maoist), including all Madhesh-based parties and indigenous organisations, have a common view in principle. They have accepted the wide variety of forms of the nationality question arising from the social, historical and ethnic diversity of Nepal, as defined by Rosa Luxemburg (2009: 101–2). There are also some fundamental differences as to the nature of the federal model.[5] The NC and the CPN (UML) are in favour of a co-operative model, rather than the competitive or mixed model. But the other parties are in favour of the mixed model. On this matter, however, there is tough debate within the NC and

CPN (UML). Most of the members among the indigenous groups, women, and Dalits appreciate the mixed model, while others do not. A similar situation is appearing among the other parties as well. All conservatives, right-wingers and old monarchists are slowly and gradually gathering in one camp against federalism, while all progressive forces are gathering in the other. Thus, the whole of society is becoming polarised on the questions of modelling and autonomy status of the federal units.

The political instability of government is a chronic problem in Nepal. Since the 1950s, no government has fulfilled its full term. The Westminster model of democracy, with the first-past-the-post electoral system, has completely failed in Nepal. As in other third world countries which have adopted the Westminster model, the electoral process revolves around personalities, money and muscle, as well as a struggle over the distribution of cabinet posts, which often leads to conspiratorial politics and fractious parties. Thus, in Nepal's current constitution-making process there is a serious debate among parties regarding the system of governance. The NC and the CPN (UML), and especially their old leadership, continue to defend the Westminster model, while the new parties, specifically the CPN (Maoist) and the MJF, are in favour of a presidential system. The latter would elect a president by a popular adult franchise system, which in turn would reduce the fractious politics of the Westminster model.

Fundamentally, all political parties have already accepted multi-party electoral competition, the protection of human and basic rights and the inclusion of all communities in the political and social institutions. But in practice, some parties are trying to create loopholes whereby some would be 'more equal than others'. What is at stake is nothing less than the restructuring of the state, the destruction of its semi-feudal and semi-colonial characteristics, and the building of a new nation-state, where all citizens would have equal access to natural resources (land, water, forests) and equal access to political and social power, in terms of representation in all state layers and opportunities in education, health care, housing, food and employment. The Dalits, Muslims and Janjaties (indigenous people), continue to have lower levels of human development and less access to opportunities and resources, and this holds for women in relation to men as well.

In the Comprehensive Peace Agreement, both sides have accepted the restructuring of the state. The meaning was clear: it meant a change in the social relations of production and drastic change in the control mechanism over the means of production. But old forces, including the leaders of the NC, the MJF, monarchists and half of the CPN (UML), that still hold and control the means of production are obstructing the programme of wealth redistribution by means of progressive taxation and radical land reform. They are even denying local level first rights of indigenous peoples over the use of natural resources, which is universally accepted under International Labour Organisation (ILO) Convention No. 169, and signed by the previous government.

It is obvious that the old forces stand against the redistribution of wealth, the sharing of power, and the strengthening of the grassroots. In this historical juncture, people of all segments of society are peacefully arguing for their rights to be assured in the new constitution. The constitution-making process itself is a process of change. However, whether it will turn into a social revolution or descend into chaos will depend on the course of the class struggle.

NOTES

1. In the Nepali context, 'supra-feudal' refers to the royal families and nobles.
2. The Madheshi had led a complementary movement during the People's Uprising under the leadership of Madheshi Jan Adhikar Forum (MJF), a non-governmental organisation.
3. Before election of the Constituent Assembly there was a provision in the interim constitution that the prime minister may by removed from his/her post by a two-thirds majority of the house of the CA, but after election the Nepali Congress and the UML were not ready to handover the leadership to the CPN (Maoist) without an amendment in the constitution that the Prime minister may be removed from his/her post by simple majority.
4. The Accord was signed in November 2007 by the then Prime Minister Girija Prasad Koirala representing the SPA government and Prachanda representing the CPN (Maoist).
5. There are three kinds of federal models practiced around the world: the cooperative, the competitive, and the mixed. The cooperative model favours a strong federal centre; the competitive model endows federal units with more power and provides nominal rights to the centre; and the mixed model seeks an equilibrium point for power sharing between centre and federal units.

REFERENCES

Bhattarai, Baburam (2004), 'Building a New Revolutionary Type of State', *The Worker*, February.

Central Bureau of Statistics (2004), *National Planning Commission*. Kathmandu: Government of Nepal.

Central Bureau of Statistics (2006), *National Planning Commission*. Kathmandu: Government of Nepal.

Luxemburg, Rosa (2009), *The National Question: Selected Writings*. New Delhi: Aakar Books.

NESAC (1998), *Nepal Human Development Report*. Kathmandu: Nepal South Asia Centre.

Rose, Leo E., and Margaret W. Fisher (1970), *The Politics of Nepal: Persistence and Change in an Asian Monarchy*. Cornell, NY: Cornell University Press.

Rose, Leo E. (1971), *Nepal Strategy for Survival*. Berkeley: University of California Press.

Stiller, Ludwig F.S.J. (1999), *Nepal: Growth of a Nation*. Kathmandu: Human Resources Development Research Center.

Sharma, Siva (2009), *Inequality and Social Justice in Nepal*. Kathmandu: UNDP.

Taneza, Nisha, and Subhanil Chowdhury (2009), 'India-Nepal Co-operation Towards the New Economy Paradigm', *The Hindu*, 23 August.

9
Neoliberalism in Turkey

Cem Somel

INTRODUCTION

The peculiarities of the transformation of the nation-state in Turkey under globalising capitalism can be understood in the light of certain features of the country.[1] First, Turkey has never been colonised outright, so there is no ingrained resentment of imperialist subjugation in the public memory. Second, there is a wide difference in development between its western and eastern regions, and the country has a sizable ethnic minority in the east. Third, Turkey is a secular state with a predominantly Muslim population, where this identity is gaining importance in politics. These contradictions have enabled the ruling class in Turkey to overcome domestic resistance against the implementation of the neoliberal project.

This chapter attempts to describe the transformation of the Turkish state, its foreign relations, and the political economy of neoliberal reforms. It begins with an overview of Turkey's history before the neoliberal era, given that current problems are rooted in this history. Then the chapter discusses the implementation of the neoliberal project in public administration and the economy, as well as the political circumstances under which reforms have been implemented. A description of Turkey's vulnerable conditions in the face of the current global recession and a conclusion are offered at the end.

PERIPHERALISATION OF THE OTTOMAN EMPIRE

The Republic of Turkey emerged from the ruins of the Ottoman Empire at the end of the First World War. The Ottoman Empire, originally a tributary social formation, underwent a gradual process of incorporation into the world economy through trade from the sixteenth to the end of the eighteenth centuries, mainly as an exporter of foodstuffs and raw materials to Europe. The integration of the Ottoman Empire into the system deepened in the nineteenth century with the advent of industrial capitalism in Europe and North America. Parts of the Ottoman territories attracted European investment in agriculture and in railways. Ottoman territories were flooded with European industrial exports, as the Ottoman state made various economic concessions to European states to maintain political support for its territorial integrity. In the 1870s a sovereign debt default was solved by establishing a 'debt administration' run by the European creditors, which directly taxed the Ottoman working population.

These processes of integration did not affect all Ottoman territories to the same extent, leading to regional differences in the expansion of capitalist production. The western and southern coastal regions of present-day Turkey expanded most in the 'development of underdevelopment'.

Several of the last sultans ruled the country with an iron fist, while carrying out modernising reforms. Political liberals fighting the sultans often had to flee to European countries, receiving support from European governments and continuing their struggle there. Thus, reformers in the nineteenth and early twentieth centuries were caught in the dilemma between, on the one hand, collaborating with European powers to 'modernise' the empire in defiance of conservative and absolutist forces and, on the other, resisting European imperialism. This dilemma continues to the present day.

At the end of the First World War, the victorious powers resolved to dissect the empire and leave a small area to the Ottoman state. A group of Turkish officers, bureaucrats and local notables established a national government in Ankara and successfully conducted a war of independence against the occupying armies. This war eventually ensured independence for the regions populated mostly by Turks and Kurds, with the Treaty of Lausanne in 1923.

LEGITIMISING A PERIPHERAL STATE AFTER INDEPENDENCE

After the Lausanne Treaty, the leaders of the national government declared Turkey a republic in October 1923. The ruling elite of the new republic had uprooted an old multinational dynastic state whose legitimacy had a religious basis. The new republic promised peace, stability, and economic and social development under one-party rule (the Republican People's Party (RPP)). Throughout the history of the republic, the ruling elite has alternately used promises of economic development and of democratisation to legitimise the regime.

The ruling elite was convinced that Islamic culture and Arab and Persian cultural influences were an obstacle to modernisation. Hence, the caliphate was abolished in 1924, the sufi orders were closed down in 1925, and the state was made secular in 1928. Actually, Turkish national identity did have an Islamic dimension. The overt preference of European businessmen for non-Muslim Ottoman subjects in building commercial partnerships and political ties during the Ottoman period had made for the emergence of a Muslim-Turkish identity. Nevertheless, the nationalist leaders, under the influence of Eurocentric modernist thinking, proceeded with reforms to introduce a new European-looking identity (changing garments, headwear, the alphabet, the calendar, and so on), rejecting Ottoman-Turkish culture which, for centuries, had interacted with Arab and Persian culture. These reforms were not easily accepted by the population.

In the drive to modernisation, the experience of European imperialism – European domination over the Ottoman economy and the exploitation of the Ottoman working people by the European debt administration – gradually receded from public memory. At the same time, core European states came to be perceived as friendly, benevolent states to be emulated. This perception has continued to this day. The result is that Turkish nationalism does not have a strong historical anti-imperialist consciousness and tradition. From the foundation of the republic, the ruling classes in Turkey have directed national and religious feelings against communism (stirring up recollections of Ottoman-Russian wars and pan-Turkic sympathy for Soviet Central Asian peoples) and against minorities and neighbouring peoples. It must be recalled that the sense of Turkish nationhood emerged in the circumstances of a crumbling multinational empire, where the 'Other' was not only Western imperialism but also the many national groups that were trying to secede from the empire to form nation-states. Hence, Turkish nationalism has an introverted orientation.

In line with this introverted nationalism, the new Turkish state reneged on promises to institute local autonomy, made during the War of Independence to the Kurds, and suppressed a series of revolts by Kurdish clans in the 1920s, 1930s and 1940s. A treaty between Turkey and Iran in 1926, and another between Turkey, Iran, Iraq and Afghanistan in 1937, included articles for containing the Kurdish problem (Gerger 2007).

In 1933, after the onset of the Great Depression in 1929, the government embarked on a policy of industrialisation led by the state. This industrialisation policy was interrupted by the Second World War. Turkey did not participate in the war but suffered huge losses in production, as the male population was conscripted into the army. At the end of the war, Turkey was still largely an agrarian society.

After 1945 Turkey began to move toward a pluralist democracy. A group of merchant capitalists and landlords formed an opposition Democratic Party (DP) to challenge the RPP. The capitalists and landlords won the political support of the working people who had suffered deprivations during the war, and unseated the RPP in the elections of 1950. In the postwar years both the RPP and DP governments used the pretext of Soviet expansionism to build closer ties with the United States and the capitalist core. With recommendations from US agencies and the World Bank, the government began to liberalise imports. Thus began Turkey's chronic current account deficits, which have served as a dependency link with the core.

The DP remained in power until a military coup in 1960. The period between 1945 and 1960 can be seen as a period of *seeking legitimacy by the rhetoric of democracy*. In 1946, the formation of workers' trade unions was permitted, but all left-wing political activities were severely suppressed throughout the period. The reason for the 1960 coup was the violation by the DP government of the constitution and economic mismanagement.

The military coup of 1960 installed a progressive constitution which consolidated bourgeois parliamentary democracy. The constitution guaranteed social, economic, individual, and collective rights, and the right to form unions and to strike; it also made provisions for a social state and established the institutions for planned industrialisation. The Turkish Republic embarked on institutionalised, planned import-substitution industrialisation (ISI) in 1963.

Turkey's ISI policies enabled the capitalist class to expand production of industrial consumer goods in a protected market. Investment carried out by the state, through state-owned enterprises (SOEs) in manufacturing, agriculture, mining, and services throughout the country, made a major contribution to industrialisation and also to the development of underdeveloped regions. However, the industries remained dependent on foreign technology.[2] Domestic markets expanded through real wage increases under collective bargaining, generous price supports for farmers' products and extension of social security. This period was marked by rising assertiveness of the growing urban industrial working class in wage disputes, and struggles over land and agricultural prices by peasants.

In the postwar decades, the foreign policy of the Turkish Republic was oriented towards linking up with the core states. The Turkish Republic sided with the core states in all international conflicts. The government sent troops to Korea to fight on the side of US-led UN forces. Turkey became a member of the North Atlantic Treaty Organisation (NATO) in 1952. In 1955, Turkey voted against Algerian independence at the UN. That same year, Turkey signed the Baghdad Pact with the United Kingdom, Iraq, Pakistan and Iran, with support from the United States. During the 1956 Suez Crisis, Turkey supported Britain and France in their attempt to regain the Canal Zone from Egypt (Gerger 2006).

The 1962 Cuban missile crisis between the United States and the USSR was resolved with the dismantling of Soviet missiles in Cuba and US missiles in Turkey, without the Turkish government being consulted. In the aftermath of Turkey's military intervention in Cyprus, the United States imposed in 1975 an arms embargo on Turkey, which lasted until 1978. The Turkish ruling circles did not allow these incidents to deteriorate relations, or provoke anti-US feeling among the population.

The oil price hikes in the 1970s and rising short-term external debt culminated in the deterioration of the balance of payments in 1977–79, intensified the struggle between classes to evade the burden of the necessary adjustment, and led to a wage-price spiral. The economic troubles fuelled domestic political violence between leftist and right-wing organisations in towns and cities.

In January 1980, a technocrat who had worked at the World Bank, Turgut Özal, was given charge of the economy. He implemented the first measures of the structural adjustment programme (SAP). With the restiveness of the working people, the programme could not go very far. In September 1980, the army took over power and retained Özal to continue the SAP without hindrance. Turkey's external debt was generously restructured. The Bretton Woods institutions saw Turkey as a suitable role model for SAPs, not least because of Turkey's position in the Western military alliance as a bulwark against both the socialist bloc and the Islamic Revolution in Iran.

TRANSFORMATIONS IN THE NEOLIBERAL ERA

The army junta that seized power in 1980 banned all political activities and strikes, closed down trade unions, and had union leaders arrested and tortured. The junta drafted a new constitution which severely restricted civil liberties and forced it through a referendum in 1981. A restricted kind of civilian rule was established in 1983. Thus began a new period wherein *restoration of democracy* became the dominant political issue once again. Turkey began a long, drawn-out process of political normalisation under the junta's 1981 constitution. Restrictions on democratic rights are often attributed to this constitution. Demands for revisions, or a complete overhaul of the constitution, are still often voiced. Throughout the 1980s, as the labouring masses struggled to regain their civil rights, the governments gradually granted the rights, in exchange for acquiescence to neoliberal economic reforms.

Judging by the Turkish experience, the neoliberal project appears as an attempt by the bourgeoisie to increase its share of the national product at the expense of the labouring classes who produce it. In Turkey, every single economic policy change and many social policy changes can be traced to, and interpreted in terms of, this objective.

It may be useful to summarise major policy changes and events that have marked the neoliberal period. They include the introduction of current account convertibility in 1984; capital account convertibility in 1989; a brief currency crisis in 1994; the signing of the World Trade Organisation (WTO) agreements in 1994; the entry into a customs union with the European Union in 1995; a staff monitoring agreement with the International Monetary Fund (IMF) in 1998; an IMF-supported stabilisation programme in 2000; a severe currency and banking crisis in 2001; and the onset of the 2007 crisis.

Transformation of the State Apparatus

The first notable transformation in the state is a shift in decision-making and regulatory power. In the 1980s, economic policy-making power shifted away from the State Planning Organisation and the Ministry of Public Finance and was concentrated in the hands of the prime minister and ministers without portfolio. The Treasury was separated from the Ministry of Public Finance. Such measures reduced the influence of the bureaucracy and of technocrats over economic policies and strengthened that of politicians. At the same time, various areas of market regulation were removed from the jurisdiction of ministries and were handed over to numerous 'independent' boards.

The public sector's personnel policy has also been undergoing transformation. In the 1980s, the Özal governments began to replace civil servants with tenure by civil servants under renewable contract. Over the last 20 years, all white-collar personnel of SOEs and many in the central government bureaucracy have become contract personnel. On another plane, in an effort to downsize the state, the positions of retiring civil servants in manual work are being abrogated, and such work in government offices is increasingly being subcontracted to firms which employ labour at minimum wage and under harsh conditions.

As a result of this process of introducing flexibility into the public sector, the personnel in government offices work under many statuses: tenured civil servants, civil servants under renewable contract, workers with indefinite contracts, workers with fixed term contracts and subcontracted workers. This policy has been effective in dividing civil servants in their interests and problems, and in preventing unionisation and collective action.

More recently, a comprehensive reform of the central government is being gradually implemented. It involves decentralisation of many government services (health, transportation, water services to rural areas, traffic and road construction). Decentralisation of the state apparatus is also promoted by the EU's system of Regional Development Agencies. Decentralisation is seen by some groups (social liberals, Kurds) as representing an increase in local control over government expenditures, hence enhancing democratic control over state activities. Critics point out that the triadic governance structures designed to oversee these services at the local level, and comprised of representatives of central government, businessmen and 'civil society' (that is, non-governmental organisations (NGOs)), will be dominated by business interests, and are but a step towards privatisation of these services.

In 2001, the Turkish Republic accepted the rule of international arbitration for disputes between foreign firms and the state. The constitution was amended to allow for this. This is seen by some as a concession of national sovereignty, as such disputes will no longer be settled in the Turkish judicial system.

The Socio-economic Transformation, 1980–2007

This section explains the attempts by the bourgeoisie to increase its share of national product through policies on wages, agricultural price support, social security, taxation, public finance, and privatisation of state enterprises. Practically all of the policy shifts in these areas have been supported and precipitated by the SAP of the World Bank, stipulations in agreements with the IMF, the WTO agreements and pressures from the EU in membership negotiations.

With the SAP of 1980, Turkey abandoned the import-substituting industrialisation strategy and switched to an export-led growth policy. This started a process of deeper integration with the world economy, that is, a simultaneous process of external articulation and domestic disarticulation. Table 9.1 shows a rough measure of this external integration. The table shows that the ratio of exports to gross domestic product (GDP) has been on a roughly rising trend; and the ratio of imports to GDP similarly.

Table 9.1   Ratio of goods exports and imports to GDP (current US$)

Ratios	1980–84	1985–89	1990–94	1995–99	2000–04	2005–06
Exports/GDP	0.08	0.10	0.07	0.11	0.16	0.17
Imports/GDP	0.13	0.13	0.11	0.16	0.21	0.24

Source: Calculated from World Development Indicators (http://data.worldbank.org/indicator).

The second implication of the switch to export-led growth is that, as the importance of the expansion of the domestic markets for capital accumulation has diminished relative to that of exports, wages have become only a cost-of-production item for capitalists. Similarly, export orientation has diminished the relative significance of expenditure out of salaries, farmer incomes, and pensions for the realisation of profits. The adjustment by the government every year of the minimum wage to the costs of living evokes references to international competition and to wages in China from the employers. The high unemployment rate (averaging 7.8 per cent over 1988–99 and 9.5 per cent over 2000–06) also presses on wages and presses workers to accept informal employment. The government passed a labour law in 2003 introducing more flexibility in employment and working conditions. The labour law, the trade union law and the unemployment rate combine to make unionisation more and more difficult; the ratio of unionised workers is diminishing.

The neoliberal reforms have included the dismantling of the price support system in agriculture. The state gradually removed the agricultural price support schemes, ended subsidies for agricultural inputs and opened up Turkish agriculture to the competition and price pressures of international trade. This process has been impoverishing Turkish peasants, speeding up the migration to cities, and pushing Turkish agriculture to give up the production of crops for domestic consumption (for example, sugar beet, maize, wheat) and to produce cash crops.

Turkey's three public social security institutions, which had been run on the principle of 'pay as you go', had been running deficits, covered by transfers from the central government budget. The deficits were due to a declining participation rate of both men and women in the labour force (in December 2008, 71 per cent for men, 25 per cent for women), a high unemployment rate (14 per cent in December 2008, 17 per cent outside agriculture), a high share of informal employment (in December 2008, the proportion of employed people not registered in social security was 29 per cent outside agriculture, 85 per cent in agriculture) and arrears in the contributions by employers, besides low retirement ages. The governments have ignored the first four problems, and have concentrated on the low retirement age. A law enacted in 2006 combined the three institutions in one, reduced the benefits of pensioners, and includes a scheme that gradually raises the retirement age to the average expected life of Turkish men and women.[3]

The political economy of the transition from a pay-as-you-go system of social security to a funded system merits analysis. The pay-as-you-go system is based on a growing labour force, so that the premium contributions of the younger generation are used to pay the pensions of the older. When the growth rate of the labour force slows down and the lengthening of expected life allows people to enjoy longer retirement years, the system can run deficits which have to be met with transfers from tax revenues. These transfers are a kind of progressive redistribution between classes, which is what *social* security should involve. In a funded system, participants are supposed to benefit from their pooled accumulated savings. This can hardly be called 'social'; it is no different from private insurance. This implicit privatisation of social security can be traced to the reluctance of the bourgeoisie, who do not need social security, to contribute through taxes to support the ailing and the elderly of the toiling people.

Since 1980, Turkey's tax system has been steadily losing its progressive structure. The share of direct taxes (taxes on income and wealth) in total tax revenues steadily increased up to 1980; since that year, the share of direct taxes has shown a decline (see Figure 9.1), while the share of indirect taxes has been steadily increasing. In 2003 and 2006, new tax laws reduced the corporate tax rate and the income tax rate on the highest income group, with no change in the rates for lower income groups.

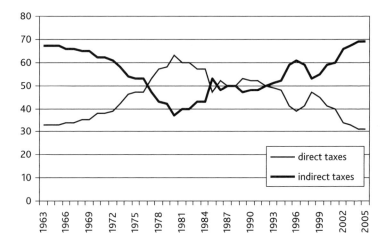

Figure 9.1   Shares of direct and indirect taxes in central government budget tax revenues (%)

Source: Revenue Administration, Republic of Turkey.

In the 1980s, the public sector's fiscal balance remained in deficit, covered by monetisation; the inflation rate began to ratchet up. In line with the monetarist theory of inflation, the government decided to check the Treasury's borrowing from the Central Bank. In 1984, the government began a new redistributive process whereby the budget law authorised the Treasury to borrow more than the projected budget deficit, and to borrow from the money and capital markets in auctions. This ended the 60-year procedure whereby the Treasury would borrow from public institutions (for example, SOEs and social security institutions) and from private banks on terms fixed by the Treasury. Thus began a process of public debt accumulation at exorbitant real interest rates determined in public auctions, subject to the demands of financial institutions (mainly banks) in the money and capital markets. The authorisation given to the government to borrow more than the estimated deficit of the budget approved by parliament represented a loosening of parliamentary control over public borrowing and public expenditures. This authorisation continued until 2002.

The interest payments on the swelling debt exceeded the primary surpluses so that public debt management degenerated into Ponzi financing: borrowing simply to pay off the interest due. The Ponzi financing was facilitated by short-term capital inflows from abroad under the capital account convertibility introduced in 1989. In 1998, the problem of debt and interest payments (Table 9.2) prompted the government to sign a staff monitoring agreement with the IMF. This was followed in 2000 by a so-called 'stabilisation programme' with an exchange rate anchor for 18 months (a programme similar to Latin American *tablita* programmes), supported by a standby agreement with the IMF.

Table 9.2 General government interest payments as percentage of GDP

1996	1997	1998	1999	2000	2001	2002	2003	2004	2005	2006	2007	2008
10.0	7.7	11.5	13.7	16.3	23.7	19.3	13.3	10.4	7.2	6.1	5.8	5.7

Source: State Planning Organisation Annual Programmes for 2004, 2007 and 2009.

The stabilisation programme of 2000 depended on sustained capital inflows which were attracted by high interest rates and confidence in the exchange rate anchor. But the inflation rate remained higher than the scheduled rate of exchange rate increases, so that the Turkish Lira (TL) appreciated in real terms and the trade deficit grew. Eventually foreign creditors lost confidence in the exchange rate anchor and inflows ceased, causing a currency crisis in February 2001 and the abortion of the programme. After the inevitable sharp devaluation, there was a surge in foreign direct investment (FDI) as foreign capital looted the (now cheapened) assets of Turkish firms that were in financial distress. The economy contracted (Akyüz and Boratav 2001). The government designed a new programme and signed a new loan agreement with the IMF. The loan provided foreign exchange to the government to sell to the private sector to pay off their foreign creditors. This was a major redistribution of liabilities, transferring to the public purse external debt that the private sector had incurred.

The government budget continues to be a device for transferring government revenues to the capitalists who hold government debt. The government is currently running primary budget surpluses to pay off the debt, averaging 5.8 percent of gross national product (GNP) over 2002–07. This policy is curtailing public services and sets the stage for their further privatisation.

In the 1980s, Özal began the programme of privatising the SOE system. The sale of state assets was slow at first, but gained speed at the end of the 1990s. Initially, the ostensible objective of privatisation was to increase the efficiency in the management of the enterprises. In time the tune changed; now the main objective is to end the economic activities of the state in sectors where the private sector can operate. The methods of privatisation have often resulted in scandalous underpricing of highly profitable enterprises. Some of the industrial enterprises, once sold, have been torn down to use the land for more lucrative service sector activities. The judiciary has prevented sales where improper procedures have been detected. No assets are deemed strategic. The SOEs – fruits of the labour and savings of previous generations – are being plundered in a frenzy of primitive accumulation.

The SOEs did not have a large share of employment overall, but in the poorer provinces SOEs made an important contribution to expanding formal employment and supporting incomes. With privatisation the state is discarding these public-sector institutions that have been instrumental in developing and providing jobs in the underdeveloped regions.

To summarise: the export-led growth strategy, the use of the public debt to redistribute income, the privatisation of public assets, the dismantling of policies that protected the livelihood of farmers, the transformation of the social security system into a virtually private one, the growing share of indirect taxes in the tax system, and increasingly flexible employment relations all spell an attempt of the propertied classes to reduce as much as possible the share of the toilers in the national product. The export-led growth policy transformed Turkey into an exporter of manufactured goods. Financial deregulation and convertibility made Turkey an 'emerging market'. Turkey is a semi-peripheral country in the world system.

The Unfolding Global Crisis

The global liquidity expansion which lay at the root of the housing and mortgage speculation in the core countries has allowed the Turkish private sector to borrow abroad beginning in 2002, causing a real appreciation of the Turkish currency (compare the stability of the dollar exchange rate and the inflation rate in 2001–07 in Table 9.3) and a mounting trade deficit.

The appreciation of the TL and consequent trade deficit might have ended earlier with a third local currency crisis (following those in 1994 and 2001) but for the liquidity expansion in the core. As it turned out, the financial meltdown in the core happened before the currency crisis. At the time of writing (April 2009), the Turkish economy has been feeling the initial effects of the slowdown in exports and difficulties in managing the external debt. Tens of thousands have been dismissed from their jobs. The government is trying to secure a new loan from the IMF. The businessmen are demanding that the borrowed foreign exchange be made available to them. This is a new attempt to transfer the external debt of the private banks and firms onto the public sector, and hence onto the people. The pundits of the Turkish bourgeoisie show no interest in questioning the wisdom of the export-led growth strategy and the switch to full convertibility, in spite of the economic vulnerability these policies have caused. How the working people will react when the full impact of the global recession is experienced, and how the bourgeoisie will try to keep order cannot be surmised.

Table 9.3   Turkey's external debt, exchange rate, inflation rate and trade balance (US$ billions)

	2000	2001	2002	2003	2004	2005	2006	2007
External debt of public sector[a]	64	71	87	95	97	86	87	89
External debt of private sector	54	42	43	49	64	83	118	158
TL/US dollar exchange rate	0.63	1.51	1.50	1.43	1.35	1.44	1.31	1.30
Annual rate of CPI increase[b]	0.39	0.69	0.30	0.18	0.09	0.11	0.10	0.08
Trade balance in goods and services	−11	6	1	−3	−10	−18	−27	−33

[a] Includes Central Bank debt.
[b] Annual growth rates by end of year.
Sources: Undersecretariat of the Treasury, Central Bank of the Republic of Turkey, Turkish Statistical Institute.

The International Links of the Turkish Bourgeoisie

Turkey's relations with the EU, which go back to 1959, culminated in a customs union in 1995, while full membership negotiations began in 2005. The customs union means free trade with EU countries and the implementation by Turkey of the EU's customs policy vis-à-vis third countries, without being represented at the bodies that make the policies – a concession of legislative power to core countries.

Different social groups in Turkey harbour a variety of expectations with respect to EU membership. Some trade unions and professional associations expect democratisation and improvements in labour relations. Bourgeois intellectuals expect democratisation, more freedom of speech, and easier travel to Europe. Many Kurds pin their hopes on EU pressures for expansion of cultural rights and stronger local government. The bourgeoisie propagates the expectation that EU membership will increase FDI and provide regional development aid. As the membership negotiations proceed at a snail's pace and as public opposition in EU countries to Turkey's membership frequently surfaces, hope among the people of Turkey for full membership is wearing thin. The leaders of the EU are interested in the Turkish armed forces for the projected EU military force. Many Europeans are wary of the social and political implications of Turkey's full membership, so they advocate a special associative relationship.

Together with the IMF, the EU is the second most important external factor used by the bourgeoisie to convince the population into acquiescing to the neoliberal reforms in Turkey. The social groups that favour pressing for integration into the EU for the purpose of democratisation choose to ignore the implications of these pressures in the economic and social spheres.

Turkey's bourgeoisie calls its relationship with the United States a 'strategic alliance'. As Turkey's geopolitical importance for the Western core countries has waned with the end of the Cold War, Turkey has assumed the role of an ally in the strategic endeavours of the core countries in the periphery: Turkey has participated in many military and peace-keeping operations of the United Nations, NATO and the United States (in Korea, the Balkans, Afghanistan and Lebanon), often using its Muslim profile to legitimise interventions in Muslim countries. The foreign policy of the Turkish Republic towards neighbouring states in the Middle East has generally been shaped by the motivation to maintain the relationship with core states, and to contain the Kurdish problem (more on this below). This policy has aligned Turkey with Israel in the region. In 1993–96, after the Oslo process began, Turkey signed a number of agreements with Israel involving the upgrading of existing weapons systems, purchase of hardware, joint production of weapons, training of staff and intelligence sharing (Pipes 1998). After the Lebanon War in July 2006, Turkey, which has an intelligence-sharing agreement with Israel, contributed troops to the United Nations Interim Force in Lebanon (UNIFIL) in Southern Lebanon. The opinion of the population for such involvements is not monitored by opinion polls.

PROTAGONISTS AND POLITICAL DISTRACTIONS IN THE CLASS STRUGGLE

The end of the multipolar world and the political confrontation between capitalism and socialism ended the class conciliation in Turkey around the national economic development idea and the social state.

Since 1980, one nationalist-leftist party, two conservative liberal parties, two Islamist parties, one fascist-nationalist party, and one social democratic party have been in power, mostly in two-party or three-party coalitions. During this time, there has been no reversal of, or even disruption in, the progression of the neoliberal project: neither in privatisation, nor in the retrogressive tax reforms, nor the increasing flexibility of employment, nor in dismantling the social security system. Parties opposed to the neoliberal project do not get votes over the 10 per cent threshold necessary to be represented in parliament. The AKP (Justice and Development Party), described as 'moderately Islamist' by the Western media, is in power and continuing the project at the time of writing. The AKP has carried on the negotiations for EU membership, the alliance with the United States and with Israel.

There are nationalist-Kemalist elements among the bourgeoisie who argue for a more independent foreign policy, oppose privatisation and sales of SOEs to foreign capital, and favour protection for domestic producers. However, they are handicapped by their negative attitude towards Kurdish demands (introverted nationalism) and their hostility towards manifestations of religious identity (see below). A number of civilian and military members of this group are on trial (the Ergenekon case) at the time of writing, on charges of plotting to overthrow the AKP government. They stand accused of organising armed attacks on state institutions and on the building of the leading Kemalist newspaper to provoke a military coup, of planning a coup, and of assassinations in South-east Anatolia.

Within the state bureaucracy, the key institutions of economic policy-making (Treasury, Central Bank) are staffed by neoliberal enthusiasts. By contrast, the judiciary, drawing on laws of a bygone era, occasionally makes rulings that aim to prevent the erosion of concepts such as 'public interest'. But it is bound by legislation which is continuously changing.

The working people are organised in three workers' union confederations (leftist, nationalist and Islamist) and three civil servants' union confederations (leftist, nationalist, Islamist). The national professional associations of engineers and architects and of medical doctors are led by groups who are trying to resist the neoliberal project. Rich farmers are organised in Chambers of Agriculture; the poor farmers who are affected by the neoliberal agricultural policies are largely unorganised.

There is little trust and co-operation among the leaderships of these mass organisations. The leftist leaderships among these comprise mainly of social liberals. Social liberals oppose neoliberal economic reforms and US imperialism, and support democratisation (including Kurdish demands) and the official policy for EU membership. The social liberals are sceptical about the idea of working people's political power, because in their view power corrupts. They hope that the advance of the neoliberal project can be stopped without assuming power, based on a conviction that 'civil society' can change government policies without using political power.[4] Social liberals prefer to ignore the EU's role in furthering the neoliberal project in Turkey. They are caught in the same trap as the Ottoman liberal reformers of the nineteenth century: hoping core countries' pressures will enhance democratisation in exchange for acceptance of economic concessions.

The leaderships of all these trade union confederations and professional organisations are responsible for the divisions among the working people in the face the neoliberal onslaught. There have been instances when the workers of a large state enterprise have occupied their factory to prevent its privatisation, only to give up when their union and confederation failed to rally the support of other workers in the same sector, let alone all the working class.

Two political issues in Turkey serve to blur the class consciousness of the toiling masses and divide them in their reactions to the neoliberal onslaught: the Kurdish question and the secularism-Islamism controversy.

The eastern region of Turkey is economically the least developed.[5] The social and economic disparity between the western and eastern parts of the country is widening (Gezici and Hewings 2004, 2007, Tosun et al. 2003). Generous investment incentives accorded to the private sector over decades have had negligible effect; and the state has given up most of the public investment instruments (mainly the SOEs) necessary for regional development. In many of the eastern provinces, the Kurds are the majority. There are also sizable populations of Kurds in towns and cities in western provinces.

Since the 1980s, a Kurdish organisation, the PKK (Kurdistan Workers' Party), has been conducting a guerrilla war in the eastern provinces of Turkey which has claimed over 30,000 lives. The political objective of the PKK is not clear, but recognition of Kurdish national identity and cultural rights are minimal demands. There is also a legal Kurdish political movement that represents similar demands. Economic issues rarely appear among Kurdish demands.

The Turkish state is gradually and reluctantly reducing restrictions on cultural rights.

Some social movements (socialists, social liberals, some Islamist parties, some trade unions, human rights organisations, and journals) advocate a 'democratic solution' to the Kurdish problem, including full cultural and language rights. Turkish nationalists (various hues of Kemalists and ultra-right-wing nationalists) depict the Kurdish demands for recognition of identity, language, and culture as an imperialist plot to 'split' Turkey. The intervention of the United States and especially of EU states and organisations in Turkey's Kurdish problem makes it difficult for those advocating a democratic solution to convince the ethnic Turkish people of the necessity of a democratic solution, as such foreign intervention adds fuel to the argument of the nationalists.

On the other hand, EU criticism of human rights violations in Turkey, as well as the US policy in Iraq of supporting the Kurdish federal state, make Turkey's Kurds view the US and the EU as their allies, and this complicates the attempts to unite the Kurdish working people with ethnic Turkish working people to achieve a democratic solution. The establishment of a regional Kurdish administration in Northern Iraq and the activities of the PKK there have strained the relations between the Turkish government, the United States and Iraq for a period.

A similar blurring of the class struggle is due to the secularism-Islamism controversy. Since the transition to a multi-party system in 1946, various bourgeois political parties have exploited the religious feelings of the working people for votes. In the 1970s, Islamist parties began to participate in political life, and since then Turkish politics has been increasingly dominated by the secularism-Islamism controversy. This is currently focused on issues such as whether women should be allowed to cover their heads in schools; how the Alevite sect should be presented in religion textbooks; and whether graduates of clerical high schools should have access to university education outside theology faculties. There is hardly any real demand for a theocracy. But the secular bourgeoisie charges Islamists of aiming to undermine the secular foundations of the Turkish state. However, even the secularists are loath to abolish the state's Directorate of Religious Affairs, which employs and controls the imams in the mosques. Both secularists and Islamists are divided within themselves on relations with the United States, the EU, the Kurdish problem, the neoliberal project, and even on capitalism.

The dominant secular and Islamist bourgeois groups are of one mind on these issues, which explains the persistence of the policies.

Ethnic and racial discrimination contradict Islamic teaching. Some Islamist movements have been critical of both the governments' repressive policies toward the Kurds and of Kurdish nationalism. They criticise Turkey for having become a nation-state based on one ethnicity and point out that a new Kurdish nation-state will simply become a new regional problem.

Islamism competes against Kurdish nationalism for the support of the Kurdish masses. Votes in the southeast and some eastern provinces have been shifting between the AKP and the Kurdish party DTP (Party for a Democratic Society).[6] A peaceful democratic resolution of the Kurdish problem requires a broad consensus among Turkish ruling government circles (including the armed forces). The ruling circles have hitherto ignored the Kurdish party as a possible negotiating partner. As the Turkish political system does not recognise 'local' parties, such a move would be a major concession. In the view of many commentators, disarming the PKK, reconciliation and peaceful resolution would necessarily involve negotiations and an amnesty. As the Obama administration in the United States is moving to disengage from Iraq, the AKP government, the government in Baghdad and the Kurdistan Regional Government in Iraq are developing cordial relations. The disclosures in the Ergenekon case on assassinations in the south-east and eastern provinces, and arrests of retired officers and even one serving officer (in March 2009) connected to them, can be seen as signs of a growing dissatisfaction in society with the official policy of insistence that the Kurdish problem is, first and foremost, the problem of 'PKK terrorism'.

THE TRANSFORMED NATION-STATE AND THE CURRENT CRISIS

Despite occasional confrontations between the government and 'big business', among government institutions, between the army and the Islamist party in power, all these groups are united in promoting the neoliberal project and maintaining Turkey's place in the alliance with the core states. With the neoliberal project, the Turkish state is in the process of shedding its *social* character as written in the present constitution. The neoliberal economic and social reforms have largely eroded the redistributive social functions and institutions of the state.

Accepting international arbitration in disputes with transnational corporations (TNCs), arranging for IMF officials to supervise economic policies, and conceding to the EU Commission the tariffs that Turkey implements with respect to third countries, all infringe on the capacity of the state to regulate the economy. In addition, capital account convertibility introduced in 1989 has subjugated economic growth in Turkey to the inflows and outflows of private capital that strongly influence the level of aggregate demand in the economy. Turkey experienced two economic contractions as a result of the reversal of foreign capital flows in 1994 and 2001. The state appears to lose its role as a *national* institution regulating a national economy.

Policies such as the harassment of Kurds who express democratic demands, or the prosecution of people who express views that do not coincide with the official line on history (such as the 1915 Armenian events), reflect the struggle between those who desire to maintain the exclusively *ethnic-Turkish character* of the state and those who desire a *democratic* state with equal rights for all ethnic and religious groups. Although progress is slow, struggles waged by some NGOs and some judgments by the judiciary (the least politicised of the branches of the state) have made landmark contributions to enhancing democratic rights.

The current global economic crisis since 2007 has made it clear that the United States is no longer a hegemon in the system, having lost all its moral standing and its role as an economic model. The EU is in disarray and cannot replace it. Since the Oslo Accords, and especially after the operation in the Gaza Strip in 2009, Israel has been rapidly eroding its own pretensions as a civilised, democratic society in the Middle East. Under the emerging power vacuum, the core states show an interest in promoting the role of Turkey as a stabilising regional power in the Middle East.[7]

If the global recession leads to increasing protectionism in the core countries and a global depression, some parts of the Turkish bourgeoisie may see in a revival of nationalism the best means to maintain power and contain discontent. This would mean increasing repression of Muslim identity, Islamic movements and the Kurds, and increasing social conflict along these lines. Although the current Ergenekon trial is a setback for such a political project, such attempts cannot be ruled out for the future. It is obvious that unless the toilers make a move to change the political balance of forces in Turkey, the neoliberal project as defined above will not be terminated by the global crisis itself.

Turkey's population and geography provide a sustainable basis for egalitarian, self-reliant development. Turkey, a semi-peripheral country, has the latitude for delinking from the world system under a popular government, especially during a crisis in the core countries.[8] So another outcome of the current crisis could be an increasing politicisation of the working people and their assuming political power, especially if similar developments occur elsewhere. Given Turkey's weight in the region, this could have region-wide popular repercussions.

CONCLUSION

Since the establishment of the Republic of Turkey, the people's vision has been blurred by the official ideology of introverted ethnic nationalism and the Eurocentric 'enlightenment' view of history. The resultant of these tendencies is a society trying to decide on its identity and to define the identity of its state. The bourgeoisie has utilised introverted nationalism and Eurocentric modernism during the Cold War to sustain capitalism in Turkey and to keep Turkey in the Western alliance. The balance of social forces during the ideological rivalry between capitalism and socialism allowed for some industrial development and the emergence of a progressive social state.

Since 1980, this nationalism and Eurocentric modernism have been utilised to push forward the neoliberal agenda – the onslaught on the working people's livelihood and security. Yet, the old politics of the Turkish ruling circles is becoming increasingly irrelevant in the face of the Kurdish reaction against Turkish nationalism and of the resurgence of political Islam with many strands, some simply rejecting the apparent features of modernisation, some rejecting nationalism, some rejecting imperialism and even capitalism.

The current global economic crisis promises a period of intensifying social conflict and tectonic political shifts, with new opportunities for overcoming the straitjackets of nation-states, ethnic, religious prejudices, and the stratified economic system that is destroying the social fabric and ruining mankind's natural habitat. At the moment, opponents of the system in Turkey do not possess a concrete social project for our age, unlike the European social revolutionaries a century ago, who had rough blueprints for constructing a new social order – guidelines such as the *Critique of the Gotha Programme* (Marx 1977). Cuba, Venezuela and Bolivia are extolled with enthusiasm, but are seldom studied to learn from their experience. Together with all other oppressed peoples of the world, the toiling people of Turkey face the task of overcoming their divisions, developing the principles for an equitable, sustainable social order, and of taking on the present system to start building a society based on justice.

NOTES

1. I owe thanks to Dr Sheila Pelizzon and Prof Eyüp Özveren at Middle East Technical University in Ankara for comments that improved this chapter.
3. Thus, Turkey's ISI in 1961–80 resulted in a similar half-way industrialisation that was criticised by Albert Hirschman (1968) in the context of Latin American ISI.
3. Working people call this 'retirement in the grave'.
4. A possible example of the 'false solutions' mentioned by Samir Amin (Chapter 15, this volume). It also attests to the anti-social character of liberalism.
5. The ratio of the per capita GDP of the 'wealthiest' province (Kocaeli in the west) to that of the poorest (Mus or Agri in the east) is 10:1.
6. The Kurdish party has been frequently closed down, reappearing under a new name. Despite the 10 per cent threshold for party representation in parliament, some DTP members got elected in 2007 by standing as independents.
7. The idea of Turkey as a regional leading power was enhanced when the AKP government severely criticised Israel for its attack on Gaza in December 2008, which raised the popularity of the AKP and the prime minister, both in Turkey and among Arab peoples. Naturally the government ignored the popular demand in Turkey to cancel the many agreements with Israel.
8. See Samir Amin, Chapter 15, this volume.

REFERENCES

Akyüz, Yilmaz, and Korkut Boratav (2001), 'The Making of the Turkish Financial Crisis', paper presented to the Conference on *Financialisation of the Global Economy*, PERI, University of Massachusetts, 7–9 December, Amherst, MA, mimeo.
Gerger, Haluk (2006), *ABD, Orta Doğu, Türkiye* [The US, the Middle East, Turkey]. İstanbul: Ceylan.
Gerger, Haluk (2007), 'Türkiye Cumhuriyeti ve Ortadoğu' [The Turkish Republic and the Middle East], *doğudan*, 1 (September–October).
Gezici, Ferhan, and Geoffrey J.D. Hewings (2004), 'Regional Convergence and the Economics Performance of Peripheral Areas in Turkey', *Review of Urban & Regional Development Studies*, 16(2): 113–32.
Gezici, Ferhan, and Geoffrey J.D. Hewings (2007), 'Spatial Analysis of Regional Inequalities in Turkey', *European Planning Studies*, 15(3): 383–403.
Hirschman, Albert O. (1968), 'The Political Economy of Import-Substituting Industrialization in Latin America', *Quarterly Journal of Economics*, 82(1): 1–32.

Marx, Karl (1977[1891]), *Critique of the Gotha Programme*. New York: International Publishers.

Pipes, Daniel (1998), 'Turkey and Israel: The Birth of a New Middle East Alliance', *Washington Times*, 5 January, www.danielpipes.org.

Tosun, Cevat, Timothy J. Dallen and Yüksel Öztürk (2003), 'Tourism Growth, National Development and Regional Inequality in Turkey', *Journal of Sustainable Tourism*, 11(2–3): 133–61.

Part III
Latin America

10
Latin American Thinking on the State and Development: From Statelessness to Statelessness

Atilio A. Boron

INTRODUCTION

The purpose of this chapter is to compare the three most important theoretical schemes in use in the Latin American social sciences in the second half of the twentieth century. More specifically, we intend to explore the ways in which the problematic of the state and development has been posed in each case.[1]

The basic argument to be developed runs as follows: from the Second World War up to the mid 1960s the social theories that prevailed in the region were variations of what C. Wright Mills called 'the grand theory'. As such, those theories were characterised by a rather pronounced disregard of the state as an institution – not to mention the critical issue of sovereignty – with other features of society occupying a much more prominent role. In the early 1960s, the dominant paradigm started to be very seriously questioned and, shortly afterwards, it collapsed. Thus, the intellectual hegemony passed to the hands of 'dependency' theory, a theoretical framework where the concerns with the state and sovereignty had a crucial, strategic role. However, by the mid 1970s, the dramatic deterioration of the social and political situation in Latin America brought about a veritable sea change in the dominant ideas, and the dependency theorists were forced either to go into exile or to put an end to their intellectual endeavours. This long intellectual night would last until the mid 1980s, when amidst the democratic recovery already in place in most countries (with the significant exception of Chile) a new wave of ideas swept the region. The distinctive feature of the new ideas was, as 30 years before, a systematic neglect of the state, this time being replaced by either the markets or civil society. With the rise of the globalisation paradigm, the state was regarded, once again, as a useless relic of the past, ready to be piously buried along with any dream of national sovereignty. In this chapter, I would like to explore the main features of this story and some of its consequences.

MODERNISATION THEORY

After the defeat of the Axis powers, the road to a precipitous race began towards the professionalisation of the social sciences, leaving behind the time-honoured tradition of the Latin American social thinkers. A process like this, of course, could not take place simultaneously in all countries, or acquire in all of them the same depth. But, in general terms, the approach, contents, and intention of the *pensadores* – the heirs of people like Joaquim Nabuco in Brazil, José Pedro Varela in Uruguay, Francisco Bilbao in Chile, the Mexican *científicos*, or Domingo F. Sarmiento and Juan B. Alberdi in Argentina – were superseded by a new 'scientific sociology' strongly patterned after the American model. While the social thinkers were intellectuals obsessed with the need to interpret a reality in order to change it, no matter how naïve their proposals may have been, the zeal of the new generation was placed in methodological rigour and data accuracy and with a significant neglect of policy implications. This shift affected the contents of the reflection, as well as the typical instrument used to communicate the ideas to the public at large. The *pensadores* wrote essays, literary pieces written in plain terms, because their work was intended to be a weapon for the transformation of their societies, in most cases, for the Euro-peanisation of their societies. The essays, Real de Azúa observed, '[are] more commentary than information, more interpretation than data, more reflection than raw material for it, more creation than scholarship, more proposition than verification, more opinion than conclusive assertion' (Solari et al. 1976: 26). For its contents, its policy intentions and its style, most of the intellectual production of the *pensadores* assigned great relevance to the study and trans-formation of the state and the politics of their time. The case of Alberdi, himself the writer of the Argentine Constitution of 1853, was by no means the exception but rather the norm.

This intellectual and political tradition was expelled from the reorganised academia of the postwar years. The professionalisation of sociology came hand-in-hand with the uncontested supremacy of a theoretical paradigm, 'structural functionalism', and very importantly, in the version devised by Talcott Parsons at Harvard.

These ideas were accompanied by the rise of a narrow-minded positivist methodology that reflected the uncritical, rather crude, adoption of the canon and procedures of the so-called 'hard sciences'. It must be observed that the diffusion of American sociology as 'the model' for the social sciences was far from being a regional phenomenon. Its theories, methods and organisational structures impacted all over the world, even in Europe, the fatherland of social theory. As it could not be otherwise, in Latin America the influence of this new situation was extraordinary. In theoretical terms, the single most important expression of these new orientations was modernisation theory, and its foremost exponent was the Italian-Argentinian sociologist Gino Germani. A considerable influence was also exerted in our region by the sociological reflections of José Medina Echevarría, a prominent Weberian Spanish sociologist recruited by Raúl Prebisch to set up the Division of Social Affairs of the Economic Commission for Latin America (CEPAL), created in 1948 and dependent upon the Economic and Social Council of the United Nations. Interesting enough, in both cases they were European sociologists who, in addition, were political refugees escaping from the dictatorships of Mussolini and Franco, respectively.

Modernisation theory was rather blind to politics and especially blind vis-à-vis the state. The underlying idea was that the developing nations would, in due time, run the same course that was run much earlier by the industrialised countries. Economic development, social modernisation, and political democratisation were part of a 'natural process'; all countries were, at one point or another, 'underdeveloped', and all had to walk along the same road. As Samuel Huntington observed, this very strong assumption, which rests on the foundations of the so-called 'scientific sociology' of the 1950s and early 1960s, was anchored in a crucial component of the American creed that assures that 'all good things come together'. Accordingly, modernisation theory portrayed the transitions from the most elementary stages to the upper levels of development as a linear and evolutionary process in which there was little room for political will and political intervention, not to speak of political conflict. Societies would 'naturally' develop in the direction of the industrial and modern world as a result of the spread of modern values, beliefs and institutions, from a core developed area throughout the backward, archaic and traditional regions. It is true that the main theorists were ready to acknowledge that all along the road the countries could stumble against different 'obstacles' that could slow down the rhythm of the march, but the final destination of the journey was never put into question. Moreover, as several authors argued in those days, it was expected that even the countries governed by 'communist regimes' would gradually converge with the developed capitalist countries.

Modernisation theory was particularly recalcitrant to an adequate understanding of the historical and structural features that sharply distinguished the societies of the periphery from those of the core of the capitalist system. The initial assumption of the theory, namely that all societies were equal, was untenable and unrealistic. The theory had no answer to the dismaying questions posed by colonialism and decolonisation, and by imperialism and neo-imperialism. Its Panglossian optimism was completely unwarranted, as the hard lessons of history would later prove in Latin America. Modernisation theory expressed the *Zeitgeist* of the postwar years, and its influence pervaded all the social sciences: in economics as in sociology, in political science as in anthropology. Walt W. Rostow's famous *The Stages of Economic Growth*, a book of the late 1950s, was echoed by numerous authors in all parts of the globe and by practitioners of the most diverse social science disciplines. That book, which carried a subtitle as striking as 'A Non-Communist Manifesto', set the model for most of the modernisation theorists. Gino Germani's *Política y Sociedad en una Epoca de Transición* (1962) and *Sociología de la Modernización* (1966) constituted enlightened reflections of this type of approach, as were Pablo González Casanova's *La Democracia en México* (1965) and a host of other similar scholarly books dealing with the problems of Latin American development.

For Germani, modernisation implies a three-headed process of change: first, a change in the type of social action passing from 'prescriptive to elective action'; second, growing structural differentiation and institutional specialisation; and third, universal acceptance of social and cultural change as a 'normal' occurrence, leaving behind the traditional adhesion to time-honoured practices and beliefs. In the tracks of Rostow, social change was perceived as the transit from traditional to modern society. But in Germani's work, the basic scheme undergoes a significant process of transformation and refinement. First, Germani introduced to it the political conflicts and social contradictions unleashed by the different rates and sequences in which the overall process of change takes place in different institutional spheres. Even within a same sphere, let's say the economy, change was said to produce a situation in which patterns and ways of living that correspond to different ages must co-exist. Additionally, modernisation implied the mobilisation of different groups, classes and sectors of society; and their reactions to the challenges posed by its more or less rapid transformation tended to have severely disruptive effects on all. Change implied the erosion of social integration and the rise of large sections of the population becoming 'available' for new political modes of action not always consistent with the rosy scenario depicted by Rostow and his followers.

Last but not least, it must be added that, already in the early 1970s, Germani progressively abandoned the major guidelines of modernisation theory, embracing an approach more linked to the 'classic' sociological tradition and marked by a sort of Weberian pessimism about the future course of the process of social development (Germani 1985). At the root of this dramatic change in mood, that put a sudden end to the unlimited optimism of his earlier writings, is the rise of the Latin American dictatorships of the 1970s. The promises of secularisation and social modernisation proved to be wrong; and the conquest of democracy was now something much more complex than arriving at the last station of a pleasant developmental journey. Even if Germani sustained that social modernisation and economic development were necessary conditions of modern political democracy, the contradictions built into these same processes could well prevent the constitution of democratic regimes, or bring them down (ibid.: 25).

Yet, even in the case of Germani, it would be useless to search for a reflection on the state, the state apparatuses, the bureaucracy, and so on. The state is a sort of 'black hole', or a 'black box', where very little is known. This does not mean that our author ignored the relevance of the political problems. His analyses of Latin American populism, especially in the Argentine case, or his reflections on the role of authoritarian political-ideological traditions, are very well known and need no further recognition. Yet, despite the depth and fruitfulness of his studies, a theory of the state and a reflection on the nature of the links between the dominant classes and the political institutions is conspicuously absent in Germani's work. This absence produced a fatal flaw in the explanatory potential of modernisation theory, completely unable to predict, much less to explain, the endless succession of military coups and authoritarian regimes that punctuated Latin American history in the postwar years; or the miserable failure of the economic policies that, inspired in the same assumptions of modernisation theory, had promised to reach the realm of economic development and prosperity; or the frustration produced by the progressive disintegration of Latin American social structures besieged by the spectres of social exclusion, marginality, mass poverty and personal insecurity. Thus, modernisation theory collapsed under the combined weight of persistent underdevelopment, mounting external dependence, political crisis, and social disintegration. The promises and expectations of modernisation theorists were unfulfilled. The scene was ready for the impetuous rise of dependency theory.

DEPENDENCY THEORY

The unremitting inability of modernisation theory to deal with key political issues and face the challenges posed by the crucial role of the state prompted the perfunctory demise of the hegemonic model in the social sciences. The political blindness proved fatal for modernisation theory. Besides, it has to be recounted that a similar frustration was experienced in the core of the capitalist system as well. We had argued that at the heart of modernisation theory was the impressive concept-building of Parsonian theory, and this edifice was also under heavy attack in the United States and Europe. In the North, the frustration of capitalist society was of much lesser importance than in the South, but it still proved to be important enough to unleash mounting criticism against the dominant paradigm in the social sciences. The social and political turmoil that affected the industrialised nations in the 1960s, the outrage over the Vietnam War, and the decadence of the political institutions (very especially, the weakening of the democratic impulse and the progressive loss of the power of parliaments), combined with the ever more visible and intolerant conservative bias of conventional wisdom, precipitated all sorts of criticisms. It would be impossible to reproduce that debate in these pages; but let us simply mention the names of C. Wright Mills and Alvin Gouldner as the two more influential figures whose criticisms to the Parsonian scheme were forcefully projected in Latin American intellectual circles: the first, by denouncing the conformist and conservative nature of the dominant paradigm; the second, by expounding the radical inadequacy of 'value-free' sociology. Similar criticisms had arisen across the Atlantic from the pen of the London-based German scholar Ralf Dahrendorf, who in the late 1950s wrote an article and a book that produced a devastating attack against the citadel of established social science (Dahrendorf 1958, 1959).

The offensive against modernisation theory was especially intense in Latin America. The neglect of the problematic of the state and, more generally, of the political dimension of social life, was instrumental in nourishing an intellectual revolt against the dominant paradigm, a rebellion that was reinforced by the strong winds of political and social change that were blowing in the region since the eruption of the Cuban Revolution. A growing corpus of theorising about the state promoted by dependency theory produced a dramatic change in the agenda of the social sciences, not only in Latin America, but also in the United States, and partly in Europe, as well. The striking fact was that, for the first time in history, a vigorous reflection on the problems of the modern state and imperialism not only gained momentum in this part of the world but played a major role in the reconstruction of the scholarly international agenda. Dependency theory was at first regarded with contempt by the scholarly community in the North, as if it were only the product of the inflamed revolutionary rhetoric of third world elites. A similar response was elicited by the growing concern in Latin America with the state, long neglected in the mainstream of the social sciences.

The fact is that, despite all these misgivings and resistances, the Latin American literature on dependence and the state made its way to the top of the scholarly agenda, becoming a critical factor in the reorientation of the themes and concerns of the social sciences all over the world. CLACSO's (Latin American Council for the Social Sciences) Working Groups on Dependency and the State counted among the most crucial actors in this process, gathering together the best of the region's minds in order to explore the multiple dimensions of these two major problematics. Distinguished scholars in this tradition were the Brazilians Fernando Henrique Cardoso, Ruy Mauro Marini, Octávio Ianni, Vania Bambirra, Francisco Weffort, Francisco de Oliveira, María de Conceição Tavares and Theotonio Dos Santos. The rest of the Latin American countries also provided names of their own: Pedro Paz, Marcos Kaplan and Amadeo Vasconi from Argentina; Anibal Quijano from Perú; Gerard Pierre Charles from Haiti; Agustín Cueva from Ecuador; Orlando Caputo and Enzo Faletto from Chile; Edelberto Torres Rivas from Guatemala; Salvador Maza Zabala and Héctor Malavé from Venezuela; Orlando Fals Borda from Colombia; José Luis Ceceña and Alonso Aguilar from México, and so on.

This complex array of theorists flatly rejected the basic assumptions of modernisation theory. For all of them, without exception, the process of capitalist development in the periphery would never be able to reproduce the features that characterised it in the countries of original development, because with the constitution of the world market, a handful of nations that never were 'underdeveloped' were able to situate themselves in a dominant position that not even remotely could be achieved by the countries of the periphery. 'The developing countries are by no means repeating the history of the developed countries. Historical conditions are different. When the world market was created along with development it was thanks to the action of the "bourgeoisie conquérante"' (Cardoso and Faletto 1967: 24). Thus, the possibilities of capitalist development of the former was strongly dependent upon the impulses and stimuli originating in the latter. As a result, the main decisions regarding what to produce, where and how, and to whom sell, where and how, were not made in the domestic arena but overseas. The very prospects of capitalist development rest in the capacity to articulate the interests and economic endowments of the peripheral nation with the necessities of the leading industrial nations that control the international markets. In this situation, the complex political arrangements which shaped the state and the state apparatuses played a paramount mediating role.

The multidimensionality of the state phenomenon was of crucial importance for dependency theorists. Among the main dimensions to be reckoned with were the following: (a) the state as a 'pact of domination', by which the classes and groups that controlled the wealth of the country and other power resources would seal an agreement that translated into a modality of accumulation best suited to the promotion of their particular interests; (b) the state as the privileged arena of the class struggle and, more generally, of all the existing social contradictions; (c) the state as the complex of apparatuses and institutions, managed by a bureaucracy that could eventually, and under some specific circumstance, develop an interest of its own; (d) the state as the symbolic representative of the 'unity of the nation', above the fractional interests in which civil society was divided, and in the international system (Boron 1995: 284).

Dependency theory gave rise to an impressive number of research projects, books, and articles dealing with the state. As mentioned above, the impetus was so strong that it pervaded American academia. By the late 1970s, 'the state was back in' – a delayed recognition of a reality that had never departed, despite the fact that mainstream social science had decided to ignore it; and studies on 'international political economy' began to flourish in the main departments and research centres. In the specific area of political studies and the state, the work of Guillermo O'Donnell and Fernando H. Cardoso was of extraordinary importance. For the former, it was extraordinary due to his effort to place the state at the centre of the debate, learning from the lessons of the past, and moved by the cruelty and sheer inhumanity of the tyrannies that harassed our countries, starting with the military coup in Brazil in 1964. O'Donnell's reflections on the 'authoritarian-bureaucratic' regimes provided a landmark in the history of the Latin American social sciences. He not only proved the continuing relevance of politics, something disregarded by the modernisation paradigm, but also the close link connecting the new phase of capitalist development – better put, 'dependent-associated' capitalist development, as Fernando H. Cardoso would say – with political authoritarianism and reaction. Yet, O'Donnell's later theorising on the dynamics of the processes of democratisation failed to achieve the same outstanding results, insofar as it paid allegiance to the narrow axioms of mainstream political science: politics is explained by politics; social reality is a collection of independent fragments; political subjects are rational actors; democracy is understood in its Schumpeterian, minimalist version, and so on (Boron 2000: 160–1).

Cardoso's contribution to the study of dependency proved seminal, notwithstanding the fact that much later, as president of Brazil, he allegedly advised his former readers 'to forget everything I wrote'. In spite of his later advice, his early work with Enzo Faletto, which first circulated as a sort of 'semi-clandestine' internal document at the headquarters of CEPAL in Santiago, Chile, in early 1967, still remains one of the landmarks of the dependency movement. Cardoso and Faletto's book superseded the 'economicism' of many of their predecessors who considered dependency as a solely economic phenomenon leaving in the shadows the political, ideological, and social dimensions of it. In all of Cardoso's work, and not only in the book he co-authored with Faletto, dependency appears as something that is not only a kind of 'external' subjection, but a much more complex arrangement of domestic factors and actors intertwined with the world markets and the international states-system. In such an arrangement, the role of the state was of paramount importance. It was important domestically, as the crystallisation of a correlation of social forces promoted a particular modality of capitalist accumulation: it organised a national alliance in which some of its members – the landed bourgeoisie, foreign capital, and banking and merchant interests – pocketed the lion's share, in association with other subordinated dominant strata, especially traditional landowners. But the state also played a key role internationally, because the smooth functioning of the 'export-oriented economies' required a stable and predictable framework and rules of the game, unthinkable without the existence of some form of state organisation.

Of course, these political and 'statist' requirements run through the diverse modalities of capitalist development in the periphery, from the oligarchic state of the export-oriented growth of the late nineteenth century until the Great Depression of 1929, passing through the import-substitution stage, and on to the latest phase marked by globalisation and the internationalisation of domestic markets. But differently from the political science literature that inspired, among others, the work of O'Donnell, in Cardoso the state and the political organisation are always intimately linked to the needs of the process of capitalist accumulation. These linkages are multiple and manifold, and the relationship between economics and politics can never be read in a 'reductionist' fashion. The rationale of the state organisation and intervention is provided by the need to uphold the continuity of an economic process based in surplus extraction, the development of the productive forces and accumulation of capital, and to devise some type of norms and procedures to ensure the smooth operation of a class-biased redistribution of the fruits of economic progress. But all these could be done in a variety of forms that precluded any kind of reductionist argument: export-oriented growth occurred with formal oligarchical democracies (as in Argentina, Chile and Uruguay, for instance) and with traditional dictatorships as in the Mexico of the 'Porfiriato'; import substitution adopted political forms as different as the Chilean Popular Front, the Brazilian corporatist state, Argentine Peronism, or the Mexican Revolution; the internationalisation of the domestic markets took place under the fierce military regimes of the 1970s in most of South America, but also under the two-party democracy in Venezuela, the archaic oligarchic state in Colombia, and the dominance of the PRI (Institutional Revolutionary Party) in Mexico. In sum: there is no room either for 'economicism' or for any sort of 'reductionism'.

GLOBALISATION

The intellectual hegemony of dependency theory was rather short, and the new ideas failed to gain the same degree of acceptance that modernisation theory had enjoyed in the late 1950s. It was short, because the rapid decay of the democratic and developmentalist regimes between the mid-1960s and the Chilean coup of 1973 rapidly destroyed the social and academic basis on which this splendid theoretical creation took place. Scholars and students were exiled, jailed, or disappeared, and public freedoms completely suppressed. On the other hand, dependency theories never reigned uncontested. The diversity of expressions of the mainstream social sciences remained entrenched in Latin America and were able to withstand the rise of their theoretical adversaries. But when the dictatorships started to withdraw from the scene, during the early 1980s, the new intellectual climate dominated by the rise of neoliberalism proved to be too hostile for dependency theorists. Hence one of the great paradoxes of our time: while the Latin American countries steadily accentuated their dependence on foreign powers and international markets, the theorisation of dependence was completely wiped out of the scholarly debate and from the public agenda as well. Instead of dependence and imperialism, globalisation and, allegedly, 'interdependence' took over. Henry Kissinger is reported to have dismissed dependency theory by saying that 'Honduras is as dependent upon American computers as the United States is dependent on Honduran bananas'.

In this world of supposedly balanced interdependence, the states came under heavy attack. Neoliberalism demonised the state and, more generally, political life. In the reactionary intellectual atmosphere of late twentieth century, politics was construed as a 'noise' that alters the calm and cold operation of the marketplace. Politics means irrationality and passions, all of which disrupt the rationality of market calculations. Political competition raises the hopes and expectations of the masses, fuelled by the ambitions and demagoguery of politicians. Little wonder that with the return of democracy, dependency theory was pronounced dead, and that the spoils of the throne began to be fiercely disputed by a variety of schools of thought, all of which were strongly influenced by the new conservative ideas that had seized the United States and most of the European countries during the Reagan and Thatcher years.

Thus, the political science that emerged in our region since the mid 1980s was quite inimical to state theorising and subservient to the neoliberal discourse that had been preaching ceaselessly that the states were institutions in retreat, that international markets had given birth to a new type of borderless capitalism, and that recent years witnessed an impressive and irreversible process of transfer of sovereignty from the old decaying national state to world markets and supranational political organisations like the European Union. Thus, instead of a reflection on the state in our reconstructed democracies, the Latin American social sciences gave rise to an inordinate effort focused on the study of the processes of democratic transition and consolidation approached from quite an orthodox theoretical perspective that largely neglected the crucial role that the states were, and still are, playing in this part of the world. The very poor results of 'transitology' – a complex mixture of rational choice theorising and neo-institutionalist scholarship – are now evident, although a few of us were aware of this already in the mid 1980s (Boron 2000).

Anyway, the predominance of 'transitology' was short-lived. By the 1990s, the insatisfaction with that theoretical scheme prompted its rather unceremonious dismissal. Its place was occupied by the neoliberal economism that asserted that one of the most distinctive aspects of globalisation was the relentless and universal trend towards the weakening role of the states, the downsizing of the state apparatuses, and the trimming of the fiscal budget. Theorists of the Washington Consensus and a host of economic analysts, bankers, public officials, and private entrepreneurs repeatedly argued about the 'reality' of this idea; and its impact in mainstream social science was considerable. In Latin America, the idea that globalisation has irreversibly undermined national states became unquestionable, and the expectations were that, sooner or later, national states would disappear and be replaced by a 'fully globalised' world market. Therefore, it would only be wise to speed up the process of economic opening and state 'downsizing' by systematically reducing governmental spending, firing 'redundant' state employees, and terminating 'populist' social programmes. A complacent political science took due notes of this nonsense.

However, even the most perfunctory analysis of the data regularly produced by the Organisation for Economic Co-operation and Development (OECD), the International Monetary Fund (IMF) or the World Bank has shown that, contrary to this kind of discourse, since the 1980s the overwhelming majority of the industrial democracies increased their public expenditures as a proportion of gross national product (GNP). Not only that; they also augmented their tax revenues, fiscal deficits and public debt, as well as employment in the public sector (Calcagno and Calcagno 1995: 29–31). This blatant disparity provides an enlightened measure of the huge gap that separates the public discourses of the first world's governments and politicians and the concrete policies they apply at home. It goes without saying that the ideological role of the IMF and the World Bank has been to ensure, thanks to the unprecedented leverage offered by the financial vulnerability of the nations in the South, that this neoliberal fairy tale is duly learnt and obeyed by the aboriginal rulers.

A quick glance to the public expenditures in the advanced capitalist nations would prove once again the mythical character of what the leading neoliberal authors have presented as some of the alleged consequences of globalisation: the downsizing of the state and the reduction of public expenditures. If we are to believe these ideologues, globalisation would imply the inexorable privatisation of state enterprises, the dismantling of the public sector, and massive cuts in the public budget. This set of policies is the only one that would make possible the mature insertion of the peripheral economies in the highly competitive world economy, a world of unfettered free markets, total mobility of capital, and a very limited range of state interventions. Yet, at shown in Table 10.1, these assertions are just ideological commonplaces of the right, unable to resist the most elementary empirical confrontation.

Table 10.1   Total governmental expenditure of industrialised countries, 1970–95 (% of GNP at market prices)

Country	1970	1980	1990	1995
Austria	39.2	48.8	49.3	52.7
France	38.9	46.6	50.5	54.1
West Germany	38.5	48.0	45.3	49.1[a]
Italy	34.2	41.9	53.2	53.5
Japan	19.4	32.6	32.3	34.9
Sweden	43.7	61.2	60.7	69.4
United Kingdom	37.3	43.2	40.3	42.5
United States	31.6	33.7	36.7	36.1

[a] Data of the unified German state.
Source: Thompson (1997: 167).

These data show that, in the 'really existing capitalisms', the size of the state, as measured by the proportion of total public expenditure to GNP, never ceased to grow. What really happened in the 1980s was that the pace of growth slowed down, especially when compared with the very high figures of the postwar years, but the size of the state did not collapse, or radically shrink, as a result of neoliberal policies (Boron 1997: 186–8, 224–8). The British case shows some peculiarities, which nonetheless fail to challenge the general conclusion. Despite their inflamed neoliberal rhetoric, the governmental record of Margaret Thatcher and John Major shows that the 'downsizing' of British public expenditure was less than 1 per cent of GNP. This proves that in consolidated democracies – as different from weak, transitional ones like in Latin America – there are severe and quite insurmountable limits to any attempt to roll back public expenditures to pre-Keynesian levels. The reason for this inflexibility is easy to understand: the popular advancements in terms of social rights and effective provision of public goods coagulated in the Keynesian state in the postwar period became fundamental, non-negotiable chapters in the new social contract of advanced capitalist nations, which no change in the electoral correlation of social forces could unmake. Thatcher was especially blind when faced with this fact, and she paid the price for this mistake. In the United States, the 'Keynesian social contract' lacked the strength and extension known in Europe. Yet, despite the electoral promises and threatening talk of Ronald Reagan and George Bush during the years of republican hegemony, total public expenditures, civilian and military, increased by three percentage points. This expansive trend was also at work in traditionally cautious Japan and, with more strident overtones, in Europe.

At the beginning of the 1990s, the proportion of public employees over the total population was 7.2 per cent in the United States, 8.3 per cent in Germany, 8.5 per cent in the United Kingdom, and 9.7 per cent in France. Meanwhile, in the lands where neoliberal adjustment reigned supreme, Latin America, the violent and irresponsible policies of state dismantling – disguised under the honourable name of 'state reform' – resulted in public employees representing only 3.5 per cent of the population in Brazil and 2.8 per cent in Chile and Argentina. It should be remembered that in these latter three countries, nearly half the population lacks sewerage or safe, clean water in their homes, and that public hospitals and public schools are scarce, understaffed and unable to cope with the popular demand. Despite all this, the pundits at the World Bank or the IMF have successfully insisted that Latin American states are 'too big' and should be downsized (Calcagno and Calcagno 1995: 29–31).

The supposedly 'technical' counsel supplied by the neoliberal ideologues has no connection with reality, and seems to be a rhetorical strategy aimed at influencing and manipulating the 'weakest links' of the imperialist chain in favour of the 'fat cats' of the international economy. As the Latin American experience shows, the liquidation of public enterprises (in almost all the cases at prices well below the real ones!) and the enfeeblement of the state produced a cascade of windfall profits for transnational firms, the creditor banks and their local allies. The comparative figures above on state expenditures strongly support John Williamson's contention that 'Washington not always practices what it preaches' (Williamson 1990: 17). Not only Washington: neither in Bonn, Rome, Paris, or Tokyo does so-called 'state reform' (a euphemism for massive lay-offs of public employees and wild budgetary cuts) command respect in governmental circles.

This was confirmed a few years ago by a special report of a journal like *The Economist*, hardly suspicious of any sympathy with any kind of socialist or *dirigiste* thought. The title of the report is quite telling: 'The Visible Hand'. After a careful analysis of the most recent data on public expenditure in OECD countries, the article concludes that 'big government is still in charge'. Despite the 'neoliberal reforms' launched between 1980, when orthodox economic policies of austerity and fiscal equilibrium were established, and 1996, the public expenditure of the 14 most advanced nations in the OECD climbed from 43.3 per cent to 47.1 per cent of GNP (*The Economist*, 1997: 8). The author of the special report, Clive Crook, regretfully concluded that '[t]he growth of the governments of the advanced economies in the last forty years has been persistent, universal and counterproductive ... In the West the progress towards a smaller government has been more apparent than real' (Crook 1997: 48).

The problem with the Latin American states is neither their sheer size nor the magnitude of their public expenditures, but the fact that they are weak, deformed, macrocephalic, plagued by a chronic financial feebleness and ridden with corruption. Compared with the European capitalist states, ours look like monstrous and vicious dwarfs: they are quantitatively small, completely out of proportion, inefficient, and corrupt. This picture recognises important national variations, especially as far as corruption is concerned, but the overall characterisation is valid.

Historical evidence shows that there is no route to development, capitalist or otherwise, that does not require a strong state as a prerequisite. By 'strong' obviously we do not mean what the Latin American right has always considered: an authoritarian or despotic government always ready to repress the popular classes, disband unions, close parliaments, suppress the freedoms, and always equally more than acquiescent to play a servile role with foreign capitalists and the local elites. By 'strong' we mean the development of the state capacities necessary to govern civil society (a society divided along antagonistic class lines) and to discipline the markets and the economic agents, including first of all the dominant classes. A state of this sort requires solid democratic legitimacy, without which its strength would be inexorably undermined (Weiss 1997: 15–17, 1998). 'Strong' to carry safe water to the 1.5 billion people in the third world who lack it and whose chances of getting it through the operation of market forces is nil. Who would invest money to carry safe water to the poorest among the poor, people living at the sheer subsistence level, housed in shacks in occupied public lands, without any kind of property title, chronically unemployed and suffering from an incredible educational deficit that made them unemployable in the current economy? In Mexico, for instance, 13 million people are in this situation, and 27 million lack sewers.[2] Who but the state, as long as it is free from mercantile logic, could be in charge to meet these demands?

Let us summarise our point by criticising the widespread belief in contemporary Latin American social theories that the main actors of the globalised economic scene, the huge mega-corporations, have become independent from any national base and achieved a truly transnational character. This misconception seems to ignore even the most elementary pieces of empirical information concerning the modern corporate world. For instance, how to reconcile these supposedly supranational features with the fact that less than 2 per cent of the members of the boards of directors of American and European mega-corporations are 'foreigners' and that less than 15 per cent of all their technological developments are carried out outside their respective home countries? In other words, despite its worldwide reach, Boeing or Exxon are American corporations, as Volkswagen and Siemens are German, and Sony and Toyota are Japanese. If their interests are threatened by unfriendly governments or disloyal competitors it is not the Security Council or the General Assembly of the United Nations which steps in, but the American, German, and Japanese ambassadors. Quoting a survey made by the business magazine *Fortune*, Noam Chomsky argued that all of the 100 more important transnational firms of the world included in the research declared that they benefited, in one way or another, by the supportive intervention of the governments of their base country. Twenty per cent of these firms were rescued from total bankruptcy by governmental intervention (Chomsky 1998, Kapstein 1991/92). With data like these, how is it be possible to talk about the 'withering away of the state'!

GLOBALISATION VERSUS SOVEREIGNTY?

The strength and pace of economic globalisation, especially in financial sectors but also affecting all the other branches of the economy in different degrees, and the persistent 'tax veto' of local financial and industrial oligarchies in Latin America, which do not feel obliged to pay taxes, brought about a radical weakening of the national states. It must be added that foreign firms quite rapidly 'adjusted' to this historical pattern by which the offspring of the Iberic *conquistadores* regarded the payment of taxes as something improper of their status. This situation prompted the lessening of their administrative and decision-making capacities, a decline in the quality of governance and growing levels of vulnerability in front of an increasingly complex domestic and international environment. The radical enfeeblement of Latin America's new democracies caused an abhorrent distortion in the order of preference of their responsiveness: governments in the region are, first and foremost, responsive to the interests of the foreign creditors and the key sections of international capital and its 'watchdogs': the World Bank and the IMF; second, they respond to the domestic 'market forces', a euphemism for big capital and firms, local or foreign, operating in our markets; third, and much less so, to the citizenry and civil society at large. The problem is that it is very hard to conceive of a solid democracy without reaching a minimum threshold of national sovereignty, where one can make autonomous decisions in crucial matters that can have alternative distributional impacts. Given the formidable reach of globalisation, and the reinforcement of financial dependence due to external debt, a democracy sitting on a weak state increasingly deprived of decisional autonomy is likely to decay.

The globalisation of economic activities caused the new Latin American democracies to surrender important margins of national sovereignty and self-determination, de facto and sometimes legally transferring decision-making powers, in a growing number of sensitive areas, to transnational firms and international financial institutions under the guise of commercial agreements, 'conditionalities' and 'country risk' evaluations. Monetary, industrial, commercial, and fiscal policies, hitherto largely decided within the national boundaries of Latin America, are today settled in distant scenarios – mostly in New York, Washington, London, Paris, Tokyo – far removed from the reach, let alone the control, of the 'sovereign' citizenry, impotent to counter the harmful effects of the globalised economy and mostly unable to take advantage of the scarce opportunities it brings to the poor.

Were these processes of globalisation and state enfeeblement neutral in terms of their distributional impacts? As a matter of fact, local capitalists and their metropolitan partners obtained several gains from the dramatic 'downsizing' of the old developmentalist state and its declining sovereign powers. First, they significantly reinforced their economic predominance by drastically reducing the public control of the markets and economic activities established in previous times, and by undermining both the consistency and scope of the public sphere itself. Today, Latin American societies have also become highly 'privatised': the state has retreated to minimal functions, and former collective goods – health, nutrition, education, housing, occupational training, and so on – have become individual problems that must be solved according to the egotistic rules of the market. The name of the game is the survival of the fittest; the rest, the poor, the elderly, the children, the sick, the homeless, the unemployed and unemployable are the new clients of the Red Cross and the host of non-governmental organisations. Private charity and altruistic associations substituted for supposedly cost-ineffective social policies and state intervention.

Second, the withering away of national states and the wholesale privatisation of state-owned enterprises (SOEs) and state-administered services transferred highly profitable monopolies to the capitalists and granted the repayment of the foreign debt contracted – as in Argentina, Brazil, Chile, Uruguay, and many others – by irresponsible, corrupt and de facto military rulers. Neoliberalism supplied the general justification for the transfer of public assets and SOEs, paid for with public savings, even in areas considered 'taboo' and untouchable until a few years ago, like electricity, aviation, oil or telephones.

Third, these reforms changed in such a dramatic manner the balance between state and markets in favour of the latter that the 'degrees of freedom' of any future government sensitive to the popular demands, or inspired by even some vague reformist vocation, will (a) immediately realise that it lacks some of the most elementary instruments of public policy-making, as well as the efficient administrative cadres to carry out these tasks; and (b) rapidly fall to its knees, overwhelmed by the weight of a formidable capitalist coalition. This is why one of the most urgent tasks facing Latin American societies is the reconstruction of the state. As a former minister of industry in Venezuela rightly observed, by the end of the 1990s, 'Washington may encounter some surprises to the South. Latin America, which has spent the last 10 years demolishing the state, will spend the next 10 rebuilding it' (Naim 1993). He was absolutely right.

CONCLUSION

In the last 50 years Latin American social thought had passed from statelessness to statelessness. The neglect of the state that modernisation theories exhibited in the 1950s and early 1960s was to be matched in the last decades of the twentieth century by a similar disregard expressed by theories of globalisation. It does not take a genius to anticipate that such neglect will not help to strengthen our intellectual capacities to understand what is going on in the world today, and much less to provide a safe 'guide for action' to the groups and organisations interested in building a new, more humane and fair, social order. An urgent reorientation is needed to meet the challenges of our time. This reorientation does not mean to assume a naive 'statist' conception that would ignore the formidable challenges affecting national sovereignty in the periphery, the complexity of modern capitalism, the vitality of markets and other types of institutions, and the growing importance of civil society. The progress made by the new theories in the 1960s and part of the 1970s provides a good launching pad for this kind of programme.

But being a necessary starting point, they are not sufficient to cope with the new challenges and contradictions facing the states in our time. Nor will they be able to provide accurate tools to recognise the changing morphology of the state apparatuses, the attack of global market forces against national sovereignty, or the new instruments of state intervention in all aspects of social life. We are, therefore, at the beginning of a great intellectual and practical enterprise, and only time will tell if we succeed or not.

NOTES

1. I wish to thank Gladys Lechini for her comments and criticisms in the preparation of this chapter. Responsibility for any errors remains my own.
2. See *Jornal Excelsior* (1999), 'Unos 500 Millones de Habitantes de 29 Países Padecen Escasez de Agua', 19 March, 3-A: 40, www.excelsior.com.mx.

REFERENCES

Boron, Atilio A. (1995), *State, Capitalism and Democracy in Latin America*. Boulder, CO: Lynn Rienner.

Boron, Atilio A. (1997), 'La Sociedad Civil Después del Diluvio Neoliberal', in *La Trama del Neoliberalismo*, ed. E. Sader and P. Gentili. Buenos Aires: Oficina de Publicaciones del CBC.

Boron, Atilio A. (2000), *Tras el Búho de Minerva: Mercados contra Democracia en el Capitalismo de Fin de Siglo*. Buenos Aires: Fondo de Cultura Económica.

Calcagno, Alfredo E., and Alfredo F. Calcagno (1995), *El Universo Neoliberal: Recuento de sus Lugares Comunes*. Madrid and Buenos Aires: Alianza Editorial.

Cardoso, Fernando Henrique, and Enzo Faletto (1979), *Dependency and Development in Latin America*. Berkeley: University of California Press.

Casanova, Pablo González (1965), *La Democracia en México*. México: Ediciones ERA.

Chomsky, Noam (1998), *Noam Chomsky Habla de América Latina*. Buenos Aires: Editorial 21.

Dahrendorf, Ralph (1959), *Class and Class Conflict in Industrial Society*. Stanford, CA: Stanford University Press.

Dahrendorf, Ralph (1958), 'Out of Utopia: Towards a Re-Orientation of Sociological Analysis', *American Journal of Sociology*, 64(2): 115–27.

Crook, Clive (1997), 'The Future of the State', *The Economist*, 20–26 September.

Germani, Gino (1962), *Política y Sociedad en una Época de Transición*. Buenos Aires: Paidós.

Germani, Gino (1966), *Sociología de la Modernización*. Buenos Aires: Paidós.

Germani, Gino, ed. (1985), *Los límites de la Democracia*. Buenos Aires: CLACSO.

Kapstein (1991/92), 'We Are Us: The Myth of the Multinational', *The National Interest* (Winter): 56–62.

Naim, Moisés (1993), 'Latin America: Post-Adjustment Blues', *Foreign Policy*, 92 (Autumn): 133–150.

Rostow, Walt Whitman (1960), *The Stages of Economic Growth: A Non-Communist Manifesto*. Cambridge: Cambridge University Press.

Solari, Aldo, Rolando Franco and Joel Jutkowitz (1976), *Teoría, Acción Social y Desarrollo en América Latina*. Mexico: Siglo XXI.

Thompson, Grahame (1997), '"Globalization" and the Possibilities for Domestic Economic Policy', *Internationale Politik und Gesellschaft*, 2: 161–71.

Weiss, Linda (1997), 'Globalization and the Myth of the Powerless State', *New Left Review*, 225: 3–27.

Weiss, Linda (1998), *The Myth of the Powerless State: Governing the Economy in the Global Era*. Cambridge: Polity Press.

Williamson, John (1990), *What Washington Means by Policy Reform*. Washington, DC: Institute for International Economics.

11
The National Question and the Autonomy of the State in Bolivia

Lorgio Orellana Aillón

INTRODUCTION

The popular uprising of October 2003, against a multinational gas project, created the opportunity for a revolutionary situation in Bolivia (Trotsky 1985: 177–8, Tilly 2006: 159, Moyo and Yeros 2007). The formation of organs of popular power, based on neighbourhood associations in El Alto and Aymara peasant unions from the Highlands in La Paz, opened the way to a duality of power.

The struggles of peasants and impoverished urban workers against multinational petroleum firms and the neoliberal government of Gonzalo Sanchez de Losada were inspired by perspectives of a democratic and nationalist character. Their slogans included, for example, the 'defence of Bolivian gas', the 'nationalisation and industrialisation of hydrocarbons', and the establishment of a 'Constituent National Assembly to reverse indigenous exclusion'.

The coming to office of the MAS (Movimiento al Socialismo), led by Evo Morales, in January 2006, signalled the end of the revolutionary situation. This meant an end to political struggles against the state and multinational companies (MNCs), even though the fundamentals of neoliberal politics had not been transformed. The preservation of 'macroeconomic stability' through restrictive monetary controls, seeking a low inflation rate, and the independence of the Central Bank, were dogmas of previous governments which became part of the ideology and political practices of the current administration. In turn, the so-called 'nationalisation of hydrocarbons' continues to cede control over gas and petroleum to MNCs for a period of 30 years (CEDLA 2006: 63–74).

Soon after the resolution of the contradictions between MNCs and the MAS government, there emerged a 'new front' in the east, in the form of civic committees and Department (provincial) governments, both led by the local bourgeoisie opposed to the central government.

Central government and opposition quarrelled over the distribution of benefits generated from the tax on hydrocarbon production, as well as the control of the state apparatus. Paraphrasing Mao Tse Tung, the Morales government resolved an external contradiction to confront an internal contradiction.

This chapter seeks to explain the specific nature of the political situation that emerged with the Morales government, as well as its relation to the revolutionary situation of October 2003. The key question is this: why has the MAS government stabilised conflicts between the state, MNCs and the subaltern classes, notwithstanding the preservation of neoliberal politics and imperialist control over raw materials?

THE ORIGINS OF THE NATIONAL QUESTION IN BOLIVIA

What was typical of the era of bourgeois democratic revolutions, affirms Lenin (1962: 610–11), was the rise of national movements and the incorporation of peasants to fight for political freedom in general and the rights of the nation in particular. National movements arose together with the struggles for freedom and equality of human beings before the law (Greenfeld, quoted in Diekhoff and Jaffrelot 2006: 16). They opposed the old regime and advocated changes of a bourgeois democratic nature (Lenin 1962: 606).

The emergence of nationalism was related to the requirements of capitalism in conquering the internal market. The political perspective of nationalism was defined by the interest of the national bourgeoisie in a process of expansion: 'for a complete victory of mercantile production, it is necessary that the bourgeoisie conquers the internal market, and it is necessary that territories with people of a single language acquire state cohesion' (Lenin 1962: 606, my translation). When the form of the national state over populations and territories was consolidated in Western Europe, the era of bourgeois democratic national movements came to an end.

But in the 'East', the national question emerged in a different way, because of the specific modality of capitalist development there. 'The main communication routes of Russian commerce', wrote Trotsky, 'led to the exterior, thereby assuring finance capital, since ages ago, the controlling position and giving all operations a semi-colonial character, in which the Russian trader was reduced to an intermediary role between western cities and the Russian village' (1985: 34, my translation).

The commitments of the comprador bourgeoisie to international finance capital and Czarism made improbable its conversion into a leader in the struggle for political independence and national self-determination. In contrast to what transpired in the 'West', in the 'East' the bourgeoisie was one of the greatest impediments to democratic transformation, as popular aspirations and struggles for independence and political equality found themselves in conflict with this class. Paradoxically, national movements of a bourgeois democratic nature were in contradiction with the bourgeoisie itself.

The complex configuration of the national question in Bolivia approximates the modalities that the classics attributed to the 'East'. Given the relations of servitude, which were the greatest obstacle to the development of the productive forces, the shortest path to capitalist development was through commercial intermediation in the world market and exploitation of raw materials (see Cueva 1982). It was neither the internal market that formed the basis of capitalist expansion, nor a revolutionary national bourgeoisie, but the relationship of the comprador class to international finance capital.

The emergence of new economic, social and political realities, tied to capitalist expropriation, enabled the revival of archaic forms of stratification, not their cancellation (Fernandez 1985). The portrait that Almaraz (1988: 89) presents of the old oligarchic power structure is illustrative in this sense: '[w]ith Arce and Pacheco and the [capitalist] miners of 1870, [political power] was almost feudal. They pass from the mine directly to the government; the boundaries are imprecise, they juxtapose and confuse … Power was exercised directly from the miner to the governor, from the oligarch to the president, without intermediate structures' (my translation).

The class and ethnic monopoly of office, that is, the status-based form of power, was one of the characteristics of the old oligarchic society, within a socio-economic structure where the appropriation of the surplus assumed specific political forms. Payment of tribute to the state by the immense native majority predominated, together with a pattern of accumulation based on the exploitation and the export of raw materials (Valenzuela 1990: 65).

The crystallisation of a stratus-based political power was intimately related to the enclaves of production and exploitation of raw materials, surrounded by feudal relations of production. National movements emerged from the inherent contradictions of this social structure. In the words of Agustin Cueva (1982: 158, my translation), the appearance of a proletarian character in the struggles of workers only happens in the post-oligarchic phase, that is, when the structural matrix itself was evolving into a class structure increasingly capitalist in its direction. Before, even the sectors that were strictly proletarian found themselves immersed in a very particular context, characterised by placing the opposition oligarchy/people in the forefront that constituted, so to speak, the location of the confluence of the distinct democratic struggles.

The era of national movements in Bolivia spans the epoch of the old oligarchic society, when the pattern of accumulation based on the exploitation and export of raw materials predominated, and where the state governed through the forms, practices, habits, and values of status-based social relations. This was a pre-democratic society, politically and juridically unequal. The structural character of this social order allows us to understand the intrinsic dynamics of the class struggles of this period, and more fundamentally, the democratic orientation of the popular movements.

According to René Zavaleta, it is with the National Revolution of 1952 that the state conquered its relative autonomy: '[n]ever was the Bolivian state so universal in this territory and over this population' (1983: 29, my translation). Until then, the power had been controlled 'without intermediate structures' by the mining oligarchy and landlords. The armed uprising by workers and the peasant occupations of *latifundios* expropriated the dominant classes, to impose a nationalisation of the mines and agrarian reform. However, the scarce surplus generated in a society in which labour of low productivity prevailed led to the restoration of the financial links with imperialism, making difficult the development of the internal market and industry; thus, the path for the development of a modern capitalist hegemony was obstructed. 'The nucleus of 1952 shows an important degree of political self-determination in a very backward scenario, even though it is certain that this self-impulsion gave way almost immediately to the coercion of the external conditions' (Zavaleta 1986: 13, my translation).

Needless to say, the Agrarian Reform of 1953 did not resolve the agrarian question, or the oppression of the native nationalities, but it did modify its terms: land distribution gave way to a large mass of small proprietors and the proliferation of the *minifundio* in the Altiplano and the Valleys. Meanwhile, in the eastern part of the country, there appeared new *junkers*, who benefited from the land donations undertaken by the military governments during the period of oligarchic restoration which began in the 1960s.

The broad relative autonomy of the state that was conquered by the revolution would be progressively restricted, first, through the credit plans promoted by US imperialism and, then, by the military regimes that, with a few constitutional lapses, extended from 1964 to 1982. The restriction of the relative autonomy of the state took place in a context of repression against working class movements and the left intelligentsia, and with the support of peasants – the so-called 'military-peasant deal'.

In a balance of power unfavourable to the subaltern classes, the 'oligarchisation of the political power' (Zavaleta 1986: 259) implied the reinstatement of class and ethnic monopoly over state positions. From 1985 onwards, the new constitutional governments did not change the power structure established under the previous dictatorships, but on the contrary, they strengthened it: the emerging political parties, now legitimated by national elections, represented the interests of the new oligarchy, formed during the dictatorships. For its part, the military abandoned political office and returned to the barracks to become the 'guarantors of the democratic regime', that is, the new power structure constituted during the dictatorships (see Orellana 2006: 20). In this restricted 'system of political parties', which political scientists call 'moderate pluralism', the elections paradoxically enabled the reproduction of the class and ethnic monopoly of office.

The deepening of the neoliberal reforms since 1986, inaugurated during the military regimes, promoted the conditions for new alliances between the new oligarchy and MNCs, within a relation of forces unfavourable to subaltern classes. It is clear that the implementation of neoliberalism in Bolivia since 1986 was the culmination of the oligarchic restoration initiated by military regimes since the mid 1960s.

From the perspective of the *longue durée*, the revolutionary situation of October 2003 should be seen as the continuation of the National Revolution of 1952. Neoliberalism updated the contradictions immanent in the old oligarchic system, which led to a new eruption.

THE NATIONAL QUESTION UNDER NEOLIBERALISM

The theoretical problem that frames the struggle of national movements for political equality and political independence in

Bolivia – self-determination – concerns the relative autonomy of the state from the dominant classes. This relative autonomy of the modern bourgeois state, in contrast to previous status-based societies characterised by a class monopoly over political office, consists in the '"apparent separation" of the state from civil society' (Clarke, quoted in Burnham 2006: 98). By fighting for self-determination, political independence and formal equality, bourgeois democratic movements fight for state autonomy, under specific conditions.

The subjection of the Bolivian economic space to North American imperialism, through the exploitation and export of raw materials during the neoliberal era, exacerbated the contradiction between the formal autonomy of the capitalist state (its political sovereignty) and its real subjection to the world economy (Evers 1989: 107). This escalated the contradiction between the functions of accumulation and legitimisation of the capitalist state, that is, between policies that promoted the expansion of multinational capital in Bolivia and the nationalist ideology which justified the supremacy of a specific alliance of classes. In this context, democratic and national movements struggled to achieve self-determination, political sovereignty, and formal equality (Lenin 1962: 606) vis-à-vis imperialism and a local oligarchy which controlled state positions, public policies, and natural resources.

The indigenous-peasant party, the MAS, led these claims, but also brought to a close the revolutionary conjuncture upon its ascent to power in January 2006, via popular elections. The basic difference between this government and previous ones, which explains the stabilisation of internal (class/race) and external (contra MNCs) conflicts, is that the Morales government has augmented the relative autonomy of the state with respect to the dominant classes. This has contributed to overcoming the conflicts between accumulation and legitimisation, that is, the struggles between the state authorities, the owners of MNCs and the subaltern classes.

Conditions of the Oligarchic Society under Neoliberalism

The uneven and combined development of capitalism, accompanied by the destruction of the productive forces, is the general condition of the historic regression that has led to the current configuration of social forces in Bolivia. Uneven development is visible through the export of metropolitan capital to Bolivia. In the beginning of the 1990s (in 1992, specifically), 22.44 per cent of foreign direct investment (FDI) was oriented towards hydrocarbons, 66.26 per cent to minerals, 10.71 per cent to industry, and 0.5 per cent to services (MCE 1999: 3). Nevertheless, at the beginning of the millennium (2003), 59.23 per cent of FDI was directed to hydrocarbons, 20 per cent to the commercial and service sectors, 11 percent to manufacturing, and 3.6 percent to mining. US firms are the main investors in Bolivia: in 1996–2003, the composition of FDI included the United States with 34 per cent, Europe with 33 per cent and South America with 25 per cent (Pereira Stambuk and Tavera Laffertt 2007: 36).

The dominance of US capital has been particularly strong in the hydrocarbons sector. For example, during the period 1996–2003, 43 per cent of US direct investments went to the hydrocarbons sector, more than double that of Argentine investments, whose participation in the sector represents 21 per cent. The climax of these investments was in 1996–97, during the privatisation of state-owned enterprises (SOEs). At that time, US investments came to represent 62–64 per cent of total FDI during those two years, while Argentine investments represented 9 per cent in 1996 and 29 per cent in 1997.[1]

These percentages demonstrate one of the essential features of the social structure of capitalism in Bolivia, that is, the exploitation of the Bolivian economic space by US imperialism through the control of raw materials. This is an essential characteristic of the oligarchic society, according to the definition of Cueva (1982: 144). The difference between the present and the past is that this domination is established through the hydrocarbons sector, while throughout nearly the whole of the twentieth century, imperial economic dominance occurred through mining. The other feature is that multinational capital has expanded into the tertiary sector, while in the 1970s it had an important participation in industry (De La Cueva 1983: 69). Both phenomena have modified the capitalist power structure in Bolivia.

Historically, the reconfiguration of the power bloc has been linked to new demands by metropolitan capital, which partly explains regional conflicts. According to Evers, the rise and fall of domestic fractions of the bourgeoisie in countries of the periphery is related to new forms of imperialist penetration (Evers 1989: 28). The privatisation of SOEs during the second half of the 1990s corroborates this observation.

Whereas in 1996, the Department (province) of La Paz captured 25.8 per cent of FDI and that of Santa Cruz, 31.8 per cent; two years later, La Paz captured only 12.69 per cent and Santa Cruz, 53.78 per cent. Since 2002, there has been a regional shift in foreign investment and consequently in private interests, local and foreign:

41.13 per cent of foreign investments were directed to Tarija, 33.92 per cent to Santa Cruz and 11.17 per cent to La Paz.[2]

These material processes have led to the historic decline of La Paz as the dominating centre of capitalists in Bolivia, allowing the rise of Santa Cruz as a regional competitor for capitalist hegemony. This is one of the principal socio-economic conditions of the regionalist movement, termed 'half moon', which in the post-insurrection period of October 2003 threatened to separate the eastern part of the country, and which today is the principal force of opposition to the MAS government. The regional conflict, therefore, has one of its roots in the dynamics of unequal development.

Another enabling condition for the current configuration of forces is the destruction of the forces of production. The neoliberal reinforcement of the pattern of accumulation based on the production and export of raw materials has disarticulated industrial activities (see Basualdo and Arceo 2006: 23) and has led to the revival of pre-capitalist forms of production. To illustrate this, we may look at the example of El Alto, the city which became the epicentre of the October 2003 uprisings. In 2003, the Census of Economic Enterprises conducted by the Chamber of Industries of La Paz (2004: 18) indicated that, of a total of 5,045 enterprises in El Alto, 4,571 were 'micro-industries', that is, economic units with less than five workers. Furthermore, 390 units were 'small-scale companies' (5–19 workers); 50 were 'medium-scale' (20–49 workers); and only 34 enterprises were 'large' companies with more than 50 workers. In 2003, in the town of El Alto, 90 per cent of economic units involved labour processes of a craft character. This reality contrasts with the high concentrations of workers which dominated in the manufacturing sector until the mid 1980s.

The case of El Alto is similar to the reproduction of small peasant and craft enterprises in other regions of the country, which have all resulted from a dynamic process of economic regression in the social structure. The neoliberal reinforcement of the pattern of accumulation based on the production and export of raw materials has modified the composition of social classes, the character of the social forces, and the configuration of political power in Bolivia.

The Oligarchic State

The nucleus of the new power structure, consolidated in August 1985, came to be organised around the two most important political parties of the neoliberal era: the Nationalist Revolutionary Movement (MNR) and Nationalist Democratic Action (AND). The interests of the mining bourgeoisie, the agro-industrial bourgeoisie in the East and the financial and commercial bourgeoisies were represented by these political parties (Toranzos 1989: 569).

Between the end of the 1970s and the beginning of the 1980s, the mining fraction of the bourgeoisie was the dominant one, evident not only in its economic power or the presence of its representatives in state offices, but principally in its influence in the definition of economic policies. In the words of Contreras and Pacheco (1989: 22, my translation),

> [w]ithout a doubt, the SD 21060 [the Supreme Decree which officially marked the beginning of neoliberalism in Bolivia] – whose formulation counted on the participation of members of the ANMM [National Medium-Scale Miners Association] and whose principal agent and advocate is a prominent member of medium-scale miners, Gonzalo Sánchez de Lozada – drew up many of the proposals implemented by medium-scale miners in 1981. Therefore, it can be argued that the greatest achievement of the ANMM, and of the medium-scale miners in general, was to contribute to the change of the model currently in force and to implement the SD 21060.

The fall in mineral prices in the international market in the 1980s also provoked the decline of mining activity in Bolivia and the modification of the upper stratum of capitalist rule. The decline of mining capital contrasts with the rise of commercial agriculture and agro-industry in the east of the country in the 1990s, devoted to the production of derivatives and the commercialisation of soy beans (Perez 2007). Today, it is in this region that the principal financial, commercial and service activities are located, as well as the headquarters of the multinational oil and gas firms. Paraphrasing Cueva (1982: 44), this is the new setting of the alliances between the local capitalist landlords, the comprador bourgeoisie, and monopoly capital in extractive activities – the power bloc that constitutes the primordial class base of the oligarchic state.

The richest men in the country have been ministers or presidents of the Republic, in one or another of the six successive governments that ruled from 1985 until 2003. They came from the banks, mining, agro-industry and commerce, and, in alliance with international monopoly capital, ruled for nearly two decades prior to the insurrection of October 2003.

Locally, private businessmen pushed for neoliberal reforms in Bolivia, together with a new bureaucratic technocracy, trained in the tradition of neoclassical economics in prestigious North American universities, or in consultancies with international financial institutions. They have constituted the fractions and intellectual leaders that, given their class interests and cultural values, have articulated with international finance capital, with multinational firms and the international credit agencies.

The relatively restricted access to high positions in the state, monopolised by a small group of privileged families, related by innumerable economic, social and cultural ties, confirms the observation by Fernandez that the type of capitalist development that unfolded in countries like Bolivia revived status-based relations, such as those that characterise the 'monopoly of office'. The higher posts of the state were largely occupied by businessmen, descendants from the old landlord classes, linked together by family relations and racial identities that until today continue to establish the criteria of differentiation and cultural and social reproduction of each dominant group in Bolivia.

The perennial character of the oligarchic ideology – 'a cast so mysteriously alien from its own place' (Zavaleta 1986: 209) – nourishes itself by the innumerable relations that the bourgeois has forged through its constant links with international finance capital. Their concept of the world and their values, that is, the basic ideology of the men of neoliberalism, has been forged through the experience defined by their own way of life and practices: 'I was bred in it [the free market economy], I have lived in it, I could not conceive of another alternative, because I saw the successes of the open economy, around the world', said an ex-Minister of Hydrocarbons of the Sanchez de Losada government, in interview.[3] His political and cultural horizon is circumscribed by his own class conditions, in general, and those of his class fraction, in particular, overlaid by international finance capital whose range of operation is precisely the world. Working as an employee of an MNC, the ex-minister has travelled so much that there is not a single country in the world that he has not known. From his perspective, something like the 'national question' would be a simple anachronism.

'I am not precisely a "Bolivian militant"', said another interviewee, the ex-Secretary of the Presidency in the last government of Gonzalo Sanchez de Losada and a descendant of the old Benian oligarchy.[4] His higher education was obtained in a prestigious Spanish university; he recounted that, from his early childhood, it was a question of common sense in his family that he would undertake his higher education abroad.

Like the rest of the neoliberal leaders of bourgeois extraction interviewed, this interlocutor undertook large part of his studies and spent much of his life overseas, a fact that permeated his values and his own view of the world. At the lunch table, the lady of the house spoke to her daughter in French. The little one attended a French school in La Paz. French culture was truly appreciated in this home. On the walls of the house there were cut-outs of magazines that related the death of the French painter Toulouse Lautrec. As in Zavaleta's (1986) characterisation of oligarchic ideology, xenophilia appeared over and over again in our interviews and ethnographic annotations, when we studied the dominant social categories.

It is understandable that a relation of international domination, such as imperialism, would be seen as natural by someone who has worked for the larger part of his life in multinational firms, or as a consultant of international credit agencies, who has been raised in an 'open economy' and has seen 'its successes' in other countries. Ideologically, this is the most adequate agent for the implementation of economic policies favourable to the established structure of power. Not only will he promote these policies, convinced that such policies will bring success to his country, he will also defend them.

His convictions reveal the hegemonic radius of US imperialism, realised in practice in the neoliberal period. Fiscal policy is an adequate variable to verify the ideological power to which we refer. According to official data, between 1980 and 1986, sales of goods and services by SOEs constituted 77.1 per cent of state revenues (CEDLA 2005: 52). After the privatisation of SOEs in 1998–2002, the contribution of privatised enterprises did not reach 5 per cent of the income of the National Treasury (CEDLA 2005: 46). The drastic reduction of state income conduced to a higher dependence by the state on international credit. Thus, based on its analysis of the Proposed General Budget (PGB) for 2002, CEDLA (2005: 31) concludes:

> Annually, from expenditures to the PGB, the state obtains more than US$1,100 equivalent to almost 40 per cent of the total income. These resources will finance the greater part of public investment and part of the expenses for public administration, and are constituted 60 per cent of external debt, 25 per cent by internal debt and the remaining 15 per cent by donations. (my translation)

In the higher levels of political power, the justification for reducing the taxation of multinational firms was to offer attractive conditions to foreign investors in a country that fell outside the international financial circuit – that is, despite the fact that the state would remain without enough resources to guarantee its normal functions. They reasoned as businessmen instead of as state authorities.

What helps to explain the crisis of 2003 in Bolivia is the restriction of the relative autonomy of the state with respect to the dominant classes. The invasion of capitalist rationality into state institutions ruptured the functional logic of the same institutions, their specificity as organs that guarantee political domination and promote the obedience of subaltern classes – that is, produce legitimacy (Orellana 2006: 22).

THE IDEOLOGY OF NATIONAL MOVEMENTS IN BOLIVIA

The contradiction between the functions of accumulation and legitimation in the oligarchic state is evident in the motives that inspired the Aymara peasant critique of neoliberal economic practices. The moral that guides these perspectives emanates from very concrete material processes and practices, which are apparent, for example, in the following statement by Rufo Calle, current Executive Secretary of the Trade Union Confederation of Peasant Workers of Bolivia (CSUTCB):

At the moment, for example, they want to sell gas to Chile, but Chile has cheated us. How many kilometres of territory did they steal? Where is our coast? And now the government is sending the gas there! First, we must have gas ourselves. This gas is ours, it is in our territory … They are selling it to Chile and the Chileans are enjoying it. Moreover, the gas will run out. When it runs out, we will have to buy it. The government has secured the external market, but has not yet secured the internal market. Choquewanca wants to negotiate with Chile, Evo Morales says, and Carlos Villegas says 'We will buy gas out there, if it suddenly ends'. It is as if they have already sold it. They have secured the external market and they have forgotten their home. This is to say, I sell my gas outside and forget of my own family. Now I will have to buy from them. This is what is happening now. They will have to buy. They do not have national patriotic sentiment. First, we should be the citizens here, the people. But such a policy does not exist anymore. Everything is for outside, outside. For the

Bolivians nothing is left. They all think towards the outside today. 'There is an outside market, therefore everything goes out'. Even the clothes that we use are foreign and we do not promote the Alpaca, the Vicuña. There is no policy with a patriotic sentiment of production for the country.[5]

To be patriotic, says the Aymara peasant leader, is to think of the internal market. To be unpatriotic is 'to think of the outside'. The national question in Bolivia is also the result of material and social experiences linked to the transformation generated by neoliberalism in production and the market, such as the economic opening towards external trade. Statements like that of Calle can be found in dozens among the leaders of the neighbourhood associations of the city of El Alto, involved in artisan activities. In their own terms, they reiterate the same 'patriotic sentiments of production for the country', of which Calle speaks.

Certainly, these socio-economic and ideological processes have updated the old caste conflicts of Bolivian society. The face of 'evil', according to Aymara revolutionaries, is not only the multinational companies and neoliberal policies, but also the 'white foreigners' (k'aras) who governed the country since the times of Spanish colonisation. According to this definition, the k'aras are descendents of Spanish conquerors, or they came from the United States, like ex-President Gonzalo Sanchez de Losada, 'the Goni gringo', who 'came to rob and become rich at the expense of the poor people of this country'.

On the contrary, the protesters claim their 'Bolivianity'. The natives of this land (Quechuas, Aymaras, and Guaranies) would be the true Bolivians. All our interviewees of Aymara origin had Bolivian flags in their houses, or another similar patriotic symbol hanging on their walls. All denounce the history of the dismemberment of the territory by foreign forces, the history learned in schools and in military service; they also share the patriotic spirit that, in the event of an invasion, they would be prepared to 'die for their country'. In contrast to the presidential secretary of Sanchez de Losada, Aymara revolutionaries would define themselves as 'Bolivian militants'.

In Bolivia, nationality has a racial meaning. The foreign k'aras are seen as white or blond. On the contrary protesters see themselves as blacks or browns: '[w]e are the blacks. They [the k'aras] have marginalised us because we are little blacks and little browns, because of our colour. We support Evo because he is from our

class, he is one of us, he is not disguised. He comes from Orinoca
[an Aymara village].'⁶

These national and racial perceptions are deeply rooted in the
social practice of class domination. First, these are the perceptions of
peasants, craftsmen, and small traders with regard to an oligarchic
government. Second, these social classes do not see themselves and
their opponents only in terms of race or nationality, but also in terms
of social condition. Last but not least, nearly all of our interviewees
were descendants of fathers and uncles that were servants in the
farms in the period prior to the revolution of 1952. The experience
of exploitation and servitude has been transmitted through oral
traditions to the current generation of peasants and craftsmen.

The image of the opponent against whom peasants and craftsmen
struggle in their direct action is that of the rich, the new lords, the
oligarchy, the landlords, and the MNC owners. This collective representation invokes the old image of the landlord of the haciendas,
renewed in the current context to assign the category of 'the new
lords' to the social actors that today occupy the higher positions
in the economic and political sphere. Thus, in our interviews,
transnational firms are referred to as the 'new lords' and the
politicians are identified as 'landlords' and members of the oligarchy.
This is how class meanings and class consciousness come to be in
the Bolivian national question.

THE PRAXIS OF THE OLD REGIME IN BOLIVIA

For Ernest Gellner, the violation of the nationalist principle assumes
a very specific, and highly sensitive, form: the governing of a political
unit by a people who belong to a nation distinct from that of the
governed. For the nationalists, this constitutes a political practice
that is absolutely intolerable (Gellner 1989: 11–12).

Certainly, the higher echelons of the leadership during the
neoliberal period were born in Bolivia. Nonetheless, not only do
their customs, habits, preferences, ways of life, and appearance
resemble more the lifestyles predominant in countries of 'the North';
but also – and this is fundamental – the subaltern classes of society
regard them as foreigners. The nationalist ideology of recent years
considers the prior, neoliberal rulers as foreigners, *k'aras*.

Following Gellner (ibid.: 12), nationalism is an ideology which
requires that, in a given state, ethnic boundaries do not separate the
rulers from the ruled. The struggle for the correspondence between
culture and political community is the nationalist struggle properly

understood. This is an assertion compatible with Lenin's theoretical conception of self-determination. The aim of Aymara peasants and craftsmen to build their own Bolivian state characterises the unsolved national question in Bolivia.

The struggle of the national movement for equality emerges from a non-democratic state that promotes political inequality and cultural discrimination. The educational system – the essential condition of the nationalist phenomenon according to Gellner – illustrates this well. In Bolivia, the educational system is divided between private education, where the descendants of the privileged classes, the upper-middle classes and some of the middle classes are trained, and public education which is for children and youth from disadvantaged families.

What is peculiar is that, since the Revolution of 1952, the state has disseminated a nationalist and patriotic ideal through public education, as well as military service. Over decades, the state has promoted the loyalty of the subaltern classes towards existing political institutions.

Ideas such as 'serving the mother country and defending it from foreign invasion' that were introduced either by the regimented system of compulsory military service, or by an educational system that enforced the 'Castellanisation and Bolivianisation' of indigenous children and youth through severe physical and psychological punishments, were all meant to instil obedience and create an abstract sense of Bolivianity among indigenous people, which at the same time expected them to forget their ethnic condition. And this system had real consequences. The social sectors which harbour the most fervent patriotic sentiments as well as hatred of 'the foreign invader' (mainly Chileans), are precisely those of the subaltern classes. For them, compulsory military service is a question of personal dignity (Quintana 1998: 112). On the contrary, for the youth of the middle classes, the bourgeoisie or the higher echelons of the state, military service is a waste of time. They simply buy out their military service certificate.

The experience of compulsory military service indicates a perpetuation of the praxis of the Old Regime: rights for certain privileged groups and obligations for the underprivileged. According to an opinion survey conducted in 1995, 78 per cent of the Members of Parliament admitted to not having undergone military service (Quintana 1998: 150). Such data reveal not only the monopolisation of state offices by certain social groups, but also their exemption from certain obligations, such as military service.

Although formal inequalities persisted between different social groups, national ideology promoted obedience among subaltern classes vis-à-vis state institutions. The historic turning point was when the power bloc abandoned nationalism to become spokespersons for globalisation. The abandonment of national ideology by the bourgeoisie and the political leaders raised the possibility of a plebeian redefinition of national ideology from an ethnic and class perspective.

THE MORALES GOVERNMENT AND THE STATE

The relative stability of the contradictions between the state, MNCs and the subaltern classes during the current government of MAS may be explained by the actions of this new government with regard to the conditions indicated above.

First, the rise of MAS to government has entailed the recomposition of the social character of the members of the legislative and executive branches. While the previous neoliberal rulers were the representatives of MNCs, the native oligarchy and international credit agencies, the new leaders come from trade unions, popular associations and peasant communities, together with middle class elements among non-governmental organisations and the academic world, with which they are allied.

The rise of the MAS government has meant the loss of the traditional class and ethnic monopoly over the highest state positions by the descendants of the old oligarchy and the landlords. This has modified the ethnic background of those occupying the commanding heights of the state. In Gellner's terms, ethnic boundaries no longer distinguish between the rulers and the ruled.

The leaders of MAS identify themselves as representatives of the 'new power bloc that expresses the interests of those who, for centuries, were marginalised and excluded' (Ministry of Development Planning 2006: 14, my translation). Enthusiastic intellectuals assert the advent of an indigenous hegemony (Stefanoni 2006: 37). In a society in which the immense majority sees itself as belonging to a native ethnic group, the 'indigenous government' has ensured that the self-image of the people be incorporated into the ideology of the state itself. Thus, in a country like Bolivia, the government of Evo Morales is better able to present itself as the 'universal representative' of the people and the spokesperson of the *national* community (Boron 2003: 274). At least it is more believable when Evo Morales says so in an Aymara accent than when ex-President Sanchez de Losada said it in an American accent.

These social features present the possibility for the new leaders to seek to expand their own interests, prestige, and power, within the limits of the relative autonomy of the political sphere that they now occupy. In order to perpetuate themselves as a government, it is necessary to augment state resources in a way that will enable the government to increase its margins for manoeuvre. The data indicate a substantive increase in state revenues as a result of the changes in the Law on Hydrocarbons. While in 2000 the revenues obtained from the production of hydrocarbons reached US$428 million, in 2006 they rose to nearly US$1.5 billion (Control Ciudadano 2007: 4).

At the same time, the renegotiation on the external debt and the substantive increase in state revenues has reduced the dependence of the state on international credit for its current expenditures. If in 2003 the foreign debt reached US$5.1 billion, in 2006 it dropped to US$3.2 billion (Control Ciudadano 2007: 12). The situation is distinct with respect to previous governments, in which even the salaries of the ministers were covered by international loans. This indicates the widening of the autonomous action of the state.

The dispute between the MAS government and foreign firms regarding the pricing of hydrocarbons (the price increased to US$5 per million BTUs – British thermal units), as well as the pressure by the government to increase state revenues by taxing the sale of hydrocarbons, indicate a change in the classic attitude of the previous neoliberal governments, which maintained low tax rates on petroleum firms in an attempt to avoid scaring away foreign investors.

Despite the importance of these changes, however, the MAS government does nothing other than quarrel over the recuperation of the normal functions of the capitalist state. The current government is managing to overcome temporarily the contradictions of the Bolivian state between the functions of legitimation and capitalist accumulation – that is, between the political form of the peripheral state (political sovereignty) and its real subjection to the world economy. This is the contradiction that stirred nationalist fervour against MNCs operating in Bolivia and led to the crisis of 2003.

However, if the government of MAS has temporarily stabilised the above contradiction, it also means that it has recovered the legitimacy that allows it to promote the interests of MNCs in this periphery, something which the previous neoliberal governments were unable to sustain. The last neoliberal governments were overthrown precisely for their defence of policies favoured by MNCs. Today, the MAS government can continue with those policies without risking a confrontation with the subaltern classes.

Certainly, the contracts for the exportation of gas to Argentina have increased the selling price of hydrocarbons considerably (from US$1.09 per million BTUs to US$5.2), as well as the projected state revenues. It is the oil companies that will exploit the gas for the next 30 years. The increase in state resources is directly related to the access by foreign firms to new markets and to the export of gas to the exterior as raw material. The current 'service' contracts establish that the greater the investments in the export of gas, the greater will be company profits (CEDLA 2006: 63–4).

According to the Ministry of National Development Planning (MNDP 2006: 214), the government has projected the net increase of FDI from 0.8 per cent of gross domestic product in 2006 to 8.65 per cent in 2011. The export of gas has also been expected to rise from US$984 million in 2005 to US$2.4 billion in 2011, and that of minerals from US$540 million in 2005 to US$ 1.7 billion in 2011. We may conclude that Bolivia's economic growth will be driven by the production and export of raw materials during the next years, under the control of multinational oil companies.

The recovery of the autonomy of the capitalist state is functional to the capitalist expansion of Bolivia's oil and gas sector. While in the recent past, multinational oil firms were seen as the 'enemies of the Bolivians', today they have became their associates. The Morales government has legitimised the presence of multinational oil companies. Thus, the MAS government has temporarily stabilised the contradiction between the functions of accumulation and legitimation of the capitalist state.

NOTES

1. INE/BCB/MDE/CEPB, *Encuesta Interinstitucional de Inversión Extranjera Directa en Bolivia*, database for 1996–2003; Instituto Nacional de Estadística, Banco Central de Bolivia, Ministerio de Desarrollo Económico y Confederación de Empresarios Privados de Bolivia.
2. INE/BCB/MDE/CEPB database, 1996–2003, ibid.
3. Interview with Fernando Illanes de la Riva, ex-Minister of Hydrocarbons, La Paz, June 2006
4. Interview with ex-Secretary of the Presidency of Gonzalo Sanchez de Losada, La Paz, April 2006.
5. Interview with Rufo Calle, La Paz, March 2007.
6. Interview with protester in the Zona de Ventilla, El Alto, February 2007.

REFERENCES

Almaraz Paz, Sergio (1988), *El Poder y la Caída: El Estaño en la Historia de Bolivia*. La Paz: Los Amigos del Libro.

Basualdo, Eduardo, and Enrique Arceo (2006), *Neoliberalismo y Sectores Dominantes. Tendencias Globales y Experiencias Nacionales*. Buenos Aires: CLACSO.

Boron, Atilio (2003), *Estado, Capitalismo y Democracia en América Latina*. Buenos Aires: CLACSO.

Burnham, Peter (2006), 'The Politics of Economic Management in the 1990s', in *Global Restructuring, State, Capital and Labour: Contesting Neo-Gramscian Perspectives*, ed. A. Bieler, W. Bonefeld, P. Burnham and A.D. Morton. New York: Palgrave Macmillan.

CEDLA (2005) *¿Para Quién Trabaja el Estado: Una Lectura Política del Presupuesto General de la Nación?* La Paz: CEDLA.

Control Ciudadano (2007), *Resultados de la Política Fiscal*, Boletín de Seguimiento a las Políticas Públicas (Segunda Época), 4(8). La Paz: CEDLA.

Contreras, Manuel, and Napoleón Pacheco (1989), *Medio Siglo de Minería Mediana en Bolivia, 1939–1989*. La Paz: Biblioteca Minera Boliviana.

Cueva, Agustín (1982). *El Desarrollo del Capitalismo en América Latina*. México: Siglo XXI Editores.

De la Cueva, J.M. (1983), *Bolivia: Imperialismo y Oligarquía*. La Paz: Ediciones ROALVA.

Diekhoff, Alain, and Christophe Jaffrelot (2006), *Repenser le Nationalisme: Théories et Pratiques*. Paris: Science Po.

Evers, Tilman (1989), *El Estado en la Periferia Capitalista*, fifth edition. México: Siglo Veintiuno Editores.

Fernandez, Florestán (1985), 'Problemas de Conceptualización de las Clases Sociales en América Latina', in *Las Clases Sociales en América Latina*, ed. R. Benítez Zenteno, Ninth Edition. Mexico City: Siglo Veintiuno Editores.

Gellner, Ernest (1989), *Nations et Nationalisme*. Paris: Edition Payot.

Lenin, V.I. (1962), 'El Derecho de las Naciones a la Autodeterminación', *Obras Escogidas, Volumen I*. Moscow: Progreso.

Lenin, V.I. (1962), 'Las Tareas del Proletariado en Nuestra Revolución', *Obras Escogidas, Volume II*. Moscow: Progreso.

MCE (1999), *Bolivia: Inversión Extranjera Directa, 1998*. La Paz: Ministerio de Comercio Exterior, Vice-Ministerio de Inversion y Privatizacion y Direccion General de Inversion.

MNDP (2006), *Plan Nacional de Desarrollo, 2006–2010*. La Paz: Ministerio de Planificación del Desarrollo.

Moyo, Sam, and Paris Yeros (2007), 'The Radicalised State: Zimbabwe's Interrupted Revolution', *Review of African Political Economy*, 34(111): 103–21.

Orellana, Aillón Lorgio (2006), 'Nacionalismo, Populismo y Régimen de Acumulación en Bolivia: Hacia una Caracterización del Gobierno del MAS', *Coyuntura*, 11. La Paz: CEDLA.

Pereira Stambuk, Juan Carlos and Humberto Tavera Laffertt, *Desarrollo de Capacidades Institucionales para la Atracción de Inversión Extranjera Directa en Bolivia*, Organización de las Naciones Unidas Para el Desarrollo Industrial, s.l., Artes Gráficas SRL.

Perez, Luna Mamerto (2007), *No Todo Grano que Brilla es Oro: Un Análisis de la Soya en Bolivia*. La Paz: CEDLA.

Quintana, Taborga Juan Ramón (1998), *Soldados y Ciudadanos*. La Paz: PIEB.

Stefanoni, Pablo (2006), 'El Nacionalismo Indígena en el Poder', in *Movimientos Sociales y Gobiernos en la Región Andina: Resistencias y Alternativas, lo Político y lo Social*, OSAL (Observatorio Social de América Latina), 7(19): 37–44.

Tilly, Charles (2006), *Regimes and Repertoires*. Chicago, IL: University of Chicago Press.

Toranzos, Roca Carlos F. (1989), 'Los Rasgos de la Nueva Derecha Boliviana', in *Nueva Derecha y Desproletarización en Bolivia*, ed. C.F. Toranzos Roca and M. Arrieta Abadía. La Paz: Unitas-ILDIS.

Trotsky, Leon (1985), *Historia de la Revolución Rusa, Volume I*. Madrid: SARPE.

Valenzuela, José C. (1990), *¿Qué es un patrón de acumulación?*. México: UNAM.

Zavaleta, Mercado René (1983), 'Las Masas en Noviembre', in *Bolivia, Hoy*, ed. R. Zavaleta Mercado. Mexico City: Siglo XXI Editores.

Zavaleta, Mercado René (1986), *Lo Nacional-Popular en Bolivia*. Mexico City: Siglo Veintiuno Editores.

12
Kirchner's Argentina: In Search of a New International Presence

Javier A. Vadell

THE ARGENTINE CRISIS OF 2001 AND THE COLLAPSE OF THE NEOLIBERAL MODEL

The Argentine economic crisis and the resulting socio-political fallout in December 2001 were paradigms for the region. This crisis signalled a break in relations between international financial institutions (IFIs), especially the International Monetary Fund (IMF) and developing nations. Argentina, which during the 1990s had been an example of 'correct' economic policies as stipulated by the Washington Consensus, entered into its worst economic crisis since the 1930s. The IFIs that had backed the structural adjustment programmes and indiscriminate liberalisation were now to blame for the crisis and the political fallout to come, as the loans they had extended were contingent upon the continuity of currency convertibility and further structural adjustments.

The exogenous causes of the socio-political crisis of the young Argentine democracy can be traced back to the crisis of global capitalism in the second half of the 1990s, whose greatest impact was felt in Mexico (the so-called 'Tequila Effect'), Thailand, Indonesia, South Korea, Russia and Turkey. This series of events put the neoliberal model to the test in various developing nations. In the case of Argentina specifically, the new crisis tested the experimental exchange rate policy, conceived in the 1991 Law of Monetary Convertibility, under the government of Carlos Menem and his Finance Minister Domingo Cavallo, which stipulated by law a fixed value between the US dollar and the Argentine peso. In January 2002, an emergency economic plan put an end to the convertibility law.

This chapter will examine Argentina's foreign policy during the four years of the government of Néstor Kirchner by analysing internal factors, specifically the troubled economic policy the government inherited, as well as external and structural factors arising from Argentina's position in the global political economy. The chapter begins with the premise that 2001 marked a break between Argentina and the international system, brought about by five political and economic factors. The first factor that ushered in this 'moment' of rupture, and had drastic implications on international security and (indirectly) on the global economy, was the 9/11 terrorist attacks on the United States and the resulting 'war on terror' declared by the administration of G.W. Bush.

The second factor was the crisis of the neoliberal model of development promoted by IFIs and the United States (Vadell 2006). The Argentine crisis of 2001 was a paradigmatic case at this juncture. The third factor has to do with the changes experienced in international finance and commerce consequent upon the rise of commodity prices, from the end of 2002, which benefited commodity-exporting countries. During this time, the US-backed policy of low interest rates and the extreme liquidity of international capital created a favourable environment for the entry of capital into emerging nations (Moffett 2004). The fourth factor was China's active commercial penetration and expansion into the South American market (Vadell 2007), which further stimulated the price of primary commodities, including cereals, minerals and oil.

The fifth and final factor was the push toward regionalism in relation to both economic and security issues, a phenomenon that flourished after the Cold War, and especially after 9/11, principally in the regions that were not implicated in the US-led 'war on terror' (Buzan and Waever 2003, Hurrell 1995, Lake and Morgan 1997). This phenomenon implied greater roles for both regional powers, such as Brazil, and mid-sized countries within certain regions, such as Argentina.

These factors strongly shaped the four years of Kirchner's Peronist-style government. Kirchner widened Argentina's margins of political manoeuvring, allowing for a greater possibility to bring about more active and interventionist economic policies, as well as a more aggressive foreign policy to confront private creditors and the IFIs, especially the IMF.

We should add that a series of changes has taken place in the politics of the region (see Villa, Chapter 14, this volume). In fact, several centre-left governments have challenged some of the pillars of neoliberal economic policies. The consolidation of Hugo Chávez's leadership in both Venezuela and the region, Luiz Inácio Lula da Silva's re-election in Brazil, and the election victories of Evo Morales in Bolivia, Tabaré Vázquez in Uruguay, Rafael Correa in Ecuador and Cristina Fernández de Kirchner (as her husband's successor) in Argentina, all highlight the critical and revisionist attitude that has been sweeping the continent at the turn of the century.

ARGENTINA'S 'CARNAL RELATIONSHIP' WITH NEOLIBERALISM

Carlos Menem, leader of the Peronist Party, was elected President of Argentina in 1989, in the midst of a heated socio-political crisis and in an international context marked by the disintegration of the Soviet Union and the end of Cold War. Optimistic intellectuals, such as Francis Fukuyama, heralded the coming of a world order in which the principles of liberal democracy and free market economics would spread across the entire planet. The centres of power, namely the United States, large banks, transnational corporations (TNCs) and the IFIs, touted economic liberalism as the solution to all the evils and vices of developing countries, but also the countries of the former Soviet bloc. These centres of power articulated themselves, with much success, through the ideological platform that came to be known as the Washington Consensus (Williamson 1990).

Confronted with such transformations within the international system, the Peronist government of Carlos Menem propped itself up on the two pillars that had sustained Argentine foreign policy, itself defined essentially in terms of economic policy. The first pillar was the policy of 'pragmatic acquiescence', which maintained a preferential relationship with the victorious power of the Cold War (Russell and Tokatlian 2003, Russell 2004).[1] Carlos Escudé (1997), an analyst and former aide in the Menem government, described the ideological foundation to this political position as 'peripheral realism'. According to this school, by recognising the hegemony of the United States, Argentina would have to maintain a posture of automatic alignment, with the objective of obtaining certain benefits that it otherwise would fail to obtain. It would be a 'realistic' acceptance of North American leadership in global political and economic issues.

From this ideological directive, the Menem government made several key decisions that signified a change in direction from the recent past. Fundamental to the redefinition of Argentine foreign policy was the re-establishment of diplomatic relations with the United Kingdom – severed since the Malvinas War in 1982 – which the government considered as an essential condition for the establishment of a new relationship with the United States. This policy of 'pragmatic acquiescence' was consolidated in the

Menem government and remained the norm during the subsequent Fernando De la Rúa government. It prioritised, on the one hand, a strategic relationship with the United States as a naïve way to incorporate the country into the first world, and, on the other hand, a relationship with Brazil as the country's privileged trading partner. This partnership materialised in the regional integration project of the Mercosur (the Common Market of the South), created in 1991 under the banner of open regionalism.

In this way, from 1989 to 2001, the Argentine government carried out initiatives that brought it ideologically and politically closer to the United States. The main examples of Argentina's new foreign policy included: (a) participation in the 1991 Gulf war, in which the country sent two warships; (b) a change of opinion toward the US-supported investigations into human rights abuses in Cuba;[2] (c) its exit from the Non-Aligned Movement in 1991; (d) the deactivation of its Condor II missile programme; and (e) the shifting of the country's voting profile in the UN General Assembly by aligning itself more closely with North American agendas (Corigliano 1990, Aranda 2004, Russell and Tokatlian 2003).

The second pillar of the Menem government was the almost unconditional acceptance of neoliberal economic ideology. Soon after taking power, Menem implemented one of the most audacious programmes of neoliberal economic reforms. These reforms were based principally on five policies: the privatisation of public firms, the opening up of Argentine markets, financial liberalisation, the loosening of labour regulations, and a stabilisation programme based on a fixed exchange rate, put forth by then-Finance Minister Domingo Cavallo, to curb inflation. This last policy received instrumental support from the Law of Convertibility of April 1991, which stipulated that, henceforth, 10,000 australes would be worth 1 peso. This new Argentina currency would have, by law, a fixed one-to-one ratio to the US dollar. This system, which came to be known as the Currency Board, obligated the Argentine Central Bank (BCRA) to maintain US dollars on reserve in relation to the circulating peso. In other words, changing parity meant having to modify the law in Congress.

The law enjoyed relative success, most notably in ending rampant inflation, a fact that gave hope to the middle and working classes, as well as foreign and national private investors who saw Argentina as an emerging economy, ripe with investment opportunities (Schvarzer 2004: 30–1).

However, the first problems arose in 1995. Argentina suffered the impacts of the Mexican economic crisis of December 2004, which provoked a rapid flight of capital and highlighted the fragility of an economic programme based on a Currency Board and a plan of indiscriminately opening Argentine markets. The Menem government, with Cavallo and his successor, Roque Fernández, did not modify the directives of Argentina's economic policy. By the end of 1998, the Argentine economy fell into a tailspin (Haslam 2003, Schvarzer 2004). The neoliberal recipe for a fixed exchange rate made the vicious cycle of rising deficits and loss of confidence unavoidable.

Meanwhile, the global economic environment proved unfavourable, exacerbating the fragilities of the Argentine economic model. As Paul Haslam (2003: 4) noted, '[t]he deterioration of commercial conditions for Argentine exports, the impact of the Russian economic crisis of August 1998, the devaluation of the Brazilian currency in January 1999, high interest rates, and the valorization of the convertible Argentine peso impeded economic growth and the ability of the government to balance the budget'. The Argentine government had lost its ability to make economic policy by exposing itself to the volatility of global markets. The valorisation of the peso, accompanied by a programme of opening up Argentine markets for foreign investment, favoured the import sector. Thus, the commercial balance of goods and services was in the red throughout nearly the entire period of convertibility.

THE BRIEF PERIOD OF '*LA ALIANZA*' – THE FAILED GOVERNMENT

In December 1999, the *Gobierno de la Alianza* (The Alliance Government), led by President Fernando de la Rúa and Vice President Carlos 'Chacho' Álvarez, assumed power after ten years of Peronist rule. *La Alianza* was charged principally with the 'need to infuse transparency into the institutional life of the country, crushed by the corruption that public opinion had associated with the previous government' (Romero and Torres 2004: 9).

Three factors prematurely hamstrung the De la Rúa government. The first was that *La Alianza* was always in the minority in the Senate, where Peronists had long enjoyed a large majority. Moreover, *La Alianza* had to govern a country with 17 out of 23 provinces held by the Peronist opposition, including the politically and economically most important provinces: Buenos Aires, Santa Fe and Córdoba. The second factor had to do with the inability of the government to win consistent political alliances to support its agenda, hampered by the lack of leadership and charisma coming from De la Rúa. The third factor was the political vacuum left by the resignation of Vice President Álvarez, who denounced corruption and bribery during the process of renegotiating labour laws in the Senate.

In terms of foreign policy, *La Alianza* toed the same general lines as the Menem government. In analysing the discourse of *La Alianza*, two fundamental points in foreign policy may be observed: the theme of regional integration, with emphasis on Mercosur, and a normative-ethical position toward the international system.

However, the economic conditions created by the neoliberal model and the international support of the United States limited *La Alianza*'s foreign policy. Even a plan to obtain a buffer of approximately US$40 billion to prepare the government to face new accords with the IMF and renegotiate the short-term debts with the private international banks failed due to Argentina's debilitated position.

Relations with Brazil exceeded expectations in the first years of *La Alianza*, mainly due to the macro-economic co-ordination accords signed during a Mercosur meeting in the Brazilian city of Florianópolis in December 2000.[3] However, this bilateral agreement suffered a new setback with the return of Domingo Cavallo as Finance Minister in February 2001. Cavallo's top priority was a closer relationship with the United States, which involved warmer overtures toward the Free Trade Agreement of the Americas (FTAA) and heavy support for a bilateral trade agreement with the United States.

Notwithstanding the attempts at strengthening regional ties, the domestic economic situation proved to be the most delicate point for the *Alianza* government, which from the start had committed itself to maintaining convertibility and upholding the neoliberal model. What resulted from this decision was the application of recessionary and deflationary policies that proved very damaging for Argentina's middle and lower classes.

It should be pointed out that beginning in 1999, when De la Rúa became president, Argentina found itself in deep economic recession. Two years later, the results of the legislative election of October 2001 reflected the social discontent aimed at the country's politicians: null and blank votes outnumbered valid votes during this election.[4]

The end of the De la Rúa government and the beginning of Argentina's moratorium took place exactly one year after the IMF granted important financial support for the convertibility plan, now in its final phase. In August 2001, four months before the country's default, the IMF disbursed US$8 million in a 'standby' programme loan (Damill et al. 2006). Just before the resignation of both Cavallo and De la Rúa in November 2001, an IMF mission visited Argentina and concluded that the country needed even more financial help. However, IMF authorities did not authorise the support (Blunstein 2005), sparking a fatal catalysing effect that rapidly turned the economic crisis into a political one. The bank run on 30 November accelerated the process of capital flight, and the government, still with Cavallo as Finance Minister, decided to limit bank withdrawals to 250 pesos per week per person, beginning what came to be known as the *corralito* (literally, 'small enclosure'). The economy, technically bankrupt, provided the backdrop for widespread protests, looting, and acts of vandalism that increased day by day as the crisis worsened.

Confronted with this new scenario, the government toughened its position and declared a 30-day state of emergency. De la Rúa's decree made an immediate impact, causing a spontaneous reaction from a wide cross-section of society – including the middle classes of Buenos Aires and other large cities – all marching to the rhythm of banging pots and pans. Soon thereafter, Cavallo submitted his resignation. The massive protests that had begun peacefully were now reaching a tragic end. Police violence and harsh repression against the protesters left dozens killed and even more wounded. At the height of the turmoil, President De la Rúa followed Cavallo and resigned as well.

Several interim presidents succeeded De la Rúa, all of them Peronists. The President of the Senate, Ramón Puerta, was the first to take up the torch, and he immediately called upon Congress to elect a new candidate. Puerta then resigned and left the interim presidency to the Governor of the state of San Luís, Adolfo Rodríguez Saá. Saá governed for one week, enough time for him to declare a moratorium on the country's foreign debt, on 23 December 2001. Saá resigned and was succeeded by the President of Congress, Eduardo Camaño, until 1 January 2002, when Congress finally nominated Eduardo Duhalde, a Senator from Buenos Aires and former Vice President under Menem, as President of the Argentine Republic.

As president, Duhalde quickly passed a public emergency law and ordered the reform of Argentina's fixed exchange rate, thus putting an end to the convertibility law. The peso was devalued, mechanisms were put in place to control capital flows, and the financial system became 'pesofied' and weaned off the US dollar, though the *corralito* remained in place. This period of transition, which marked the end of Argentina's neoliberal phase, lasted until the 2003 elections, which ushered the Peronist Néstor Kirchner – politically supported by Duhalde – into the presidency.

The crisis of the late 1990s left a dramatic impact on Argentine society. The unemployment rate climbed above 20 per cent of the active population in 2002, while gross domestic product (GDP) fell at a rate of 16.3 per cent during the first trimester of 2002, an ignominious record for the country. Real wages fell 18 per cent in 2002. The rates of poverty and indigence reached unprecedented levels: according to official data, 53 per cent of Argentines lived below the poverty line, while 25 per cent of the population was living in a state of indigence, with their most basic needs for survival going unmet. In 1998–2002, extreme poverty rose 223 per cent, an unprecedented event for such a short span of time. And in 2001, labour's share of GDP fell to the lowest level in Argentina's history.

KIRCHNER IN POWER: A NEW ROLE FOR THE STATE?

Is a New Argentine Foreign Policy Possible?

Influential analysts and investigators have questioned Kirchner's foreign policy. Some complained of a lack of grand strategy for the country (Tokatlian 2004, 2005a), while others simply and more definitively have argued that the government never had a foreign policy to begin with. Notably, Pérez Llana (2006), analyst and former ambassador, claimed in *La Nación* that the government 'has no foreign policy; it does not know who its partners are, who its allies are, and it has not decided whether it wants to be on the side of populists or social-democrats'. According to this view, three political models are taking shape in Latin America: one conservative, another social-democrat, and another populist. And within this realm of change in the region, continues Pérez Llana,

> there exists a great ignorance of the world and a great ignorance of the importance of the world. No correct evaluation exists regarding what the international agenda is, what world tendencies are, or how Argentina can come out ahead. No one knows who Argentina's partners are, who its allies are, and with whom Argentina should sympathise: with populists or social-democrats. (2006, my translation)

Similarly, Carlos Escudé (2006), a specialist in international relations and a former aide to the Chancellery under Menem, has argued in the same journal (*La Nación*) that the death of Argentine foreign policy has been reflected especially in the conflict between Argentina and Uruguay over the cellulose industrial plants belonging to the firm Botnia, on the shores of the Uruguay river – a dispute known as 'the pulp mill conflict' (*conflicto de las papeleras*). Escudé has argued that Argentina has been living in a latent and permanent crisis of governance since 2001, in which popular organisations, 'manipulated by political *caudillos*' (or oligarchs), have gained 'the same partial veto power that the military wielded between 1930 and 1983'. The case of the popular organisations and assemblies of Gualeguaychú, in the Entre Ríos province, would stand out as the clearest example of an absence of foreign policy in Argentina. According to Escudé, environmentalists 'usurped a dimension of Argentine foreign policy', damaging regional commerce and generating a political crisis within Mercosur.

On the other hand, Tokatlian (2004: 14) recognises that the key question surrounding Kirchner's apparent lack of foreign policy has more to do with the possibility of 'developing an independent foreign policy for Argentina in the new international context of economic and financial globalisation … a period of reconstruction that will be slow and painful' (my translation). According to the author, the present external conditions are favourable for Argentina to revise its model of international involvement.

However, the critics do not acknowledge the fact that significant changes have occurred during the Kirchner government, as much in relation to foreign policy as to the way in which the government understands and controls the economy. According to Tokatlian (2004), these changes are based on three new realities.

The first is the perception of wide segments of society and part of the government regarding the enormous failure of a foreign policy based on 'special relations with', or 'pragmatic acquiescence toward', the centres of international economic and political power. Throughout the 1990s, the IFIs and private international capital presented the Argentine state to the world as an exemplary student. However, when Argentina fell into its worst crisis, it found no help, support or solidarity from these centres of economic power.

The second important reality is that, given the weakness of Kirchner's mandate, the President-elect felt obligated to give clear signals of assertiveness and determination. Besides, Kirchner always demonstrated strong personal appeal, with little time for following protocol, which strengthened the 'personalist' character of his mandate.

The third variable is linked to Kirchner's own political making and the characteristics of his generation. As others have also argued, Kirchner 'is a son of the generation of the 1970s, which has a worldview marked by a historical moment of change' (Corigliano 2004); he has been influenced by a '1970ist' Peronism, which identified ideologically and symbolically with reformist politics of an anti-imperialist character (Altamirano 2004). This worldview 'seeks to rescue in symbolic form the ideas and reformist postures of the Peronist left that Kirchner and his [first] Chancellor Rafael Bielsa identified with in their youth' (Corigliano 2004).

Russell and Tokatlian (2003: 79) define the new Argentine foreign policy paradigm as 'responsible participation' oriented by six directives: a high profile in the construction, defence and reform of international political and economic institutions with the objective of reaching greater democratisation; a firm commitment to democracy, peace, the fight against terrorism, protecting the environment and defending human and humanitarian rights; creating a strategic society with Brazil, open to all other South American countries; a connection with the United States geared toward securing positive ends and oriented by specific objectives; supporting plans for intra- and extra-hemispheric economic integration that are compatible with domestic politics; and the realisation of a development strategy open to the world that at the same time applies the principals of 'selective protectionism'.

Considering that the country found itself in a critical economic situation in 2003 – although by then it was showing signs of recovery – one of the aspects of Kirchner's foreign policy that must be pointed out was the clear priority placed on economic concerns. In this regard, by contrast to the policies of the 1990s, Kirchner's government defended a more interventionist perspective. In this sense, one of the virtues of the Kirchner government was that it found out how to take advantage of a favourable climate for negotiating with international creditors and the IMF, whose prestige had already taken a terrible blow. The dynamic nature of this policy over the course of Kirchner's four years in power created new favourable opportunities for Argentina in regional politics.

Kirchner's Policies: A 'New' International Role?

In this way, the directives of 'responsible participation' discussed by Russell and Tokatlian became crystallised in a chorus of five relations and actions that defined the four years of Kirchner's relationship with the rest of the world.

First, Kirchner's state visits to Brazil, the United States, and Spain, immediately after becoming president, signalled the priorities of the new government. The first trip was to Brazil, meant to re-establish and solidify relations, with the ultimate objective of strengthening Mercosur. Kirchner's second trip was to the United States to participate in a previously scheduled meeting with G.W. Bush, in a quite complicated context for Argentina and its negotiations with the IMF. In the meeting, the US president expressed his clear support for his Argentine counterpart.[5] The third visit was to Spain, where Kirchner defended the renegotiation of contracts with privatised service companies, many of them Spanish-owned (Godio 2006: 206). Together, these presidential visits revealed the priorities of 'Kirchnerist' foreign policy. However, new priorities have since arisen in regional politics. Presently, solidifying ties with Brazil, attempting to strengthen Mercosur, and the warming of relations with Venezuela are the events that have stood out.

The second element of foreign policy was to make a top priority the establishment of special relations with Brazil. In the Southern Cone sub-region, ties between Argentina and Brazil were elevated to the status of 'strategic relations', a political tool meant to maximise the margin of Argentina's manoeuvring in relation to the United States and the European Union, specifically when it came to trade negotiations within the scope of the World Trade Organisation (WTO). This new stance implied a clear preference on the part of the Argentine government for regional politics, ideally as a foundation for an alternative means of development to that proclaimed by the Washington Consensus. Thus, the Argentine official view of Mercosur is that it is 'above all a political project, a space to widen state autonomy and guide our countries to greater positions in the world. We have the conviction that in the world of today there are no development projects of a strictly national scope, and therefore we give our beloved bloc a more endearing feeling than a mere commercial accord' (Bielsa et al. 2005: 49, my translation).

The official position recognised, as those of the Argentine governments of the 1990s did, that the development projects of an exclusively national character no longer had a place in the contemporary world. The only difference was that the Kirchner administration emphasised development on an essentially regional plane, spurning the notion of development within the virtual space of globalisation and the idealisation of the free market as the only path to the first world. The inherent contradiction of this regionalist revisionism is that the answers to the crisis of 2001–02 were limited in scope to purely national means and abilities. For the Argentine government, there were not many alternatives beyond a purely regionalist strategy, a fact derived from a series of consequences that negatively impacted the other Mercosur members, especially Brazil. A clear example of those effects was the alteration of the trade rules within the jurisdiction of the bloc. At any rate, one must recognise that since the Duhalde government – due, among other factors, to the intransigence of international financial institutions (Blunstein 2005) and the US government – Argentina has turned its gaze toward Brazil with the objective of strengthening a strategic economic and political relationship.

The third element has been the negotiation of Argentina's foreign debt. The resolution on ending the default came about after difficult negotiations with private creditors and, concomitantly, with the IMF. Argentina released itself from the uncomfortable circumstances of the moratorium, securing a seemingly better agreement with the IMF than other developing nations, including Brazil. Many sectors of the Argentine population viewed as a success the restructuring of Argentina's foreign debt with private creditors in 2005 and the release from the moratorium. This success allowed Kirchner and then-Finance Minister Roberto Lavagna[6] to reinsert Argentina into the global economy. In January 2005, the government put forth a hefty exchange offer for one part of its debt with both national and foreign private creditors. To reach this objective, the government issued new bonds to replace those which had not yet been paid. There existed more than 150 types of bonds in a state of moratorium. Creditors were given the opportunity to choose between three new categories of bonds, with a deadline of 25 February stipulated by the government. After this date, creditors that did not accept this proposal could make the necessary appeals.

On 3 March 2005, Finance Minister Lavagna announced that 76.07 per cent of private creditors, holding a total of 152 titles of Argentina's debt in moratorium, agreed with the government's proposal to cancel the debt, despite the loss of approximately 63–68 per cent of the bonds' original value. The recuperation of economic growth that had begun in 2002, even amid the moratorium situation, subsequently bolstered Lavagna's position in negotiations with the IMF and private foreign creditors.

The fourth element has been the forging of ties with Chávez's Venezuela. Relations between Argentina and Venezuela began warming at the turn of the millennium. This strengthening of ties between these two countries, which traditionally had seldom engaged in commercial relations with one another, can be considered one of the most significant of geopolitical changes in the region, and it can be interpreted by way of various dimensions.

The first dimension is ideological, observed within the context of the collective shift to the left of the majority of Latin American countries. Kirchner's Argentina is evidence of this tendency that has led to a scenario of ideological and political convergence in the sub-region. As a result of this tendency, debates have arisen throughout Latin America surrounding which of the various types of leftist and populist governments will prove most successful for the region and its nations (Castañeda 2006, Paramio 2006).

The second dimension, arguably the most relevant in this conjuncture, is the growing complementary dependence between Argentina and Venezuela with relation to strategic commodities, which has had implications on the energy and food security of both nations, as well as the nature of each country's foreign investment. This growing reciprocal need exposes deep economic vulnerabilities in both countries, in that both are dependent on the rise of the prices of oil, minerals and other commodities. Argentina, propelled by elevated growth in the last few years, is headed toward severe energy problems. At the same time, although the country began regulating its delicate financial situation as it faced down the IMF and other private investment banks, Argentina's financial condition has proven neither strong nor reliable. Faced with such financial difficulties, the Kirchner government found in Hugo Chávez a kind of 'lender of last resort' who could help give a new impulse to the Argentine economy.

Likewise, Venezuela faces serious problems in feeding its own population.[7] Thus, a fortified partnership arose between the two countries, founded on the real worries bubbling up from their respective energy and food security issues. Certainly, if Argentina's economy continues to grow at a high rate, the country will face critical problems with regard to its energy supply. Taking this issue into account, Argentina and Venezuela have signed various trade agreements outlining a commercial exchange in which basically a barter system prevails: oil for food.

The final dimension concerns regional geopolitics, reflected in the negotiations between state actors in the Mercosur sub-regional bloc. This incomplete integration process, which has a low degree of institutionalisation, depends above all on presidential diplomacy between principal members. The warming of relations between Argentina and Venezuela will have inevitable repercussions on Brazil, as it plays the role of regional power and the most important member of the bloc, according to the criteria of Buzan and Waever (2003). However, the energy card is the trump card in this triangular relationship, and it conditions the actions of Brazil, which are defined by the regional giant's own ambition for regional leadership. Brazil's interest lies in co-opting new actors in its zone of political and economic influence – such as Venezuela – while at the same time avoiding the estrangement of Argentina, the member that holds the key to any hope of viable regional integration.

The fifth and final element of Kirchner's foreign policy is the new relationship with China. Since 2002, the People's Republic of China has become one of the most important foreign actors in South America (Vadell 2007). The Asian global power, which since the 1990s has surged forward on the wings of unprecedented economic growth rates, has re-entered the world stage with a more active and 'institutionalist' profile, beginning with its induction into the WTO in 2001. China has set itself up for a giant leap forward in international commerce, especially with developing countries in Africa, Asia and Latin America. It is in these regions that China is realising its global strategy of procuring the energy resources and vital commodities it needs to fire the engines of its economy.

Within this context, taking into account the chief characteristic of the Argentine economy as producer of commodities, China has proven itself a formidable trade partner for Argentina at the turn of the millennium. The Kirchner government has taken full advantage of this opportunity, and consequently Argentina has greatly benefited from commercial relations with the Asian giant. Thus, from a negative trade balance of US$322 million with China in 1995, Argentina began to obtain a trade surplus in 2001, which then peaked in 2003 at US$1.7 billion, only to decrease significantly since 2005.[8]

There has been no lack of opportunity for the government to politically exploit this new relationship; as the public caught wind of the negotiations with China, the government announced grand investment plans for Argentine infrastructure. Expectations were especially high when Chinese President Hu Jintao visited Buenos Aires in November 2004. Hu publicly affirmed China's plans to invest US$100 billion in the region. Since this declaration, the Argentine government leaked the information (later denied) that China would invest US$20 billion solely in Argentina. Whatever the actual figures were, the agreements signed between Argentina and China proved immensely important, as they represented the first great opportunity for significant foreign investment in Argentina since the moratorium of December 2001.

Another interesting point that reveals the Kirchner style of government is that these agreements were conducted without the direct participation of either Argentina's Finance Minister or Foreign Minister. The ministers were relegated to secondary negotiations, leaving direct relations with Chinese authorities in the hands of the president. This event is no anomaly in Kirchner's decision-making process, but rather another example of his characteristic presidential diplomacy.

Independently of the expectations surrounding Chinese investment, China has become Argentina's third largest trading partner. Also important is the fact that 80 per cent of the value of exports to China has a direct or indirect relation to soy beans, which in turn satisfies one-third of all Chinese imports (Vadell 2007). There are also plans in the works for Chinese investment in the Argentine steel industry. The Chinese firm Sinosteel has been studying the possibility of investing in Argentina's Hiparsa iron mine, with the specific objective of increasing production in order to meet China's growing demand for steel (Ellis 2003: 4).

Two years after Hu's visit to Buenos Aires, amid all the expectations and enthusiasm surrounding this historic event, the reality is that Chinese investment has been far below the magic mark of US$20 billion. What Argentina has seen instead has been investment in very specific areas such as railroads and mining, to the tune of around US$500 million.[9]

OVERLAPPING REGIONAL POLITICS AND DOMESTIC POLICY

In regional affairs, changes in economic policy show a sharp rejection of the principles of open and hegemonic regionalism of the 1990s, imbued with the ideals of economic liberalism. According to Lima and Coutinho (2006: 1), 'open regionalism' is a contradictory expression, 'since the [second] term shows a preference for the region, while the [first] term negates and qualifies this very preference'. Thus, regional integration must, and should be, the platform for opening up national markets throughout the region, favouring competitive sectors, and not an obstacle for the process of opening up to trade and foreign investment.

The Argentine crisis of 2001 acted as a catalyst for domestic political transformations, reconfiguring political alliances between social sectors. The left wing of the Peronist movement won substantive support, and it consolidated its power around President Kirchner. On the other hand, Lavagna, ex-Finance Minister for both Duhalde and Kirchner, had always been tied to the petty bourgeoisie and the industrial business class.

This 'nationalist' economic turn naturally had its consequences in regional politics. The Duhalde-Kirchner worldview parted ways with the principals of open regionalism, which depended heavily on the economic agents of the market and private financial capital. However, the new characteristics of a different type of regional integration enjoys the support of a new brand of politics which calls for a more active role of the state in the economy, with the specific objective of diminishing the region's historic social inequalities.

Does this imply that these changes are exempt from contradictions? If the expression 'open regionalism' comes across as a contradictory term, whose results have shown alarming degrees of social fragmentation and disarticulation, the paradoxes are not found merely in semantics. Other contradictions remain on the horizon at the dawn of the twenty-first century.

The application of an extreme programme of neoliberal economic reforms in the 1990s, especially the fixed exchange rate, had decisive effects on Argentine industry. The higher international competitiveness of Brazilian industry would send ripples throughout Mercosur. President Kirchner, Lavagna, and fellow ex-Finance Ministers Felisa Miceli and Miguel Peirano, were all fully aware of this asymmetry. With the new nationalist and 'developmentalist' focus of the Kirchner government, the outcome would be no different than a conflict of interests and some harsh negotiations between the diverse sectors affected by 'intra-bloc' trade, which since 2003 has created a growing trade deficit for Argentina. Specifically, Argentina's surplus with Brazil of US$2.5 billion in 2002, entered a secular decline to US$112 million in 2003, followed by a deficit of US$112 million in 2004 and US$3.6 billion in 2005.[10]

NEO-DEVELOPMENTALISM, NEO-NATIONALISM AND SOME FINAL REMARKS

The four years of Kirchner's Peronist government signalled a change in Argentina's economic path within a propitious foreign context. This shift called for a return to the state on matters that had traditionally been left to the market under neoliberal ideology. The creation of a new state energy firm, ENARSA (Energía Argentina S.A.), the implementation of price controls and a growing distrust of orthodox economic policies all have marked the path that some authors have termed 'neo-developmentalism' (Bresser Pereira 2007, Godio 2006, Ferrer 2006).

Grugel and Riggirozzi (2007) have questioned the degree to which Duhalde's and Kirchner's policies can be considered a new type of developmentalism. In spite of the fact that this question deserves a more detailed investigation, one can affirm that if neo-developmentalism indeed does suppose a national development strategy, the features of the Argentine version of that strategy are not yet clearly defined. Certainly, there were pragmatic national responses to neoliberalism in the context of growth, whose clearest traits have been an energy-based nationalism and a reinsertion into the world economy on the basis of agricultural export commodities.

The current government of President Cristina Fernández de Kirchner is now receiving the political blows of the after-effects of growth, in which inflation is the most worrisome consequence, as well as the more fragile global economic environment ushered in by the financial crisis in the United States. To this we may add the sharp jump in food prices throughout 2008, which forced the current president to raise taxes on agricultural exports, which in turn sparked mass protests in a rural sector that had already been growing restive during Néstor Kirchner's administration.

The Argentina of the twenty-first century is exhibiting its deepest social contradictions, which must also be comprehended within the context of the nation's political history. The still half-hearted push for development suffers from its dependence on the agribusinesses sector that drives the country's dynamic export sector, whose health determines that of industrial growth and consumer confidence. Thus, whereas Venezuela and Bolivia are clear examples of the nationalisation of energy resources, in Argentina nationalism is closely correlated with the state's control of the wealth derived from the commodities market.

The current conflict between the government and farming and ranching sectors, the mounting energy problem, and high inflation rates have polarised the Argentine population. The rise in commodity prices and Argentina's resulting economic growth, which until only a short time ago seemed to be part of a virtuous upturn for the country, is no longer a reality. Today, this relationship presents itself simply as an inverted mirror in which external conditions reflect themselves in the constriction of the Peronist government's margins for manoeuvre. Moreover, they reflect a distributive dispute that, as is the case of other South American countries (namely Venezuela, Ecuador and Bolivia), reveals a process of social polarisation that will affect not only the internal social fabric of Argentina, but also the process of regional integration.

NOTES

1. This policy is also popularly known as a 'carnal relation' with the United States, a term coined by the Argentine ex-Chancellor Guido Di Tella. In an interview in the news daily *Página12* on 9 December 1990 (www.pagina12.com.ar), Di Tella declared, 'I want to have a cordial relationship with the United States and we do not want platonic love. We want carnal love with the United States; it interests us because we will obtain benefit.'
2. In this case, Argentina estranged itself from its traditional defence of non-intervention in the internal affairs of other nations.
3. One cannot underestimate the important commercial role that Brazil played for Argentina during this time of economic weakness. Brazil was the principal buyer of Argentine products, incurring commercial deficits with Argentina between 1995 and 2002.
4. Argentina has a compulsory electoral system, and thus null votes and blank votes – the former a non-institutional and often illegal voting method; the latter a legal, institutional method – often serve as vehicles for citizens to protest against politicians who are not worthy of what might otherwise be a guaranteed vote by default.
5. Bush encouraged Kirchner with the famous phrase 'fight to the last penny' with Argentina's creditors.
6. A former aide to the Raúl Alfonsín government, he was Finance Minister in Duhalde's transition government, and continued in the same post under Kirchner.
7. Venezuela's special condition as an 'oil state' provides incentives for investments to be funneled toward the petroleum export sector. The political consequences of this phenomenon are observable in many other similar cases, as analysed in Karl (1997).
8. See ALADI database at www.aladi.org.
9. See 'Inversiones Chinas: En Dos Años, de la Euforia a las Dudas', *Clarín*, 14 November 2006, www.clarin.com.
10. See ABECEB/*Jornal Clarín*, http://www.clarin.com.

REFERENCES

Altamirano, Carlos (2004), 'Kirchner Trae Una Visión Estilizada de los Años 70', *Página12*, 17 February 2004, www.pagina12.com.ar.
Aranda, Ramón Alberto (2004), 'La Política Exterior Argentina: de Menem A Kirchner', *IDELA/UNT*, November, www.idela.org.
Bielsa, Rafael, Roberto Lavagna and Horacio Rossatti (2005), *Estado y Globalización: El Caso Argentino*. Buenos Aires: Rubinzal-Culzoni Editores.

Blunstein, Paul (2005), *And the Money Kept Rolling In (and Out): Wall Street, the IMF, and the Bankrupting of Argentina*, first edition. New York: Public Affairs.

Bresser Pereira, Luís Carlos (2007), 'Hay Espacio para un Nuevo Desarrollismo', *Nueva Sociedad*, 29 April, www.nuso.org/upload/opinion/bresser.php.

Buzan, Barry, and Ole Waever (2003), *Regions and Powers: The Structure of International Security*. Cambridge and New York: Cambridge University Press.

Castañeda, Jorge (2006), 'Latin America's Left Turn', *Foreign Affairs*, May–June, www.foreignaffairs.com.

Corigliano, Francisco (2003), 'La Dimensión Bilateral de las Relaciones entre Argentina y Estados Unidos durante la Década de 1990: El Ingreso al Paradigma de las "Relaciones Especiales"', in *Historia General de las Relaciones Exteriores de la República Argentina*, Part IV, Volume XV, ed. C. Escudé. Buenos Aires: GEL.

Corigliano, Francisco (2004), 'La Política Latinoamericana de Kirchner', *Revista Criterio*, December, www.revistacriterio.com.ar.

Damill, Mario, Roberto Frenkel and Roxana Maurizio (2006), 'Macroeconomic Policy Changes in Argentina at the Turn of the Century', mimeo.

Ellis, Evan R. (2006), 'El Nuevo Romance Chino con América Latina: Comprendiendo la Dinámica y las Implicaciones Regionales', *Air & Space Power Journal*, 21 September, www.airpower.maxwell.af.mil.

Escudé, Carlos (1997), *Foreign Policy Theory in Menem's Argentina*. Gainesville: University of Florida Press.

Escudé, Carlos (2004), 'A Río Revuelto: Autonomía Periférica en un Contexto de Desorden Global', *Agenda Internacional*, 1(1), www.geocities.com.

Escudé, Carlos (2006), 'La Muerte de la Política Exterior', *La Nación*, 1 August, www.lanacion.com.ar.

Ferrer, Aldo (2006), *Hechos y Ficciones de la Globalización: Argentina y el MERCOSUR en el Sistema Internacional*. Buenos Aires: FCE.

Godio, Julio (2006), *El Tiempo de Kirchner: El Devenir de una Revolución desde Arriba*. Buenos Aires: Letra Grifa.

Grugel, Jean, and María Pía Riggirozzi (2007), 'The Return of the State in Argentina', *International Affairs*, 83(1): 87–107.

Haslam, Paul Alexander (2003), 'Argentina: Governance in Crisis', *FOCAL: Canadian Foundation for the Americas*, February, www.focal.ca.

Hurrell, Andrew (1995), 'O Resurgimento do Regionalismo na Política Mundial', *Contexto Internacional*, 17(1): 23–59.

Karl, Terry Lynn (1997), *The Paradox of Plenty*. Berkeley: University of California Press.

Lale, David A., and Patrick M. Morgan (1997), *Regional Orders: Building Security in a New World*. University Park: Pennsylvania State University Press.

Lima, Maria Regina Soares, and Marcelo Vasconcelos Coutinho (2006), 'Integração Moderna', *Análise de Conjuntura* (Observatório Sul-Americano), January, http://observatorio.iuperj.br.

Moffett, Matt (2004), 'Latin America is Aided by Weak Dollar', *Wall Street Journal*, 3 December.

Paramio, Ludolfo (2006), 'Giro a la Izquierda y Regreso del Populismo', *Nueva Sociedad*, 205, www.nuso.org.

Pérez Llana, Carlos (2006), 'Este Gobierno Carece de Política Exterior', *La Nación*, 2 September.

Romero, Estela, and Miguel Agustín Torres (2004), 'La Constante Búsqueda de una Identidad: Una Mirada Hacia la Política Exterior Argentina desde Menem a Kirchner', *IDELA/UNT*, November, www.idela.org.

Russell, Roberto (2004), 'Política Exterior y Veinte Años de Democracia: Un Primer Balance', in *La Historia Reciente: Argentina en Democracia*, ed. M. Novaro and V. Palermo. Buenos Aires: Edhasa.

Russell, Roberto, and Juan Gabriel Tokatlian (2003), *El Lugar de Brasil en la Política Exterior Argentina*. Buenos Aires: Fondo de Cultura Económica.

Schvarzer, Jorge (2004), 'Poder Político-social, Condições de Mercado e Mudança Estrutural', in *Brasil e Argentina Hoje: Política e Economia*, ed. B. Sallum, Jr. Bauru, SP: EDUSC.

Tokatlian, Juan Gabriel (2004), *Hacia una Nueva Estrategia Internacional*. Buenos Aires: Grupo Norma Editorial.

Tokatlian, Juan Gabriel (2005a), 'No se Gestó una Estrategia Internacional', *Página12*, 7 May, www.pagina12.com.ar.

Tokatlian, Juan Gabriel (2005b), 'La Argentina, Brasil y la ONU', *La Nación*, 19 May, www.lanacion.com.ar.

Vadell, Javier A. (2006), 'A Política Internacional, a Conjuntura Econômica e a Argentina de Néstor Kirchner', *Revista Brasileira de Política Internacional*, 49(1): 194–214.

Vadell, Javier A. (2007), 'As Implicações Políticas da Relação China-América do Sul no Século XXI', *Cena Internacional*, 9(2): 194–214.

Williamson, John (1990), 'What Washington Means by Policy Reform', in *Latin American Adjustment: How Much Has Happened?*, ed. J. Williamson. Washington, DC: IIE.

13
State and Nation in Brazil:
Old Questions, New Challenges

Sebastião C. Velasco e Cruz and Reginaldo C. Moraes

INTRODUCTION

In his provocative way, just before he died, Darcy Ribeiro (2000) – anthropologist, educator, institution builder, politician, novelist, Renaissance Man gone astray – often referred to Brazil (the Brazil of his dreams) as the 'New Rome'. His reasoning: it was the only country in the Americas with the conditions to become the locus of a genuine civilisation. This possibility did not present itself in the United States, a mere extension of Europe in the Western Hemisphere. Nor did it present itself in Mexico or Peru, countries of 'witness peoples', whose mission was to rescue the extraordinary patrimony of their primal cultures and adapt them to the radically alien context of the modern world.

Exaggerations aside, there is a bit of truth in Ribeiro's provocation. Indeed, from a distance, Brazil comes across as an anomaly. To begin, there is the size of its territory: 8.5 million square kilometres, almost as large as the whole of Europe. With its enormous climatic diversity – the equatorial, super-humid, rainforest climate of the Amazon Basin, the dry tropical and semiarid zones of the north-eastern *sertão*, and the subtropical zone that predominates in the central and south-east of the country – the vastness of Brazilian territory is occupied today by nearly 200 million people of different ethnic lineages and diverse cultural backgrounds, yet who all speak – albeit with different accents – one common language, Portuguese. The third peculiarity is Brazil's imperial past: while the fragmented Spanish dominion in the Americas became republics soon after independence (with the brief Mexican imperial experience being the only exception), the political formation of Brazil, with the territorial unity that it preserves to this day, came about under monarchic rule, which lasted until the proclamation of the First Republic on 15 November 1889. But there's more than that: the fourth, and most sombre, peculiarity of Brazil is that the construction of this immense country was based on the exploitation of slave labour, whose heaviest influence was in those regions which were at the forefront of distinct cycles of the colonial economy: sugar in the north-east; gold in Minas Gerais; coffee in Rio de Janeiro, a region which already had distinguished itself because of its privileged position in the slave trade circuit. The slave regime was extinguished only in 1888.

Naturally, there is much more than mere chance in the convergence of these characteristics, and the exact definition of their mutual relations has been, for more than a hundred years, the primordial task of scholars and essayists, suggestively denominated by someone as the 'interpreters of Brazil' (*explicadores do Brasil*). Joaquim Nabuco (2003 [1883]), Manoel Bomfim (1996 [1931], 1993 [1905]), Oliveira Vianna (1987 [1920]), Caio Prado Júnior (1967), Gilberto Freyre (1986), Sérgio Buarque de Holanda (1997 [1936]), Florestan Fernandes (1975) and Ribeiro himself – in spite of their differences, they all dealt with these elements, synthesising them in their own ways. We are not so bold as to insert ourselves in this tradition with this modest chapter. But we shall take from it a common element: the question of the 'absence of the people' – or rather, in the progressive tradition, of the intermittent presence of the people, with the strong reaction that it always stirs. Brazil appears in this literature as a country endowed with a strong state, highly centralised in certain periods; however, it also appears as a country with a weak collective identity, low social articulation and pronounced inclination toward 'privativism' (*privatismo*). It is a national state, but only very precariously a nation-state.

Whether interpreted by conservatives, liberals or revolutionaries, this is the crux of the question posed by this tradition (of Ribeiro et al.), and to this day it remains the most challenging question, both intellectually and politically.

FROM EMPIRE TO REPUBLIC

With the exception of Joaquim Nabuco and Manoel Bonfim, the intellectual and political biography of the above mentioned authors is marked by the epoch ushered in by the Revolution of 1930. And this is no mere coincidence. As it occurred in so many other countries during the Crisis of 1929 and the Great Depression that ensued, the disorganisation of the pattern of insertion into the world economy exacerbated pre-existing tensions, leading to a rupture in the preceding socioeconomic and political organisation. We can describe this organisation succinctly as the combination of an agro-exporting economy with an oligarchic republic: prosperity rested on the control of the world coffee market and the 'politics of governors' (*política de governadores*) – the decentralised system of governance by the elite of each state. Both features were rooted in the situation that saw the crisis and downfall of the Empire.

Which situation was this? The slave trade had been abolished in 1850 by decision of the imperial elite, made under strong British pressure, amid the unrest provoked by slave revolts in various parts of the country. This period bore witness to the decadence of traditional regions and the flourishing of new ones, where the land was cultivated with the labour of 'free' colonists. The urban population was growing, and within it, there appeared new middle sectors with some level of education, influenced by the new ideas that were arriving from Europe, where evolutionism and Comtean positivism were in vogue. Put together, these circumstances eroded the bases that had sustained Imperial politics. One year after the abolition of slavery, the higher echelons of the army sponsored the *coup d'état* by which the Republic was installed in Brazil.

However, contrary to what liberals and radicals imagined momentarily, what assured the political stability of the country were not the republican virtues of the constitution of 1891, but rather a peculiar political compromise in which the oligarchies that controlled the republican parties in each state mutually recognised their supremacy, committing themselves to respect the unwritten rule of non-interference in the internal affairs of another state in the federation. Under a strongly decentralised constitution, this rule – founded on an extremely restrictive electoral system, the open-vote system and the 'verification of powers' mechanism which endowed Congress with the power to decide the legitimacy of mandates – established a one-party system (or dominant-party system). That is, a one-party system in each state of the federation, the latter being governed by an alliance of the two strongest state parties: São Paulo and Minas Gerais.

It was in this extremely exclusive political context that coffee production spread throughout the state of São Paulo and the first seeds of light industry were sown – as in so many other countries on the capitalist periphery – with the relative disorganisation of commercial flows occasioned by the First World War. With the expansion of industry, the figure of the organised worker burst onto the national scene, with the characteristic demand for a voice of its own, either socialist or anarchist at the time, and in diverse accents, national and European.[1]

During this time, the shift in the foreign relations of Brazil, which had begun at the end of the Empire, was reinforced. Formed with British blessings, the imperial state experienced a moment of crisis with England in the mid-nineteenth century over the issue of the slave trade. But this was not the determining factor that compelled Brazil to opt strategically for an alliance with the giant in the North. At the end of the century, Brazilian diplomacy recognised the United States as the emerging power in the international system and wisely concluded that the strengthening of 'friendly' relations with the United States was the best way to assert itself vis-à-vis its primary rival in the region, Argentina, which was much more prosperous at the time and was virtually married to the old hegemonic power.

With the advent of 1929, all of these elements underwent deep changes. Strictly speaking, we can say that it was at this time that Brazil encountered the first of several great waves of transformation that turned it into what it is today.

THE FIRST WAVE OF TRANSFORMATION

Between 1930 and 1945, under the command of Getúlio Vargas, former governor of the state of Rio Grande do Sul – a permanent counterpoint to the *café com leite* ('coffee with milk') alliance between São Paulo and Minas Gerais – now transmuted into the leader of an anti-oligarchic revolution, Brazil saw itself pushed into the first phase of industrialisation through import-substitution. This take-off was in large part conditioned, first, by the circumstances of the global depression, and, second, by the relative isolation (and supply shortage) of Brazil provoked by the Second World War. Accompanying this process of industrialisation and urbanisation, another process would leave its equally important mark on the formation of the political framework: the federalisation or nation-alisation, de facto, of national politics. A series of political elements – institutions, organisations, successive and extensive regulations – became, in fact, national. The 'politics of the governors' gave way to state politics and to nation-building. A few important innovations of this period deserve some attention.

First, there was a strong concentration of power in the hands of the national executive. A direct result of the Revolution, which sought the immediate overthrow of the governors linked to the old order, was the suppression of the constitutional autonomy of the states. This was established in the juridical order of the *Estado Novo* ('New State') in 1937, after a brief constitutional, democratic interlude.

The second great novelty was the creation of numerous regulatory codes and mechanisms of economic intervention – public enterprises, foundations, independent authorities (*autarquias*), planning councils, and management organs – as well as the rationalisation of public administration, whose most emblematic expression was the Department of Public Service Administration (DASP, Departamento de Administração do Serviço Público) and the adoption of an examination system for the appointment to public office.

The third institutional innovation of the Vargas regime, and by far the most long-lasting, was the creation of a corporativist system of representation of societal interests – legally recognised trade unions and federations, with differential treatment for workers, whose organisations were supervised by the Ministry of Labour – and the Consolidation of Labour Laws in 1943, which established a series of social protection provisions, including the right to a pension and 30 days' annual leave.

It should be pointed out that these provisions benefited only urban workers in formal employment. The great masses of the urban sub-proletariat and the entirety of rural workers were placed beyond the reach of such provisions. Rural workers, in particular, remained under the direct authority of landowners, whose highly concentrated power was unaffected by the policies of the regime. Be that as it may, the advances made in this area fulfilled the original purpose proclaimed by the regime, to promote social harmony and subdue class conflict.

Pari passu, modernising intellectuals, many of them closely linked to the *Estado Novo*, proceeded on a complex intellectual operation whose result – soon to become a basic ingredient of state politics – was the redefinition of Brazilian national identity, which now proudly declared itself *mestiço*. Gone was the ideology of the inherent inferiority of the country due to the racial impurity of its population. Explicit manifestations of racism were banned from the official discourse of the state, though they survived more or less overtly in the actions and the discourse of some branches of the state apparatus (most notably the police).

Born at a time of intense turbulence in the international scene, the Vargas regime also stood out by the innovating character of its foreign policy. Here, the element to point out is not so much the policy of neutrality in the war – a policy which was followed by other Latin American countries – but the bargaining undertaken by Vargas with the Franklin D. Roosevelt administration, which led Brazil to declare war on the Axis powers. Thus, besides benefiting from a rearmament programme foreseen by the Lend-Lease Act of 1941, the Brazilian government received from the United States the approval and the human and material support necessary for the implantation of the National Steel Company, which played an immense role in the subsequent industrialisation of Brazil.

But in May 1945, the Allied victory sounded like an elegy for the Vargas regime. Obliged to convoke general elections in February of that year, Vargas was toppled in October by a military coup, with ample civilian support, during which his officers stood by without even a gesture of resistance.

With the liberal Constitution of 1946, Brazil entered into a new era. Nonetheless, the progressive sectors of the civilian opposition soon saw their most generous expectations frustrated. In the climate of the Cold War that soon followed, conservatism became the dominant mark of the Eurico Gaspar Dutra government. This conservatism was expressed in economic policy, in the extinction of the Communist Party and the retention of the system created some years earlier to control organised labour. The agrarian question remained off the horizon, and, by way of constitutional provisions, illiterate people (nearly 50 per cent of the adult population in 1950) were deprived of the right to vote.

THE SECOND WAVE

It was under this system of limited political competition that the second wave of structural changes swept through. Once again under the leadership of Getúlio Vargas, returned to the presidency, this time by the ballot box, a powerful programme of economic modernisation sought to build the infrastructure for a new period of growth. Large investments in the areas of electricity, petroleum, steel, and transportation, stimulated and enabled the establishment of industries of durable consumer goods, intermediate goods and even serial capital goods. The emblematic expression of this orientation, as well as the key instrument of all the subsequent development policies adopted in the country, was Petrobras, the state-owned enterprise founded in 1952, under the impetus of a broad popular campaign with a strong nationalist character. Less spectacular in its origins, yet equally emblematic, was the founding of the National Economic Development Bank (BNDE, Banco Nacional de Desenvolvimento

Econômico, later renamed BNDES, with the inclusion of the term 'Social'). A public finance institution, the BNDE soon began to play a decisive role in the financing of infrastructural projects, and more generally, in the provision of resources for long-term investments, both public and private, in Brazil.

This system would bear fruit under the presidency of Juscelino Kubitschek, with his slogan of condensing 50 years of development into the five years of his term, which he sought to do with a strong policy of attracting foreign investments. It was during Kubitschek's presidency that the embryo of Brazil's automobile industry was implanted, along with a clear division of labour that was characteristic of the industry for many years to come: a small number of foreign assembly lines, supplied by a relatively de-concentrated auto-parts sector, where national capital had primacy. Also established at this time were the petrochemical and home appliance sectors, among other 'modern' branches of industry.

But the achievements did not end there. The years 1955–60 were a time of high cultural creativity in all areas. Bossa nova, the fruit of musical experimentalism, constituted perhaps the most widely recognised example of this phenomenon. Introducing programmatically elements of jazz into the vast musical tradition of Brazilian samba, the seductive appeal of bossa nova was felt as much within the country as abroad, marking the tune of Kubitschek's Brazil. The decision to move the capital from Rio de Janeiro to Brasília, a city built from scratch in the middle of nowhere, at the central point of Brazil's territory, is an eloquent expression of the confidence of this time. The incredible cost of this venture did not dampen the spirits. For Brazil, the country of the future, the future appeared at arm's reach.

Not everything, however, conformed to this vision. As the heir to the two-party political system put together by Getúlio Vargas – with the Social Democratic Party (PSD, Partido Social Democrata) representing the conservative face and the Brazilian Labour Party (PTB, Partido Trabalhista Brasileiro) the national-popular face – the Kubitschek government was the target of an intense defamatory campaign promoted by the liberal-conservative opposition, frustrated by its repeated inability to take power by means of the vote. The hate unleashed by such a campaign translated into two military mutinies, which were quickly contained. It was nothing that would cause the government to lose sleep. But the signal had been sent.

More worrisome were the growing disequilibria in the external accounts and the inflationary tendency. The government began negotiations with the International Monetary Fund (IMF) in the hope of a loan, yet these did not move forward. Faced with the austere requirements of the IMF, which implied sacrificing many of his goals, Kubitschek broke with the Fund, to the delight of the nationalists and to the great dismay of the 'sell-outs', the representatives of the opposition as they were referred to by the nationalist left.

A polarisation was clearly taking shape, which would lead to the 1964 military coup, after a quick succession of events. Jânio Quadros rose to the presidency as a figure uncommitted to organised political forces; he was adopted by the liberal-conservative opposition as a springboard to power, but he resigned in the seventh month of his term after Congress denied him the extraordinary powers he had sought. The legal successor to the presidency was Vice President João Goulart; he had previously been Minister of Labour during the second government of Vargas, to whom he was closely linked and considered to be his legitimate heir in the *Estado Novo*. However, in the current transition, Goulart would suffer a veto by several leaders of the armed forces who sought to block his legal ascent to the presidency. In the event, the veto failed, due to the deep cleavages that existed in the army at this time, and this in turn gave way to a political pact and a constitutional reform – the adoption of an improvised parliamentary regime – which avoided constitutional rupture. In October 1962, a referendum confirmed Goulart as president, but again he would not exercise his powers for too long. With inflation out of control, in the midst of an open clash with the United States, and with escalating mobilisations and counter-mobilisations – especially as rural workers entered the fray, organised in rural unions and, more threateningly, in 'Peasant Leagues' – the Goulart government collapsed a day after rebel troops began to move. Hence the ambiguity that surrounds the episode: it is known as the 31 March Revolution for the victors and the 1 April coup for the vanquished.

THE THIRD WAVE

The incoming military regime remained in power for 20 years, and it was under its yoke that the third wave of transformations took place in Brazil. These began with the institutional modernisations promoted by the government of Castello Branco (1964–67), the first of five president-generals. The first of these modernisations included monetary reform and restructuring of the capital market, which saw the creation of the Central Bank, the introduction of a mechanism for the indexation of public debt, the centralisation of the banking sector, and the diversification of the financial system (which made room for one segment geared toward the direct financing of durable consumer goods and another toward the financing of homes for the middle classes). Next, the labour market was made more flexible by extinguishing the law that ensured severance pay proportional to the time of service and job security for workers after ten years of employment; this was replaced with a deceiving mechanism: the Guaranteed Time of Service Fund.[2] A new statutory wage policy would also substitute the practice of negotiation, mediated by the Labour Justice Department, with the application of a correction index derived from a mathematical formula established by the government. Finally, a series of broad public administration reforms were implemented, along with the restructuring of the fiscal system, which created new taxes and led to the strong centralisation of fiscal power in Brasília.

The years of strong growth after 1968, and especially the period until 1973, known as 'the economic miracle' for its annual growth rates above 10 per cent, prolonged the developmentalism of the 1950s and stretched it to its limits. Due to a range of circumstances, which cannot be fully examined here, the military regime in Brazil assumed a different role and character than those of neighbouring Argentina or Chile. Industrialist and driven by the idea of 'Great Power Brazil' (*Brasil-potência*), the regime did not destroy the apparatus of state intervention created under Vargas. On the contrary, it strengthened existing state-owned enterprises (SOEs), starting with Petrobras, and created many others, thereby transforming the state business sector into a powerful system of production and regulation. In the same vein, it widened enormously the resources of the BNDE, ascribing to it new and more important functions. Moreover, the mechanisms of compulsory savings were accentuated in such a way as to finance a new push toward industrialisation and modernisation.

But another equally relevant element in this 'great transformation' must be brought to attention: the compulsory modernisation of agriculture, implemented by the strong intervention of the military state. Acts such as the Land Statute and, especially, the Rural Credit System, pushed the country toward a path of agricultural development *without* reducing the concentration of landownership; on the contrary, land concentration increased. Mechanisation, the introduction of chemicals, and the expansion of agribusiness produced a new agrarian elite and a new contingent of dispossessed peasants, turning the countryside into a breeding ground of new political actors. By the mid 1980s there emerged movements of rural landless workers set against a modern, aggressive 'rural lobby', strongly connected to influential urban sectors (banks, industry and media).

An important element in this aspect of the process of change is the internalisation of agricultural development. Concomitantly with innovations in cultivation methods and the reconfiguration of relations between agricultural, industrial and commercial sectors, there was a profound shift in the geography of agricultural production, involving the expansion of new crops, such as soy beans, as well as cattle-raising in previously unutilised spaces in the central and eastern parts of the country. The future that Kubitschek had dreamed of when he created Brasília was now becoming a reality.

This should not come as a total surprise. In effect, in spite of all the violence that resulted from the 1 April coup, between the period of military rule and that immediately preceding it, the continuities are very clear. We already alluded to this when we mentioned the use of Petrobras and the BNDES. Something similar can be seen in the management, supervision and control of labour relations. Here, too, what the military regime did was to utilise fully the institutional resources available to achieve its ends: it was not necessary to change the labour laws to repress labour unions or to purge union leaders who had led the pre-1964 mobilisations and replace them with subservient leaders.

From 1964 to 1984, the Brazilian economy made a leap in its productive system, extended and deepened its industrial sector, and relied heavily on the incorporation of foreign capital. Yet the passage from this 'dependent associated' model of development, to use terminology that is out of vogue, did not occur in the post-1964 period. If we were to look for a dividing line, we would have to go back to the 1950s. And if we follow the arguments of Carlos Lessa, author of a brilliant study co-authored with Sulamis Dain (1980), we may even have to go back to the 1920s. In this work, which considers the economic role of the state in Latin America, especially Brazil, the authors show that since the 1920s the relations between the state, national capital and foreign capital were regulated by a kind of pact. Accordingly, dominant groups – generally businessmen and propertied classes in general – would cede space in certain sectors for the leadership of foreign firms (especially in industry), and would keep for themselves the control over those areas of activity that provided positional returns. These remained reserved areas for a long time, which foreign capital could not penetrate, or at most did so to a very small degree. The military regime retained this scheme, and here, too, there was little innovation.

Regarding foreign policy, continuity also predominated. After a period of nearly unconditional identity with US foreign policy in the years following the coup, the second military presidency would evidence a hesitant autonomy. But it was in the Ernesto Beckmann Geisel government (1974–78) that this impulse became the nexus of a coherent strategy of the country's affirmation on the international stage. 'Responsible pragmatism', as the policy was called, translated into a reaffirmation of the ties of friendship with the United States, but also a denunciation of the nuclear oligopoly and the consequent refusal to sign the Nuclear Non-Proliferation Treaty (NPT). It would also translate into the immediate recognition of the independence of Angola and other former Portuguese colonies, when the United States was still betting on the possibility of vetoing their respective governments, and in the denunciation of the Military Co-operation Treaty with the United States, in reaction to the pressure by the Jimmy Carter administration against human rights violations and the nuclear accord that Brazil maintained with Germany.

The new policy turn was further reflected in Brazil's leadership, alongside India, in the GATT (General Agreement on Tariffs and Trade) negotiations (Tokyo Round), in which the two countries represented the bloc of developing countries opposed to the agenda of the great powers. Thus, there was a resumption, in grand style, of the 'independent foreign policy' whose contours had first been sketched during the Kubitschek government. In the government of João Batista Figueiredo, the last of the president-generals, the rhetoric of diplomacy became more opaque, but the general lines of diplomatic conduct remained the same. This could be seen in the policy of exporting armaments, in the investment incentives given to Middle Eastern countries and, above all, in the support, more than just rhetorical, given to Argentina in its war with Britain over the Malvinas Islands (the Falklands, as they are known in the UK).

In foreign policy, just as in economic and social policy, the military regime deepened a model whose profile had already been clearly designed in the prior period. If we abstract from it the element of political change, it would be possible to narrate the historic trajectory of the country in way that renders the coup as a minor occurrence.

THE FOURTH WAVE

But this abstraction we cannot make. One of the fundamental characteristics of pre-1964 Brazilian society was its strong democratising dynamic. From 1946 to 1964, Brazil experienced enormous economic growth, and with that growth the participation of the popular classes in the political process grew as well. The intervention of these sectors in political life was not a new phenomenon, as has already been shown. After Vargas' suicide in 1954, and largely because of it, the popular classes returned to the political scene to become a central element in the crisis situation that led to the 1964 coup. That coup aimed to suffocate the demand for greater political voice and to triumph over this disturbing force, that is, the democratic impulse of Brazilian society. The architects of the 1964 coup set out from the start to fulfil this task, and with refined zeal. When it came to the popular sectors, particularly in the countryside, violence was the rule. In dealing with politicians and organisations that served as channels of expression for the middle classes, the actions of the regime were much more contained, hesitant. Violence was more surgical in nature, limited in its time and its reach. But soon it began to surge in waves, culminating in December 1968 with Institutional Act No. 5 and the establishment of a dictatorship *sans phrase*.

Yet, contrary to what some analysts have come to believe, the military men that led the coup did not intend to send the country back to the past. They were authoritarian, yet they were modernisers. They wanted strong industry and a robust capitalist economy. Thus, they delegated command of economic policy to civilians, and created a security cordon to insulate them from all forms of pressure, even those that came from the barracks. And in this strategy, they were very successful.

The cycle of growth that began in 1968 and continued until the beginning of the 1980s came as the result of a series of factors, both internal and external, a large part of which had no relation to the orientation of the country's economic policy. What mattered was that, by way of its duration and intensity, this growth implied profound changes in the structure of the Brazilian economy and society. The accelerated urbanisation of this period is one example; the enormous expansion of the waged middle classes and the workforce employed in industry are two further examples. And here lies the great irony. By changing ways of life, opening new horizons and redefining the expectations and worldviews of a large part of the population, these structural changes threw up new social forces which would give new impetus to the democratic dynamic that the architects of the coup had originally sought to extinguish. This dynamic manifested itself from the beginning of the Geisel government in 1974, with the large and unexpected electoral victory of the opposition. Three years later, the labour movement returned to the stage with a campaign for wage readjustment. In 1978, such actions multiplied. In 1979 came the political amnesty; in 1980, the third and longest strike by metallurgical workers in São Bernardo (greater São Paulo). In 1984, the campaign for direct elections exploded onto the scene. At this rate, the military no longer had the conditions to stay in power, nor even to appoint a civilian successor.

Beyond the unanticipated effects of Geisel's liberalising policy, which was transformed into a 'political opening' at the end of his term, as well as the impact of the debt crisis, which struck with full force during the government of his successor, the exhaustion of the military regime was driven by a structural problem that fuelled the critique of the opposition. Along with denouncing the autocratic character of the regime, the democratic opposition denounced the economic model for being exclusive, centralising and dependent – a condition that was becoming critical with regards to technology and, as the 1970s unfolded, to finance.

The opposition had a further criticism. Its target was state interventionism, and its greatest expression was the 'campaign against nationalisation', which mobilised the liberal-conservative press and wide sectors of the Brazilian business community during Geisel's government. But the social and political reach of this criticism, at the time, was limited. When the civilian opposition finally conquered the presidency of the country in 1985, the mottos of its programme were democracy and the sustained expansion of the economy, within the terms of a socially inclusive and autonomous model of development.

Had it been successful, this programme would have been a decisive step in transforming Brazil into a nation. Unfortunately, expectations of this kind were quickly frustrated. Constrained by the commitments assumed by the 'forces of the past' and confronted with a hostile external environment – the debt crisis and the new rules of the game in the international economy, which began to give substance to the neoliberal restructuring of capitalism – the government of the 'New Republic' was paralysed after the unsuccessful attempt to curb rampant inflation by means of shock therapy: the Cruzado Plan of 1986.

During this agonising period, the civil government of José Sarney (1985–89) witnessed the intensification of social unrest, the explosion of the inflationary process – which elevated repeatedly the monthly index above 50 per cent (the conventionally accepted annual rate of hyperinflation) – and an external stand-off with the United States and Europe that worsened day by day.

Three positive elements must necessarily be included in the balance sheet of this period. First were the democratic victories, especially the immediate suppression of the numerous provisions of political control implanted during the military regime (the removal of the 'authoritarian debris', in the language of the time). Second were the important advances in the area of social policy. And third, the work of the Constituent Assembly (Constituinte Cidadã).

Installed in 1987, at the exact moment that the inflationary process was escaping control, the Constituent Assembly, in its process of elaboration and in its results, condensed the contradictions and impasses of this epoch. Not by accident, its text was seen by the representatives of all political quarters as repulsive, incoherent, a provisional fix, a simple truce. Yet, this constitution left an important legacy that survived every revision that the document would later undergo: it institutionalised many of the recently introduced innovations in the area of social policy; and it universalised the vote, incorporating tens of millions of illiterates into the electoral and political dynamic.

Ironically, many of these 'new voters' helped elect Fernando Collor de Mello, responsible for introducing neoliberal reforms in Brazil. We will not go into the details of Collor's short presidency – he resigned from office in December 1992 to avoid impeachment on corruption charges, but even so, he had his political rights revoked for eight years. But we must add that his reform agenda was implanted – and this is another irony of the time – by Fernando Henrique Cardoso, the sociologist known worldwide as the author of 'dependency theory'.

THE FIFTH WAVE

Ironies aside, it was in Cardoso's government that Brazil entered fully into the era of neoliberal reforms. Without a doubt, the biggest feat of this period was the management of the Real Plan (*Plano Real*), a stabilisation programme launched when Cardoso was Minister of Finance and which became the flagship of the electoral campaign that won him the presidency. His intellectual conception of the plan was of some significance, but its success can only be explained in the context of the changing behaviour by international investors, who were turning to 'emerging markets', and the partial transformation introduced by the Collor government – the first important measures towards commercial opening and financial liberalisation.

This intimate association between short-term policy and the transformation of the institutional framework of the Brazilian economy was well understood by Cardoso's team, which bet on the deepening of these 'reforms' to guarantee simultaneously monetary stability and growth. This is not the place to discuss the details of either one of these objectives. But it is worth noting that, during this time, Brazil became the centre of one of the largest privatisation programmes in the world, as well as one of the principal destinations for foreign direct investment (FDI) outside of the Organisation for Economic Co-operation and Development (OECD).

However, the application of neoliberal reforms in Brazil was not as extensive as one would imagine, nor was it marked by an accentuated radicalism. Privatisations were of great importance, and they were carried out to the limit in strategic sectors such as steel, petrochemicals and telecommunications. But the electricity sector ended the period with a mixed profile, while Petrobras, BNDES, Banco do Brasil and Caixa Econômica Federal, along with other banking institutions in certain states of the federation, remained in government hands. There was an attempt to implement sweeping reforms in the social security system (*Reforma da Previdência*), but the initiative did not make it through Congress, which also blocked more ambitious attempts at tax reform.

In terms of foreign policy, we again encounter this sort of mixed game. Cardoso's diplomacy continued the *aggiornamento* begun in the Collor administration: Brazil would accept the agenda of the central states (economic liberalisation, non-proliferation, environmentalism, provisions for human rights, anti-terrorism) and would prove its worth as a respectable member of the 'international community' by signing the NPT, among other symbolic gestures. But it would also reiterate its commitment to principals that Western powers now denounced as obsolete in the post-Cold War world, such as non-intervention in the internal affairs of other countries. In another dimension, Brazil would remain very reticent in the negotiations surrounding the formation of a Free Trade Area of the Americas (FTAA), whose outcomes it would seek to postpone on procedural questions, while investing instead in Mercosul (the Common Market of the South) as a base for building its own international economic space, partially outside the control of the superpower to the North.

In these and other policy areas, what resulted from such crossed signals was an intermediary line that pleased few. And this contradictory approach would not be alien to the politics of his successor.

Luiz Inácio Lula da Silva was elected in November 2002, after a long campaign from which he emerged as leader of a broad developmentalist alliance which called for the reconstruction of the country on more equitable terms, but without sacrificing the hard-won monetary stability. He began his first term extremely cautiously, at least with respect to economic policy. In effect, on this terrain, the continuity of the directives that marked the politics of his predecessor is notable: commitment to ambitious goals of budgetary surpluses, strict control of inflation and the independence of the Central Bank. Such was the 'conservative' face of the Lula government, for which he earned scathing criticism from his opponents on the left, and also from some sections of the business community.

This choice made by the ex-leader of the metallurgical union and founder and leader of the Workers' Party (PT, Partido dos Trabalhadores), a leftist party with a trajectory of unprecedented success in Brazil and Latin America as a whole, took many by surprise. But a brief look at the context in which Lula won the elections might help to clarify his choice.

In many ways, the context was very adverse. With the stabilisation plan (the *Real*) and the structural adjustments of the 1990s, the inflation had been curbed. But the therapy adopted had as its side effects a policy of high interest rates and mediocre economic growth, which translated into alarming indicators of unemployment and income (in terms of level and distribution). Public property had been sold off in order to reduce a skyrocketing debt, with enormous short-term interest payments. And SOEs had been privatised without a previously defined regulatory framework, such that the state monopoly regime was followed by another, of private monopolies operating in a savage environment, which stimulated the search for quick profit, not efficiency. The social crisis was flagrant. In 1994, there were around 800,000 unemployed in the greater São Paulo region. In 2002, there were almost 2 million. Across the country, a period of so-called long-term unemployment was setting in. There were 50,000 detainees in the prisons of the state of São Paulo in 1994, rising to more than 100,000 in 2001. Today, Brazil and Colombia are the only two countries in Latin America that have mass criminal organisations. The culmination of a process that had been building for some time, organised crime permeated all social spheres and all classes and groups, and also extended itself through the different instances of public power. In a perverse allegory of competitive society, organised crime seemed to reveal the recondite truth of the modern market that had been presented as the bright horizon of competitive integration into globalisation.

This 'cursed inheritance', denounced and lamented by the new government, was nonetheless decisive for the change in command. Lula's victory depended heavily on a crisis within the reigning conservative coalition and the disastrous effects of its economic policy, in practically all aspects of national life. In the last year of the Cardoso government, the country found itself literally on the brink of darkness as it faced an unprecedented energy crisis. Affecting the daily life of the whole of the population, the 'blackout crisis' (*apagão*) carried powerful symbolism: contrary to the pretension of competence of a government of 'PhDs', the crisis exposed the bankruptcy of the state, which was defeated by the undoing of its own public machinery.

These are some of the elements of the social crisis that struck the country at the beginning of the millennium. But – and we place great emphasis on this – these elements combined with other elements that made the hypothesis of rupture very problematic. Despite the pitfalls, political institutions functioned regularly, and mutually supported each other, having passed the crucial test of Collor's impeachment and the broad constitutional reforms put forth by the Cardoso government. In Congress and among the state governments, the centre-right forces enjoyed ample majorities. And with each passing day, the weight of the judiciary in the resolution of critical issues grew heavier, reproducing in Brazil a process also observed in many other countries, the 'judicialisation of politics'. And in a conjuncture of retreat or stagnation of mass movements and the weakening of leftist movements, not only in Brazil but throughout the world, with only timid attempts at recovery, the PT went to the polls once again with an extremely moderate coalition.

THE LULA GOVERNMENT

In contrast to the other leftist governments of the continent, Lula won the presidency in conditions of political and institutional normality, a fact that was equally expressed in the behaviour of the voters: in voting overwhelmingly for a leftist candidate, now dressed in elegant suits and using a laid-back discourse, the electorate chose the path of tranquil change. The economic policy could be less conservative, despite this. But we cannot understand this option if we abstract it from the above context.

However, not everything in the Lula government was continuity – not even in the area of economic policy. In the Lula government there was a sensible reduction in interest rates (although they still remain very high); a systematic policy of extending the country's debt profile and reducing external vulnerability, which culminated in March 2005 with the settlement of the country's debt with the IMF; and funding policies by the BNDES (in productive sectors, infrastructure, credit and micro-credit) that have yielded positive results in terms of growth in employment and income. By the way, a significant indicator of the reorientation of economic policy, even if partial, is the restoration of the BNDES into a genuine development bank, after being disguised as an investment bank under the Cardoso government.

In other areas, the differences are clearer. In social policy, we have had a limited reduction of inequality and a significant reduction of poverty and misery. The policies of inclusion were reasonably successful, and with reduced leakage (efficient targeting). Programmes of access to credit and banking services, agrarian reform (financing, credit, assistance), support for family agriculture (credit, marketing facilities) – these resulted not only in a reduction of the desperation of the poorest. According to Paulo Singer, these are 'emancipatory programmes' and should 'result in a significant expansion of the processes of community development, which constitute the best way effectively to fight poverty and avoid the creation of new social and economic inequalities' (2005, our translation). This remains to be seen.

'Palliative measures', 'mere patchwork', the critics mutter. But on the back of ten years of falling employment rates and wage stagnation, some improvements, though seemingly small to the distant observer, can be quite significant for the masses of the excluded. These improvements certainly affect the mood and the way in which these citizens receive signals from the world, including televised signals. And these changes in daily life, though small on the scale of values held by the more demanding activists, or on the wealth scale of the social analysts, mean nothing less than the difference between life and death for millions of Brazilians. And it was largely on the grounds of these meanings and representations that the political judgment was passed that resulted in Lula's re-election in November 2006.

One cannot underestimate the importance of this element. Small policies – which one analyst ingeniously called 'the hidden side of government' – have enormous implications. Some of these are material, as simple examples indicate, such as the increase in the consumption of so-called 'white line' home appliances, construction material and popular furniture. Or the number of 'urbanised' *favelas*: with a street name and postal code, the residents can receive post, purchase orders and buy furniture on credit, as well as seek employment, without having to provide the address of a 'legalised' relative. Or the persistent fall in the price of essential foodstuffs, the so-called 'basic basket of consumption' (*cesta básica de consumo*) of the popular classes. Federal banks were instructed to popularise the access to personal checking accounts, which meant, for millions of people, gaining access to cheaper and more secure forms of credit, and with lower rates than the personal credit of conventional banks or usurers. There are also symbolic implications: through such policies, there is the chance of 'becoming a person'. It is for such reasons that an analyst like Paulo Singer calls such policies emancipatory: they liberate not only the body, but also the soul of the subject-turned-citizen.

Lula was elected for a second term (2007–10) in adverse conditions under an enormous media siege. The victory had a logic that can only be understood amid the pains of the inherited structures and the remedies, small but significant, that the Lula government applied in its first four years in power.

Therefore, there have been changes. But it is in the realm of foreign policy that they have been most evident. The first indications in this sense arose even before the transfer of office, with the dispatching of Lula's personal emissary to Venezuela – at the time submerged in a deep crisis, with the supply of oil cut and the economy in a state of paralysis – and the proposal for the creation of the 'Group of friends of Venezuela', whose activity contributed to overcoming of the political impasse. This was only the beginning. Soon after, the new orientation of Brazilian foreign policy – new in the much more assertive style and the way in which it defined its objectives – came to express actively its condemnation of the war in Iraq; to give emphasis to economic and political integration in the South American sub-continent; to strengthen ties with other 'large countries of the periphery', especially India, China and South Africa; and to adopt an independent position on the commercial negotiations in progress. With this new posture, Brazil made a decisive contribution to the virtual shelving of the FTAA project, and took on a leading role in the alliance that has assured developing nations a vigorous voice in the Doha Round.

The conduct of foreign policy supposes the possibility of changing the architecture of world order in the direction of a multi-polar configuration and seeks to contribute to such a change as quickly as possible. But it seeks to do so by operating within the existing institutions, avoiding a course of conflict that could turn the country into a 'revisionist nation' (in the jargon of the discipline). It is no surprise, therefore, that despite the clear manifestation of divergences, Brazil maintains today a relationship with the United States that is seen by both sides as excellent. The reorientation of foreign policy is obvious, but here too we will find no ruptures.

THE UNFINISHED CONSTRUCTION: OLD QUESTIONS, NEW CHALLENGES

In recent years, Brazil has appeared increasingly in the international media alongside China, Russia, and India as an emerging power, with growing influence in the conduct of global affairs. Apart from the effects of an exceptionally favourable economic conjuncture, this fact reflects an external perception of some economic and social tendencies that have been mentioned, the assessment with regards to the potential of the country – which appears to grow to the extent that the preoccupation with the ecological situation of the planet grows – and the successes of Brazilian diplomacy.

However, the enthusiasm of some must not breed illusions. The fragility at the foundations of Brazil's success is great. Brazil's exporting sector is still greatly dependent on agricultural and mineral commodities, and it is vulnerable to the protectionist movements in the North. Agribusiness accounts for 30 per cent of Brazilian exports – and exports account for more than half of the revenue of the sector. A burdensome public debt still weighs heavily on national finances, even though today it is less bound by short-term consideration, especially with the increase in foreign reserves. External payments are still aggravated by the enormous expenditures with remittances, profits, interest, royalties, in an industry fundamentally serving the internal market, but with ownership strongly concentrated in the hands of non-residents. The financing of infrastructure projects for a new leap in development runs into great difficulties – including embargos imposed by conservative reaction in the legislature and judiciary.

Social disparities continue to be very high, with one of the highest polarisations in the world, when considering the relation between the richest 20 per cent and the poorest 20 per cent. In a feedback effect, the ideological impact of such inequality is brutal: there is enormous resistance to redistributive policies, which is legitimated on the basis of values which are supposedly 'meritocratic' but which, in fact, are almost aristocratic.

To make matters worse, the political system is very resistant to change. Congressional representation is one example. Fifty years ago, Celso Furtado pointed out the persistent conflict between the presidential mandate, the result of a national election in which each head is a vote, and the congressional mandate, with its distortions in representation which favour enormously the less populated states and the oligarchies. In 1964, on the eve of the reactionary military coup supported by the United States, this conflict spawned a popular leftist slogan: 'progressive President, reactionary Congress'. The president embodied reformist hopes, while the parliament assumed the furious defence of the status quo. Decades later, the reality is not all that different. Add to the reactionary and conservative front a judiciary profoundly attached to oligarchic interests and practically immune to any change. The initiatives for agrarian reform and access to rights, for example, encounter, in every corner of the country, the door of the judiciary to halt their entry.

Some time ago, when it was common to speak of the Brazilian economic model, by many considered a 'miracle', Furtado warned that this case demonstrated the insufficiency of industrialisation as the means to overcome underdevelopment; in the last years of his life, he referred to the Brazilian trajectory as an 'interrupted construction'. In his writings (Furtado 1966: 101–2) he would design the development model that he judged both desirable and possible, combining four large vectors:

1. sustained growth: constant (not cyclical), durable, and not based on the predatory use of natural and human resources;
2. reasonable national integration and reduction of regional inequalities;
3. internalisation of dynamisms (economic, technological) and of decision-making centres; and
4. significant incorporation of the masses in the economic, social, and political process.

In general, in the so-called hard sciences, in a vector sum, we can suppose these components as independent. However, such is not the case on the terrain of human history. The four above mentioned vectors are conditioned by one another. Thus, for example, if social and political incorporation of the masses is, or can be, the result of the three other goals, it is also a political condition to enable the first three. And in a certain way, the result, envisioned and presented as a project to the New Prince, acts as a real force.

Reviving the interrupted construction implies confronting old questions. In the conditions of present-day Brazil, these questions translate into a series of challenges, of which the following appear to us as of special importance.

First, there needs to be advance on the technological frontier, so as to create one's own capacity of generating knowledge and innovations. This has to do with the urgent necessity of expanding and diversifying education and research, including that which is essentially incremental and adaptive in nature. Given the profile of the technological frontier, Brazilian development has no option but to be knowledge-based if the country wishes to shed the reflexive and dependent nature of its economy and politics.

On the other hand, this technology does not refer only to the most obvious field of application, industry. Considering the sheer size and the profile of the country, development cannot but be rural-based as well, taking advantage of the country's vast agricultural potential and energy base. The application of technological and scientific research could make Brazil a pioneer of a new sustainable development model that combines both the urban and the rural.

Second, there needs to be a strengthening of the role of the state as guarantor of the civil, political, and social rights of the destitute layers of society. The state not only needs to fulfil the role of the ideal collective capitalist, according to Friedrich Engels' celebrated image. We can add a bit of Karl Polanyi to this Marxist vision. To enable economic development and prevent that it be affected by political resistances and turbulence, generated by the great transformation, the state needs to guarantee 'compensation for the losers' through bold social policies. And we should reinforce the dosage, when we take into account the abysmal inequalities that are the sad mark of the country and the furious resistance that changes, even miniscule ones, tend to provoke. The emancipatory nature of the policies of social and economic inclusion cannot be underestimated. Escaping poverty means, very frequently, escape also from servile obedience. In this sense, we can say that the strengthening of state is the condition, simultaneously, for both development and democracy.

Third, the rule of law must be bolstered in order to fight diffuse criminality and organised crime, this darker side of 'globalisation'. We could say that there already exists in Brazil 'mass' organised crime, with large organisations that dominate the peripheral neighbourhoods of the urban centres. However, organised crime is not a characteristic of the 'poor side' of the country; organised crime traverses society and is certainly co-ordinated from its 'refined' centres. In this sense, it is, fundamentally, a crime 'of the elite', with a wide network of agents in the banking system, commerce and the political apparatus – the legislatures, judiciary and local executives. The challenge here is to promote the required changes in the police and judicial systems in order to do away with its class bias, preparing them to fight crime in the most privileged sectors of Brazilian society and to respect the civil rights of the country's marginalised, the customary victims of unchecked police violence.

Finally, in the area of foreign policy, Brazil must combine the role it is playing – and increasingly tends to play – by its own weight in the world with its disposition to contribute to the process of regional integration (in South America, particularly), as a condition for the realisation of the potential autonomy of all the countries involved.

Overcoming these challenges will not transform Brazil into a 'New Rome' – in the end, there was something assumedly humorous in the metaphor – but it will certainly provoke a satisfactory smile on the face of the restless Darcy Ribeiro, wherever he might have gone.

NOTES

1. From the 1880s onward, the incorporation of immigrants from various European countries, especially Italy, was one of the components of the 'solution' to the problem posed by the transition from slave to free labour. The inverted commas are justified, because the corollary to this process was the mass exclusion of ex-slaves from the labour market, who suddenly saw themselves thrust in the competitive world without the least bit of preparation in order to insert themselves in a stable way.
2. Under this system, an enterprise would contribute the equivalent of 9 per cent of the wages of each employee, who in the event of a lay-off could withdraw the accumulated amount, corrected according to the official inflation index and capitalised at 3 per cent per year.

REFERENCES

Bomfim, Manoel (1993 [1905]), *A América Latina: Males de Origem*, fourth edition. Rio de Janeiro: Topbooks.
Bomfim, Manoel (1996 [1931]), *O Brasil Nação: Pealidade da Soberania Brasileira*, second edition. Rio de Janeiro: Topbooks.

Buarque de Holanda, Sérgio (1997 [1936]), *Raízes do Brasil*. São Paulo: Companhia das Letras.

Fernandes, Florestan (1975), *A Revolução Burguesa no Brasil: Ensaios de Interpretação Sociológica*. Rio de Janeiro: Zahar Editores.

Freyre, Gilberto (1986), *The Masters and the Slaves: A Study in the Development of Brazilian Civilization*. Berkeley: University of California Press.

Furtado, Celso (1966), *Subdesenvolvimento e Estagnação na América Latina*. Rio de Janeiro: Civilização Brasileira.

Furtado, Celso (1968), *The Economic Growth of Brazil: A Survey from Colonial to Modern Times*. Berkeley: University of California Press.

Lessa, Carlos, and Sulamis Dain (1980), 'Capitalismo Associado: Algumas Referências para o Tema Estado e Desenvolvimento', in *Desenvolvimento Capitalista no Brasil*, ed. L.G. Belluzzo and R. Coutinho. São Paulo: Brasiliense.

Nabuco, Joaquim (2003 [1883]), *O Abolicionismo*. Brasília: Editora UNB.

Prado, Caio, Jr (1967), *The Colonial Background of Modern Brazil*. Berkeley: University of California Press.

Ribeiro, Darcy (2000), *The Brazilian People: The Formation and Meaning of Brazil*. Gainesville: University Press of Florida.

Singer, Paulo (2005), 'O Lado Oculto do Governo', *Teoria e Debate*, 61 (February–March). São Paulo: Fundação Perseu Abramo.

Vianna, Oliviera, and José Francisco (1987 [1920]), *Populações Meridionais do Brasil, Vols I and II*, seventh edition. Belo Horizonte, MG, and Niteroi, RJ: Itatiaia and Universidade Federal Fluminense.

14
South American Cleavages and Venezuela's Role

Rafael Duarte Villa

INTRODUCTION

The Andean region has attracted attention by the intensity of its political instability, in contrast to the more stable Southern Cone of South America (with the exception of Paraguay). While the intensity may vary from case to case, it is possible to make some general observations regarding the sources and character of stability and instability in South America as a whole.

South America exhibits a mixture of inequality, poverty, violence and unemployment. The broader Latin American region began the millennium with a remarkable poverty rate, whereby 45 per cent of the population earned up to two dollars a day, and with one of the highest rates of daily violence in the world. Regional imbalances are also stark. Whereas the Southern region of Brazil may give the impression of being on a par with modern advanced countries, this perception vanishes when considering the Northern and North-eastern regions, which are economically weak and socially very imbalanced. Even when considering countries like Bolivia, it is not surprising to find regional divisions, such as between the highlands region of gross social imbalances and the eastern region of great economic strength and quite a modern agribusiness sector.

In principle, it would be possible to ascribe these asymmetries to the weakness of the traditional political agents, such as political parties and leaderships, in completing successfully the modernisation process. Modernisation remains incomplete in the sense that there has been an effective fulfilment neither of the land reform promise nor of industrialisation through import-substitution.

With respect to the first problem, this dates back to the time of Simon Bolivar. The land promise to millions of needy people has always been a constant in Latin American politics. It was also the great promise of the Mexican Revolution, as well as of the democratic

299

and authoritarian governments that took hold in the region since the 1950s and 1960s. At the beginning of the new millennium, it is evident that land reform, one of the main promises of the nationalist and reformist governments of the 1960s, has hardly materialised. In fact, history seems to have gone in an opposite direction. Instead of a fair and equitable redistribution of land, we are confronted with a vast concentration of land in latifundios.

With respect to the second problem, it is important to remember that in the 1950s and 1960s there was an almost mystical faith in industrialisation as the answer to our political and social problems. This thinking was firmly represented by the Economic Commission for Latin America (ECLA, or CEPAL in Spanish and Portuguese). It sprang from the positivist hypothesis which held that political and social underdevelopment was a result of economic underdevelopment. Thus, industrialisation appeared as the pioneer of modernity, which Latin Americans had not yet attained. At the same time, this process was to be driven by the state, in partnership with the national bourgeoisie.

Oddly, although the promise was not fulfilled, Latin America grew at an impressive annual rate of 7 per cent. But growth did not mean proper industrialisation. The result was that Latin America reached the 1980s and 1990s semi- or unindustrialised, but indebted, with high rates of unemployment and inflation, increased levels of poverty, and a decline in gross domestic product (GDP) growth. These decades were certainly 'lost decades'. Thus, it is not surprising that, today, out of a total population of 530 million in Latin America, nearly 34 per cent lives in poverty (with incomes less than twice the cost of the basic food basket) and 12.6 per cent in extreme poverty (below the cost of the basic food basket) (CEPAL 2008). Latin America also leads the world in homicides, with 25 per 100,000 inhabitants in the late 1990s, as compared to 22 for Africa, 1.4 for Western Europe, and 8.8 for the rest of the world.[1]

This incomplete modernisation is a highly seductive variable in explaining the reasons for the demand for political change by both organised and less organised sectors of society. But this sociological variable is not sufficient to explain political stability or instability, or why political stability co-exists with political continuity in the medium and long term.

Although I continue to have my doubts about the term 'radicalised states', with regards to both its theoretical status and its political implications, we may observe four cleavages that are behind the new wave of political radicalism in South America and which help us approach the question of stability and instability. These cleavages include the following: an elite renewal through the ascent of new lefts of diverse hues; a politicisation of socio-ethnic identities; a socio-political polarisation of a class nature; and the politicisation of foreign policies, on the basis of internal and external dynamics.

ELITE RENEWAL AND THE ASCENT OF LEFTS OF DIVERSE HUES

The first cleavage in South American political systems concerns the circulation of elites. This is not explainable by generational change, that is, by the aging of traditional leaderships, such as of Raúl Alfonsin in Argentina, Paz Estenssoro in Bolivia, Rafael Caldera in Venezuela and Leon Febres Cordeiro in Ecuador, among others. This elite circulation reflects the persistence of politico-institutional and social deficits which the democratic regimes failed to address, or which the authoritarian experiences aggravated.

This factor is responsible for the rise of a series of leaderships that include a moderate leftist tendency (Luiz Inácio Lula da Silva, Tabaré Vasquez and Michele Bachelet) and a stronger leftist tendency fused with nationalism, as in the case of Hugo Chávez, Evo Morales and Nestor Kirchner, but also others who, despite not having obtained electoral success, have gained some political legitimacy at the polls, as in the case of Ollanta Umala in Peru and Manuel López Obrador in Mexico.

A number of these leaderships have been called 'neo-populist'. Although the term is inaccurate, neo-populism has been the object of interpretations ranging from the more sophisticated to the more impassioned. In its more sophisticated version, neo-populism appears as a compensatory movement 'to the losers of economic change in Latin America' (Lodola 2004: 16), and this can be defined as a *strategic style* of politics characterised by a five-point agenda: personalised leadership, not necessarily charismatic; a coalition of multi-class support; a strong top-down social mobilisation; an eclectic and anti-establishment ideology; a systematic use of redistributive methods.

The second interpretation involves a binary typology. Jorge Castañeda (2006) placed the new lefts in Latin America within two camps, one 'radical and populist', the other 'modern'. However, the continuities between the new leaderships cannot be reduced to a new binary difference between the 'correct' left and the 'wrong' or 'bad' left. Such categories have no capacity for generalisation or explanation. For example, they cannot explain the immense disrepute of the traditional parties in Venezuela in the eyes of both the middle class and the poor. The contempt for traditional political parties in Venezuela is less related to populism than the lack of legitimacy of the political system. The above categories also cannot explain the success of a right-wing leader, such as Álvaro Uribe in Colombia, who might also be called neo-populist.

THE POLITICS OF SOCIO-ETHNIC IDENTITIES

A second important cleavage concerns the emergence of social and ethnic identities among some of the new leaderships and certain social sectors. A new element is that social and ethnic identity became congruent with political identity. From a social point of view, there seems to be emerging a very strong perception among socially excluded sectors that 'their time has come'. Cases like that of Chávez in Venezuela, Lula in Brazil, or Morales in Bolivia indicate that social sectors, generally the poorest, view the new leaderships through the prism of social identity, such that they may even minimise the absence of broader public policies and accept welfarist policies, along with the continuity of patrimonial admin- istration of the state apparatus, corrupt practices and authoritarian behaviour by some of the new leaderships.

In the case of the Andean region, there is also a specifically ethnic dimension in the political relations established between the leaderships and excluded social sectors. This is not surprising given that, in its ethnic and demographic composition, the region has a significant number of indigenous people. This is especially so in Bolivia and Ecuador, where the proportion of the indigenous population is 55 per cent and 25 per cent, respectively. In Peru, 45 per cent of the population is considered *mestiço* (Villa 2005). In Colombia and Venezuela the indigenous population is 1 per cent and 2 per cent, respectively. As for the Afro-descendant population, this is very low in Bolivia and Peru, and 10 per cent or below in Ecuador, Venezuela, and Colombia.

There is a new trend emerging in the way in which indigenous sectors perceive political representation. The case of Bolivia exemplifies the argument. Since 1978, indigenous parties, the *kataristas* and *indianistas*, participated in electoral contests, but without success. Since the conquest of universal suffrage in the National Revolution of the 1950s, the indigenous Bolivian voter had a strong tendency to vote for the Revolutionary National Movement (MNR, Movimento Nacional Revolucionário). According to Andrés

Aranda (2002: 85, my translation), '[t]his was possible because the electoral support used to be approved by the assembly of the indigenous community. Thus, inside the communities the unanimous vote was above 80 per cent.' However, in the 2002 elections, the indigenous-peasant sectors, led by the leftist indigenous leaders such as Morales and his party Movimento al Socialismo (MAS), as well as by Aymara leftist Felipe Quispe of the Pachakuti Indigenous Movement, obtained 31 per cent of the vote in Congress. And in the presidential elections of 2004, the MAS managed to elect an Aymara indigenous president, Morales. In the case of Venezuela, this ethnic component is also present, as it is in Peru, where the emergence of a political figure such as Umala reveals a tendency to identify the ethnic with the political.

It would not be an exaggeration to affirm that this identity between the ethnic and the political has to do with the fact that the demands for legal equality by ethnic and social sectors may be better translated and mediated by the new leaderships. This hypothesis is supported by the findings of the United Nations Development programme (UNDP) in its research on democracy in Latin America, which concludes that the indigenous people of the Andean regions have quite a negative perception of legal equality. Only 27.8 per cent believe that 'they always or almost always manage to fulfil their rights', which is higher than in Mexico, where only 7.5 of indigenous people perceive legal equality positively (PNUD 2004: 108).

The indigenous constituencies have been emerging in the political systems and societies of the Andes and have been making two basic types of demands. The first demand is for 'constitutional recognition ... as bearers of rights in the nation' (Iturralde 2001: 55, my translation). The second is for changes in the political and legal frameworks, both at national and local levels, in which their political representation is inserted; this implies that the reform process must necessarily involve the inclusion of indigenous demands for political representation. These two demands, in turn, have resulted in political tension, given that the traditional elite created neither the conditions, nor the institutions for welfare and representation necessary to fulfil such demands.

SOCIO-POLITICAL POLARISATION

As a consequence of the socio-ethnic cleavage, a socio-political cleavage has emerged around the new leaderships, whereby electoral preferences coincide in some cases, for example, those of Chávez,

Lula and Morales, with the social origins of candidates. The presidential elections held in Venezuela since 1998, and in Brazil and Peru in 2006, reinforce the notion that the poorer social sectors tend to vote for leaders with popular origins, while the higher-income sectors tend to vote for candidates of their own social status.

In the case of Brazil, the distribution of votes in the 2006 presidential election tends to confirm a social cleavage when we correlate the votes in the first round of the elections to the Human Development Index (HDI) by municipality. In 104 national municipalities with the lowest HDI, the incumbent candidate, President Luiz Inácio Lula da Silva (Workers' Party, PT), received practically three out of four votes in the first round, while in 104 municipalities with the highest HDI, Geraldo Alckmin (Brazilian Social Democratic Party, PSDB) received 48 per cent, against Lula's 37 per cent.[2]

In the case of the presidential referendum in Venezuela in August 2004, it has similarly been argued that '[t]he electoral results provide evidence as to how class identity functioned as a formative element of the so-called "political polarisation" which is expressed symbolically and territorially in the city of Caracas among voters' (Sierra 2005: 31, my translation). The official data clearly show a class cleavage. In the municipality of Libertador, home to the lower-income sectors of Caracas, 68 per cent of the voters favoured 'No' with regard to the revocation of the presidential mandate, while in the middle-class and higher-income municipalities (Chacao, Baruta, El Hatillo), voters overwhelmingly favoured the 'Yes' vote (ranging from 79 per cent to 82 per cent). The municipality of Sucre, which is socially mixed, confirmed the class cleavage by yielding a balanced vote: 53 per cent versus 47 per cent for 'Yes' and 'No', respectively (ibid.).

Nonetheless, if social identity can explain the emergence of new leaderships, it does not sufficiently explain the vote of confidence given to the new leaderships, as expressed in successive electoral victories in legislatures and the executive, as in the cases of Brazil, Venezuela and Colombia. In the case of Lula and Chávez in the first two, the social cleavage has been accompanied by public policy initiatives with both short-term objectives – attending to the immediate needs of the more vulnerable social layers – and longer-term objectives. Chávez's public policies are perhaps exemplary. Although the 'missions' (*misiones*) have a strong emergency character, certain public policies, such as in health and education (which succeeded in eradicating illiteracy in the country), have had a longer-term perspective. Similarly, in Brazil, programmes like the school fund (*bolsa escola*), the family fund (*bolsa familia*), and others targeting employment creation (*renda Brasil*), have managed to redistribute incomes such that, in 2004 alone, the income of the poorest rose by more than 14 per cent.[3]

Certainly, the relation between political stability (or continuity) and new leaderships also has its origin in the manner in which some of the new leaders have dealt with the problem of political violence. In the 1990s, an authoritarian populist like Alberto Fujimori managed to obtain enormous popularity in Peru on the basis of his intensive fight against the terrorist group Sendero Luminoso ('Shining Path'). In 2000, on the heels of Fujimori's success, Alvaro Uribe in Colombia went forward with his own particular crusade against guerrilla groups and drug-traffickers. Uribe, also considered a right-wing populist, rose to power at the end of Andres Pestrana's government, a time marked by economic stagnation and the outburst of political violence. Uribe defined his objective as the reunification of a country that was politically fragmented and consumed by the violence of various groups (guerrillas, paramilitaries and drug-traffickers). He capitalised on the results of his policy of 'democratic security' to receive widespread support and credit from the Colombian people for recovering the legitimacy of a state that, until 2002, was on the verge of collapse. In the trade-off between peace and security, the Colombian people, fatigued by so many years of conflict, were disposed to ignore the immense political costs of Uribe's solution, specifically the internal repression that would violate the human rights of civilians in conflict zones (Villa and Ostos 2005).

On the basis of the above, we may reach a preliminary conclusion: that the leaderships that have emerged on the left in South America – whatever the qualifier used, modern, populist or nationalist – build their political legitimacy on public policies that confront social inequality, as the cases of Lula, Kirchner, Chávez and Morales demonstrate. Meanwhile, the leaderships on the right, such as those of Fujimori and Uribe, have placed their emphasis on the fight against political violence.

A final cleavage is manifest in the new models of foreign policy, which are highly politicised and substantively different among South American states. We will approach this cleavage by considering Venezuela's South American policy and the impact of internal dynamics on foreign policy.

THE IMPACT OF INTERNAL DYNAMICS ON VENEZUELA'S FOREIGN POLICY

The unfolding of certain events in domestic politics is important to understand Venezuela's position in relation to South America. At the level of ideas, the government is convinced that it is possible to convert the country to its project of 'twenty-first Century Socialism'. Although it may not be clear what this really means, it is clear that an ideological radicalisation occurred after the 2004 presidential referendum, culminating in the founding of the United Venezuelan Socialist Party (PSUV) in early 2007. Certainly, its close relationship with the Cuban government helps to explain the radicalisation, but the latter is founded on some internal developments of greater importance.

First, Chávez has a history of successful electoral confrontations. After winning the 1998 presidential elections, he was confirmed in 2000, in accordance with the transitional provisions of the Constitution of 1999; in the 2004 presidential referendum, he managed perhaps his most decisive victory over the opposition; and in December 2006, he was re-elected for a second term with almost 63 per cent of the votes. Second, Chávez overwhelmingly controls the state machinery, both at the state (provincial) and municipal levels. Nineteen out of 23 state governments are dominated by *Chavistas*. And given that in the prior elections for the composition of the National Assembly, in late 2005, the opposition did not field candidates of its own, the legislative chamber is entirely *Chavista*. Third, the social programmes under the rubric of the *misiones*, which have had a significant impact on the reduction of poverty, are still very well received by the under-resourced sections of the population. Add to this the new oil-driven cycle of consumption which has been beneficial to these social layers; as well as the split in the opposition between those that recognise the need to confront the forces of *Chavismo* on a democratic playing field and those that have been taken over by a culture of destabilisation.

The Venezuelan government has also a very strong nationalist inclination, which reinforces the ideological radicalisation. This nationalism expressed itself more clearly in the beginning of the second presidential term, in the process that sought to reverse the privatisations that had occurred during the 1990s, in the last governments of the *Punto Fijo* pact of Carlos Andrés Perez and Rafael Caldera.[4] The announcement of the nationalisation of some electricity and telecommunication companies should not have surprised anyone. Despite the delay, they were realised when the moment was right, after Chávez's overwhelming re-election in December 2006 and his dominance of Congress. Thus, Chávez managed to pass the enabling law that was missing for the re-nationalisations.

However, the impact of the renationalisations may have been more political than economic. The impact on the Venezuelan economy is likely to be small. And the loss to the multinational firms, such as the Spanish *Telefônica*, must also have been small. However, from a political point of view it would consolidate the fears of foreign investors that Venezuela is not reliable regarding their capital and it would increase the fears of the United States and Europe that Venezuela is advancing towards a nationalist radicalisation. It would equally spark fears among neighbouring states, especially those of Mercosur (the Common Market of the South), regarding possible difficulties in dealing with a leader who takes internal measures without taking into account the impact of the integration process.

This is not to lose sight of the role of ideas in Chávez's decision. Given his socialist convictions, he perceives state control over strategic sectors, such as telecommunications, electricity, the issuing of currency, or the oil strips that remain in private hands, to be fundamental. But, certainly, the success of his project will depend more on the manner in which Venezuelan society reacts, which is so socialised in liberal values and the American way of life.

ACTIVISM, OIL AND VENEZUELA'S LACK OF STRATEGIC VISION

Under Chávez, Venezuela's foreign policy began to grant higher priority to Latin America, and especially South America, which has resulted in a contradictory dynamic of co-operation and conflict, especially with Brazil, although the conflict in this case is more veiled than declared. There has been some estrangement in the Brazil-Venezuela relationship, whose inflexion point was Venezuela's decisive support for Bolivia's decision to renationalise its gas and oil industry in May 2006. Also irritating to the Brazilian government has been Venezuela's interventionist behaviour in the domestic affairs of South American states, especially in electoral processes, such as in the case of Peru and Ecuador. Moreover, the Brazilian government has also viewed with dissatisfaction Chávez's own attitude in establishing preconditions for Venezuela's definitive entry into Mercosur, especially Chávez's argument that Venezuela is not interested in integrating into the 'old Mercosur', referring to the strongly commercial nature of the integration of the Southern Cone up to the present.

Moreover, Venezuela has supported, together with the more radical leftist governments in Latin America, such as Cuba, Nicaragua, Ecuador and Bolivia, the regional bloc known as the Bolivarian Alternative for the Americas (ALBA). But Chávez's foreign policy agenda is still wider. Chávez defends an alliance of state-owned Latin American oil companies, Petrosur, which would speed up the regional integration of the energy sector, and has further proposed, among other initiatives like the Bank of the South as an alternative to the World Bank and the International Monetary Fund (IMF), a nuclear consortium among Argentina, Brazil and Venezuela, the development of a Mercosur gas pipeline, the integration of Latin American armed forces, and the creation of a regional defence alliance that would exclude the United States. He has also supported the creation of Petrocaribe (a Caribbean multi-state oil company) and Telesur (a South American multi-state television company). In the wider global context, Chávez continues to slam the United States in his speeches as he simultaneously strengthens his ties with China, Russia and Iran, with which he supports a multipolar world (Villa 2004, 2007).

What are the roots of this intense diplomatic activism? It is necessary to clarify that Venezuelan foreign policy activism has been a constant throughout the democratic period that began in 1959. In the 1960s, the social democratic Venezuelan president Rómulo Betancourt, the great architect of Venezuelan democracy under the *Punto Fijo* pact, became notorious for his diplomacy of proclaiming the so-called 'Betancourt doctrine' which denied recognition to any government that came to power on the basis of foul play. In the 1970s, the government of social democrat Carlos Andres Pèrez, architect of the nationalisation of the oil industry in 1976, always nurtured the dream of becoming one of the main leaders of the third world. Chávez's government has given continuity to this tradition since the beginning of 2000, that is, a tradition of coveting a role as a regional player which does not correspond to its power resources, or its geographic or demographic size, or the size of its internal problems.

Apart from Venezuela's traditional activism – which some authors (Romero 2007: 1) even date back to the times of Simon Bolivar – it is not surprising that oil resources have been mobilised as a political instrument to serve a hemispheric foreign policy, that is, for the realisation of political projects of regional influence, or as a bargaining chip. This is the second constant in Venezuelan foreign policy.

During the two decades of the *Punto Fijo* pact, the greatest volume of oil income (the main instrument of regional influence) was directed towards Central America and the Caribbean. In so doing, Venezuela competed with Mexico for regional influence, although this competition had outstanding moments of co-operation, such as the San José Treaty, which supplied oil to Central American and Caribbean countries at prices protected from the contingencies of the world market, and the Contadora Group, in which Colombia and Costa Rica also took part, which played a frontline role in the mediation of the armed conflict in Central America in the 1980s.

The novelty of the foreign policy of the Chávez period is that, on the one hand, Venezuela no longer has a strong competitor in Mexico, whose foreign policy activism ceased in the early 1990s; and on the other, it has redoubled its interests in Central America and the Caribbean, through the intense relations with Cuba and the creation of Petrocaribe in 2006 as an instrument of aid and co-operation. At the same time, a further novelty is Venezuela's growing interest in playing a protagonist role in South America, thereby also confronting Brazil's agenda in the region. This objective combines the mobilisation of ideological elements with pragmatic political resources. The image of a man moved by ideas and a Bolivarian historical mission has nurtured suspicions among domestic sectors in some South American countries, such as Brazil, Chile and Peru.

The most co-operative of objectives with regards to South America have often been confusing, as was the case of the failed proposal of an oil pipeline that would cross South America from Venezuela to Argentina. This amounted to a lack of strategic vision, a deficiency nurtured by Chávez's personalist style. Just like in domestic politics, in foreign policy Chávez could justly claim that 'foreign policy is me'. It is true that Chávez inherits a tradition that is, in fact, constitutionalised, and that strongly tends to concentrate foreign policy-making in the hands of the President of the Republic. But the personalism of Chávez in foreign policy can only be compared to the first government of Carlos Andrés Perez (1973–78). The lack of strategic vision in foreign policy is reflected in the constant change of Foreign Affairs ministers, which does not allow for the consolidation of aims and procedures in the ministry. The concentration of power is very possible in presidential regimes, but it does not necessarily imply constant changes in its bureaucracy. Until mid 2007, six chancellors had passed through the *Casa Amarilla* ('Yellow House', or Ministry of Foreign Affairs) under Chávez. Chávez also inherits a foreign policy apparatus whose diplomatic and bureaucratic corps are hardly professionalised, when compared to that of the Itamaraty (Brazilian Foreign Ministry) in Brazil, for example. None of Chávez's chancellors have been career diplomats.

In addition, the paucity of strategic vision has caused tensions with other South American governments, especially those with which, in theory, the Venezuelan government would have an ideological affinity, such as that of Brazil. Chávez's foreign policy for South America has led to the revisiting of some common liberal ideas which postulate that governments of states with similar political regimes tend to be more co-operative with each other, while governments with different political regimes tend to be more antagonistic. Liberal thought conceived of this as the theory of 'democratic peace', which, since Immanuel Kant, has affirmed that democratic governments do not go to war with one another. We may twist this theoretical premise to say that leftist governments with substantial ideological coincidences should tend to be more co-operative with each another, even if the content of their leftism may be of different intensity.

With the current trend of emerging leftist governments in Latin America, and especially in South America, this notion made a great deal of sense; it was expected that the strategic goals of South American countries, such as regional integration, would find a more favourable environment among leftist governments. This was a strong bet by Brazilian foreign-policy makers in relation to the new nationalist governments with leftist hues, such as that of Chávez in Venezuela.[5]

TENSIONS WITHIN SOUTH AMERICA

In principle, the overlap of positions between the Brazilian and Venezuelan governments tended to confirm the premise regarding the higher convergence among governments of similar political character. These coincidences were not few. Amado Luiz Cervo (2001) summarised this close diplomatic relationship some two years after the beginning of the Chávez administration:

> Effectively, insofar as differences of style in external action is concerned, no other South American country presents, compared to Brazil, in the beginning of the millennium, so many common variables in its vision of the world and in its external strategy as

Venezuela. The convergence establishes itself within the following parameters: (a) the concept of asymmetrical globalisation as a correction to the concept of beneficial globalisation; (b) the political and strategic concept of South America; (c) the reinforcement of a robust central nucleus in the national economy as a conditioner of global interdependence; (d) the prior integration of South America as a conditioner of hemispherical integration; (e) a perception about the harmfulness of ALCA [Área de Livre Comércio para as Américas, or Free Trade Area of the Americas, FTAA], in the case of its establishment without prior conditioners and without effective commercial reciprocity; (f) reservations towards the military aspect of Plan Colombia; (g) repudiation of any North American military presence and over flights in the Amazon; (h) the decision not to privatise the oil sector. (ibid.: 19, my translation)

Cervo also highlights that during the administrations of Caldera, Chávez and Cardoso, from 1994 to date, 'the personal effort of the heads of state was the main engine of co-operation that was enhanced in the spheres of political and economic action' (ibid.: 7–10).

What then has changed and what is the limit of this change? First, it is necessary to say that the differences between Brazil and Venezuela are at a level that can still be treated diplomatically. But the differences are not of diplomatic style, they are substantive. Certain issues are no longer relevant in the original overlap; for example, with the almost definitive freezing of the ALCA project and the multilateral efforts of Brazil to secure a position adequate to its status as a middle power in the 'asymmetric globalisation', two points that offered good arguments for a solid bilateral relation vanished. But the substantive causes of differences are to be found on the binomial of ideas and interests that now dominate the Venezuelan elite in power and the manner in which the latter views its role in South America, which does not coincide with Brazilian ideas.

The distancing of Brazil and Venezuela reveals some important differences. First, South American countries, even if they appear to have a certain ideological convergence, they do not have a common foreign policy project. Within the different hues of left politics that exist in South America – that span a spectrum from the more radical to the centre-left – there appear to be three foreign policy projects: one represented by the founding states of Mercosur, which, despite successive crises and different government styles, agree that it is necessary to maintain the autonomy of the bloc with a positive agenda towards the United States; a second project which is more orientated towards a strong relationship with the United States, and is advocated by Chile and Colombia;[6] and a third project, which is the perspective of the ALBA bloc, that is, a more radicalised proposal that includes three Andean countries, Venezuela, Bolivia and Ecuador, but whose main promoter is the Venezuelan government.

Another important aspect revealed by the diplomatic estrangement is the existence of substantive differences between Venezuela and Brazil in their conception of the process of integration. There is a strong difference over what the political nature of the regional integration process must be. Venezuela conceives of the integration process as resting on a foundation that is not only economic but also profoundly political. It also conceives of the integration process as anti-capitalist, in accordance with its vision of 'Twenty-first Century Socialism', which differs from the moderate centre-left view, which places a strong emphasis on the commercial nature of the integration process and which is sustained by Brazil and the rest of the original Mercosur nations. As Carlos Romero, an important scholar of Venezuelan foreign policy, has observed, this alternative model of integration proposed by Venezuela is concerned with

> defining an integration that in the medium term is based on non-capitalist foundations, in the exercise of a participative democracy, in the promotion of an economy that combines state property with social and co-operative property, and in the regulation and reduction of foreign direct investments. (2007: 7, my translation)

Actually, ALBA was in principle an initiative of the Cuban president, Fidel Castro, but it found in Venezuela its most enthusiastic proponent and financial supporter. ALBA was initially conceived of as an alternative to the ALCA project promoted by the US government. Its declared objective is to widen integration and resist US influence in the region, on the basis of the elements mentioned above by Romero. Perhaps the alternative character of ALBA will sooner or later come into conflict with the more pragmatic Mercosur. During the first meeting of the member states of ALBA in mid 2007, the Venezuelan government sent clear signs of this estrangement by announcing the creation of the Development Bank to fund joint projects among ALBA members. And in a clear reference to Mercosur, Chávez himself said that 'we are forced to advance more rapidly every day and in a more precise way'.[7] Meanwhile, the members of the treaty have already sketched out for the future the institutional structure of the integration mechanism, aspiring to turn ALBA into 'a confederation of states'.

Perhaps the premises on which this alternative model of integration is based could explain the ambiguous and vacillating discourse that the Venezuelan government has adopted since the first semester of 2007, that sets as a condition for its definitive entry in Mercosur the profound reformulation of the latter, as it is no longer of interest to Venezuela to join the 'old Mercosur', as the president calls it. The Venezuelan president could have been signalling the possible withdrawal of Venezuela's candidature, since his vision of a substantive Mercosur would be based on ideological alignments, in addition to a substantive and structural convergence of interests (such as the common front against ALCA or globalisation).

On the other hand, although Fidel Castro continues to be an important reference for part of the Latin American left, Venezuelan leadership would find, without a doubt, more space for action in a bloc like ALBA. In fact, until now ALBA subsists on the basis of the mobilisation of Venezuelan oil resources, capable of subsidising the oil consumed by Cuba and part of the social programmes underway in Bolivia, Ecuador and Nicaragua. In other words, ALBA is a kind of foreign policy clientelism that works on the basis of the exchange of influence for oil (or its resources). Meanwhile, this foreign policy clientelism has received very little enthusiasm from key countries like Argentina, from which Venezuela purchased 5 per cent of its external debt in 2006, and with which it signed important energy agreements in 2005. In the Argentine case, the discrepancy between the enormous co-operation efforts by the Venezuelan government and the small returns for its plans of an alternative integration project is an additional reason for *Chavista* presidential diplomacy to prefer substantive agreements based on ideological preferences.

But why would Chávez's diplomacy turn into an interesting victory, as was the case with the signing of the Mercosur Adhesion Protocol in 2006 to become an integral member of the bloc, in a fleeting passage, without objective results for the country? When the Venezuelan government decided to abandon the Andean Community of Nations (CAN, Comunidad Andina de Naciones) in 2006, the argument was that the Community had been weakened by US interference through commercial mechanisms, such as in the areas of trade promotion and drug eradication, a free trade proposal which had already been signed by Colombia and Peru, and additionally through military and political mechanisms, such as Plan Colombia, which is seen as a future bridge for US intervention in Venezuela.

The Venezuelan government did not have such strong arguments to pull out of Mercosur, of which, in any case, it is not even a full member. The accusations against the Brazilian Congress of being 'a parrot of North American imperialism', or even the deadlines given to Brazil and Paraguay to approve the definitive entry of Venezuela into Mercosur,[8] was no more than ambiguous rhetoric showing lack of a strategic vision by the Venezuelan president.[9] This resulted in internal problems for the heads of state of Mercosur, and especially for Lula, who was strongly criticised by certain sectors for supporting the entry of a country whose president is perceived as a threat to internal democratic principles and who constantly violates the most basic principles of non-intervention in the internal affairs of other nations.[10]

Nonetheless, the lack of strategic vision, which is partly explainable by the absence of a more professionalised and less politicised structure at the helm of the Foreign Affairs ministry and partly also by the voluntarism of presidential diplomacy, does not lead the Venezuelan executive to lose sight of certain strategic objectives for the country. It must not be forgotten that since the last days of the *puntofijista* democracy, Venezuela defined South America as an important alternative for the diversification of its economic and political relations. And with the arrival of Chávez to power, Mercosur was defined as a 'strategic objective' by Venezuela (Villa 2004: 110).

Either because of pragmatism or because such an objective is still valid for *Chavista* diplomacy, Chávez showed signs of understanding what was at stake for Venezuela. The visits by the Venezuelan ambassador to the Brazilian Congress in July 2007, and the statements made at the same time by the president himself excusing the Brazilian executive for the delays in Congress, attenuated the estrangement between the two countries. The Venezuelan ambassador, putting aside his ideological convictions, expressed that '[t]here was no intention whatsoever by President Chávez to give an ultimatum to Congress. The fact is, there is a Venezuelan market interested in joining Mercosur.'[11]

The dynamics of approximation and distancing between Venezuela and Brazil must be considered in a series of broader aspects. The first aspect to be considered is the pressure by Chávez on the internal political institutions of the Venezuelan opposition. Certainly, given the doubts and reservations, especially in the United States and in the European Union, raised about the uncertainties created by Chávez's internal policies with respect to the Venezuelan democratic system, the proximity of Lula to the Venezuelan leadership could eventually affect Brazil's image negatively. But the episode that involved Venezuela, the Brazilian Congress, President Lula himself and Itamaraty can be interpreted as a message sent by the Brazilian government to other governments, that even though Brazil remains politically close to Chávez's Venezuela, it does not approve of internal actions by Chávez that would destabilise domestic institutions in the opposition. At the same time, Brazil may fulfil an important role in relation to Venezuela, exercising a 'moderating power' to the *Chavista* excesses against Venezuela's internal political institutions, given that it is well known that Brazil, since Fernando Henrique Cardoso's second term, remains one of the few countries to which Chávez tends to listen, even in times of diplomatic tension.

The second aspect to be considered has to do with the commercial question. This theme is quite complex because, even if Brazil wishes to distance itself politically from Chávez, this would be contrary to the Brazilian foreign policy of transforming South America into the principal area of Brazilian exports. It should be recalled that in late 2006, South America represented over 20 per cent of Brazilian exports, just below that of the European Union, which was at 22 per cent. With respect to Venezuela specifically, until the government of Cardoso in Brazil, trade with Venezuela was hardly dynamic or significant. But in the last four years, Venezuelan imports from Brazil have acquired an unprecedented dynamism. Brazil's trade with Venezuela is growing faster than that with the other South American countries. In 2006, Brazil became Venezuela's second most important commercial partner, displacing Colombia; today Brazil is second only to the United States. And certainly the trade balance is favourable to Brazil. Of the US$4.2 billion negotiated in 2006, Brazil exported US$3.5 billion, while Venezuela exported only US$600 million (VENBRAS 2006: 2–5).

Similarly, some internal policies by Chávez, especially in the food and civil construction sectors, are favourable to Brazilian capital and certain states of the Brazilian federation. For example, states like Amazonas and Roraima have in Venezuela their main export market for their timber, while the state of Paraná and private firms like Sadia export huge amounts of food, especially chickens, that are destined for the popular markets created by the Chávez government. Finally, over the last five years, Venezuela has been an important destination for Brazilian finance through the BNDES (Banco Nacional de Desenvolvimento Econômico e Social, or National Bank of Economic and Social Development), which has enabled

Brazilian building contractors to carry out some of Venezuela's main public works, such as the construction of bridges and the enlargement or construction of new subways in various cities of the country.

The third issue involved in the relations between Venezuela and Brazil has to do with regional leadership. In this case, we certainly cannot speak of approximation but, on the contrary, distancing. And the highlight of this distancing was certainly Bolivia's rena-tionalisation of its gas and oil sector in May 2006. This moment is symbolic in the relations between Brazil and Venezuela, not only for the participation of Venezuela in the consultations over the Bolivian nationalisation decree, but also because Venezuela's participation revealed three relevant aspects of its foreign policy for South America.

First is that Chávez had a real influence over certain politicians in the region, especially in the Andean countries of Bolivia, Ecuador and Peru. That which may possibly concern the Brazilian government most is that this influence might not be exercised in a responsible manner, in which case it could lead the Venezuelan government to lose sight of the political consequences of openly interventionist postures, as occurred in Ecuador and Peru during their presidential elections.

Second, although the nationalist reaction among some Brazilian opinion-makers called for more drastic measures against Venezuela for its role in the renationalisation of the Bolivian oil, the Brazilian government was not so totally naïve as to overlook that states, even when they preach co-operation and integration, simultane-ously pursue an egoistic agenda. For over two decades, whichever Venezuelan elite has been in power has always sought to promote the internationalisation of its oil sector. Even though the last *puntofijista* governments of the late 1980s had a different philosophy on the functioning of democracy – the model was one of representative democracy and not participative, as in the Chávez era – there is a line of continuity in the objective of internationalising Venezuelan oil that runs though Chávez's governments. Thus, Chávez, despite his sharp criticisms of the United States and of neoliberalism, never seriously proposed winding down Citgo, a subsidiary of PDVSA (Venezuela's state-owned energy company) in the United States, or Veba Oil (another PDVSA subsidiary) in Germany; in all cases, his policy has always gone towards restructuring these subsidiaries and articulating their functions with the new government philosophy, before getting rid of them.[12]

Thus, the renationalisation of Bolivian gas and oil presented an opportunity for the Venezuelan state to promote its policy of inter-nationalisation, given that it would mean the expansion of trade and investment for PDVSA, the only Latin American oil company with high technology and investment portfolios capable of competing with the Brazilian Petrobras. However, the manner in which this was done was diplomatically disastrous because it clashed with Brazilian interests, just as Venezuela appeared to be the South American country with a foreign policy close to that of Brazil. Also, the Venezuelan government opted for promoting its own business interests in South America, at the expense of the co-operative discourse and projects, such as the proposal to create a South American supra-state company, Petrosul. In addition, Venezuela took advantage of the old image of Brazil as 'sub-imperialist', which re-emerged among sectors of Bolivian society and which identified Petrobras as the ultimate expression of this behaviour.[13]

Finally, Chávez has shown significant capacity to assume economic and diplomatic initiatives which clash with Brazil's aspirations for South American leadership. This fact has awakened Brazil's perception that Chávez is serious about building a project of regional leadership; that he is not just an ally, but also a potential competitor. In practice, this capacity to take initiatives has included the purchase of part of the foreign debts of Argentina and Ecuador, the proposal for financing Bolivian gas and oil production, the proposal of a southern pipeline,[14] and the latest proposal for creating a funding organ known as Bank of the South.

Added to these is Chávez's financial assistance to the electoral campaigns of candidates close to his ideas in countries that have recently held elections, such as Mexico, Nicaragua, Peru and Ecuador. Chávez seems to have turned himself into an inexhaustible factory of regional initiatives. All in all, the consequence has clearly been an increase in the Venezuelan government's political influence, which has become a constant reference in domestic political affairs in the countries of the Andean region and Mercosur. Such activism may have nourished Chávez's belief that he could transform himself into the latest and most outstanding leader of the Latin American left, as a Fidel Castro replacement.

Despite some diplomatic setbacks, like the southern pipeline and the Bank of the South, if the Venezuelan leadership carries on with its initiatives, Brazil has little chance of neutralising Venezuela in the short term, because Chávez's Venezuela has something that Brazil does not: the flexibility of using or providing huge economic resources rapidly.[15] For its part, Argentina is less concerned with regional leadership and does not give priority to neutralising Venezuela's activism. At the least, the mobilisation of Venezuelan resources leaves certain countries like Argentina (Venezuela bought 5 per cent of Argentina's foreign debt) with less possibility of playing a critical role against Venezuelan initiatives, even against those acts which constitute intervention in the internal affairs of neighbours or that destabilise the long-term project of regional integration.

It is also true that the Venezuelan government takes advantage of the great discrepancy between discourse and concrete action on the part of Brazilian diplomacy. In this sense, Brazil has a problem similar to that of the United States. It offers much on a discursive level to South American countries and very little on the level of concrete initiatives. In contrast, the Venezuelan government, among its initiatives, has used a social agenda that serves to legitimatise itself internally, through public policies like the *misiones* to affirm itself externally (Maya and Lander 2007). The export of the social agenda as a diplomatic bargaining chip works well with some South American partners, like Bolivia and Ecuador, to which it has exported its social co-operation programmes in collaboration with Cuba. Even the initiatives of the George W. Bush government seemed to recognise, paradoxically, that the social co-operation initiative is correct, and the Venezuela-Cuba pair must be neutralised in the field of social initiatives. In his last visit to South America, Bush defined as one of his objectives the support for programmes in education, health, and housing. According to the US president, the amount of US$385 million was to be allocated to family housing programmes in Mexico, Brazil, and Chile. Countries like Brazil and Argentina promise investments and social aid initiatives, and open their markets to South American products in the medium term, while Chavez invests, assists, and buys in the short term.

CONCLUSION

The activism of Venezuela in South America, heavily charged with nationalism and commonplace references of the traditional left, encounters resistance in some countries of the region, while the pragmatism of the Venezuelan leader keeps the doors open for cooperation. This is true both for the countries with ideological affinities to Chávez, and for those without them. With regard to the group of South American countries as a whole, the reaction to Venezuela's activism in Brazil and in some other countries has served to show the Venezuelan government the limits of its external actions based on oil and the export of ideas.

But Venezuelan leadership is also complex. Take, for example, the case of Colombia: despite diplomatic tensions between Colombia and Venezuela in early 2008 when the Colombian army invaded Ecuadorian territory in order to eliminate members of the FARC (Revolutionary Armed Forces of Colombia), this has not impeded the signing of treaties for the development of energy integration or the coincidence of positions in some multilateral forums, like the Organisation of American States. Currently, the two are constructing a binational gas pipeline, an investment of US$100 million, that will unify western Venezuela with Colombian territory.

But the main dilemma of Chávez's diplomacy is to decide whether to opt for the leadership of a group with little capacity to influence substantively the external agendas of South America, this being the case of ALBA, or to participate in a bloc of countries, specifically Mercosur, in which its leadership aspirations will have to pass through the maze of interests and expansive regional tactics of more heavyweight countries like Brazil and Argentina. Alternatively, in the last instance, it could assume the moral leadership of social movements in South America, an option of limited ambitions, not only for the Venezuelan leader but also in light of historical precedents in Venezuelan leadership, marked by surges of grandeur in regional foreign policy.

With few political resources but with an excess of economic resources, the Venezuelan leadership has acted with little strategic vision of what must be an exercise in cohabitation and use of consultative mechanisms with its South American neighbours. On the other hand, however, the Venezuelan leader has not lacked in pragmatism, and this could be positive in relations with South American countries, insofar as it helps him to understand the limitations of an activist agenda based strictly on values.

NOTES

1. See the Interpol database at www.Interpol.int/Public/ICPO/GeneralAssembly/AGN73/Gallery.asp.
2. See http://noticias.terra.com.br/eleicoes2006/interna/0,,OI1188143-EI6652,00.html, accessed on 12 October 2006.
3. See www4.fgv.br/cps/simulador/impacto_2006/ic239.pdf, accessed on 12 October 2006.
4. The *Punto Fijo* was a pact among liberal political elites that governed between 1959 and 1990.

5. It is important to remember that the left in Venezuela only ascended to power during Chávez's administration, which was incorporated as one of the fractions in power, the other fraction being the military.

6. In Colombia's case, this convergence is based on ideological, security and economic reasons, while in Chile's case, it is based less on ideological and more on economic reasons, mediated by the convergence of the Chilean elite with the United States regarding the modus operandi of their insertion into the global markets.

7. Quoted in 'Chávez Propõe Pacto Militar na Alba', *O Estado de São Paulo*, 8 June 2007 (my translation).

8. Argentina and Uruguay had approved Venezuela's entry as a permanent member by July 2007.

9. In July 2007, the Venezuelan president even signalled Venezuela's return to CAN, on the condition that Colombia and Peru ended their negotiations for a Free Trade Agreement with the United States.

10. However, in 2009, the Brazilian Congress finally approved the entry of Venezuela into Mercosur.

11. See *Folha Online*, www.folha.uol.com.br, accessed on 21 July 2007 (my translation).

12. The new management philosophy of PDVSA is to serve as an instrument of social policy by means of the Social Investment Fund of the company, through which the government finances most public policies within the ambit of the *misiones*.

13. According to Moniz Bandeira, this negative image was construed since the 1950s, by means of funding of nationalist sectors by multinational oil firms that feared competition with Brazil in the future; see interview with Moniz Bandeira, 'Seria Difícil para Chávez Sustentar Qualquer Guerra', *A Tarde* (Bahia), 8 July 2007.

14. The Venezuelan government seems to have halted this project on announcing, in late July 2007, that it would not go on with the initiative which was facing resistance by South American partners (Brazil, Argentina, Bolivia and Uruguay); see *O Estado de São Paulo*, 28 July 2007.

15. Not surprisingly, President Lula, during an interview with the BBC, in the context of the regional debate on Venezuela's decision not to grant a concession to the private television station RCTV, called Venezuela a regional 'partner'. This change in diplomatic terminology could mean that Brazil no longer views Venezuela as a 'strategic ally', as in the recent past. And certainly one cannot call a country that is disputing one's regional leadership a 'strategic ally'.

REFERENCES

Aranda, Andrés (2002), 'A Questão Étnica e Cultural na Política Boliviana no Cenário do Pós-Guerra Fria', PhD thesis, University of São Paulo.

Castañeda, Jorge (2006), 'Latin America's Left Turn', *Foreign Affairs*, 85(3): 28–43.

CEPAL (2008), *Anuario Estadístico de América Latina y el Caribe*, http://websie. eclac.cl/anuario_estadistico/anuario_2008/esp/index.asp.

Cervo, Amado Luiz (2001), 'A Venezuela e os seus Vizinhos', *Revista Cena Internacional*, 1: 7–10.

Iturralde, Diego (2001), 'Pueblos Andinos en América Latina y Reformas Neoliberales', *Anuário Social y Político de América Latina y el Caribe, FLACSO/Nueva Sociedad*, No. 4.

Lodola, Germán (2004), 'Neopopulismo y Compensaciones a los Perdedores del Cambio Económico en América Latina', *Diálogo Político*, 21(92). Buenos Aires: Konrad Adenauer-Stiftung.

Maya, Margarita Lopez & Luis Lander (2007), 'Venezuela, em Direção ao Socialismo do Século XXI?', *Política Externa*, 15(4): 7–22.

PNUD (2004), *A Democracia na América Latina: Rumo a Uma Democracia de Cidadãs e Cidadãos*. São Paulo: Programa das Nações Unidas para o Desenvolvimento.

Romero, Carlos (2007), 'Venezuela en el Contexto Global', mimeo.

Sierra, Rosaura (2005), 'Tensiones y Conflictos entre las Ciudades que se Globalizan y los Estados Nacionales: Estudio de Caso de Caracas, Venezuela', mimeo.

VENBRAS (2006), *Revista Brasileira da Câmara Venezuelana-Brasileira*, 3: 2–5.

Villa, Rafael Duarte (2004), 'Dos Etapas en la Política Exterior Venezolana Frente a Estados Unidos en el Período de Hugo Chávez', *Cuadernos del CENDES* (Caracas), 21(55): 21–45.

Villa, Rafael Duarte (2005), 'Los Países Andinos: Tensiones entre Realidades Domésticas y Exigencias Externas', in *América Latina a Comienzos del Siglo XXI - Perspectivas Económicas, Sociales y Políticas*, ed. G. Dupas. Rosário: Homo Sapiens Edicione.

Villa, Rafael Duarte (2007), 'A Política Externa Venezuelana de Chavez para a América do Sul: Entre a Ideologização das Identidades e as Necesidades do Pragmatismo', *Análise de Conjuntura* (Observatorio de Política Sul-americana), 10 (October): 2–32.

Villa, Rafael Duarte, and Ostos M. del Pilar (2005), 'As Relações Colômbia, Países Andinos e Estados Unidos: Visões em Torno da Agenda de Segurança', *Revista Brasileira de Política Internacional*, 48(2): 86–110.

Conclusion

15
National States: Which Way Forward?

Samir Amin

INTRODUCTION

Global capitalism is actually a complex construction of states (formally sovereign), peoples, and nations ('homogeneous' or not), and social classes articulated around the capital/labour conflict which defines the essence of capitalism. As such, conflicts between states and classes are interwoven in a close relationship of inter-dependence. The interdependence of social struggles in the various countries of the world therefore depends on how the dominant blocs will exploit the margins of manoeuvre at their disposal on the international scene. This for its part will depend on the content of their political and social projects. The establishment of global alliances of dominated classes which constitute the objective of creating a 'better global alternative' is therefore confronted with serious obstacles which must be analysed carefully.

The states and societies of Africa, Asia and Latin America are fully integrated into the process of globalisation. They are in no way 'marginalised', as is often hastily concluded, especially with respect to Africa. Indeed, Africa is even more integrated than the other regions of the world, even though it occupies a lower position in the global hierarchy (Amin 2003a). In all cases, the national question today is a direct consequence of the history of global integration. The national question, in turn, due to the nature of global integration, remains confounded by the agrarian question, on which depends the future of the peasant communities of the peripheries, nearly half of humanity (Amin 2004; see also Moyo and Yeros, Chapter 1, this volume).

GLOBAL REALLY EXISTING CAPITALISM IS IMPERIALIST IN NATURE

The Objective Foundations of the Diversity of Globalised Capitalism

The diversity of the social and political conditions of the states constitutive of the world system stems from the types of developments which define the global expansion of capitalism. Subjected to the demands of accumulation in the centre, social groups of the peripheries have never been part of the central position occupied by proletarian workers in the general production network. The victims of the system are the peasant communities which are integrated and subjected to the logic of imperialist expansion, as are, in varying degrees, many other classes and social groups. Moreover, the history of the making of each country, be it dominant or dominated, has always been characterised by features which are unique to each. As such, the hegemonic blocs of classes and interests that have enabled capitalism to assert its domination, as well as the victims of the system that have established, or tried to establish, in order to face the challenges, have always been different from country to country and from one period to another.

This evolution has shaped specific political cultures, setting up in their own ways, value systems, and 'traditions' of particular expressions, organisation, and struggle. These diversities are equally objective, just like the cultures through which they are expressed. Thus, the development of the forces of production, through scientific and technological revolutions, has for its part dictated changes in the organisation of work and various forms of its subjection to the demands of capitalist exploitation. All these different realities prohibit the reduction of political actors to the bourgeoisie-proletariat conflict.

Capitalism is founded on a market integrated in its three dimensions: market for the products of social labour, capital markets, and the labour market. But really existing capitalism as a world system is based solely on the global expansion of the market in its first two dimensions as the establishment of a real global labour market is hindered by the persistence of state barriers at the detriment of economic globalisation, which is, as such, always limited. For this reason, really existing capitalism is necessarily polarising at the global level, and the uneven development it creates is the most violent and growing contradiction of modern times which cannot be overcome within the framework of the logic of capitalism.

Development and 'underdevelopment' are two faces of the same reality. The dominant discourse that associates capitalism with the affluence of the countries of the centre and qualifies others (developing countries) as 'retarded' has no scientific basis. Consequently, national liberation struggles of the people in the peripheries have always been, objectively, in conflict with the logic of capitalism. They are 'anti-systemic' (anti-capitalist), although, evidently, in different degrees in accordance with the conscience of the actors and the radicalism of their projects. This situation calls for a long-lasting transition to global socialism. If capitalism has set the foundation of an economy and a planetary society, it is, however, unable to carry out the logic of globalisation to its conclusion. Socialism, conceived as a qualitatively higher level of humanity, can, for this reason, be considered universal. However, its construction will have to go through a very long historical transition, requiring a strategy of negation of capitalist globalisation.

In terms of a political and social strategy, this general principle means that the long transition requires an obligatory and inescapable passage towards a national popular society based on an autocentric national economy. Such a process is contradictory in every aspect: it associates the criteria, institutions and operational modes of a capitalist nature with the social aspirations and reforms which are in conflict with the logic of global capitalism; it also associates external forces with the demands for progressive social transformation which conflict with dominant capitalist interests.

Due to their historical nature, governing classes generally formulate their visions and aspirations within the perspective of really existing capitalism; willingly or not, they subject their strategies to the constraints of global capitalist expansion. This is the reason why they cannot really envisage delinking (Amin 1990). Such a vision is left to the popular classes that must use political power to transform their conditions and liberate themselves from the inhuman consequences to which the polarising expansion of capitalism subjects them. The strategic choices of the states and movements of the dominated masses in Africa, Asia and Latin America must be appreciated on the basis of these criteria.

Autocentric and Peripheral Accumulation

Autocentric (or inward-looking) development constitutes, historically, a specific feature of the capital accumulation process in core capitalist countries which conditions the modalities of the resulting economic development and is led mainly by the dynamics of internal social relations, reinforced by the external relations at their service. By contrast, capital accumulation in the peripheries is mainly derived from the evolution of the countries of the centre, in a type of 'dependence'.

The dynamics of the autocentric model of development are founded on a major articulation, one which brings into a close interdependence the expansion of the production of capital goods with that of the production of goods for mass consumption. To this articulation corresponds a social relationship whose main terms are constituted by the two fundamental blocs of the system: the national bourgeoisie and the world of labour. Autocentric economies are not closed in themselves; on the contrary, they are aggressively open to a world system moulded, by them, to enable their own political and economic intervention. However, the dynamics of peripheral capitalism – by definition, the antinomy of autocentric capitalism – are founded on another major articulation which associates the capacity to export, on the one hand, to the consumption – imported, or locally produced by import-substitution – of a minority, on the other. This model defines the comprador nature – by contrast to the national – of the bourgeoisies of the peripheries.

This contrast results in a divergent tendency: the integration of nations in the centres, where centripetal forces prevail in the process of autocentric accumulation; and a permanent threat of disintegration in the peripheries, due to the centrifugal forces of dependent accumulation (see Moyo and Yeros, Chapter 1, this volume). This explains why warlords operated in China in the past, as they do in Africa today. Imperialist policies encourage such tendencies, instrumentalising them with arrogance and cynicism, invoking in the process the 'right to interference', 'humanitarian' intervention and (abusively) the right 'to self-determination'.

EXTERNAL AND INTERNAL COLONIALISM

The centre-periphery contrast is inherent in the global expansion of really existing capitalism at all stages of its deployment. The imperialism that is specific to capitalism has assumed different forms, depending on the specific features of the successive phases of capitalist accumulation: mercantilism (1500–1800), classical industrial capitalism (1800–1945), the aftermath of the Second World War (1945–90) and the ongoing 'globalisation'.

Beyond the specificity of each of these phases, really existing capitalism has always been synonymous with the conquest of the world by the dominant powers. It is therefore no surprise that 'colonialist' dimensions (the general term with which I will designate the conquest), constitute an important element in the establishment of the political cultures of the nations concerned. Nevertheless, the articulation of this colonialist dimension to other aspects of the political culture is specific to each of the regions and countries in question. For Europe, colonialism was rather 'external', while in America and South Africa it was 'internal' – a very significant difference.

In this analysis, colonialism is a special form of expansion of imperialist powers based on the subjection of conquered nations to their political power. Colonisation is 'external' where the metropolis and the colonies are distinct entities, even if the latter are integrated into the political space dominated by the former. The imperialism in question is capitalist in nature and should not be confused with other, previous, forms of the eventual domination practised by one power over other people. The argument that treats the imperialism of modern capitalism in the same way as Roman imperialism does not make much sense. Multinational states, such as the Austro-Hungarian, Ottoman and Russian Empires, and the USSR, are also distinct historical phenomena: in the USSR, for example, financial transfers went from the centre, Russia, to the Asian peripheries, the inverse of what is the rule in the colonial system.

Capitalist colonialism concerns, in the first instance, the Americas, conquered by the Spaniards, the Portuguese, the English and the French. In their respective American colonies, the ruling classes of the colonial powers set up specific economic and social systems, conceived to serve the accumulation of capital in the dominant countries of the time. The asymmetry between Atlantic Europe and colonial America is neither spontaneous nor natural (produced by the 'market', as commonly claimed), but perfectly constructed. The submission of the conquered Indian societies falls within this asymmetry. The grafting of the trafficking in slaves onto this system was equally intended to consolidate its effectiveness as a peripheral system, subjected to the demands of accumulation in the major countries of the period. Black Africa, the source of the enslaved, was transformed into the periphery of the American periphery. Colonisation was rapidly deployed beyond the Americas, through, inter alia, the conquest of English India and Dutch India, and thereafter, towards the close of the nineteenth century, the conquest of Africa and Southeast Asia. Countries not completely conquered – China, Iran and the Ottoman Empire – were subjected to unequal treaties which properly qualified them as semi-colonies.

Colonisation is 'external' when viewed from the metropolitan countries, the most industrialised and advanced in terms of social modernisation, itself conquered by the democratic struggles of working-class and socialist movements. However, these developments never benefited the people of the colonies. Slavery, forced labour and other forms of super-exploitation, as well as administrative brutality and colonial massacres, have marked this history of really existing capitalism. One should therefore be speaking of a veritable 'black book' of capitalism which counts dozens of millions of victims (as in the Indian famine, for example).

Such practices, frankly, have also had certain devastating consequences in the metropolitan countries themselves. For they have provided the basis for the racialisation of the cultures of the ruling elites and even the popular classes, which has legitimated the divergence between democracy in the metropolitan countries and brutal autocracy in the colonies. The exploitation of the colonies benefited capital as a whole, while metropolitan powers derived benefits in accordance with their position in the global hierarchy; Britain defended its hegemony by exploiting the sheer size of its empire, at the same time as Germany aspired to catch up.

'Internal' colonialism was the result of specific combinations of settler colonialism and the requirements of imperialist expansion. The process of primitive accumulation in the centres assumed the form of a systematic expropriation of the poorer layers of the peasantry, which created an excess population that local indus- trialisation was never fully able to absorb; this, in turn, created powerful pressures for emigration. Subsequently, the demographic revolution associated with social modernisation, manifest in the decline of death rates over birth rates, reinforced the same emigration pressures. England furnished the precocious example of such an evolution with the generalisation of 'enclosures' from the seventeenth century onwards.

The United States created in its evolution a new capitalist-imperi- alist centre with its own internal colony. The late abolition of slavery did not in any way wipe out this internal dichotomy, but endowed it with a new form associated with the massive migration of blacks from the American South towards the industrial cities of the North, which was followed by that of poor people from European regions hit by capitalist development. One finds similar features in Latin America and South Africa.

Internal colonialism in Latin America led to political and social consequences similar to those generated by colonisation in general: racism against blacks (especially in Brazil) and contempt for the Indians. This internal colonialism was challenged directly only in Mexico, where, for this reason, the Revolution of 1910–20 constitutes one of the 'great revolutions of modern times'. The legacy of internal colonialism is, perhaps, on the verge of being challenged in the Andean countries today, with the rebirth of contemporary 'indigenous' claims, but of course in a new local and global conjuncture.

In South Africa, the first case of settler colonialism, that of the Boers, was more in line with establishing a 'pure white' state by the expulsion (or extermination) of Africans rather than their subjection. By contrast, it was the British conquest which set as its objective the subjection of Africans to the demands of the imperialist expansion of Britain, primarily by the establishment of mines. Neither the former settlers (the Boers), nor the new arrivals (the British) were authorised by the metropolis to establish themselves as autonomous centres. After the Second World War, the Boer apartheid state sought to do this by asserting its power over its internal colony, essentially the black population. They, however, did not succeed in their mission, given their numerical disadvantage and the growing resistance of the subjected people, who eventually triumphed. The powers in place after the fall of apartheid inherited this question of internal colonialism, but without having been able to find a radical solution, to this day. But the victory has constituted a new chapter in history.

The South African case is particularly interesting from the point of view of the effects of colonialism on political culture. This is not only because internal colonialism here is visible even to the blind, or because it produced the political culture of apartheid. It is also because the Communists in this country arrived at a lucid analysis of what really existing capitalism was all about. In the 1920s, the South African Communist Party (SACP) was the promoter of the theory of internal colonialism – incidentally, a theory adopted in the 1930s by a black leader of the Communist Party in the United States (Harry Haywood), but not followed by his 'white' comrades. The party reached the following conclusion: that the high incomes of the minority 'whites' and the incredibly low incomes of the majority 'blacks' were two sides of the same coin.

Taking the argument a bit further, the Communist Party even attempted to make an analogy with the situation holding within the British Empire by contrasting English wages and labour earnings in India. For the SACP, as for Third International of the time, these two sides of the same question – at the heart of really existing capitalism – were inseparable. The SACP theory of internal colonialism arrived at the conclusion that, at the level of the global capitalist system, colonialism, though considered external by major imperialist powers, was evidently internal. The SACP and the Third International internalised this conclusion in the political culture of the (Communist) left. And this broke radically with that of the socialist left of the Second (social-colonialist) International, whose political culture denied this association inherent to the global reality.

I have argued that 'South Africa is a microcosm of the world capitalist system'. It brings together on its territory the three components of the system: a minority, in the imperialist centres, benefiting from the rent of its advantageous position; plus two majority components, almost evenly split between an industrialised 'third world', analogous to the emerging countries of today, and an excluded 'fourth world' (as in the former Bantustans), analogous to the non-industrialised regions of contemporary Africa. Whatever the actual proportions may be between the numerical size of the populations in these three components and their per capita income, they are almost the same as those which characterise the current world system. This fact undoubtedly contributed to the lucidity obtained by the SACP at the time. This political culture today is lost: not only in South Africa, with the (late) rallying of the SACP behind certain banalised theses on 'racism' (which impute the status of cause to what is an effect); but also on a world scale, with the social democratic co-optation of the majority of the communists.

It is important to add that internal colonialism and accumulation by dispossession are still going on before our very eyes in Palestine, where the Palestinian people continue to face extermination, much like the 'Red Skins' of America (see Hilal, Chapter 7, this volume).

We may ask the question: is the contemporary global system evolving towards a new generalisation of types of internal colonialism? The deepening of the social crisis in the peripheries – which harbour the peasantries of the world, that is, half of humanity – brought about by the generalised offensive of capitalism (a strategy of 'enclosure on a world scale'), engenders a gigantic migratory pressure that could come to compensate for the relative demographic stagnation of the countries of the Triad (the United States, Europe and Japan). The hypothesis of a generalised internal colonialism that would characterise the future phase of global capitalism remains debatable, given the real political and ideological resistance to the adoption of such a model in Europe, which would imply the institutionalisation of 'racism'. However, the 'communitarian' model inspired by the United States appears to constitute a very real danger of an 'Americanisation of Europe'.

THE AWAKENING OF THE SOUTH

The deployment of imperialism translated from 1492 (the date not of the 'discovery' of America but of its conquest and the destruction of its peoples), and during the ensuing four centuries, in the conquest of the world by Europeans. The peoples of Asia and Africa, American Indians who survived the genocide, and later the new nations of Latin America and the Caribbean, had to adjust to the demands of this subjection.

This globalised deployment of capitalism/imperialism constituted for the peoples concerned the greatest tragedy in human history, thus demonstrating the destructive character of the accumulation of capital. For this reason, capitalism cannot be but a parenthesis in history, whose further deployment would lead to barbarism. It is an unsustainable system in the long run, not the 'end of history'! This is so, not only for ecological reasons – tardily acknowledged – but, above all, for the devastating effects of the commercialisation of individuals and the peoples rendered 'useless'.

The catastrophe manifested itself in the destruction of entire peoples and the numerical reduction of non-European peoples from 82 to 63 per cent of the world's population from 1500 to 1900. The catastrophe of some was simultaneously the delight of others. Accumulation by dispossession of entire populations enabled not only the creation of wealth for the dominant classes of the *ancien régime*, but above all, the administrative and military strengthening of European centres. The industrial revolution at the end of the eighteenth century would have been unthinkable without this first period of imperialist deployment. On its part, the military superiority of the new Europe lifted nineteenth-century capitalism to its apogee. The North-South gap widened, the apparent wealth ratio rising from 1:1.3 in 1800 (a ratio not always favourable to Europeans) to 1:40 today. The law of pauperisation formulated by Marx manifested itself even more violently at the systemic level than the father of socialist thought could have imagined!

This page in history has now turned. The people of the peripheries no longer accept the fate reserved for them by capitalism. This fundamental change in attitude is irreversible. This means that capitalism has entered the phase of its decline. A decline initiated in the twentieth century by the Revolution of 1917, followed by the socialist revolutions of China, Vietnam and Cuba, and by the radicalisation of national liberation movements in the rest of Asia and Africa.

The concomitance of the rise of the periphery and the decline of capitalism is not coincidental. Of course, this does not exclude the persistence of various illusions: that of reforms capable of giving capitalism a human face (something it has never been able to do for the majority of the people); that of a possible 'catching up' within the system, which nourishes the dreams of ruling classes in the 'emerging' nations, exhilarated by the success of the moment; and that of a backward-looking salvation (para-religious or para-ethnic), a trap into which many among the 'excluded' have fallen. Such illusions appear tenacious because we are passing through a low point. Although the revolutionary wave of the twentieth century is over, the modern radicalism of the twenty-first century is still to come; and as Antonio Gramsci wrote, in the twilight of transitions there will be monsters.

The awakening of the peoples of the peripheries in the twentieth century is manifest not only by their demographic growth, but also by their expressed will to reconstruct their states and societies, which have been disarticulated by the imperialism of the four preceding centuries.

Bandung and the First Globalisation of Struggles (1955–80)

The governments and peoples of Asia and Africa proclaimed at Bandung in 1955 their will to reconstruct the world system on the basis of the recognition of the rights of nations previously under domination. This 'right to development' constituted the foundation of the globalisation of the period, implemented within a negotiated multipolar framework, and by imposing constraints on imperialism, which was forced to adjust to the new demands.

As I have repeatedly argued, the progress of industrialisation initiated during the Bandung period was not the result of the logic of imperialist deployment, but was imposed by the victories of peoples of the South. Such progress undoubtedly nurtured the illusion of 'catching up', which appeared to be underway, while imperialism, obliged to adjust to the demands of development in the peripheries, was recomposing itself around new forms of domination. The old contrast of imperialist-dominated countries which was synonymous with industrialised-unindustrialised gave way, gradually, to a new one founded on the centralisation of advantages associated with the 'five new monopolies of imperialist centres': the control of modern technologies, natural resources, the global financial system, means of communication, and weapons of mass destruction (Amin 2003b).

The Bandung period is also that of African Renaissance. Pan-Africanism should be situated within this perspective. Initially the product of the American Diasporas, Pan-Africanism achieved one of its main objectives, the independence of the countries of the continent; if not the other, their unity, as Mkandawire has put it (Chapter 2, this volume). It is not by chance that African countries are involved in renovation projects inspired by socialist values, for the liberation of the people of the peripheries is inscribed necessarily in an anti-capitalist perspective. There is no reason to denigrate these numerous attempts on the continent, as is the case today: even the hated regime of Mobutu managed in 30 years to create educational capital in Congo that was 40 times higher than what the Belgians achieved in 80 years. Whether we like it or not, African countries are at the beginning of the formation of veritable nations. And the 'trans-ethnic' options of the ruling classes favoured such a crystallisation; ethnic deviations came later, caused by the erosion of the Bandung models, leading to the loss of legitimacy of powers and a recourse to ethnicity by some so as to reconstitute power in their own interests (Amin 1994).

New Era, New Challenges?

As we have argued, the centre/periphery contrast is no longer synonymous with industrialised/unindustrialised. But the centre/periphery polarisation which gives the expansion of capitalism its imperialist character is still underway, and is deepening, by means of 'five new monopolies' (mentioned above) from which the imperialist centres maintain their advantage. In such conditions, the pursuit of accelerated development projects in emerging peripheries, which has had an undisputable immediate success (in China especially, but also in other countries of the South), does not abolish imperialist domination. Instead, this deployment sets up a new centre-periphery contrast.

Imperialism can no longer be conjugated in the plural, as in the previous phases of its deployment; it is, henceforth, a 'collective imperialism' of the Triad. In this way, the common interests of the oligopolies, which have their roots within the Triad, triumph over ('mercantile') conflicts. This collective character of imperialism can be seen in the control of the world system by the common instruments of the Triad. At the economic level, there are the World Trade Organisation (WTO) (Colonial Ministry of the Triad), the International Monetary Fund (IMF) (Collective Colonial Monetary Agency), the World Bank (Ministry of Propaganda), the Organisation for Economic Co-operation and Development (OECD) and the European Union (set up to prevent Europe from escaping liberalism). At the political level, there are the G7/G8, the armed forces of the United States, and their subaltern instrument represented by the North Atlantic Treaty organisation (NATO), while the marginalisation/domestication of the United Nations completes the picture. The deployment of the hegemonic project of the United States, put in motion by the military control of the planet (involving among others, the abrogation of International Law and the right that Washington has arrogated to carry out 'preventive wars' of its choice) is interwoven with collective imperialism and gives the American leader the means to overcompensate for the US's own economic deficiencies.

Objectives and Means of a Strategy to Develop Convergence in Diversity

The people of the three continents, Africa, Asia and Latin America, are confronted today with a project said to be neoliberal and globalised, but which is nothing else but the construction of 'apartheid on a world scale'. The new imperialist order in place will be challenged. But who will challenge it? And what will be its outcome?

Without a doubt, the self-image of the dominant reality does not permit imagining an immediate challenge to it. The ruling classes of the countries of the South, defeated, have largely accepted their positions as subaltern compradors; the people crippled, engaged in the struggle for daily survival, appear to accept their fate; or, even worse, nurture new illusions which these same ruling classes shower on them – with political Islam being the most dramatic example (see Boratav, Hilal and Somel, Chapters 5, 7 and 9, respectively, this volume). However, from another angle, the rise of movements of resistance and of struggle against capitalism and imperialism; the successes recorded, at least in electoral terms, by the new leftist governments in Latin America and Nepal (whatever the limits of their victories); the progressive radicalisation of many of these movements, as in Zimbabwe, as well as the increasingly critical positions taken by governments of the South within the WTO, are proof that 'another world', a better one, is effectively possible. The offensive strategy necessary for the reconstitution of the front of the peoples of the South requires the radicalisation of social resistance against the offensive of capitalist imperialism.

The governing classes in some countries of the South have visibly opted for a strategy that is one neither of passive submission to the dominant forces in the world system nor of declared opposition: it is a strategy of active interventions on which they base their hopes of accelerating the development of their countries. China has been better equipped than others to positively exploit this option and to draw unquestionably brilliant results. But these are due to the solidity of the nation-building project that the revolution and Maoism produced, by the choice to preserve controls over its currency and the flows of capital, and by its refusal to challenge the collective ownership of land (the main revolutionary gain of the peasants). Can this experience be followed elsewhere? And what are some of the possible limits?

An analysis of the contradictions inherent in this option has led me to conclude that the project for a 'national capitalism' capable of obtaining equality with the dominant powers of the world system is very much an illusion. The objective conditions inherited from history do not permit the implementation of a historic social compromise of capital/labour/peasantry to guarantee the stability of the system, which, for this reason, would drift to the right and be confronted by growing popular resistance, or otherwise evolve towards the left by constructing a 'market socialism' as a stage in the long transition to socialism. The apparently similar options formulated by the governing classes of other so-called 'emerging' countries are even more fragile. Neither Brazil nor India – because they did not experience radical revolutions as in China – are able to resist effectively the combined pressures of imperialism and reactionary local classes.

Meanwhile, the societies of the South – or at least some of them – now have the means to reduce to nought the 'five monopolies' of imperialist countries. They are capable of developing on their own, without falling into dependence. They have the potential to master the technology that would permit its use for one's own purposes. They can also compel the North, by recuperating the use of their natural resources, to adjust to a less harmful consumption mode. They can equally exit from financial globalisation. They have already begun to challenge the monopoly over weapons of mass destruction that the United States intends to preserve. They can develop South-South exchanges – of goods, services, capital and technology – which could not have been imagined in Bandung in 1955 when all these countries were deprived of industries and the mastery of technology. More than ever before, delinking is within the realms of the possible.

Can the societies of the South achieve this? And who will achieve it? Will it be the ruling bourgeoisies in power? I strongly doubt it. Will it be the popular classes that have come to power? Perhaps they can, as a first measure, by consolidating the transitional regimes of national-popular character.

The agrarian question is at the heart of the problems to be resolved, and this constitutes the central axis of the national question. The capitalist path of the private appropriation of land by a minority and the exclusion of others is a path entirely borrowed from Europe. But this was only feasible there thanks to the possibility of massive emigration by the peasantry. Capitalism is unable to resolve in the same way the peasant problem of the peripheries today, whose peasantries constitute half of humanity. To do so, the peripheries would need at their disposal four Americas for their emigration! The *only* alternative is the peasant path, founded on access to land for all peasants.

In fact, the possibility of progress on this basis is potentially higher than that of the capitalist path. For if the growth in productivity of modern farmers, who are few in number, were to be divided amongst the millions who become 'useless', it would appear much more modest than is imagined. The peasant path is one of 'socialist orientation', to recall the Chinese and Vietnamese formula, which is superior and the sole guarantor of the solidity of nation-building (Amin forthcoming).

NATIONAL STATES: WHICH WAY FORWARD TODAY?

According to the dominant discourse of the day, the national state can no longer be the place for the definition of the major choices that determine the evolution of the economic, social, and even political life of societies, due to the 'globalisation' produced by the expansion of the modern economy. There is, therefore, 'no alternative', as Margaret Thatcher used to say. In reality, there are always other alternatives which, depending on their character, will endow the national state with functions and define its margin of manoeuvre within the world system.

The effective response to the challenges facing societies can only be discovered if one understands that history is not determined by the infallible deployment of the laws of 'pure' economy. History is the product of the social responses to the tendencies expressed by these laws, which in turn define all social relationships within the framework in which these laws operate. 'Anti-systemic forces'

– if one could label as such the organised, coherent and effective refusal of a unilateral and total subjection to the intentions of these laws (in fact, simply the law of profit proper to capitalism as a system) – shape real history as much as the 'pure' logic of capitalist accumulation. They determine possibilities and forms of expansion which are thus deployed within the framework in which they are organised.

The state may be, as is presently, the unilateral mouthpiece of the interests of the dominant interests of 'transnationalised' capital (of the countries of the imperialist Triad), or its subaltern comprador allies (in the countries of the periphery). In such a conjuncture, the role of most countries has been reduced to the maintenance of internal order, while the superpower (the United States) exerts alone the responsibilities of a sort of 'para-world state'. The United States thus disposes alone of a large margin of autonomy, while the others, none.

But, evidently, the development of social struggles can bring to power alternative hegemonic blocs, based on compromises between social interests known to be diverse and divergent: capital-labour compromises in the capitalist centres and national-popular-democratic blocs (that is to say, anti-comprador) in the peripheries. In such a case, the state would retrieve a large margin of manoeuvre. It is necessary to strive for this to happen.

The older world systems were always multipolar, even if such multipolarity had never truly been equal. For this reason, hegemony has always been a desired ambition of states, rather than a reality. Hegemonies, even when they have existed, have always been relative and provisional. The partners of the multipolar world of the nineteenth century (extending until 1945) were scarcely the 'hegemons' of their time, always in struggle against one another. We might add that, within the contemporary Triad, there are probably those who remain nostalgic of that epoch of 'balance of power' politics. But this is not the multipolarity desired by the majority of the peoples of the planet (85 per cent!).

The multipolar world inaugurated by the Russian Revolution and later imposed, partially, by the liberation movements in Asia and Africa, was of a different nature. We cannot analyse the postwar period in the conventional terms of 'bipolarity' and 'Cold War', which deny the countries of the South and the advances they made their rightful place. I see this multipolarity within the terms of a fundamental civilisational conflict which, beyond distorting ideological expressions, concerned the conflict between capitalism and the possibility of its overcoming by socialism. The ambitions of the peoples of the peripheries, whether they obtained a socialist revolution or not – to abolish the effects of polarisation – are inscribed necessarily in an anti-capitalist perspective.

Multipolarity is thus synonymous with the real margin of autonomy of states. This margin will be used in accordance with the social content of the state in question. The Bandung period (1955–75) enabled the countries of Asia and Africa to forge new paths, which I have analysed in terms of autocentric development and delinking, in accordance with the national-populist project of power ushered in by national liberation. There is certainly a link between the 'internal' conditions defined by the social alliance of the national liberation project in each country and the favourable external conditions whereby the East-West conflict would neutralise the aggressiveness of imperialism. I am refereeing here to an autonomy which is, by definition, relative independence, whose limits are determined jointly by the nature of the national project and by the margin of manoeuvre permitted by the world system.

The question of autonomy remains very present and pressing (globalisation is not a new thing!). In this regard, there is a tendency in schools of International Political Economy and world economy to deny the importance of the margin of manoeuvre in question, and reduce it to nought. In other words, they restore the view that within the system of globalisation (at all times) the 'whole' determines the 'parts'. I prefer an analysis which restores the autonomy social and political struggles, national and international.

The postwar period (1945–80) has drawn to a close. The current deployment of the collective imperialist project of the Triad and, within this, the hegemony of the United States, abolishes the autonomy of the countries of the South and reduces them to associates of Washington within the imperialist Triad.

The current moment is characterised by the deployment of a project of US hegemony on a world scale. This project is the only one that occupies centre stage today (Amin 2006). There is no longer a counter-project to limit the spaces subjected to the control of the United States, as was the case in the postwar period. The USSR has come undone, while the European project, beyond its original ambiguities, is itself fading out. The countries of the South (the Group of 77, the Non-aligned), which once had the ambition to mount a common front against western imperialism, have renounced it. For its part, China is going it alone, interested only in protecting its national project (itself ambiguous) without becoming an active partner in the transformation of the world.

The collective imperialism of the Triad is the result of a real evolution of the productive system of capitalist countries which has produced not the emergence of 'transnationalised' capital – as Hardt and Negri (2000) would have it – but the solidarity of the national oligopolies of the centres of the system expressed in their desire to 'jointly govern' the world for their own profit. But if 'the economy' (understood as the unilateral expression of the demands of the dominant segments of capital) brings together the countries of the Triad, politics divides their nations. The deployment of social struggles can thus challenge, particularly in Europe, the role the state plays at the exclusive service of big capital. Within this hypothesis, one would expect once again to see the emergence of a new polycentrism which would accord Europe a margin of autonomy. But the deployment of 'the European project' does not fall within this framework, necessary to bring Washington to reason. In reality, this project is nothing but 'a European wing of the American project', with the 'constitution' project itself stuck in the dual option of neoliberalism and Atlanticism. The potential borne by the conflict of political cultures, effectively calling for an end to Atlanticism, remains mortgaged by the options of the left majorities (in electoral terms, the European socialist parties), which rally behind social-liberalism. These two terms are in themselves contradictory, given that liberalism is by nature non-social – indeed, anti-social.

Russia, China and India are the three major strategic adversaries of the Washington project. The ruling governments in these three countries will increasingly become conscious of this. But they still seem to believe that they can manoeuvre without directly colliding with the US administration, or even 'take advantage of their friendship with the United States' in conflicts between one another. The 'common front against terrorism' – to which they appear to subscribe – sows such confusion. The double game of Washington is clearly visible here: the United States, on the one hand, supports the Chechens, Huigurs and Tibetans (just as they support Islamist movements in Algeria, Egypt and elsewhere!), while on the other hand, it waves the flag of Islamist terrorism in order to rally Moscow, Beijing and Delhi behind it. This double game seems, more or less, to be working up to now.

A Eurasian rapprochement (including Europe, Russia, China and India), which would certainly carry with it the rest of Asia and

Africa and isolate the United States, is certainly desirable. There are some signs in this direction. But we are still very far from seeing the end of Europe's Atlanticist choice.

Can countries of the South play an active role in the necessary defeat of the US military project and ambition? The peoples that have been attacked are, presently, the only active adversaries capable of curbing the ambitions of Washington. Even so – and partly because they are the only ones active, and feel it – their methods of struggle remain of questionable effectiveness, while their 'fundamentalist' appeals do not elicit the solidarity of the peoples of the North in their rightful struggle. Meanwhile, the 'generaralised compradorisation' of dominant classes throughout the South leads us to conclude that no great contributions will be made by them in this struggle, or those likely to be in place in the near future, even if they are evidently 'fundamentalists' (Islamists, Hinduists or ethnicists). These governments are caught between the endless arrogance of Washington and the hostility (not to say, hatred) of their peoples towards the United States. Is there anything they can really do other than to accept their fate?

For the time being, the South in general no longer has its own project, as was the case during the Bandung era. No doubt, the ruling classes of the so-called 'emerging' countries (China, South Korea, Southeast Asia, Brazil, and some others) have objectives they have set for themselves and which their countries are working to achieve. The objectives can be summarised by the maximisation of growth within the globalisation system. These countries have – or believe they have – a power of negotiation that will permit them to benefit more from this 'egoistic' strategy than from a vague 'common front' formed with countries weaker than them. But the advantages they might obtain are specific to particular domains of interest to them, and do not take issue with the general architecture of the system. They are thus not an alternative; and they do not endow this vague and illusory project of 'national capitalism' with the consistency that defines a veritable societal project. The most vulnerable countries of the South (the 'fourth world'), do not even have analogous projects of their own, and the eventual result of 'substitution' (religious or ethnic fundamentalism) does not merit to be qualified as such. Thus, it is repeatedly the North that takes the initiative 'for them' (one ought to say 'against them'), such as in the EU-ACP (African, Caribbean and Pacific countries) association (and 'economic partnership agreements' to replace the Cotonou Agreements), the 'Euro-Mediterranean dialogue' or the

American-Israeli projects with regards to the Middle East, and even the 'Greater Middle East'.

The challenges facing the building of an authentic multipolar world are more serious than what many of the 'anti-globalisation' movements can imagine. The most immediate challenge is to defeat Washington's military project. This is the inescapable condition to open up the necessary margin of freedom, without which any social and democratic progress, and any advance towards a multipolar world, will remain extremely vulnerable. Because of its inordinate nature, the US project will ultimately fail, but certainly at a terrible human price. The resistance of its victims – the peoples of the South – will be reinforced to the extent that the Americans get bogged down in multiple theatres of war in which they will be compelled to engage. Such resistance will end up defeating the enemy, perhaps by awakening public opinion in the United States, as was the case with the war in Vietnam. It would, however, be better to stop the catastrophe sooner, which international diplomacy can do, above all if Europe grasps the weight of its responsibility.

In the longer term, 'another globalisation' implies challenging the options of liberal capitalism and the management of the planet's affairs by the collective imperialism of the Triad within the framework of an extreme Atlanticism, or of its 'rebalanced' version.

An authentic multipolar world will not become a reality unless the following four conditions are met.

First, that Europe genuinely advances on the path of 'another Europe' that is social (and thus engaged in the long transition to global socialism) and that it initiates its disengagement with its imperialist past and present. This implies, obviously, more than simply exiting from Atlanticism and extreme neoliberalism.

Second, that in China, the path of 'market socialism' is not swept away in the strong currents of the illusory construction of 'national capitalism', which will be impossible to stabilise as it excludes the majority of workers and peasants.

Third, that the countries of the South (people and states) rebuild a 'common front', a necessary condition which will permit a margin of manoeuvre for popular classes not only to impose 'concessions' in their favour, but also to transform the nature of the powers in place, substituting dominant comprador blocs with 'national, popular and democratic' blocs.

And fourth, at the level of the organisation of the systems of rights, national and international, that there is advance in the direction of building respect for national sovereignty (moving from the sovereignty of states to that of peoples) and for all rights, individual and collective, political and social.

REFERENCES

Amin, Samir (1990), *Delinking*, trans. M. Wolfers. London and Atlantic Highlands, NJ: Zed Books.

Amin, Samir (1994), *L'Ethnie à l'Assaut des Nations*. Paris: Harmattan.

Amin, Samir (2003a), 'Is Africa Really Marginalized?', in *History and Philosophy of Science*, ed. H. Lauer. Ibadan: Hope.

Amin, Samir (2003b), *Obsolescent Capitalism*, trans. P. Camiller. London and New York: Zed Books.

Amin, Samir (2004), 'The New Agrarian Question', in *Globalizing Resistance*, ed. F. Polet. London: Pluto Books.

Amin, Samir (2006), *Beyond US Hegemony*. London: Zed Books.

Amin, Samir (forthcoming), *Land Tenure Reforms: A Proposal for Asia and Africa*.

Hardt, Michael, and Antonio Negri (2000), *Empire*. Cambridge, MA: Harvard University Press.

Notes on Contributors

Lorgio Orellana Aillón is Lecturer in Social Movements at the Faculty of Social Sciences, Universidad Mayor de San Simon, Cochabamba, Bolivia. He has also been a researcher at the Centre for the Study of Labour and Agrarian Development (CEDLA) in La Paz.

Samir Amin has been Director of the Third World Forum in Dakar, Senegal, co-founder of the World Forum for Alternatives, and Director of IDEP (United Nations African Institute for Planning). He has published widely on the political economy of development. His recent books include *Beyond US Hegemony?* (London: Zed Books, 2006) and *A Life Looking Forward: Memoirs of an Independent Marxist* (London: Zed Books, 2006).

Korkut Boratav retired from his post of Professor of Economics at the University of Ankara in 2002. Currently he is with the Turkish Social Science Association and an active member of the Group of Independent Social Scientists, Ankara, Turkey.

Atilio A. Boron is Director of the Latin American Programme of Distance Education in Social Sciences (PLED), Professor of Political Theory at the Faculty of Social Sciences, University of Buenos Aires, Senior Researcher of the National Council of Science and Technology of Argentina and Chairman of the Scientific Committee of CROP, the Comparative Research on Poverty Programme based at the University of Bergen in Norway.

Sandeep Chachra is a social anthropologist and development activist. He is Executive Director of ActionAid India and former Head of Governance for ActionAid International. He is actively involved in developing the Global Economic Literacy and Budget Accountability Platform, the South-South Peoples Solidarity Forum and the World Forum of Alternatives for South Asia.

Jamil Hilal has been Senior Research Associate at the Law Institute of the Development Studies Centre and at the Institute of Women Studies of Beirzeit University. Among his recent books is the edited volume *Where Now for Palestine* (London: Zed Books, 2007).

Mahmood Mamdani is Executive Director of the Makerere Institute of Social Research at Makerere University, Kampala, Uganda, and Herbert Lehman Professor of Government at Columbia University, New York. He has published widely on African politics and culture. His most recent book is *Saviors and Survivors: Darfur, Politics, and the War on Terror* (New York: Pantheon Books, 2009).

Thandika Mkandawire is Professor of African Development at the London School of Economics. He has been Director of the United Nations Research Institute for Social

Development (UNRISD) and Executive Secretary of the Council for the Development of Social Science Research in Africa (CODESRIA).

Reginaldo C. Moraes is Professor of Political Science and International Relations at the State University of Campinas (UNICAMP), Brazil. His recent publications include *Estado, Desenvolvimento e Globalização* (São Paulo: UNESP, 2006) and *As Cidades Cercam os Campos: Estudos sobre Projeto Nacional e Desenvolvimento Agrário na Era da Economia Globalizada* (São Paulo: UNESP, 2009).

Sam Moyo is Executive Director of the African Institute of Agrarian Studies (AIAS), Harare, Zimbabwe, and President of the Council for the Development of Social Science Research in Africa (CODESRIA). He has published extensively on land, agrarian and environmental issues and is co-editor of *Reclaiming the Land* (London: Zed Books, 2005).

Hari Roka is Member of the Constituent Assembly of Nepal since 2008, and a regular columnist in the *Kantipur Daily*. Previously, he was Member of the Legislative Parliament (2007–08) and has also spent seven years in prison for his political activism against the Shah dynasty.

Cem Somel studied Economics at Istanbul University, obtained his PhD at Ankara University and teaches at Abant Izzet Baysal University in Bolu, Turkey. He edits the bi-monthly political journal *doğudan* ('From the East') and is a fortnightly columnist of the daily *Evrensel*.

Javier A. Vadell is Adjunct Professor of International Relations at the Catholic University of Minas Gerais (PUC Minas), Belo Horizonte, Brazil. He has a doctorate in the Social Sciences from the State University of Campinas (UNICAMP), Brazil.

Sebastião C. Velasco e Cruz is Professor of Political Science at the State University of Campinas (UNICAMP), Brazil. Among his many works on the politics and economics of contemporary Brazil and international relations are the recent books, *Trajetórias: Capitalismo Neoliberal e Reformas Econômicas nos Países da Periferia* (São Paulo: UNESP, 2007) and *O Brasil no Mundo: Ensaios de Análise Política e Prospectiva* (São Paulo: UNESP, 2010).

Rafael Duarte Villa is Professor of Political Science in the Department of Political Science and the Institute of International Relations at the University of São Paulo (USP), Brazil. He is also Co-ordinator of the Nucleus for Research in International Relations (NUPRI). His publications include the recent book *Ensaios Latino-americanos de Política Internacional* (São Paulo: Editora Hucitec, 2007), and numerous journal articles on foreign policy and Latin American politics.

Paris Yeros is Adjunct Professor of International Relations at the Catholic University of Minas Gerais (PUC Minas), Belo Horizonte, Brazil, and Research Associate of the African Institute of Agrarian Studies (AIAS), Harare, Zimbabwe. His main areas of research are the agrarian question and the new South-South relations. He is co-editor of *Reclaiming the Land* (London: Zed Books, 2005).

Index

accumulation, 13–16; autocentric and peripheral, 128, 141, 327–8; disarticulated, 13; disarticulation of formerly autonomous development *with* state control, 15; disarticulation of formerly autonomous development *without* state control, 15; enhanced disarticulation, 15; partially articulated *without* structural reform, 14; partially disarticulated *with* structural reform, 13; planned and articulated *from above*, 14; planned and articulated *from below*, 14

African Diaspora, 32, 44

African Union, 39, 41, 48, 51

Africa's borders, 36–8

Andean Community of Nations (CAN), 313

apartheid, 14, 20, 51, 86, 98, 331

Arafat, Yasser, 155, 157

Argentine politics, *corralito*, 261–2; Currency Board, 258–9; *Gobierno de la Alianza*, 259–60; Malvinas War, 257; Peronist Party, 257; peronists in government, 261; Peronism, 264

Association of Southeast Asian Nations (ASEAN), 144

Atlanticism, 343

Balfour Declaration, 152

Bandung, 141–2, 334–5

Barak, Ehud, 155

'bipolarity', 339

Bolivar, Simon, 299

Bolivarian Alternatives for the Americas (ALBA), 143, 308, 312–13

Bolivian politics, Movimiento al Socialismo (MAS), 235–6, 240, 250–2, 303; National Democratic Alliance (AND), 242; Nationalist Revolutionary Movement (MNR), 242, 302; National Revolution, 238–9

'bonapartism', 79, 82

Brazilian politics, *bolsa familia*, 305; *Brasil-potência*, 283; Brazilian Labour Party (PTB), 281; Cruzado Plan, 287; *Estado Novo*, 279, 282; National Economic (and Social) Development Bank (BNDES), 280–1, 283–4, 289, 292, 315; 'Peasant Leagues', 282; Real Plan, 290; Social Democratic Party (PSD), 281; Workers' Party (PT), 290–1

Caldera, Rafael, 306

Capitalism, mercantile, 7; industrial and monopoly, 8–9; and systemic rivalry, 9–12

Camp David, 155, 166

Cardoso, Fernando Henrique, 221, 223, 288–9, 291, 291, 315

Castro, Fidel, 312–13

Cavallo, Domingo, 255, 258, 260–1

Chávez, Hugo, 256, 265, 301, 303; and *chavismo*, 306; and foreign policy, 310–17

China, Chinese Communist Party, 119; Cultural Revolution, 81; development, 14–15, 110, 115–20, 130; and India, 144; and Nepal, 175, 185–6; and Argentina, 268–9

Collor de Mello, Fernando, 288–9

colonialism, 7–8; and ethnic identity, 35–6, 54, 60–6; external, 329; internal, 8, 63, 330; semi-, 8, 175, 188, 235; settler-, 25, 85–6, 151–3, 158, 331–2

Common Market for Eastern and Southern Africa (COMESA), 96